SEMINAR PAPERS 4
Center for Advanced Study in the Visual Arts

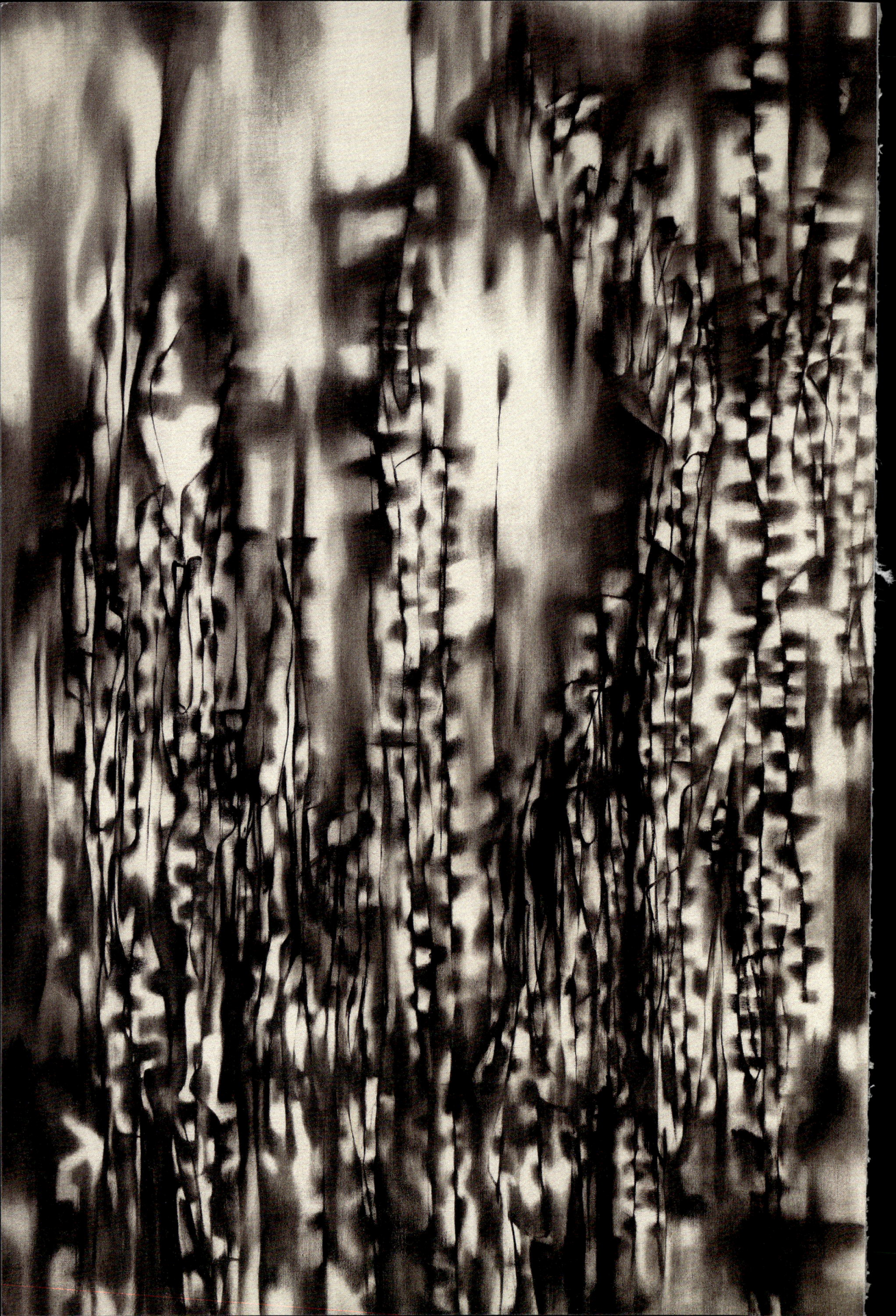

BLACK MODERNISMS IN THE TRANSATLANTIC WORLD

Edited by Steven Nelson and Huey Copeland

NATIONAL GALLERY OF ART, WASHINGTON
Distributed by Yale University Press
New Haven and London

CONTENTS

PREFACE — vi
STEVEN NELSON

INTRODUCTION: A TROUBLED CONJUNCTURE — 1
HUEY COPELAND AND STEVEN NELSON

SIMONE LEIGH: ACTS OF TRANSFORMATION — 19
STEVEN NELSON

LEAVE NO MARK: BLACKNESS AND INSCRIPTION IN THE INQUISITORIAL ARCHIVE — 35
MATTHEW FRANCIS RAREY

BARE FEET, OR, THE AMBIVALENCE OF EMANCIPATION: CAMILLE PISSARRO AND THE CARIBBEAN — 57
C. C. MCKEE

ON EUROPEAN MODERNISM AND BLACK BEING — 79
SIMON GIKANDI

NANCY ELIZABETH PROPHET AND AUGUSTA SAVAGE: SCULPTURAL HABITS OF BLACK MODERNISM — 103
KELLIE JONES

NUMINOUS AFFECT IN BLACK ATLANTIC MODERNISMS — 129
SYLVESTER OKWUNODU OGBECHIE

DARKNESS AND THE *UNVISIBLE*: NORMAN LEWIS, ROY DECARAVA, AND POSTWAR ABSTRACTION — 153
KOBENA MERCER

AT THE THRESHOLD OF WITHHOLDING: STANLEY BROUWN'S MODERNIST REPETITIONS — 179
ADRIENNE EDWARDS

SPACES IN THE SHADOWS: ARCHIVES AND ARCHITECTURES IN THE WORK OF CARRIE MAE WEEMS — 199
MABEL O. WILSON

NOTES — 228
CONTRIBUTORS — 248
INDEX — 250

PREFACE

Black Modernisms in the Transatlantic World is the fourth installment of the Seminar Papers series, produced by the Center for Advanced Study in the Visual Arts. Inaugurated with the publication of *The Dada Seminars* in 2005, this series brings diverse groups of people together to explore subjects of mutual interest. The present volume began to take shape in late 2017, in tandem with my invitation from dean emerita Elizabeth Cropper to be the Center's 2018–2020 Andrew W. Mellon Professor.

I was excited about the idea of hosting discussions and producing a text focused on Black art, but I felt unsure about how to frame such an endeavor. Wanting the project to be truly collaborative in nature, I asked Huey Copeland, BFC Presidential Associate Professor of Modern Art and Black Study at the University of Pennsylvania, to scheme with me, to dream about what this seminar volume could be. We talked little about Black art as a stable category. Indeed, it proved to be an uninteresting starting point for us. Instead, we discussed the capricious nature of Blackness and its foundational role in the formation of the West as we know it.

Enslaved Black bodies made possible the efflorescence of modern capitalism. Moreover, they were necessary to the formation of modernism and modernity. Black artists and thinkers participated in these innovations, culturally and formally. They also created their own modernisms that diverged from white formations, understanding Black worlds, Black experiences, and Black cultures as central tenets of modern life.

Through Huey's and my conversations, the topic "Black modernisms" was born. We assembled a group of scholars and curators whose work highlights how Black artists have actively engaged with modernism and modernity. We challenged them to ask how the many experiences of being Black in the world can be understood as fundamental in the forging of Black modernisms. The volume's resulting contributions respond to our queries beautifully, exploring myriad encounters in art and representation between the early eighteenth century and the present with an eye towards the multiple artistic, cultural, and political forces within and without Black cultures that have produced various modernisms. In addition to the group assembled at the National Gallery of Art, we invited artist Simone Leigh and art historian C. C. McKee to contribute to the project. Taken as a whole, *Black Modernisms* asks how the field has been defined by Black production across the transatlantic world and forces a reassessment of the history of Western modernism.

I am enormously grateful to the many people who contributed to the publication of this text. Special thanks are due to Elizabeth Cropper, whose leadership created the perfect conditions for *Black Modernisms* to take shape. I would also like to thank former associate dean Therese O'Malley, who provided a wonderful roadmap for the group's 2018 and 2019 seminars and expertly supervised the book's preliminary editing and production. Therese was supported by Annie Miller, who served as the touchstone for the authors and scholarly editors. Megan Driscoll supported the seminars at the National Gallery and the early stages of the editorial process. Jen Rokoski and Frances Grant coordinated with authors and institutions to secure permissions for images. Helen Tangires, Jeannette Ibarra Shindell, and Nathalie Meza managed the budget and administration. Sarah Battle provided much-needed support as we came to the end of production.

The Center has wonderful partners in the National Gallery's office of content strategy, publishing, and branding. These colleagues were critical to the success of *Black Modernisms*, and I am grateful for their extraordinary contributions. I extend appreciation to Emiko K. Usui for her continued support of the Center's publishing program. Cynthia Ware was the project's original managing editor. Lisa Shea and Emily Zoss expertly guided the process upon Cynthia's retirement. Magda Nakassis provided editing support. Peggy Martin oversaw the design of the book, and Christina Wiginton and Mariah Shay ensured it was produced to the highest standards. The 2018 and 2019 seminars were made possible by the Center's Arthur Vining Davis Foundations endowment. Support for the resulting publication comes from the Center's Andrew W. Mellon endowment for scholarly publications.

Finally, I am grateful to the authors, for their dedication to this project, and to Simone Leigh, who enthusiastically shared her work and her ideas with us. Their brilliance leaps from the pages that follow. I am deeply indebted to my coeditor and compatriot Huey Copeland. *Black Modernisms* would never have happened without his inspiration, camaraderie, incisiveness, and rigor. This volume reflects our shared commitment to Black studies and the role it can play in the expansion of art history's intellectual possibilities and relevance in today's troubled world.

Steven Nelson
Dean, Center for Advanced Study in the Visual Arts

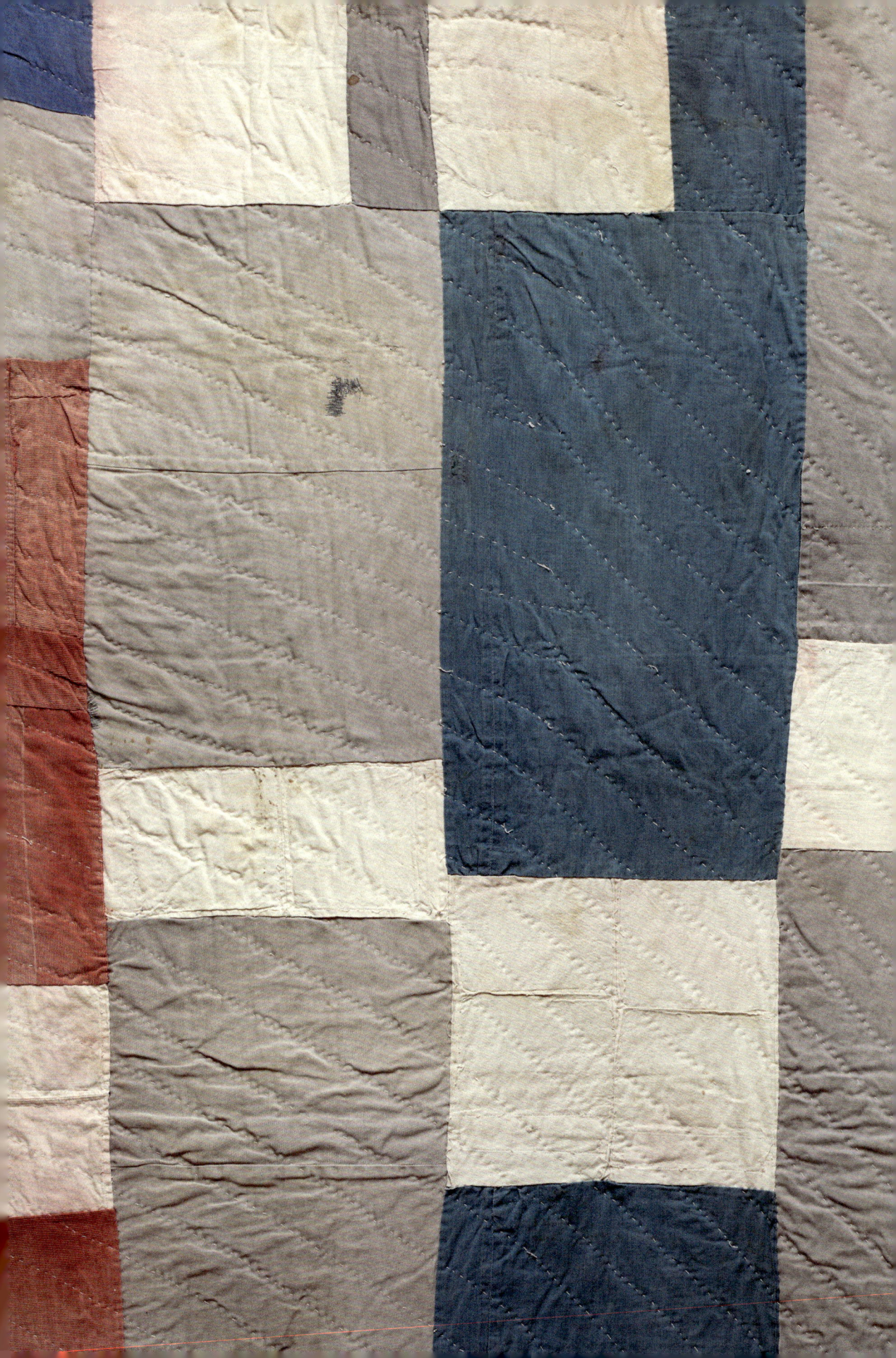

INTRODUCTION: A TROUBLED CONJUNCTURE

HUEY COPELAND AND STEVEN NELSON

Over the last three decades, scholars in the humanities have turned increasingly critical eyes to hegemonic histories of modernism in order to grapple with the often repressed diversity of its meanings, participants, and practices across the globe and beyond disciplinary boundaries.[1] At the same time, Black radical study, which focuses on the constitutive import of transatlantic slavery in the making of the modern world, has emerged at the forefront of ethical, historical, and theoretical debates with transformative implications for every field it touches.[2]

Despite their considerable temporal and conceptual overlaps, the two discourses have often seemed to operate in discrete, if parallel, universes, underlining the persistent force of racial segregation in the organization of knowledge in the United States. As a result, "black modernisms" remains an unnaturalized and indeterminate conjuncture with multiple valences in art historical praxis. The extant literatures tell the tale, each with their own conceptual implications. For any number of "mainstream" art historians, black modernism might simply refer to modernist art that is chromatically black—think here of the emblematic canvasses produced at mid-twentieth century by Ad Reinhardt (fig. 1)—signifying negation, exhaustion, and a dialectics of extremity that are part and parcel of oppositional culture's melancholic project of resisting industrial capitalism and the terrors it has come to visit upon the world.[3] Scholars of African/diasporic art have taken a rather different tack. By these lights, black modernism can be understood as an umbrella term referring to work in whatever form—from a painterly homage to Haiti's founding fathers by Guillaume Guillon Lethière (fig. 2) to a Gee's Bend quilt by Missouri Pettway made from her late husband's work clothes (fig. 3), to the legendary master key used by Jafta Masemola while imprisoned on South Africa's Robben Island—that was made by peoples of African descent and that challenges any pre-given sense of the who, when, what, where, and why of "advanced" artistic praxis.[4]

Perhaps most radically, "Black" may be situated as one of many qualifiers that speak to the multiplicity and uneven development of global modernisms and their operative conditions of possibility: namely, colonialism, conquest, and transatlantic slavery. Indeed, African captives came to provide the models through and against which Western notions of the commodity, the object, and the work of art were organized. In this framework, the phrase "black modernisms" seems less like an oxymoron and instead resonates as a kind of redundancy, since any form of the modern is always already *blackened*, even if that fact is limited to the literal footnotes of the discipline.[5] Just recall, as we often have, the American critic Clement Greenberg's famous 1939 justification for the maintenance of modernism's aristocratic values in the face of an ersatz capitalist culture in a paean that operatively links racist and aesthetic discrimination. The critic shows his hand in a closing note, an aside that, to Greenberg's mind, barely needed saying: "In Africa today," he scoffed, "we find that the culture of slave-owning tribes is generally much superior to that of the tribes that possess no slaves."[6] In contrast to his usual line of critique, Greenberg's

Fig. 1 Ad Reinhardt, *Abstract Painting, No. 34*, 1964, oil on canvas, National Gallery of Art, Washington, Gift of Mr. and Mrs. Burton Tremaine

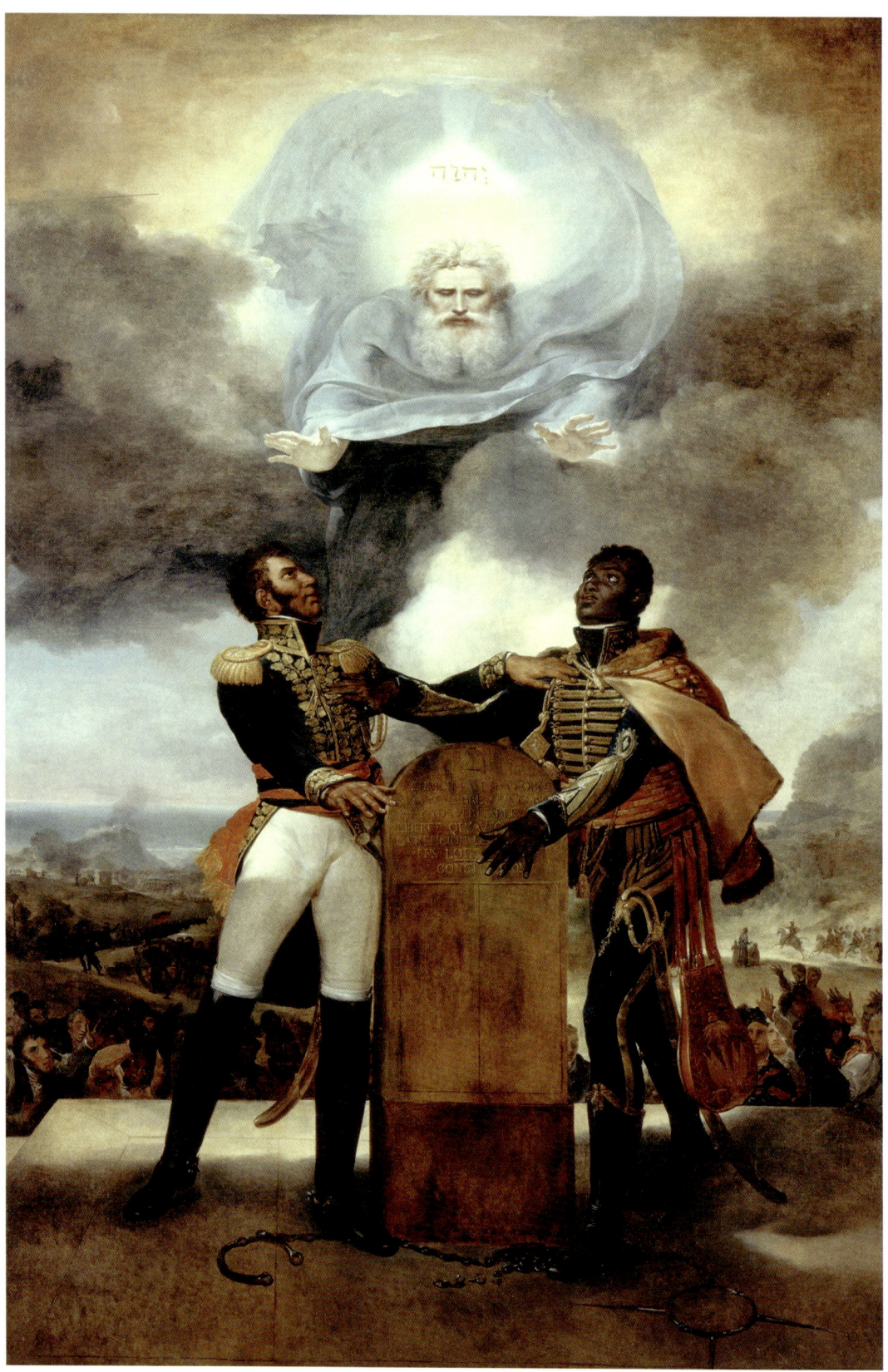

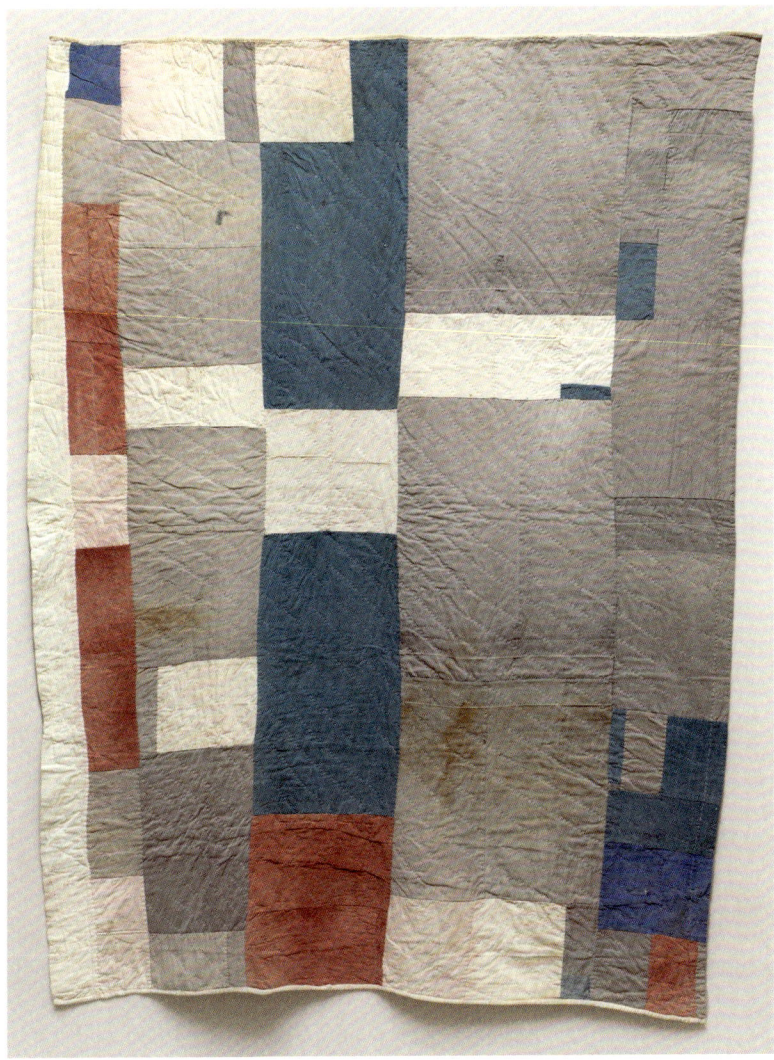

Fig. 2 Guillaume Guillon Lethière, *The Oath of the Ancestors*, 1822, oil on canvas, Musée du Panthéon National Haïtien, Port-au-Prince

Photo by Gérard Blot. © RMN-Grand Palais / Art Resource, NY

Fig. 3 Missouri Pettway, *Blocks and Strips Work-Clothes Quilt*, 1942, cotton, corduroy, and cotton sacking, National Gallery of Art, Washington, Patrons Permanent Fund and Gift of the Souls Grown Deep Foundation

assessment here suggests that any modern art worth the name must be considered in relation to histories of enslavement and racialization, through which Blackness and modernism were at once mutually constituted and fractured from each other.

Chromatic, cultural, structuring, deformative: the present volume aims to hold these multiple dimensions of black modernisms—as well as the different protocols of reading that they elicit—in productive tension. At the same time, our conjoining of Blackness and modernism is both newly inflected by the past and foundationally informed by contemporaneous practices. Consider, in this light, American artist Ellen Gallagher's more recent abstract, large-scale canvases (2016, fig. 4), almost reflective dark topographies that recall the monochrome tradition in order to rethink it in deed as well as word. The title of this quartet, *Negroes Battling in a Cave*, pointedly recalls an 1898 racist joke by the French artist Alphonse Allais, who printed a solid black rectangle with the caption "Negroes Battling in a Cave at Night," as a way of lambasting the ways that avant-garde painting in his time had grown increasingly illegible so that even blank blackness

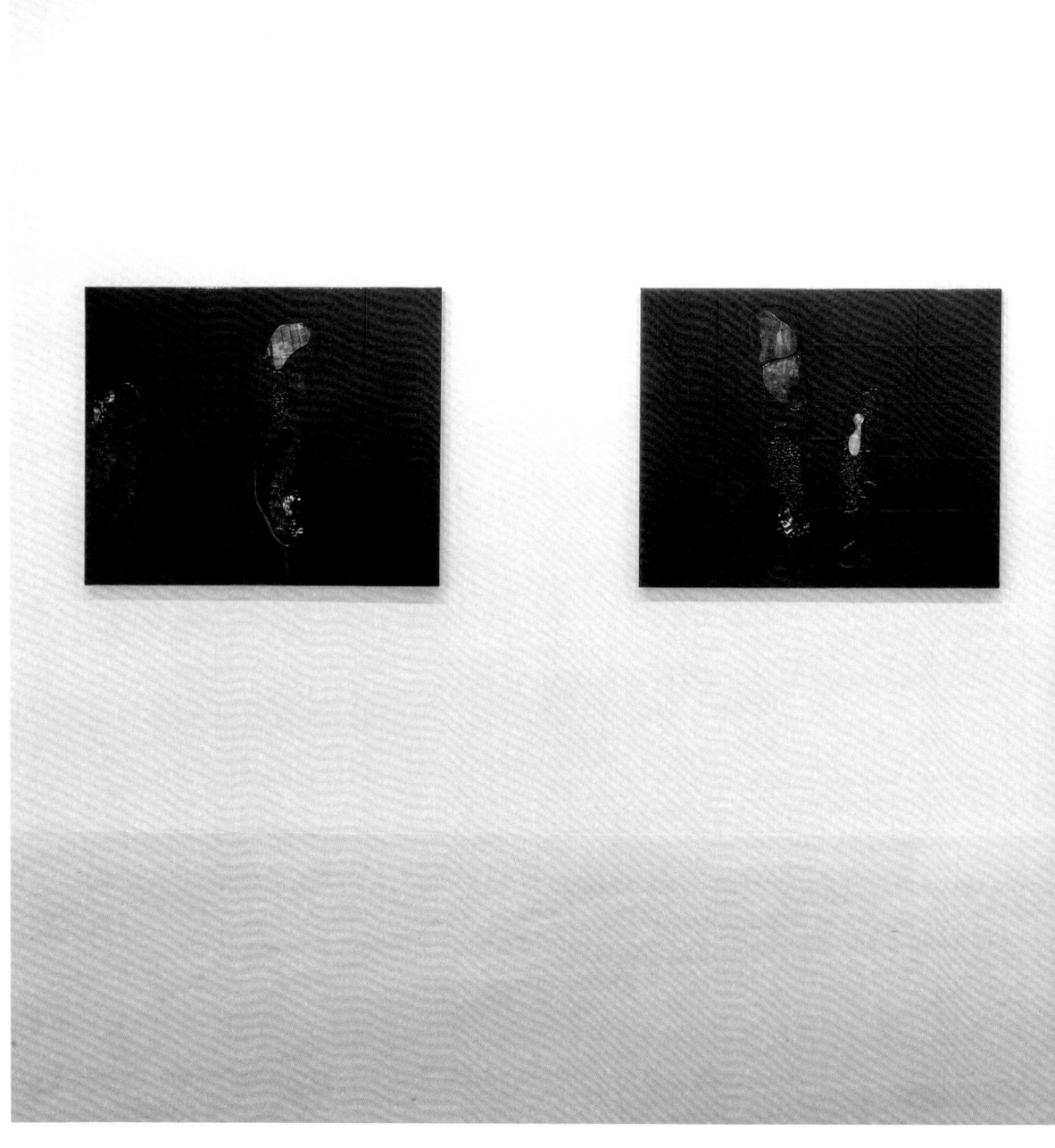

Fig. 4 Ellen Gallagher, *Negroes Battling in a Cave*, 2016, enamel, ink, rubber, and paper on linen

Courtesy of the artist and Gagosian.
Photo by Charles Duprat

might be imbued with depictive meaning. The Russian avant-gardist Kazimir Malevich, always in on the joke, would inscribe a translated snippet of this phrase onto a canvas in 1915 before covering it entirely in paint to produce his iconic *Black Square* (fig. 5), which has long enjoyed a totemic status within accounts of modernist abstraction as the ultimate sign of painting reduced to its barest means. In recovering the racial grounds of his intervention—revealed on the one-hundredth anniversary of the work with the aid of X-ray technologies—Black women artists on both sides of the Atlantic, like Gallagher and Hannah Black, immediately grasped the tremendous implications for the history of modernism, facts that so-called mainstream art historians have thus far resoundingly failed to address in print.[7]

This example clearly demonstrates that thinking black modernisms demands novel encounters among various knowledges—of art, art history, and Black studies with a queer feminist bent—that require us to move in and out of the discipline's boundaries as well as back and forth in time to understand those sites of conjuncture, displacement, and erasure that have the potential to both deform and reshape our habits of seeing and thinking the modern. This ambition, a weaving together of discourses rather than the supplantation or supplementation of existing structures, animates the present volume and sets it apart from prior like-minded attempts aimed at thinking "race" and "representation." By homing in on Blackness and modernism, which we take to be embodied and entangled material-discursive phenomena, our approach aims to put pressure on simplistic divisions that would place words, works, and actions in opposition to each other.[8] In this spirit, unlike, say, Darby English's *1971: A Year in the Life of Color*, *Black Modernisms in the Transatlantic World* insists that the two terms belong together and refuses to prioritize a narrowly defined art historical canon ultimately predicated on the denigration of African cultural intelligence.[9] Nor do we promise a comprehensive survey of "Black art," as Richard J. Powell provides in his indispensable volume of that name, which also tends to give pride of place to twentieth-century African American fine arts.[10]

For us, black modernisms provide an avenue for coming to a new understanding of the past and present, as well as the determinative historical forces that engender them, enabling interventions in and deossifications of hegemonic notions of modernism, which time and again focus on the singular white male European artist. In this sense, our approach embraces what theorist Karen Barad calls "ontological indeterminacy" and "a radical openness" to the range and multiplicity of modernism's various iterations.[11] Indeed, signaling "black modernisms" in the lower case in this introduction encompasses its capacious nature while pointing to Black modernisms as a field in which the subsequent essays insert themselves. Accordingly, we have attempted to sit with and test the various lenses through which black modernisms can be seen by leaning into the Black anthological modalities so cogently theorized by Brent Hayes Edwards. In *The Practice of Diaspora*, his magisterial 2003 book focused on the rise of Pan-Africanist literatures in 1930s Paris, Edwards argues that the (Black) anthology, which often founds the tradition it is ostensibly meant to document, is "a means more broadly to grapple with *modernity* itself: the form serves to 'mark time'. . . . [and to] delimit the borders of an expressive mode or field, determining its beginning and end points, its local or global resonance, its communities of participants and audiences."[12]

With these operations in mind, we here gather interventions by nine leading scholars and practitioners of African and diasporic art and culture who each explore Black practitioners' multifarious approaches to the contradictions of modernity and to the myriad traces of Black agency, both seen and unseen, that continue to haunt and define the Western world.

As such, the book aims to pose a set of fundamental questions: When was/is modernism, and how do different cultural, economic, regional, political, and social contexts inflect its temporality? What does modernist artistic practice look like on either side of the northern Black Atlantic, that crucible of enslavement, especially when considered in relation to understudied areas such as Black cultural production in South America and the Caribbean? How do the intersections of gender, sexuality, and race influence our understanding of both modernity and modernism? To what extent does Black artistic production force a reassessment of the history of Western modernism, especially if we insist that any aspect of the modern is necessarily bound up with histories of racial enslavement? Consequently, how might we reassess what Black practitioners have done

Fig. 5 Kazimir Malevich, *Black Square*, 1915, oil on canvas, State Tretyakov Gallery, Moscow

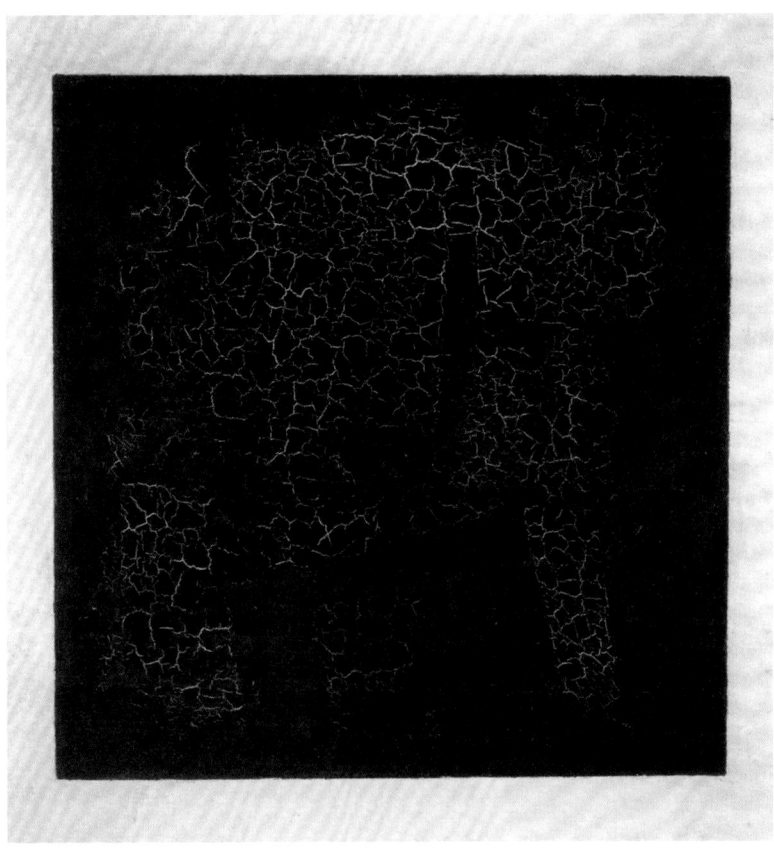

in, on, and to a field of inquiry predicated, simultaneously, on the utter availability of Black bodies and artifacts and the devaluation of Black artistry and agency? Finally, what if anything—or many things—distinguishes a Black modernist artistic response to the conditions of modernity? While following Edwards in our approach to Pan-Africanist worlds, each undergirded by the globe-straddling hierarchy of racial value in which Blackness is compulsively seen as the nadir, we acknowledge that those worlds take form differently in different places and at different times. Notably, they share the ability to submit modernism to new scrutiny and to remake its boundaries with another set of imperatives, ethics, and histories in mind.

Mama's Idea, Papa's Farewell

To model the kinds of scholarship that we hoped to educe, we prompted our collaborators to consider what might emerge from an encounter between two related scholars—whose divergent works, on their face, represent a clash between the purported grand narrative of modernism and its raced and gendered other—on the suspicion that they might, in fact, be two sides of the same coin. To wit, T. J. Clark's introduction to his watershed 1999 collection, *Farewell to an Idea: Episodes from a History of Modernism*, read alongside Hortense J. Spillers's landmark 1987 essay, "Mama's Baby, Papa's Maybe: An American Grammar Book," provided the ground in which our initial conversations took root.[13] The work of these two scholars, without whom their respective fields would be unimaginable today, is rarely considered in tandem, despite Clark and Spillers's generational proximity, as well as their parallel efforts to work with and against the grains of post-structuralist orthodoxy in the 1980s. Clark operates within disciplinary parameters, while Spillers presumes their dismantling, each differently enabled by the 1960s cataclysms—renewed modes of historical materialism and interdisciplinary Black study, respectively—that transformed the academy in the ensuing decades. The disconnect between Spillers and Clark not only serves to underline how the logic of racial segregation continues to inform American thought more generally, but also speaks specifically to the limits of the art historian's vision and to the cultural theorist's deep understanding of the implications of those limits for Black folks in life and in representation.

Now, while Clark would eventually admit that "the snake of ideology" prevented him from reckoning with Laure, the African maid in Édouard Manet's *Olympia* (1863, fig. 6), the painting whose analysis helped cement his art historical reputation in the mid-1980s, Spillers would go on to identify how such blindness in the face of Black women's forthright appearance informs the "image anxiety" that foundationally influences the African American "critical posture."[14] Throughout her work, and particularly in "Mama's Baby," a text that has opened entire fields of inquiry within Black studies, Spillers centers captive Black flesh in her description of a modern world in which the question of modernism seems, at best, a distraction, if not altogether beside the point. Taken together, these two texts are at

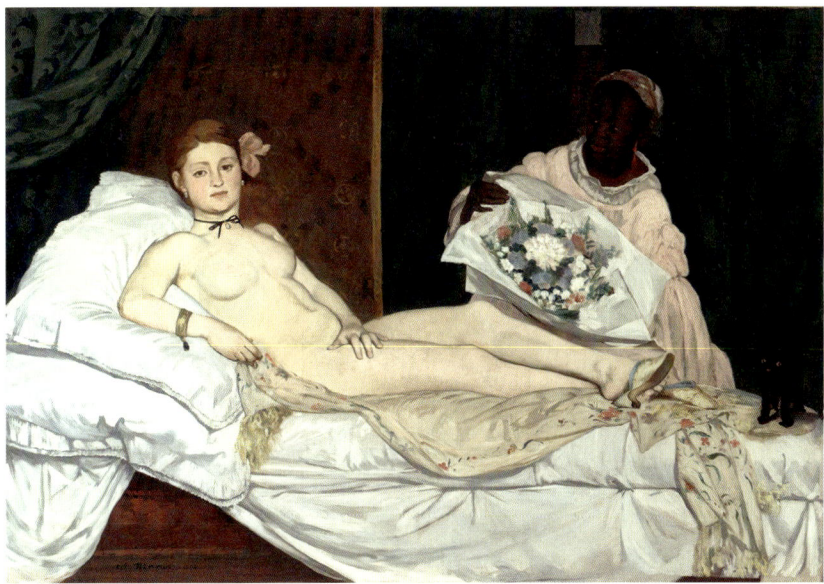

Fig. 6 Édouard Manet, *Olympia*, 1863, oil on canvas, Musée d'Orsay

© RMN-Grand Palais / Art Resource, NY. Photo by Patrice Schmidt

once necessary and insufficient; neither of their approaches, in and of themselves, can address the intersecting movement of Black and non-Black cultural workers or the function of representation in the context of conquest, colonialism, slavery, and racial capitalism over the last three centuries.[15] Yet thinking about them relationally enables us to fully reckon with both the blind spots of canonical artistic modernism and the radicality of Black cultural procedures, which have long been relegated to the margins but that, we would argue, are the heartbeat of modernist inquiry.

Although Clark's project, as enunciated in *Farewell*'s introduction, combines ways of seeing formal qualities of artworks and the structural presumptions of the societies that produce them, it also erases the Black female body even as the very terms of his arguments speak to, and indeed depend upon, her predicament. For Clark, ontologically speaking, modernism is a ruin that represents "the disenchantment of the world," just as it does for Édouard Glissant, Toni Morrison, and many other Black radical thinkers who have centered the Black (and the fem) in their understandings of what such disenchantment entails.[16] At the same time, according to Clark, modernism belongs politically with socialism, because the latter "occupies the real ground on which modernism could be described and opposed."[17] This suggests that it is indeed Black women's resistive struggles that ought to be placed near the heart of modernist inquiry: African female captives have historically needed to oppose the constitution of the world tout court without a politics proper, let alone a party, to claim as their own.

From this vantage we can begin to consider how Clark's interpretation of modernism's most radical dreams—of freedom and autonomy glimpsed through the reconfiguring of signification itself—might resonate with Spillers's accounting of the African American liberatory project, which she describes as aiming "1) to break apart, to rupture violently the laws of American behavior that make such *syntax* possible; 2) to introduce a new semantic field/fold more appropriate to his/her own historic movement."

Spillers's insistence that we face the fact that "dominant symbolic activity, the ruling episteme that releases the dynamics of naming and valuation, remains grounded in the originating metaphors of captivity and mutilation" means we must grapple with modernism's structural contiguity with, as well as its means of dissenting from, ongoing regimes of despotism and racial terror.[18]

These considerations proved invaluable for the participants of the seminar as we worked to refine and articulate what black modernisms could do and be, both individually and collectively. For us as editors that meant acknowledging, as Spillers shows, that modernity has been configured on and through the bodies of Black subjects denuded of gender and reduced to mere flesh long before "modernism" proper was even imagined.[19] By the late nineteenth century, Afro-Atlantic artists had actively engaged with modernities and modernisms as they would come to be defined by scholars like Clark. In addition to inserting themselves into modernist discourses, Black cultural practitioners have also intervened in Western modernism itself, rupturing its paradigms as well as its temporalities and geographies both formally and conceptually. Indeed, throughout the Afro-Atlantic diaspora, Black artists have long made use of the splitting, separation, and experimentation that have historically come to define modernist activity and structured Black being since the advent of transatlantic slavery. Such diasporic works, we would argue, are based not only in Western modernisms but also in variously classed, sexed, and gendered experiences of being Black, opening channels to consider the role of Afro-Atlantic discourses as a fundamental part of the formation of the modernist enterprise.

Toni Morrison brilliantly puts paid to this contention in a 1993 interview with Paul Gilroy:

> From a woman's point of view, in terms of confronting the problems of where the world is now, black women had to deal with "post-modern" problems in the nineteenth century and earlier. These things had to be addressed by black people a long time ago. Certain kinds of dissolution, the loss of and the need to reconstruct certain kinds of stability. Certain kinds of madness, deliberately going mad in order not to lose your mind. These strategies for survival made the truly modern person. They're a response to predatory Western phenomena.[20]

Two further examples suffice to make the case. On the one hand, consider how theorist Fred Moten productively recast Piet Mondrian's *Broadway Boogie Woogie* (1942–1943) as a specifically American and diasporic object that points out how the artist and his work became infected with the pulsatile energies of Black musical cultures upon his arrival to the United States.[21] On the other hand, think back to the ruse invented by an enslaved Harriet Jacobs and detailed in her astonishing narrative *Incidents in the Life of a Slave Girl* (1861). While hiding in her grandmother's attic for seven years, just a stone's throw away from her erstwhile master's house, Jacobs nonetheless was able to send out letters in her own hand that were then ferried to locations across the eastern seaboard and mailed back to her grandmother where she knew her master would intercept them. In so doing, she produced an illusion of herself elsewhere as a mobile free agent to preserve her bodily autonomy even though constrained in a space hardly larger than a coffin, a paradigmatic example of using a visual conceit to hold onto the actual self.[22]

Produced as a ready-made, fantasized as a part-object, and forced to bodily enact her own "social death," to borrow sociologist Orlando Patterson's apt phrase, Jacobs faced, and developed means of resistance to, conditions whose structures anticipate much of what we take for granted as modernist aesthetic innovation.[23] Viewed in this light, the most vaunted achievements of the twentieth-century Euro-American avant-garde, from Marcel Duchamp's 1917 *Fountain* to Robert Morris's 1961 *Untitled (Box for Standing)* (figs. 7, 8), cannot help but read as aestheticized rehashings of Jacobs's survival tactics, now enacted with uncanny objects in the gallery rather than upon fleshly things on the plantation. What would our modernisms look like if these were the facts with which they began?

Toward Intersectional Futures

Clark's erasure of Laure, the African-descended model who posed as the maid in Manet's *Olympia*, is perhaps the most concrete instance of white modernist art history's erasure of Black women. She is, in a sense, the most preeminent peripheral Negro, that sexed and racialized figure who, art historian Judith Wilson reminds us, looms "in the shadows of European and Euro-American aristocratic portraiture" and is "perpetually cast in supporting roles in allegorical works."[24] Clark's approach not only renders Laure invisible but also masks Manet's use of her as a foil for white womanhood. As African American conceptual artist Lorraine O'Grady would go on to note, in the hands of both "masters," Laure "is outside what can be conceived of as woman." The Black woman is, O'Grady continues, "the chaos that must be excised, and it is her excision that stabilizes the West's construct of the female body."[25] Spillers perhaps put it best in the unforgettable opening lines of "Mama's Baby":

> Let's face it. I am a marked woman, but not everybody knows my name. "Peaches" and "Brown Sugar," "Sapphire" and "Earth Mother," "Aunty," "Granny," God's "Holy Fool," a "Miss Ebony First," or "Black Woman at the Podium": I describe a locus of confounded identities, a meeting ground of investments and privations in the national treasury of rhetorical wealth. My country needs me, and if I were not here, I would have to be invented.[26]

Although specifically focused on the United States, Spillers's argument pertains on a global and nearly transhistorical scale given the Black

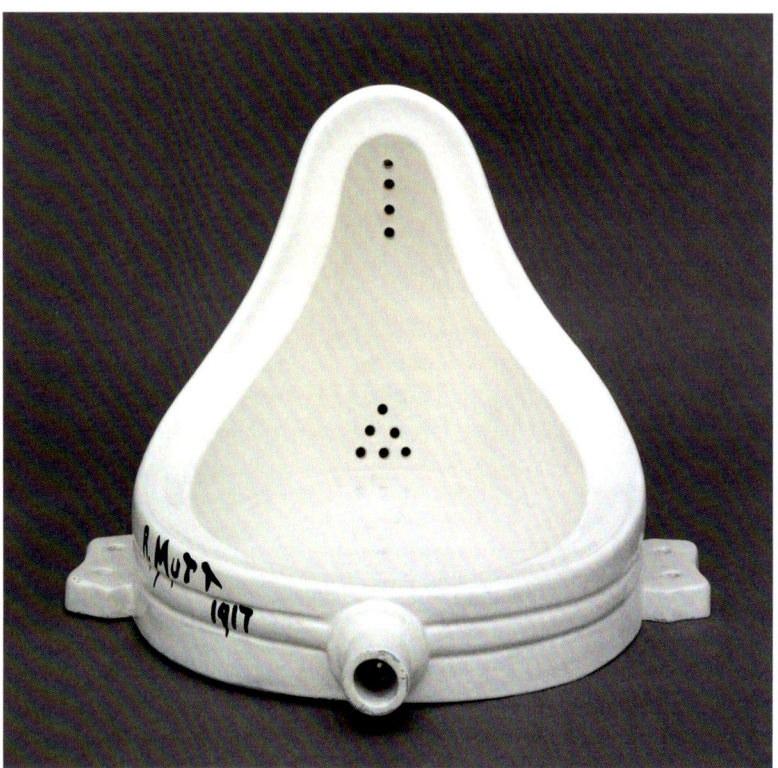

Fig. 7 Marcel Duchamp, *Fountain*, 1917, replica 1964, porcelain, Tate

© 2023 Association Marcel Duchamp / ADAGP, Paris / Artists Rights Society (ARS), New York. Photo: Tate

woman's paradoxical structural position: she is placed at the nadir of gendered and racialized hierarchies, yet is mined as an inexhaustible site for the extraction and production of value.[27] In other words, modernism, like modernity, was built on the backs and through the bellies of Black women.[28]

The present volume, however, does not merely mark the return of modernism's repressed other; rather, in doing so *Black Modernisms in the Transatlantic World* aims to question the operations that have so long sublimated Black fems and discounted Black artistic and intellectual production. Our contributors have focused on the kinds of complexity, multiplicity, and rhizomatic movement—whether in engaging canonical figures or nameless practitioners—that are central to the intersectional approaches advanced by Black women scholars such as Kimberlé Crenshaw to overcome the tunnel vision inherent in viewing the world from a single axis.[29] Accordingly, the essays move across geography and chronology, re-covering various points of the triangular trade from the eighteenth century to the present, as they explore modernisms' fissures and contradictions, always with an eye toward reframing our understanding of Black cultural intelligence, both in terms of artistic producers and those represented, figured, indexed, or suppressed within modern art and its histories.

The volume begins with a photo essay of recent work by Simone Leigh. Exalting the power and agency of Black women, the artist places them at the center of her practice as subjects, spectators, and audience members. Deeply engaged with Black feminism, African, African American, and diasporic histories, anthropology, architectural history, art history,

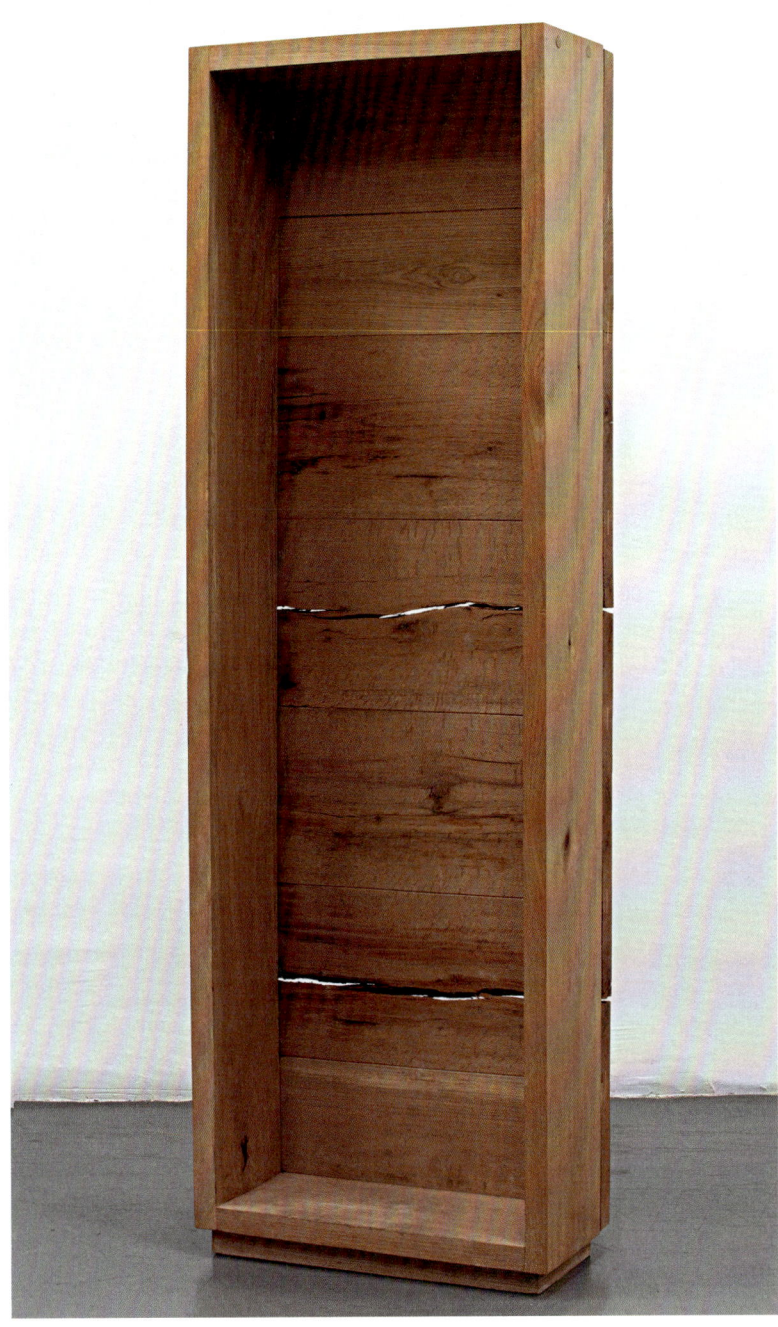

Fig. 8 Robert Morris, *Untitled (Box for Standing)*, 1961/1994, reconstruction of 1994, oak wood, Museo Nacional Centro de Arte Reina Sofía, Madrid

© 2023 The Estate of Robert Morris / Artists Rights Society (ARS), New York

and European colonialism, Leigh's oeuvre performs the kind of desublimation and reconstellation that is at the heart of *Black Modernisms in the Transatlantic World*. Her works change our understanding of the modernist project while closing off the availability of the Black female body for white delectation.

Matthew Francis Rarey's study details the contradictory visual condition so often accorded to enslavement (and to contemporary Black life) through his analysis of a small group of visually unassuming eighteenth-century pouches called *mandingas*, which were made and used by enslaved Africans in Brazil. Considering these objects and the Portuguese Inquisition records that made them somehow legible against the backdrop of an archive that records Black bodies through the denial of subjectivity and humanity, Rarey details how Black men's use of *bolsas* empowered them. He also explores how these makers and users were enmeshed in a gendered crisis of representation in the early 1700s.

C. C. McKee's essay looks at the centrality of Black women in Camille Pissarro's Caribbean images of the 1850s and early 1860s. Questioning the supposed neutrality ascribed to the work by earlier commentators and considering the position of Black women as leaders in ending slavery in the Danish West Indies, McKee analyzes two conceptions of Black femininity in the work: one that renders Black women as a fixture of the Caribbean landscape and another based on the history of representing laboring freedwomen as symbols of erotic fantasy. By putting these differing conceptions in conversation, McKee locates traces of modern Black female agency while theorizing the emergence of "the contradictory visions of a post-emancipation modernism."

Simon Gikandi's contribution focuses primarily on late nineteenth- and twentieth-century African American artists, in particular the sculptures of Meta Vaux Warrick Fuller, to explore the emergence of black modernism in the face of art history's erasure of Blackness and the unimaginable violence wrought on Black people through European colonization and American lynching. Understanding modernism and racial violence dialectically, Gikandi looks at the strategies Black artists have deployed to make modernist languages their own while asserting Black humanity and reimaging Black modern life beyond the reach of white violence.

In a similar vein, Kellie Jones's essay restores to our field of vision the pioneering modernist practices of Black artists through an examination of Nancy Elizabeth Prophet and Augusta Savage. Employing Black feminist and intersectional methods of analysis, Jones links the artists' experiences in Paris to their sculptural treatment of Black bodies, showing not only how their figures derive from a Black internationalism but also how they exist at the intersection of race, gender, and fluid sexualities. Modernisms here are Black, female, queer, and multitudinous, pressuring us to rethink a modernism coded as white and a black modernism construed as male.

At the same time, Sylvester Okwunodu Ogbechie's contribution reconsiders the implications of the numinous on Black Atlantic men's modernisms through the examples of artists Wifredo Lam, Ben Enwonwu, and James Hampton. Looking at the intersection of art making and religious practices, the author traces the tension between the material and the numinous in modernist painting and sculpture, providing a reading of black modernisms that does not proceed from the viewpoint of negation by the West. Instead, Ogbechie offers a genealogy of modernisms that acknowledges and reestablishes the role of the spiritual in their making, while he theorizes a Black Atlantic modernism that centers African religious practices and cultural registers.

Kobena Mercer's essay explores the interplay of darkness and luminosity, which he calls the "defining concern" that Norman Lewis and Roy DeCarava shared. Expanding our terms of engagement with darkness and luminosity beyond a reductive understanding of black and white as always referring to raced identities, the author posits a shift of this nexus to include perceptual qualities of shadow and light to allow a novel phenomenological perspective to emerge. With Lewis and DeCarava as models, this shift allows for an opening of possibilities for the interpretation of Black abstraction that moves beyond the straitjacket of representational politics.

Adrienne Edwards's contribution examines Afro-Dutch artist Stanley Brouwn's work *This Way Brouwn* (1964) through the lenses of errantry, migration, and immigration. Understanding that these conditions take place in and through bureaucratic systems and structures, Edwards posits that Brouwn's works seek out affinities between Dutch/Surinamese histories and his practices and ultimately show the state apparatus to be inert. At the same time, Brouwn's transgressive works create new systems of indeterminate signs in which Blackness is always already conceptual, providing a powerful means to interrogate modernisms and their conventions.

Mabel O. Wilson's essay explores Blackness, place, and memory in the work of Carrie Mae Weems, considering how her 2006 series *Roaming* and related photographic projects recalibrate Western notions of history through the figure of the witness, a doppelgänger for Weems herself, who guides viewers through space and time. Wilson uses architecture and space as part of the armature that serves as Weems's targets of critique, showing how the artist interrogates hegemonic modernism by insisting on the fundamental role that race, the bodies of Black women, and traumatic encounters have had in its construction.

We hope that this volume, taken as a whole, opens new avenues of intersectional and interdisciplinary thought and inquiry that both enable a broader understanding of the when and where of modernisms and take as a given the many locations and actors that have defined art of the last three centuries in its ongoing permutations. We are invested in space-clearing, space-creating, and a decolonization of modernism's discourses. To be clear, *Black Modernisms in the Transatlantic World* has no investment in a facile rescripting of a center/periphery model. Nor is it interested in models of "diversity" or "inclusion" that bring more speakers to the table without undoing the table's fixed structures of thought and practice.[30] Rather, if art history is to survive as a fertile place of intellectual and political engagement and to become relevant to the many rather than an elite, self-selecting few, then the kinds of thinking modeled by this volume's contributors must be placed at the forefront of art historical analysis. All to say, dear readers, that the future of modernist art histories is now in your hands, and, to riff on James Baldwin, "You need not take or leave it as it was when you came in."[31]

What will you do?

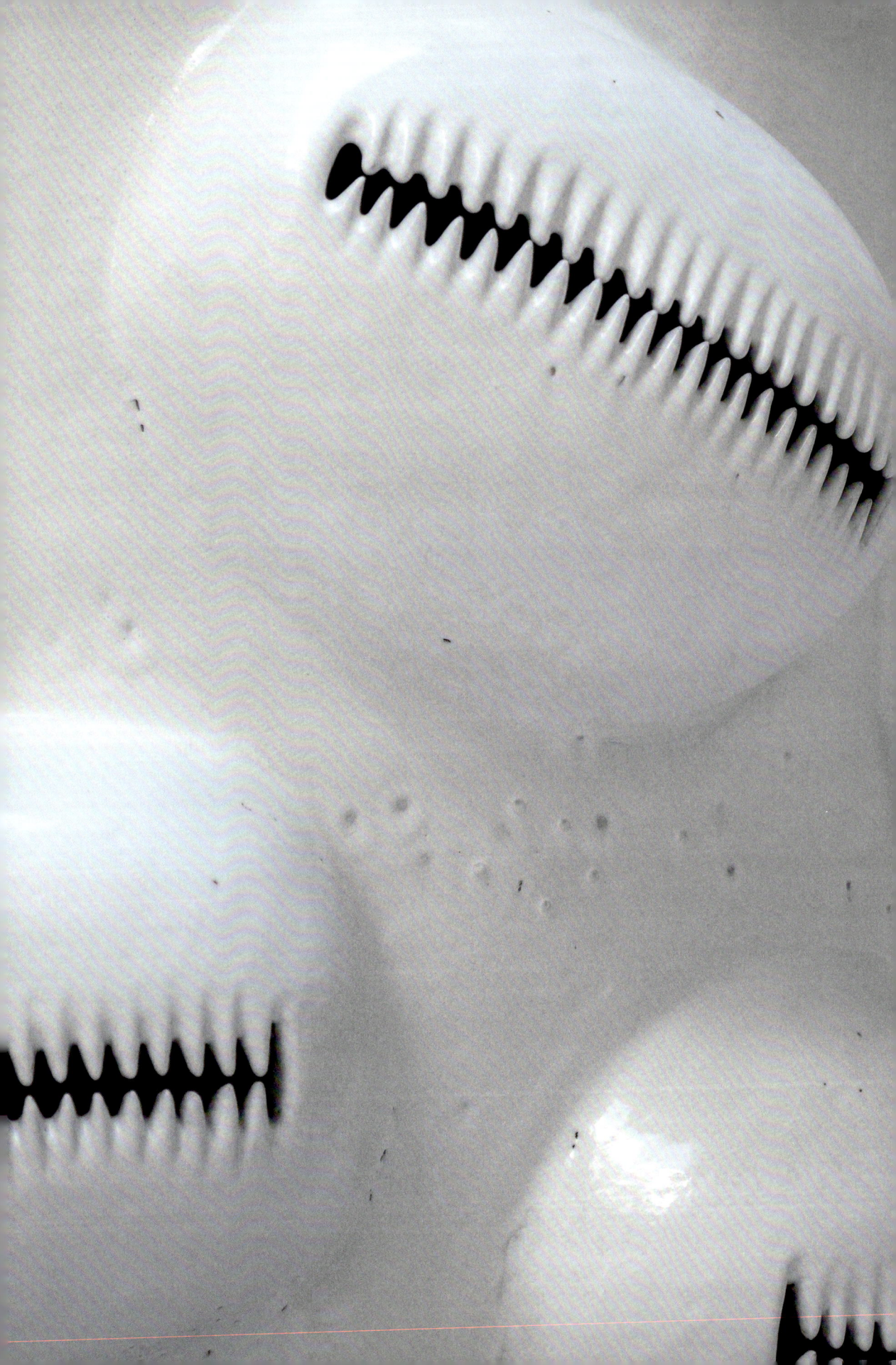

SIMONE LEIGH:
ACTS OF
TRANSFORMATION

STEVEN NELSON

Detail, *Jug*

In April 2019 Simone Leigh installed her first monumental sculpture, *Brick House*, on the High Line, an elevated park that threads through the west side of Manhattan. Sixteen feet tall, the work fuses the body of a Black woman with an iconic Mousgoum domed house (*teleuk*). Its form recalls Mammy's Cupboard, a roadside restaurant in Natchez, Mississippi, built in the shape of a giant, stereotypical Aunt Jemima figure holding a tray. Towering over 10th Avenue, *Brick House* presented an extraordinary example of Leigh's centering of Black women in a world where they have too often been treated as maids, mammies, or muses. Leigh's work combines a reverence for Black women with a deep engagement with Black feminism, African, African American, and diasporic histories, art history, anthropology, architectural history, and European colonialism. *Brick House* and the other pieces illustrated on the following pages are Black women's bodies created for Black women, and as such they reclaim and hold space while deconstructing histories of imperialism and modernism.

Leigh arrived at her practice of transforming houses, jugs, pots, spoons, and more into the bodies of Black women largely through her research on African art and architecture. During her tenure as a student at Earlham College, the artist happened upon a book called *Nigerian Pottery*. Compiled by British anthropologist Sylvia Leith-Ross, the volume is a detailed catalog, including essays that provide cultural context, overviews of pottery techniques, and more than five hundred illustrations. Leigh was particularly struck by the water pots. "Many of them," she has noted, "are perfect formally."[1] Wanting to learn how to make similar pots, Leigh secured an internship at the National Museum of African Art (NMAfA) and "[xeroxed] everything I could find on making an African pot."[2] She noted that many of the pots she studied had rounded bottoms and could balance on uneven surfaces. She was also fascinated by their transformative properties, observing, "Evaporation in terracotta purifies water and also cools the remaining water."[3] As examples of African women's visual acuity and material virtuosity, these pots offered Leigh alternative models to traditional Western understandings of form and formalism.

Leigh connected the materials, shapes, and possibilities of the pots she studied with ideas gained from her reading of Black feminists Zora Neale Hurston, Audre Lorde, Lorraine O'Grady, and others. In their writing she found clarion calls for Black women to think critically about the problematic histories of their representation. Following Hurston, Leigh adopted autoethnography as an artistic strategy.[4] She understood Lorde's insistence that the communities of nurturing created by Black women could be sources of redemption as well as power. Leigh's practice inhabits Lorde's dictum: "Interdependency between women is the way to a freedom that allows the *I* to *be*, not to be used, but to be creative. This is a difference between the passive *be* and the active *being*."[5] Leigh heeded O'Grady's call to give the Black female body, routinely "raped, maimed, and murdered," a healthy present.[6]

The records that Leigh examined at NMAfA were written by white anthropologists and Christian missionaries. She quickly understood that these documents were part of European colonial projects defined through racist lenses and aimed at convincing a white audience of the vital importance of empire and imperial dominion over others. The diagrams and texts she perused, Leigh writes, "had nothing for me that wasn't tainted."[7] These tools suppressed the histories and deeds of the colonized, rendering them as cogs in the wheels of imperialism. Leigh filtered these discourses through an ecosystem of the self as a means of disarming their power and releasing herself from the straitjacket they created.

Leigh's oeuvre is deeply involved in the politics of race and representation. Her centering of Black women counters the use of Black women's bodies by modernist artists to find their own voices. Black women are widely represented in modernism's annals, most often in the binary O'Grady so brilliantly describes as "Jezebel and Mammy, prostitute and female eunuch, the two in one."[8] Such depictions of Black women have served to highlight whiteness and the avant-garde enterprise.[9] Stripped of their humanity and individuality, Black women in the realm of white modernism have been naturalized, to invoke Black feminist literary critic Hortense J. Spillers, "as a metonymic figure for an entire repertoire of human and social arrangements."[10] In Leigh's hands, the Black woman is no longer modernism's mammy, maid, or muse. Her Black female subjects' transformed and abstracted bodies are opaque, retaining their power and unraveling modernism's desire to extract knowledge and reduce Black women to types and specimens upon which to project white fantasy, fear, loathing, and longing.

Leigh's diasporic lens, her research, and her understanding of colonialist discourse dovetail beautifully with her understanding of the Black female body as a repository of complex lives and incredible power. Nowhere is this clearer than in *Sovereignty*, Leigh's installation for the 2022 Venice Biennale, which transformed the US Pavilion from a temple of modern American art into a space that holds and celebrates Black women's strength, perseverance, and humanity. Moreover, her work creates settings that nurture Black women while calling out histories of their marginalization. Highlighting Black female subjectivity on the artist's own terms, Leigh has created a body of formally extraordinary work by a Black woman, unabashedly and unapologetically for Black women.

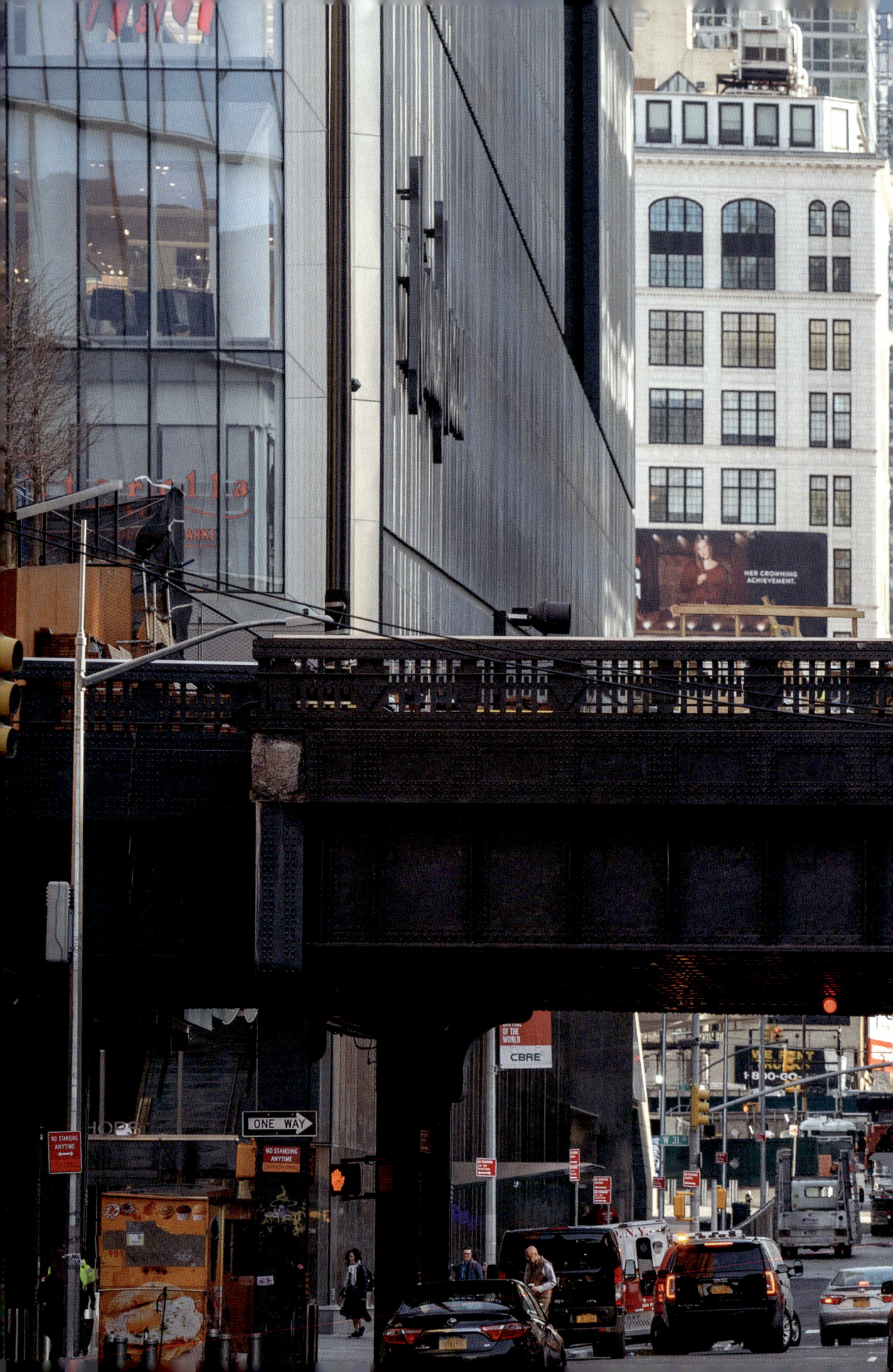

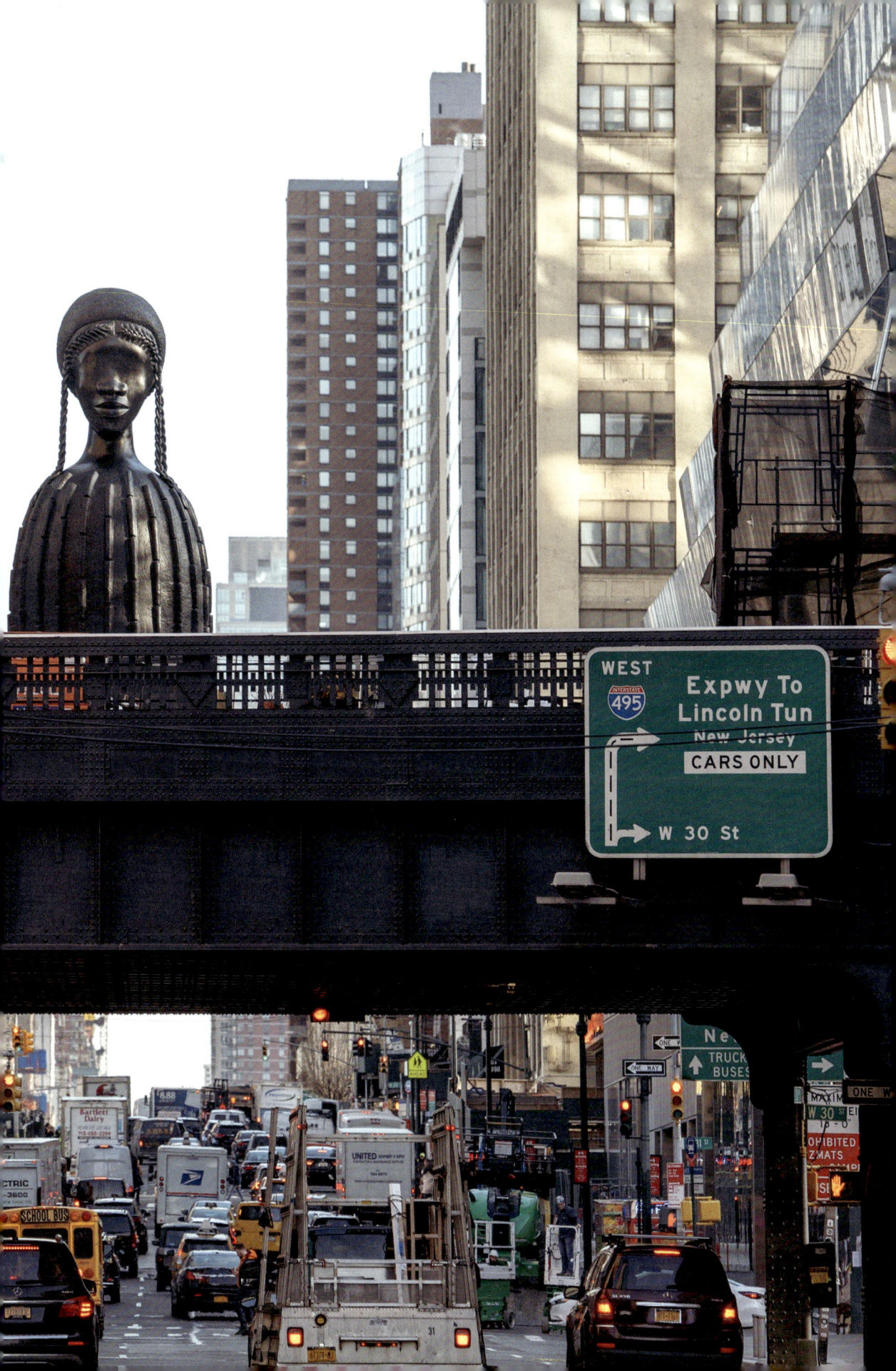

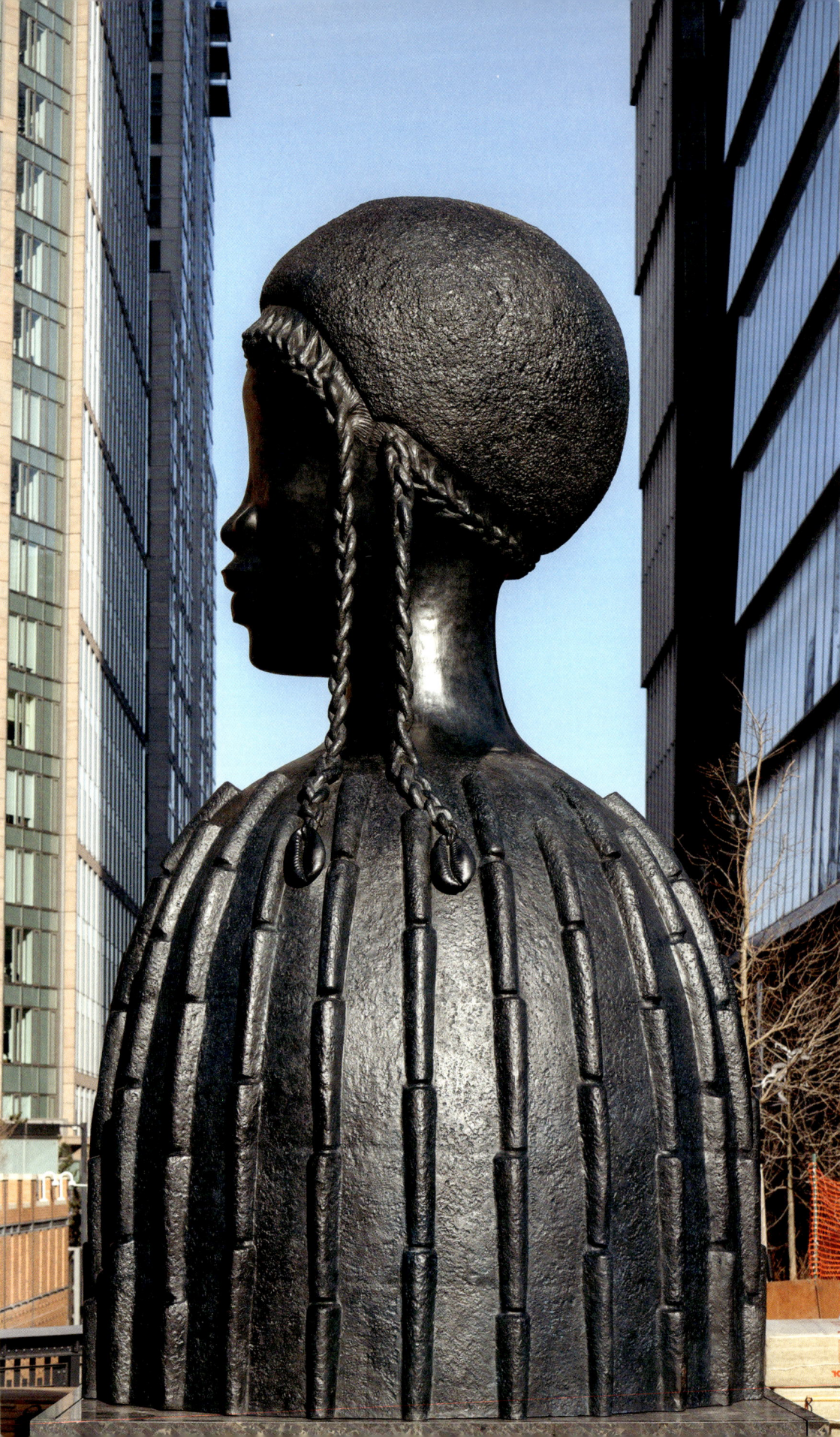

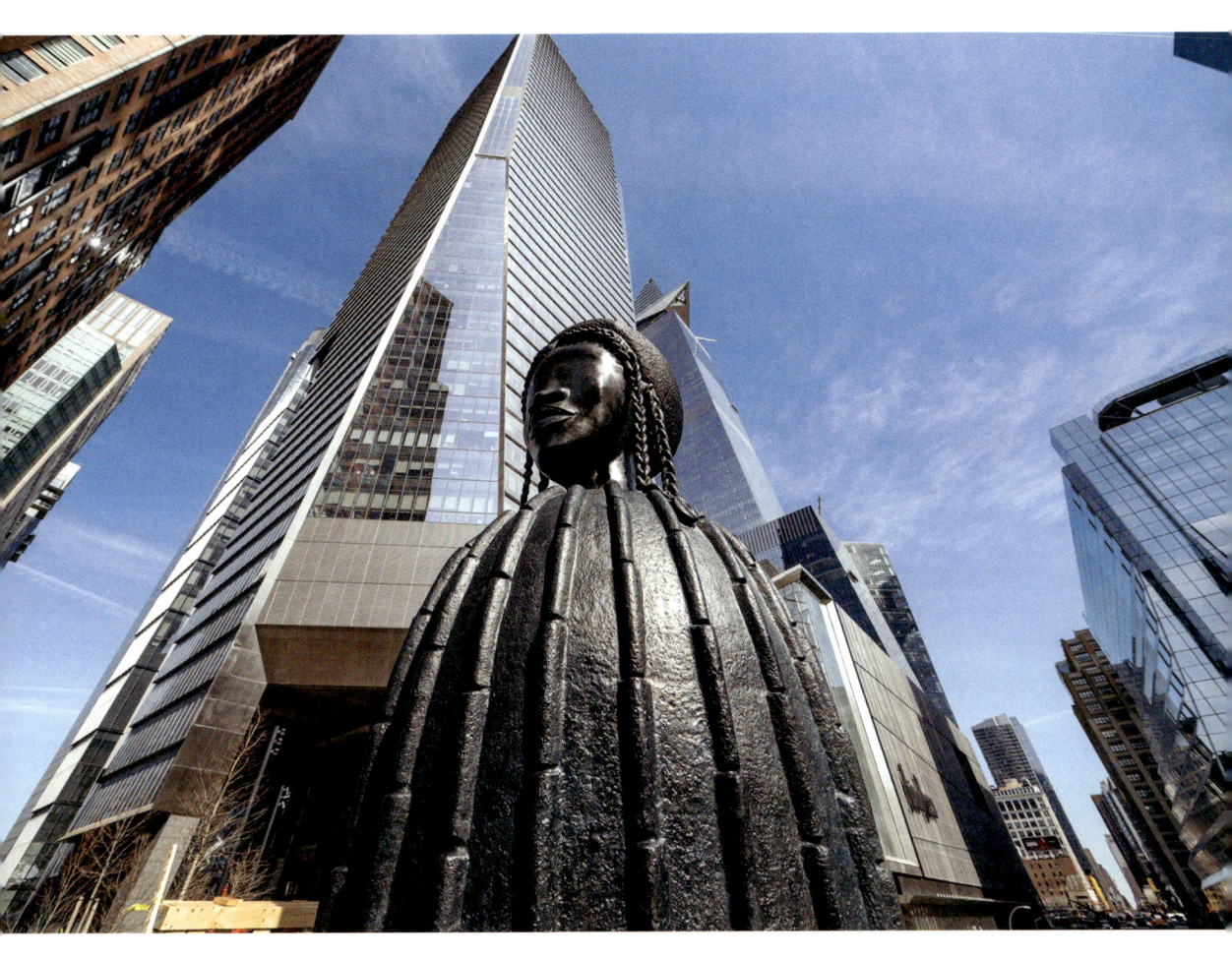

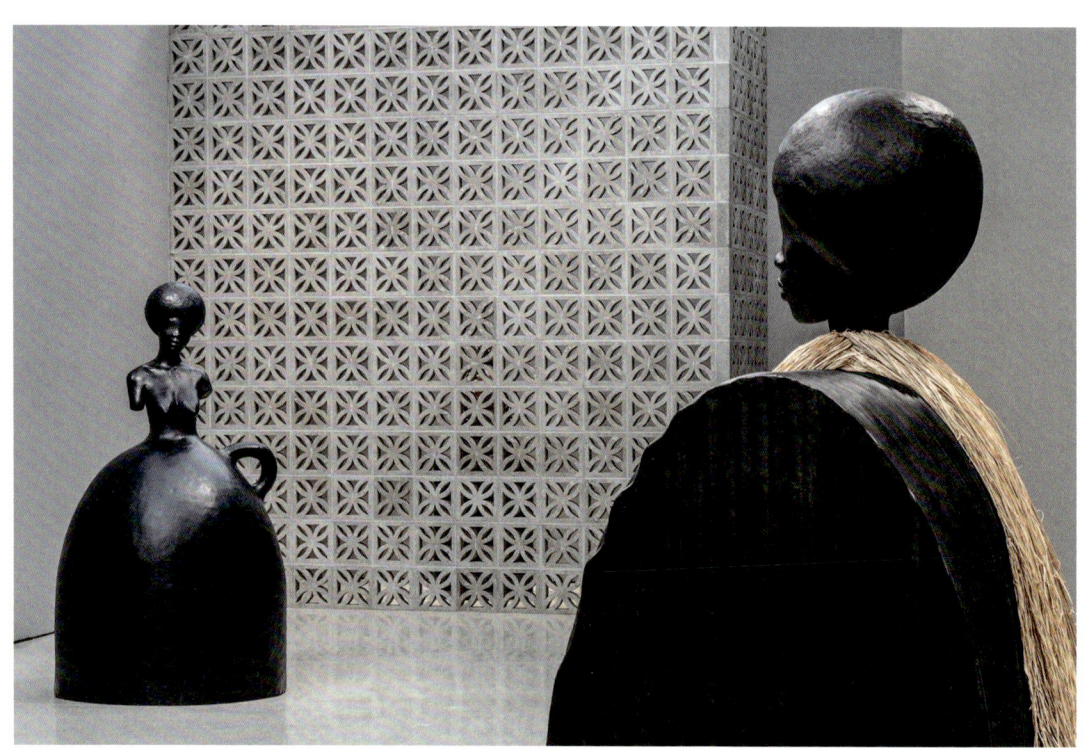

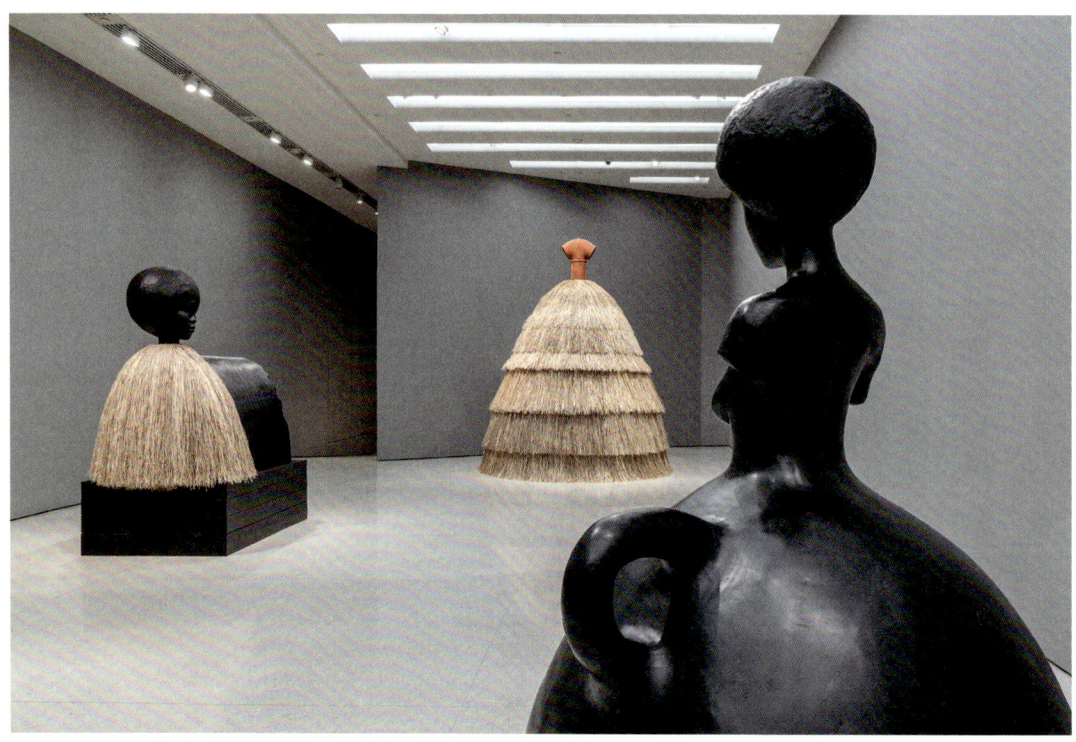

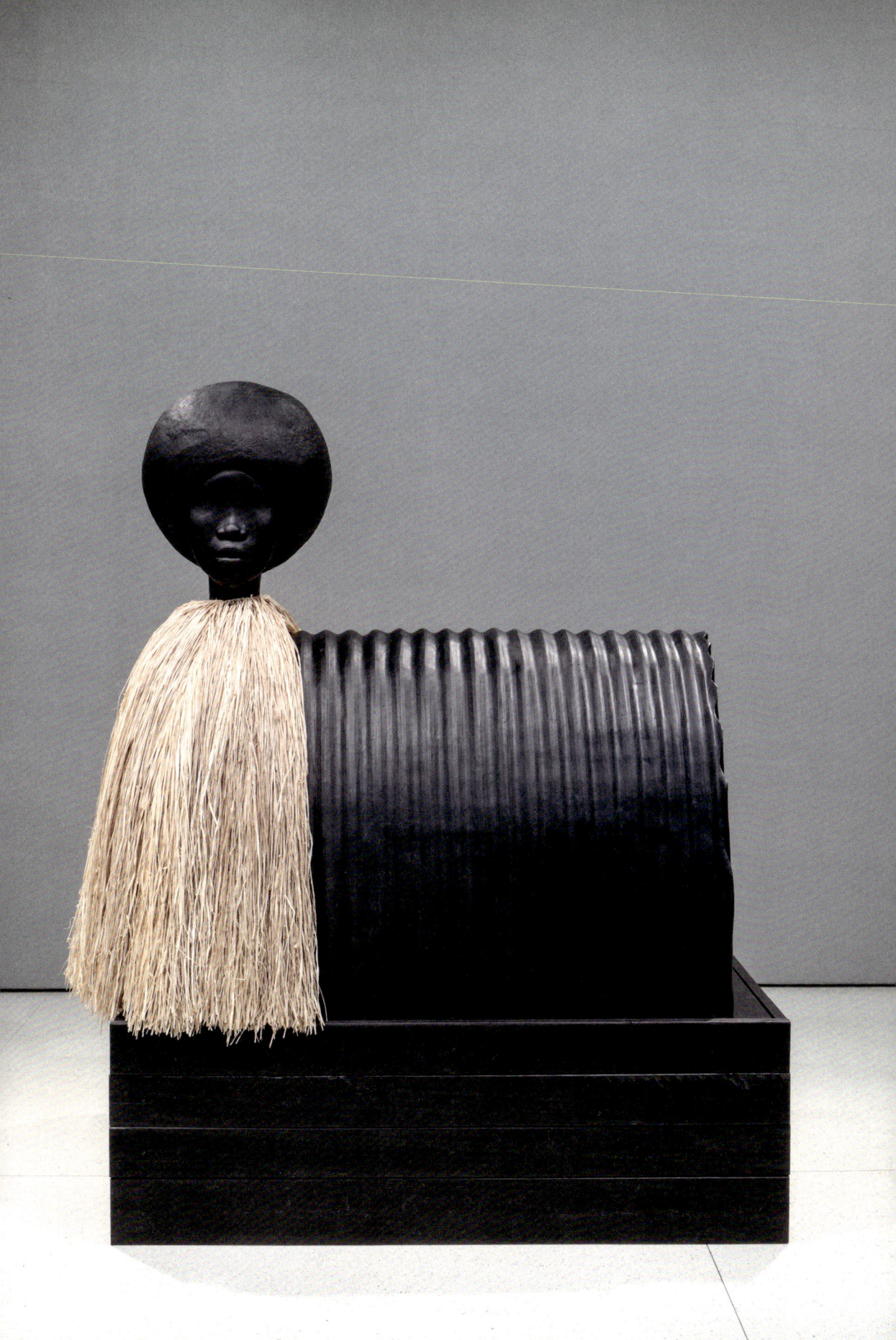

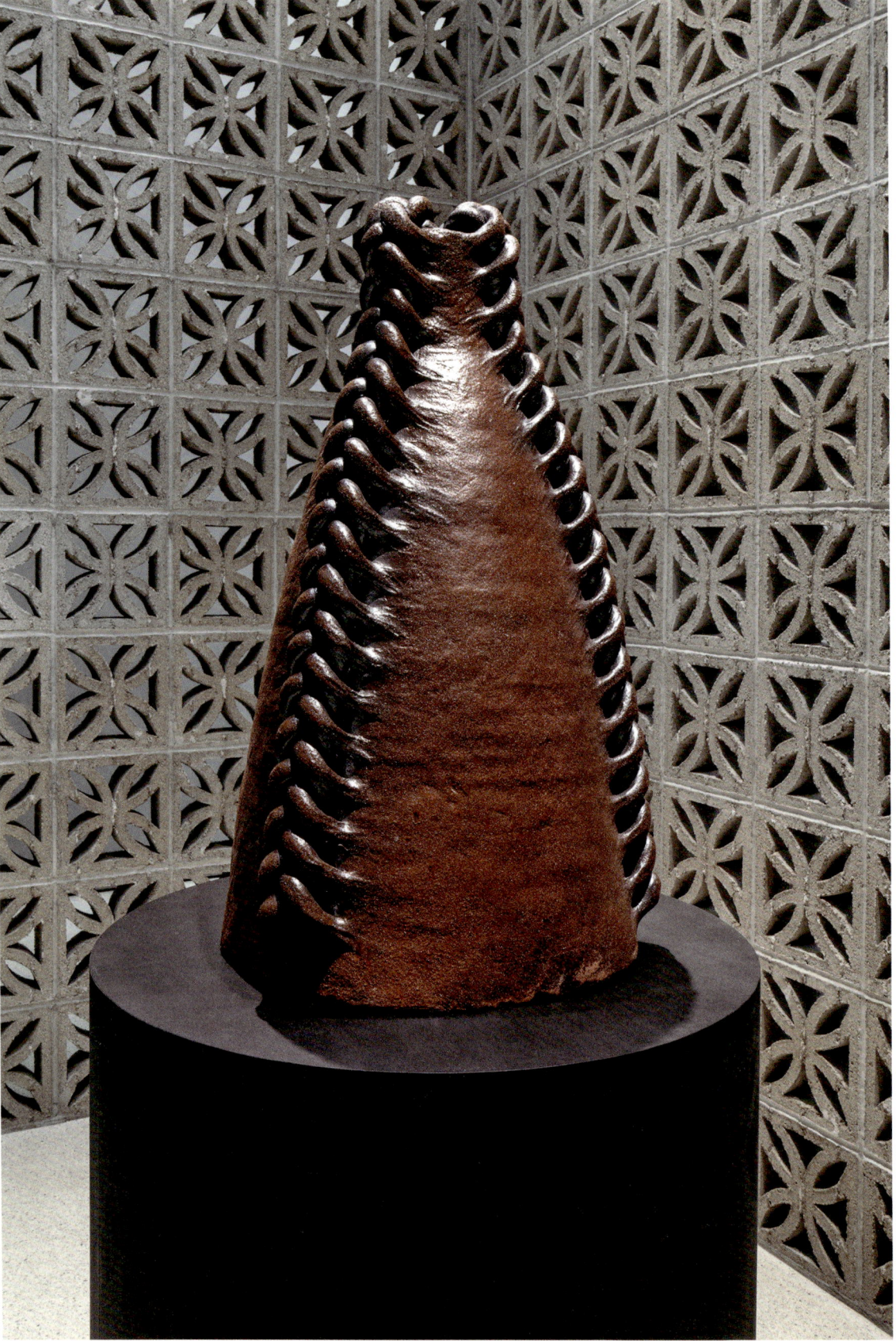

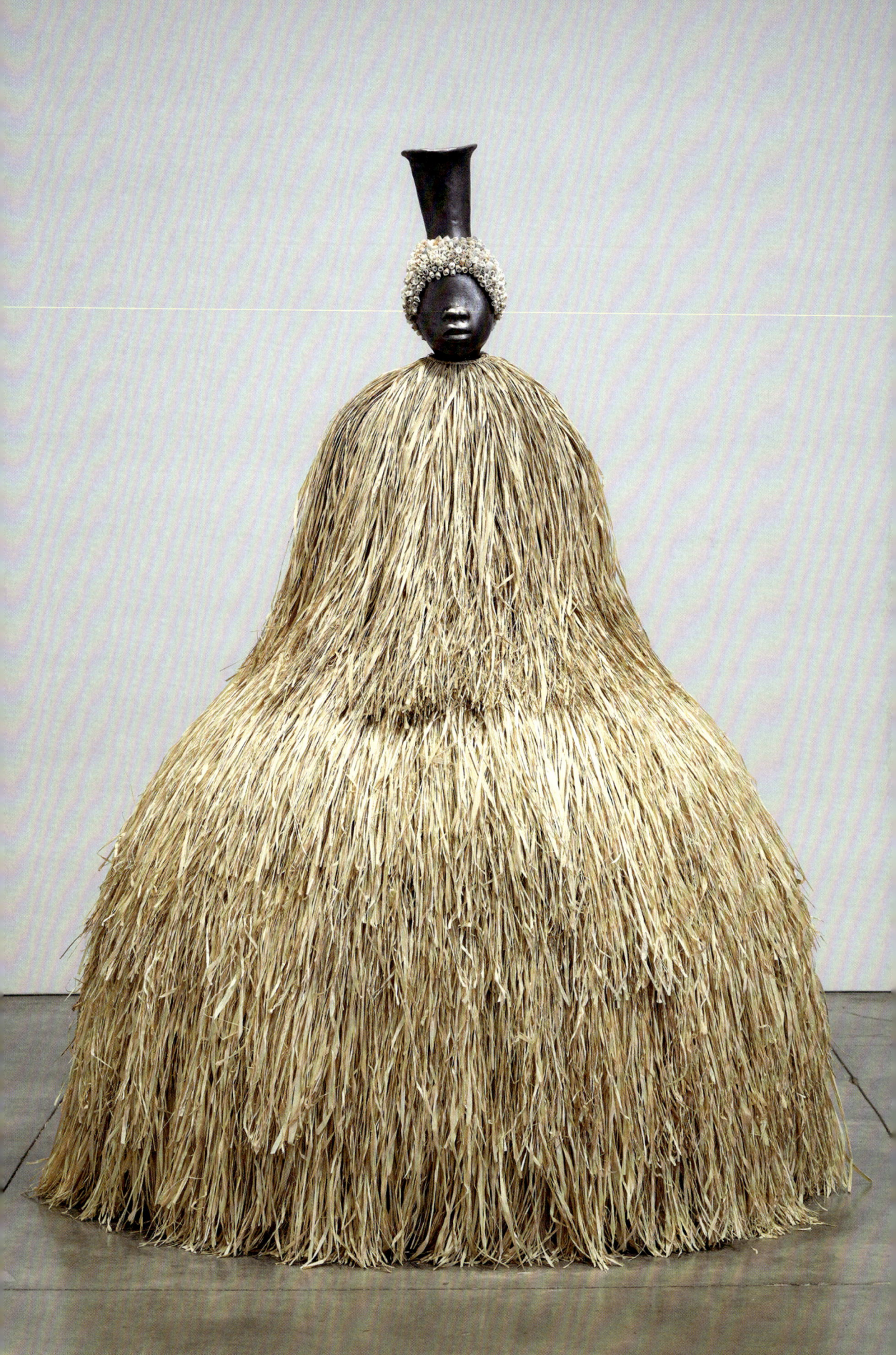

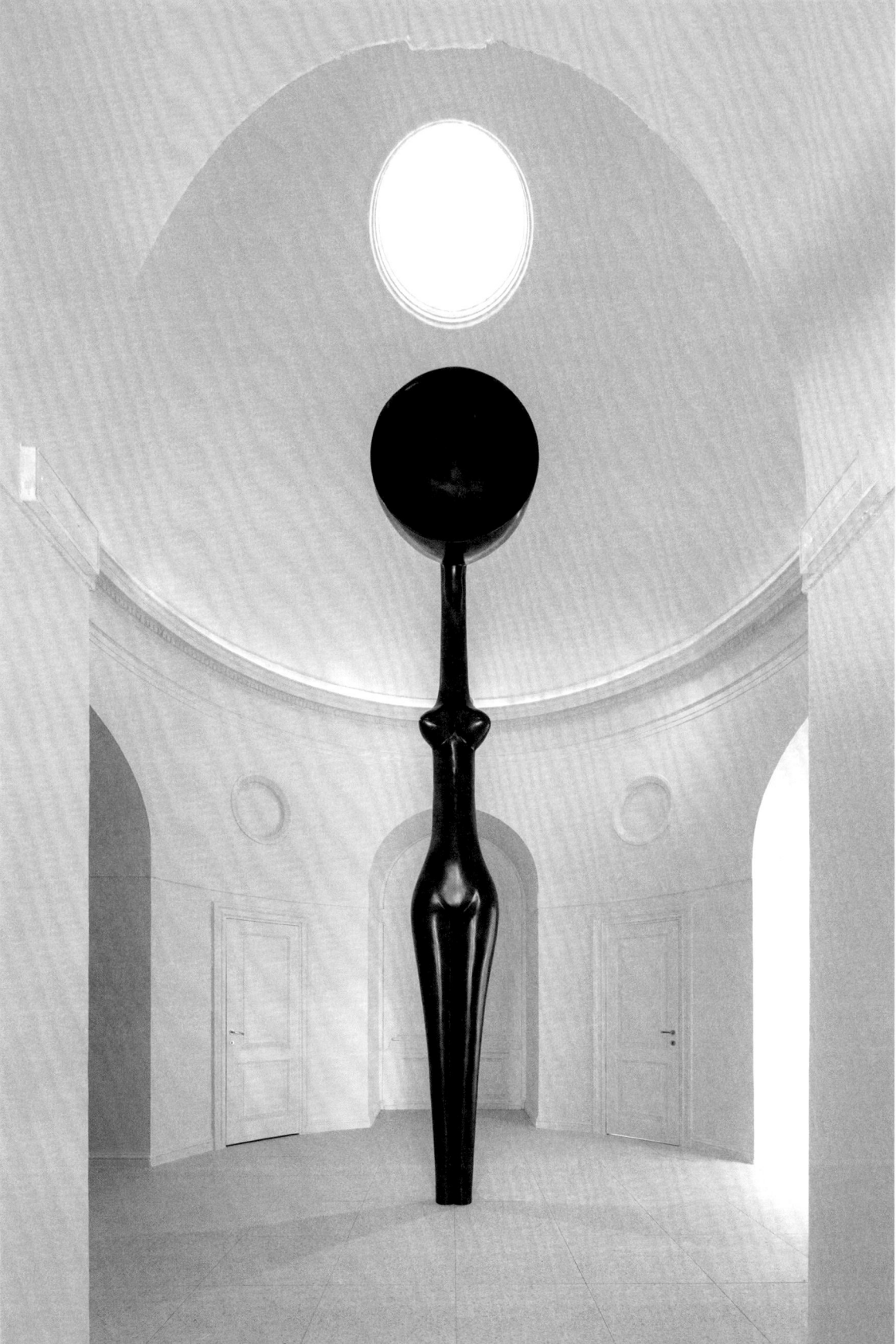

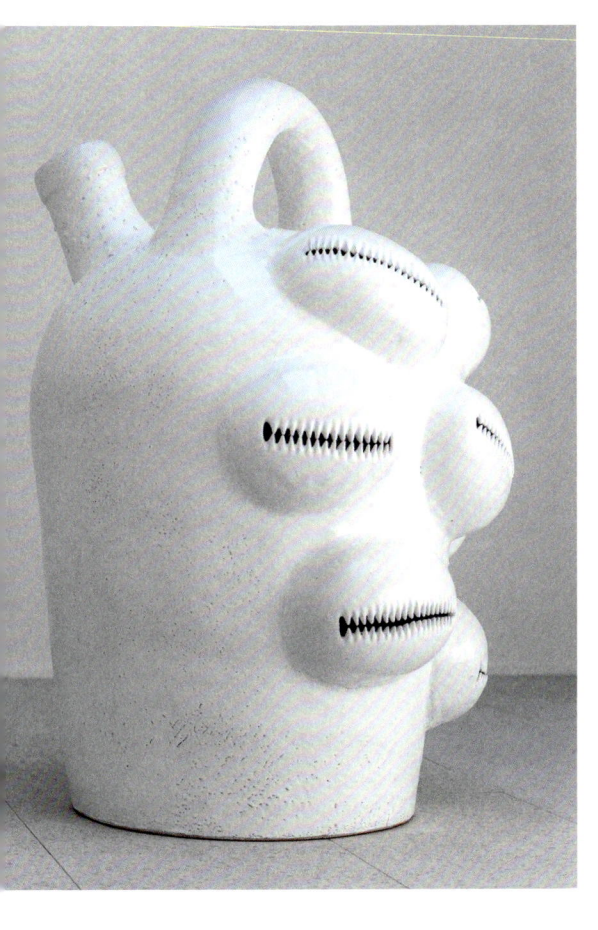
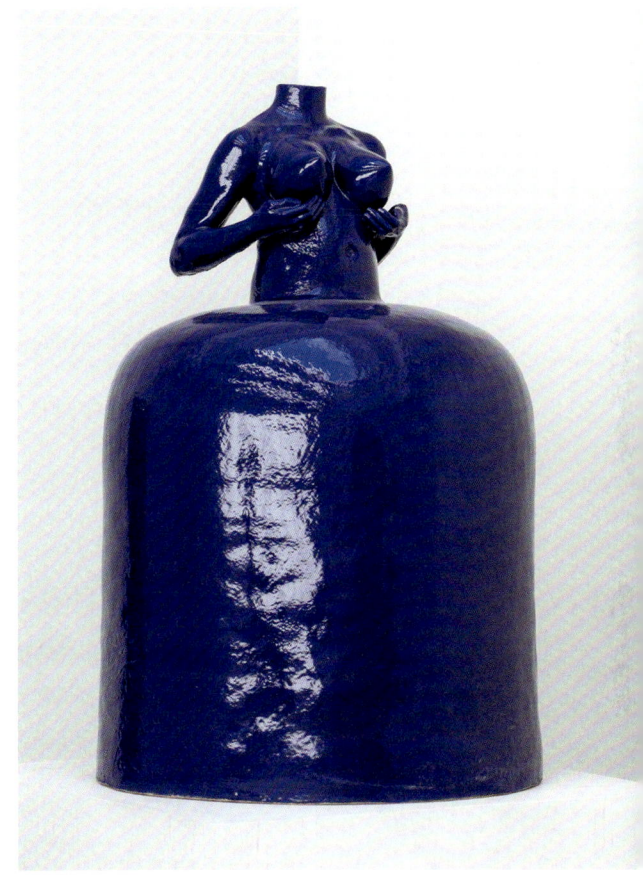

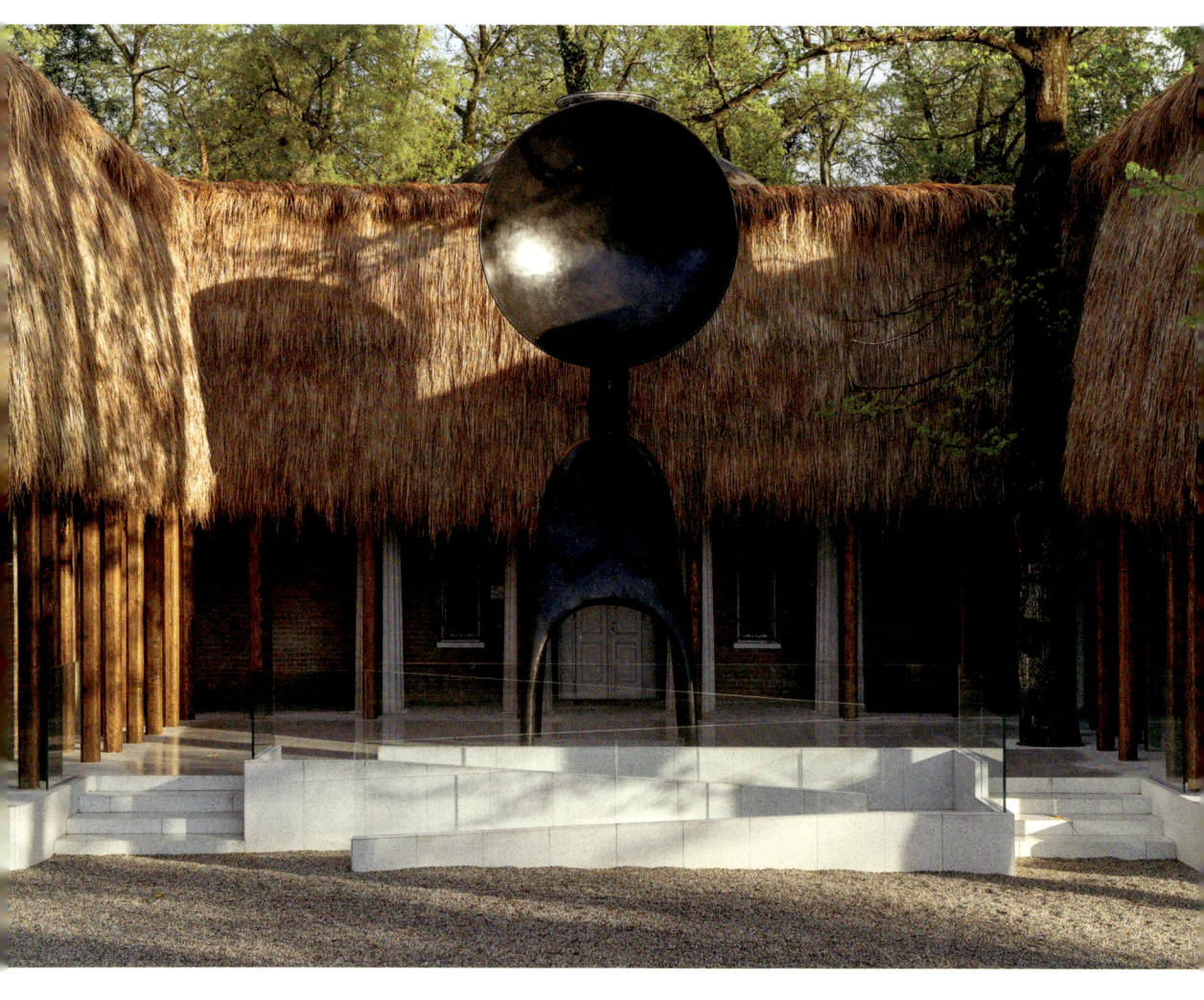

In order of appearance

Brick House, 2019, bronze, temporary installation at the High Line, New York
Photos by Timothy Schenck

Installation photos, *The Hugo Boss Prize 2018: Simone Leigh, Loophole of Retreat*, Guggenheim Museum, New York, 2019
Photos by David Heald. © 2019 The Solomon R. Guggenheim Foundation, courtesy of the artist and the Guggenheim Museum, New York

Sentinel, 2019, bronze and raffia
Photo by David Heald. © 2019 The Solomon R. Guggenheim Foundation, courtesy of the artist and the Guggenheim Museum, New York

Loophole of Retreat (detail), 2019, concrete blocks, bronze, and sound, 6:44 minutes
Photo by David Heald. © 2019 The Solomon R. Guggenheim Foundation, courtesy of the artist and the Guggenheim Museum, New York

Figure with Skirt (Face Jug Series), 2018, terracotta, graphite, salt-fired porcelain, steel, and raffia
Photo by Farzad Owrang, courtesy of the artist and Luhring Augustine Gallery, New York

Sentinel, 2022, bronze
© Simone Leigh, courtesy Matthew Marks Gallery. Photo by Timothy Schenck

Jug, 2022, glazed stoneware
© Simone Leigh, courtesy Matthew Marks Gallery. Photo by Timothy Schenck

Martinique, 2022, glazed stoneware
© Simone Leigh, courtesy Matthew Marks Gallery. Photo by Timothy Schenck

Façade, 2022, thatch, steel, and wood, with *Satellite*, 2022, bronze
© Simone Leigh, courtesy Matthew Marks Gallery. Photo by Timothy Schenck

coal seu coura q me fes, ne so mo fasa coura de su
nao far meu de pe vir a mão ainda q eu não saiba
de vem quero fazer mal sei ti sos vem quero Luira m
do prigo dom paliaçar p euu q he sa q no brasil
fora della me não mordao Bisar e deos me de ver
e Moços de men Euma Casta mas q fusao de min
que o q q me juda como perder logo a pareça quero q
o q se tras a ver ão manda po vos o men sinco sa boa
o sor tou e Ne mem Jesus

LEAVE NO MARK: BLACKNESS AND INSCRIPTION IN THE INQUISITORIAL ARCHIVE

MATTHEW FRANCIS RAREY

Senhor

Mandado da obidiencia do perlado fui com outros companheiros fazer missão ao termo de Sintra e estando ẽ hũa quinta hũa legoa da dita villa q̃ he de Sebastião de Carualho achei nella a seu filho Manoel de Carualho capitão q̃ he da Caualaria do qual soube q̃ hũ negro forro q̃ eu ui e elle tem em seu seruisso trazia bolça, e se prouou porq̃ metendolhe em certa occazião hũa adaga pela gragante com toda a força a adaga torçeo q̃ ebrou como se topara em pedra sem deixar o menor sinal.

O dito negro disse diante de min (seg.do eu mal entendi porq̃ não falaua claro) q̃ tinha tres cada qual q̃ seu ministerio e estranhandolhe me respondeo q̃ m.ta gente em Lx.a trazia bolças, e nomeou alguãs pessoas q̃ a min me não embrão o dizer agora elle o poderá dizer examinado.

Também me dicerão q̃ o d.to negro dicera q̃ hũ negro seu cunhado as fazia; e o furriel da companhia do dito capitão Manoel de Carualho me dice a min q̃ lhe achara hũa uez hũa bolça q̃ ao negro cahio e lançandoa no fogo foi notauel a fumaça e fedor q̃ de si lançou, outras m.tas coizas me dicerão e elles poderão referir perguntados porq̃ a min me não lembrão agora em firma q̃ as possa escreuer.

E porq̃ entendo q̃ pelos decretos desse S.to Tribunal estou obrigado a denunciar specialm.te por hũ q̃ o poucos anos sahio a cerca destas bolças em special (não obstante q̃ eu dice ao sobredito capitão e sua familia estauão obrigados todos a denunciar) eu por esta carta denuncio p.a descargo da minha conciencia e de meus companheiros.

On June 11, 1700, João de São Boaventura—a missionary then stationed in central Portugal—sent a letter to the *comissários* of the Lisbon Inquisition denouncing a Black man he knew (fig. 1).[1] In the text, São Boaventura attests that this man wore an object described as a "pouch" (*bolsa*) that, despite its seeming visual banality, functioned as a shield against physical violence.[2] On one memorable occasion, São Boaventura recounted, this man took a dagger to his own neck "with such force, but the dagger bent back as if it had struck stone, without leaving any mark."[3]

São Boaventura's words recall Hortense J. Spillers's classic essay "Mama's Baby, Papa's Maybe," in which she argues that efforts to articulate Black identities remain haunted by the captivity, mutilation, and marking of Black bodies, a kind of inherited "hieroglyphics of the flesh" that inaugurates histories of racial inscription and subjectivity.[4] For Spillers, Black people's formation of and entry into the modern world originated from, and depended on, literal and figural de-gendering, dismemberment, and marking of their flesh. Sherwin K. Bryant elaborates on this argument when he describes the status of enslaved people in the colonial Americas as "an act of archival inscription. . . . The practice of subjecting the bodies of enslaved African captives to inspection, documenting their 'marks,' including scarification, wounds received in the transatlantic passage, smallpox marks, brands of the licensed trading companies, and their overall physical conditions were more than acts of power, these were ways of forming, expanding, and legitimating the race relation of governance that slavery installed."[5] In this way the archive symbolically substitutes the visceral violence Spillers describes, giving it the form of "laboratory prose" and calculated, facile regulation.[6] For Spillers, one thus cannot easily disentangle the endless shelves of imperial decrees, registers of enslaved people, and trial records that form the archival accumulations of Church and Empire from the "marking and branding" of Black bodies.[7]

I read Carrie Mae Weems's *Black and Tanned* (1995) as one effort to grapple with this tension (fig. 2). A circular window—evoking a camera, a peephole, and a gun's sight—zeroes in on the scarred back of an enslaved man identified as both "Gordon" and "Peter" in extant records. In 1863, after this man reached a Union camp at Baton Rouge, Louisiana, a photograph of his "Scourged Back" quickly emerged as one of the most widely circulated abolitionist images of its day, reproduced as a carte-de-visite and a shocking insertion in abolitionist lectures.[8] In *Black and Tanned*, Weems tries to address and redress this viral conversion of the subject's identity into his wounds. The white text imposed over the red background—itself an evocation of blood and warning—creates a slippage between the text's inscription, the new voices it may grant its subject, and the archival-corporeal violence inherent to its production.

It is against this backdrop of archival lack created in service of racially deterministic histories of violence; against recent reckonings with modernity's dependence on the disarticulation of Black lives; and against ongoing efforts to redress that disarticulation by counter-narrating the archives of Atlantic slavery, that I read São Boaventura's three-centuries-old

Fig. 1 Letter by João de São Boaventura denouncing an unnamed Black man to the Lisbon Inquisition, 1700, Arquivo Nacional da Torre do Tombo, Lisbon

Courtesy of ANTT

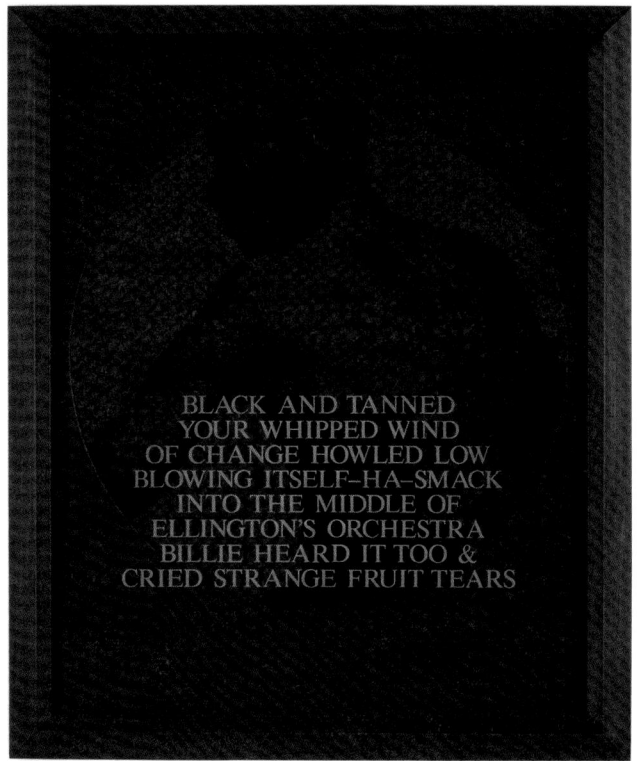

Fig. 2 Carrie Mae Weems, *Black and Tanned Your Whipped Wind of Change Howled Low Blowing Itself-Ha-Smack into the Middle of Ellington's Orchestra Billie Heard It Too & Cried Strange Fruit Tears*, from the series *From Here I Saw What Happened and I Cried*, 1995, chromogenic color print with sandblasted text on glass, Museum of Modern Art, New York, Gift on behalf of the Friends of Education of the Museum of Modern Art

Digital image © The Museum of Modern Art / Licensed by Scala / Art Resource, NY

account of a Black man publicly performing his own body's inviolacy. São Boaventura's letter is one of scores of similar eighteenth-century testimonials describing the use of bolsas filled with unseen activating contents—objects often called *mandinga* on account of their presumed African and sorcerous associations.[9] While São Boaventura wrote that in Lisbon "many people use them,"[10] other records testify to their use in Angola, Cape Verde, Madeira, and especially Brazil.[11] Though they possessed a diverse range of powers, including the ability to attract new lovers or grant luck in games of chance, most often, awestruck Europeans and Africans alike attested that these amulets protected their users from intimate personal violence, a function proved through spectacular public demonstrations of their efficacy. In April of 1700, two white men in Lisbon denounced Francisco, an enslaved Black Cape Verdean man, for selling them bolsas; they lodged a complaint because his wares did not work as described.[12] In August of 1700, another enslaved Black man attested that Jacques Viegas, an enslaved "*natural* of Mina," boasted that he could not be harmed.[13] The man took up the challenge and ran at Jacques with a sword, but could not penetrate Jacques's exposed skin because of a bolsa he wore.[14] In January of 1702, a carpenter testified that his friend put the base of a sword in the floor and fell on it, but survived unharmed because of the mandinga he had.[15] In September of 1702, a priest in Portugal denounced "a black man who carried a mandinga with him," its effectiveness proved when he stabbed himself in the arm.[16] And in June of 1704, the Inquisition once again charged Viegas with using a mandinga pouch, this time to protect him during knife-fights in a local church.[17]

Today, Jacques's green fabric mandinga pouch, sewn into the binding of his Inquisition trial record held at Portugal's National Archive, is one of the few extant examples (fig. 3).[18]

The stated ability of these bolsas to protect their users from physical violence can arguably be seen as a reflection of the logics of enslavement—the presumption of the enslaved person's heightened capacity for pain and consent over bodily violation. It is thus unsurprising that almost all recorded users of bolsas identified as men and openly discussed their sexual attraction to women, for they allowed their users to participate in a particular performance of masculinity tied to the racial-sexual dominance of others' bodies.[19] As Spillers defines Blackness as a series of othered subject positions that function outside of legal orders of race and gender, the "marks" on papers inside the pouches provided one of the few mechanisms through which the enslaved could attempt to inhabit positions as gendered subjects. In the case studies discussed below, this device manifests as a temporary masculinity dependent on the ability of those using mandingas to dominate others while preventing domination of one's own body.

Another level of the argument to be pursued here, however, is an interrogation of the forms of inscription, which not only appear in the bolsas but also provide the archival information that makes them known in the present. Almost all information about these objects comes from the records of the Portuguese Inquisition, which, beginning in the late seventeenth century, circulated *editais* (printed paper decrees) decrying the use of bolsas across Portugal and its overseas colonies.[20] In response,

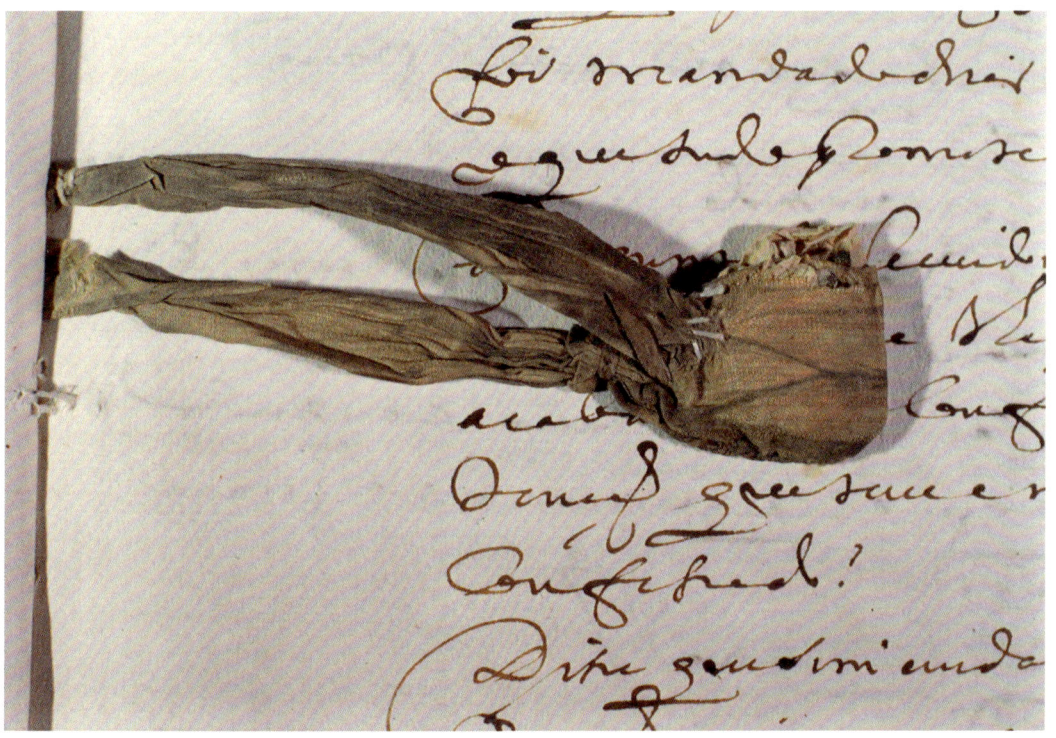

Fig. 3 Mandinga pouch attached to the 1704 Lisbon Inquisition trial of Jacques Viegas, Arquivo Nacional da Torre do Tombo, Lisbon

Courtesy of ANTT

suspicious onlookers, neighbors, and trusted confidants sent letters to Lisbon denouncing suspected criminals against the Church. Indeed, São Boaventura wrote his own letter in response to a decree requiring the empire's subjects to denounce anyone using a bolsa. I reproduce São Boaventura's letter here to call attention to its letter-ness, to emphasize how the creation, transit, and archiving of written denunciations sustained the Inquisition's fledgling global surveillance system. In reproducing first-person testimonies of assumed crimes and suspects' biographical information, paper emerged as the medium that defined imperial subjects as witnesses, suspects, and heretics. It also transformed bolsas into Inquisitorial evidence by ritually converting their contents into paper in the Inquisition file. When they could obtain the amulets, Inquisitors often feverishly opened them to reveal their contents and wrote ekphrastic descriptions of the assembled mélange they found. Consider this list of contents from Inquisition trials, which upends assertions of cultural origin or artistic hierarchy: hair, sticks, cotton, sulfur, gunpowder, a piece of lead, a bullet, a silver coin, "some red feathers from a Brazilian bird,"[21] "some human fingernails and pieces of flesh, which appear to be from a dead man,"[22] and "other little things."[23] Inquisitors typically discarded most of the amulets' contents, despite the attention paid to them. But they kept the papers, orations, and drawings that were common, and sometimes singular, inclusions inside of the pouches, incorporating them into the Inquisition files.

The aforementioned contemporary arguments that bookend this essay aim to address the production of Blackness over the long duration by tracing the intimate relationships between corporeal violence, absence, and the legibility of Black histories in Atlantic slavery's archives. If one agrees (as I do here) with Spillers's argument that the initial moment of archival-corporeal inscription and violation inaugurated Blackness and modernity and Blackness *as* modernity, then we may neither close off nor finalize the "where" and "when" of modernism. What, then, might it look like to present a conception of modernism that takes Black people's subjection to, and active aesthetic-political work against, those metaphors of violation and marking as its origin and constitution?

To flesh out such an argument would require more space than available here. But the talismanic papers that survive in the Lisbon Inquisition's archives present a series of possible responses to this provocation, since they remain some of the only extant texts authored by enslaved Africans in the Lusophone world prior to the middle of the nineteenth century. I analyze three of these texts on the pages that follow. Each was once contained inside a bolsa, was eventually confiscated and sent to the Inquisition, and is now attached to the trial record of the person who made or used them. I argue that these documents show how enslaved mandinga-makers and users, whose biographies crossed Africa, Brazil, and Portugal, knew of the transformative role papers played for officials and elites and that they understood the ways the perceived power of writing could inscribe Blackness and define the status of "slave." While this argument provides fresh historical and geographic context to Spillers's articulation of modernity, I add here that the bolsas also make visible forms of resistance to it by strategically dis- and re-articulating the perceived relationships between writing and literacy that undergird the act of racial inscription. As such, while the bolsa-papers described below make clear how writing could inscribe an enslaved person, they also illuminate attempts to de-inscribe that status—a move that maps modernity as a fraught and fragile endeavor. At the same time, the continued survival of these objects and papers depends, once again, on the subjugation of their owners, and so I conclude with a meditation on the possibility of archival recovery.

Harnessing the Word: José Francisco Pereira, 1730–1731

In the summer of 1731, Inquisitorial agents arrested and confiscated mandinga pouches from José Francisco Pereira.[24] Born in 1704 in or near Dahomey and captured around 1718, he spent about a decade laboring in Brazil before being taken to Lisbon in the late 1720s. There, he quickly established himself as a sought-after mandinga-maker, partnering with his friend and confidant José Francisco Pedroso.[25] One of José Francisco Pereira's papers stands out for its intriguing integration of word and image (fig. 4). The image's iconography points to José Francisco's efforts to represent, or even capture, the critical and transformative symbols of the Catholic Mass, and thus the ritual authority they conveyed. At bottom, José Francisco depicts the Caravaca Cross. The original, housed in a church in Spain, had in the seventeenth century developed a new origin story describing how its miraculous appearance convinced Zayd Abu Zayd, the last Almohad governor of Valencia, to convert to Christianity in 1231.[26] The cross was associated with religious conversion, particularly in post-Reformation Iberia, which made it a popular fixture on Catholic altars across the peninsula. Its powers, too, depended on ritual knowledge: as José Francisco likely knew, during Mass priests often carried these crosses over *pedras d'ara*, the specially prepared stones placed inside altars to sanctify what was placed on them. Not coincidentally, José Francisco also placed pieces of altar stone inside his mandingas, for they played a key role in converting quotidian materials into empowered intercessors.

At center, José Francisco renders a circular design with a small cross, likely representing a Eucharistic host. Used during the most sacred moment of Catholic ceremonies, the Catholic doctrine of transubstantiation—codified and widely upheld during this period—declares that this small wafer invisibly transforms into the body of Jesus, usually by passing over an altar stone. The Inquisition considered hosts as deeply sacred, inviolable objects, and severely punished those who stole them. This image, then, reappropriates the host's powers within mandingas' charge to protect their users from human violence and to invoke the invisible transformations of its other empowering contents, while also pointing to the potentially transgressive dangers of Catholicism's most sacred objects.

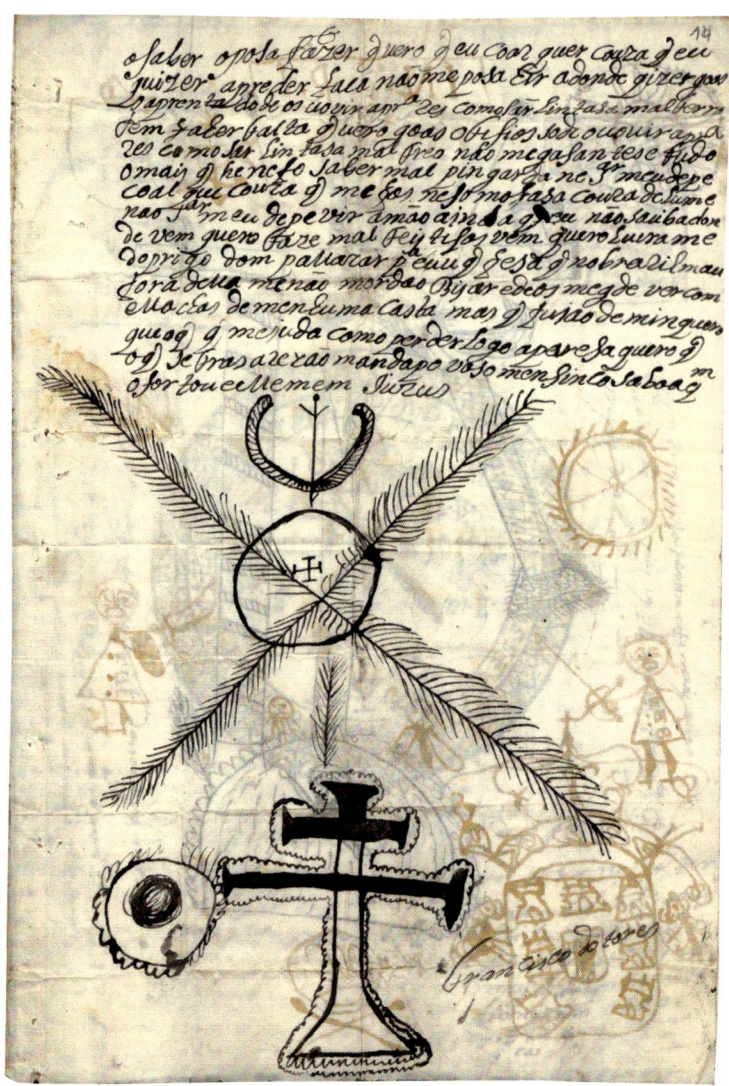

Fig. 4 Paper once contained inside a mandinga pouch made by José Francisco Pereira, 1730, Arquivo Nacional da Torre do Tombo, Lisbon

Courtesy of ANTT

The paper's top third, covered with fifteen lines of handwritten text, alludes to the paper orations and Catholic prayers commonly included inside mandinga pouches. But while eighteenth-century Portuguese writing often lacks strict structure and grammar, the inventive spellings that appear in this single run-on sentence make translation particularly difficult, even given its uncommonly legible handwriting. Words like "Brazil" and "feitissos"—the latter term describing bolsas and the unseen forces they negotiated—appear in the text, but the complex syntax obscures the wishes and desires invoked here. Perhaps this obfuscation is the point. In its simultaneous evocation and denial of legible text, José Francisco's document explicitly decouples writing from literacy, and thus points to his understanding of the power inherent in the written word itself. As outlined below, such an understanding may derive from José Francisco's own religious and cultural background, but it may also have emerged as his response to the new forms of legal and racial status inscribed on him during his life in Brazil and Portugal.

By their own testimonies, neither José Francisco Pereira nor José Francisco Pedroso knew "how to read nor write."[27] When questioning enslaved Africans who had spent time in Brazil, Inquisitors could all but assume such a response. For centuries, the export of Brazil's economic output inhibited the development of a settler population with the means to invest in local education. While the United States often had local laws preventing enslaved people from learning to read or write (because literacy provided access to power), such laws were never necessary in Brazil, where only a small minority of the population had access to literacy training. In an 1872 Brazilian census, fewer than 1 in every 1,000 enslaved people registered as literate, compared to 1 in 20 in the United States in the previous decade.[28] While one could assume the syntactical obscurity of his papers as symptomatic of José Francisco Pereira's lack of formal education, why would he seek out writing as a constitutive element of his mandinga pouches at all?

In 1730, José Francisco recruited António Guedes, a servant at a local church, to transcribe orations for him; it is likely António's handwriting preserved on José Francisco's papers.[29] While using mandinga pouches in proximity of Catholic priests carried serious risks, José Francisco closely identified the power of writing with Catholic ceremony. His own baptism at the Igreja do Corpo Santo in Recife, Pernambuco, was likely his first exposure to the written word.[30] Though José Francisco's account of this ceremony does not survive, James H. Sweet considers James Albert Ukawsaw Gronniosaw's 1772 narrative as a kind of interpretive substitute, wherein Gronniosaw describes his early life in Borno (present-day northeastern Nigeria), his enslavement by the Dutch, and his first encounter with the written word.[31] "[My master] used to read prayers in public to the ship's crew every Sabbath day," Gronniosaw wrote, "and when I first saw him read, I was never so surprised in my life, as when I saw the book talk to my master, for I thought it did, as I observed him to look upon it, and move his lips. I wished it would do so with me. As soon as my master had done reading, I followed him to the place where he put the book, being mightily delighted with it, and when nobody saw me, I opened it, and put my ear down close upon it, in great hopes that it would say something to me; but I was very sorry, and greatly disappointed, when I found that it would not speak."[32]

Gronniosaw's description of writing's power in the hands of a select few provides one model for considering José Francisco's orations. Gronniosaw suggests an understanding of spoken language as an ephemeral invocation: once transformed into ink and paper, it could be ensnared and transported. Critically, he seems most interested in how and why written text may provide access to certain forms of ritual power. José Francisco's design, however, suggests his desire to capture the *act* of writing as a way of accessing the forms of ritual authority it provided, as opposed to the specific meanings of written words. As Cécile Fromont notes in her study of José Francisco's use of writing, the four feathered quills emanating from his depiction of a host may also point to a longer history of Afro-Atlantic practices of inscription to protect the body.[33] Fromont notes that in a mid-eighteenth-century report published in Lisbon, Catholic priest Nuno Marques Pereira described his admonition of central African religious practitioners in northeastern Brazil in 1728. In his sermons, Father Pereira noted the role of "geomancy, which uses certain drawings, circles, and spots [*pontos*] drawn on the ground," stressing how "this [geomancy] still today is practiced" among Africans in Brazil.[34] Umbanda practitioners to this day use similar markings called *pontos riscados* (scratched points) to call forth spirits and ritually cleanse practitioners. Made of chalk, sulfur, or gunpowder—substances also included inside José Francisco's mandinga pouches—they are lit on fire to purify celebrants. An 1828 watercolor by French artist Jean-Baptiste Debret accents Father Pereira's observations (fig. 5). The depicted "Black Sorcerer" traces a circular design on the ground. His elite garb may speak to his role as a spiritual medium or high priest, a position confirmed by his placement inside the circle, while the staff he uses to trace a circular design evokes the same design at the center of José Francisco's paper.

Taken as a whole, José Francisco's use of writing, along with visual references to the act of writing, seems to reckon with the spectacular transformation and harnessing of the awe-inspiring forces he encountered. As such, his creations expand definitions of literacy to account for how he understood the acts of inscription and orality that played broad roles in his own spiritual life and the lives of other Africans similarly displaced. In turn, José Francisco's writings suggest his efforts to disarticulate the relationship between writing and literacy, and, potentially, the claims to ritual and political power on which that presumed relation depended. Indeed, José Francisco may have tried to do so because he knew that writing carried other powers, including the capacity to authorize and enact punishments and to confirm legal and racial status. It is this reckoning that comes through inside a mandinga pouch used by António de Sousa.

Appropriating Spectacle: António de Sousa, 1732–1733

On January 6, 1733, two white men denounced António de Sousa, who was enslaved by a fabric merchant in Lisbon. The previous month, they attested, António got into an argument with a group of people in his neighborhood, telling them that "he did not fear anyone," and "even if twelve people came at him they could not do anything bad to him," all because of a bolsa he possessed.[35] In contrast to his boasting, when one of his later denouncers learned of the existence of the pouch, António told him "not to say anything to anyone."[36] But on Christmas day, the men attested, the brother of António's enslaver punished António harshly by whipping him on his hands, a beating to which António reacted with some surprise, given the bolsa he owned.

António de Sousa's story walks a line common in bolsa denunciations. On the one hand, his accusers depict António as cocky and confident, routinely boasting of his possession and the protections it granted him. On

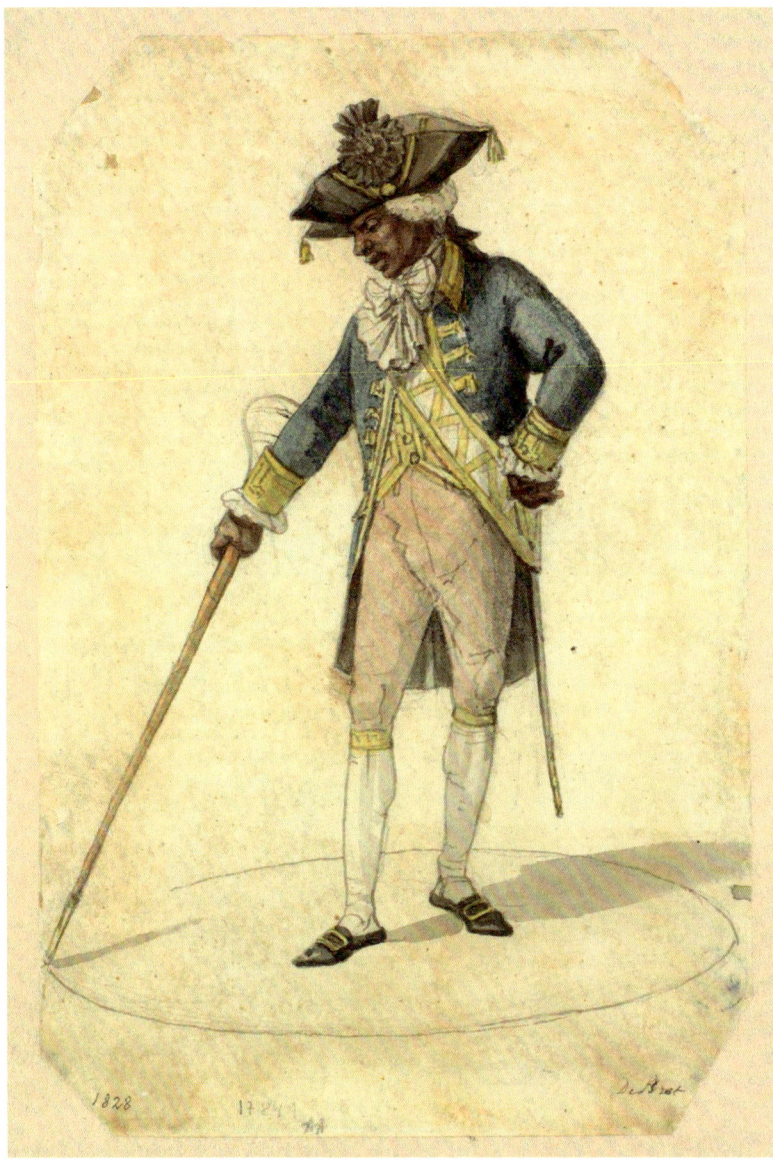

Fig. 5 Jean-Baptiste Debret, *Untitled* (*Black Sorcerer*), 1828, watercolor on paper, Fundação Biblioteca Nacional, Rio de Janeiro

the other hand, António takes pains to keep the amulet's existence hidden from the wrong ears. António's concerns parallel Laura de Mello e Souza's observations that these objects' "sorcerous" powers were a necessity across colonial power structures, for they "not only furnished weapons with which slaves could wage a silent battle against their masters," but "also legitimized repression of and violence against these captives."[37] António's story thus resonates with those of multiple enslaved people who specifically utilized mandingas in order to protect themselves from the punishment of their enslavers.[38] At the same time, António's story builds off a longer history of Black men publicly performing their bolsas to repel violence while also navigating the potential attraction and suspicion such a power aroused. Critically, these performances upended typical expectations of Black people's servitude and capacity for pain, while making clear how a culture of denunciation framed Black masculinity as a kind of always-possible performance of embodied violence. Unsurprisingly, Inquisitorial records identify all these users as men. In 1672, for example, Manuel, an enslaved man in Lisbon, was accused of using a bolsa tied around his wrist in order to protect himself from knife slashes, a theory he proved by stabbing himself in a public square.[39] In 1730, Luís de Lima, an enslaved "*natural* of Ouidah," West Africa, confessed to using mandinga pouches in Brazil and Portugal that protected him from injury.[40] And in the first half of the eighteenth century in Brazil, a rather bombastic white man named João de Siqueira proclaimed, in the home of an acquaintance, that "nothing of iron could enter him," and showed as proof the mandinga that hung around his neck. Putting the pouch around the neck of a man enslaved to his acquaintance, Siqueira ordered a sword to be pushed into his body. Siqueira's friend, fearing the loss of his property, pleaded with him to stop. Instead, Siqueira then put the pouch back around his own neck and pushed the sword into his own chest. Like the others, he emerged unharmed.[41]

Striking in António de Sousa's denunciation, as well as those cited above, is how such performances situate enslaved men as fitting test subjects for bolsas' ability to protect from bodily penetration regardless of who uses the pouch.[42] António, for example, explicitly dares other people to harm him. This statement publicly undermined conceptions of his own Black body as always ready for violation. Manuel, in turn, used his own body as a public test subject, whereby the confirmation of the amulet's effectiveness lay in not only its capacity to stop the routinized violence feared daily, but also the expectation that bodies like his were meant to receive such violence. Similarly, Siqueira called for "a slave," a move that emphasized his power to call forth others' bodies for violent uses, but also indicated his seeming lack of confidence in the ability of the mandinga to protect him. António and other Black men's use of bolsas thus confounded relations between embodiment, racial inscription, and violence in slavery societies: while bolsa demonstrations relied on, and even confirmed, the perceived capacity of the enslaved body to tolerate violence and pain, enslaved persons could overcome the systematic violence of enslaved life in Portugal and its colonies by demonstrating the amulets' effectiveness.

These performances, however, also risked attracting the attention of onlookers who could turn them in to the Inquisition, where the accused would again be subject to a different public spectacle of bodily and ritual violation. Indeed, the contents of António de Sousa's bolsa suggest that its maker knew of this possibility and attempted to deflect it. Inquisitors recorded the contents of a blue bolsa found in his bed as "some red feathers of a Brazilian bird, a piece of bull's horn, and some small pieces of white paper, and other pieces of the Auto-da-Fé list, all of which is suspected to be Mandinga."[43] An *auto-da-fé*, literally an "act of faith," was a lavish, all-day ritual during which convicted heretics marched through Lisbon's central plazas as their crimes were read aloud. Most were Jewish, but a litany of other crimes—particularly sorcery and "recourse to fetishes"—occurred with increasing frequency in the early eighteenth century. Led

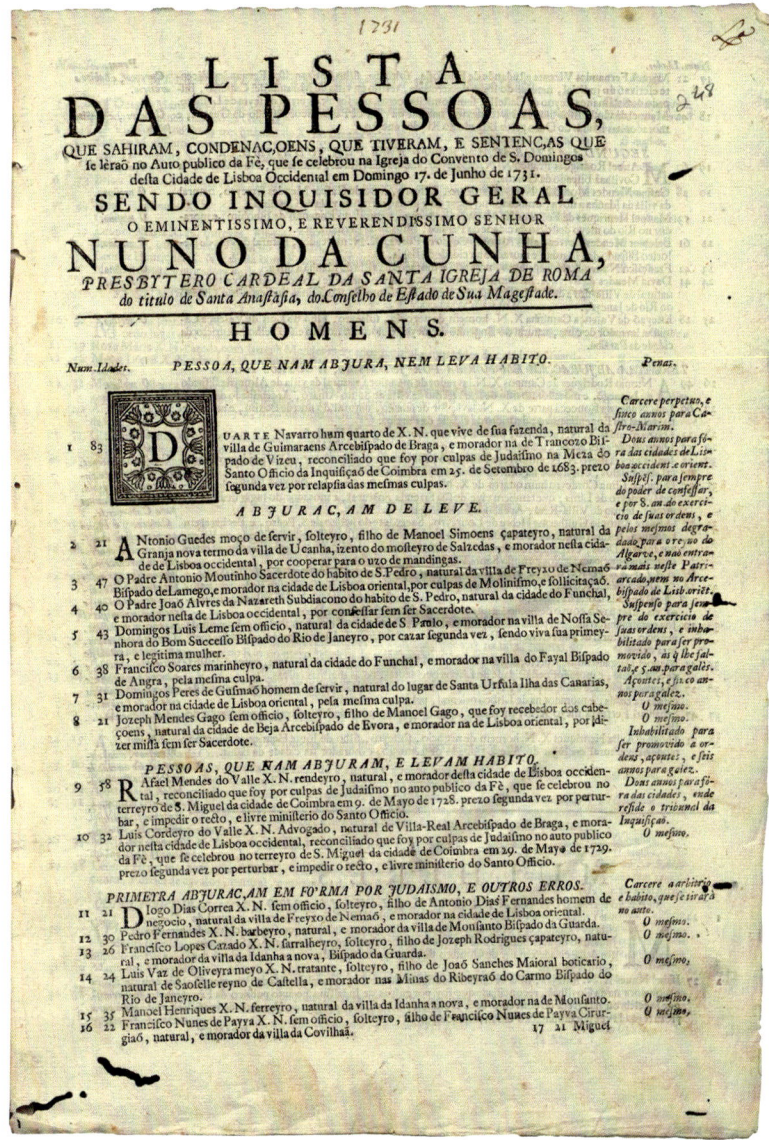

Fig. 6 Front page of the Lisbon auto-da-fé list of June 17, 1731, Arquivo Nacional da Torre do Tombo, Lisbon

Courtesy of ANTT

by friars carrying a flag with the Inquisition's seal, prisoners donned specially made robes with designs symbolizing their punishments (those condemned to death by burning, for example, had robes embroidered with flames).[44] This "all-consuming diversion," as António José Saraiva describes it, afforded the Holy Office the opportunity "to show off its ghastly supremacy."[45] Indeed, Inquisitors intentionally delayed autos-da-fé by stockpiling convicted heretics until they amassed enough people—usually a few hundred—so that "an adequate scenography made evident the reality and persistence of the danger combated by the Inquisitors."[46]

The Inquisition built up anticipation a few weeks ahead of each ceremony by printing and distributing lists with the names, ages, crimes, and punishments of the convicts marching in the auto-da-fé. Given the date of António de Sousa's denunciation, the "pieces of the Auto-da-Fé list" inside his mandinga likely dated from June 17, 1731 (fig. 6). The eighty-six names

> QUARTA ABJURAÇAM EM FORMA POR FEYTIÇARIA, E JUDAISMO.
> 33 26 Jozeph Francisco Pereyra homem preto, solteyro, escravo de João Francisco Pedrozo, natural de Judà Costa da Mina, e morador nesta cidade de Lisboa occidental, por culpas de feytiçaria, e ter pacto com o demonio, a quem reconhecia, e adorava por Deos.
> 34 19 Jozeph Francisco homem preto, solteyro, escravo de Domingos Francisco Pedrozo homem de negocio, natural de Judà Costa da Mina, e morador nesta cidade de Lisboa occidental, pelas mesmas culpas.
> 35 42 Manoel Delgado homem preto, escravo do Capitaõ Jozeph Rodrigues de Oliveyra, natural da Ilha de S. Thomé, e morador nesta cidade de Lisboa occidental, pelas mesmas culpas.
> 36 27 Manoel da Piedade homem preto, solteyro, escravo do Capitaõ Gaspar de Valladares, natural da cidade da Bahia, e morador na de Lisboa oriental, pelas mesmas culpas.

Fig. 7 Detail of the second page of the Lisbon auto-da-fé list of June 17, 1731, showing the names of José Francisco Pereira, José Francisco Pedroso, and Manuel da Piedade, Arquivo Nacional da Torre do Tombo, Lisbon

Courtesy of ANTT

Fig. 8 Paper once contained inside a pouch used by João da Silva, before 1742, Arquivo Nacional da Torre do Tombo, Lisbon

Courtesy of ANTT

on it included the notorious mandinga-makers José Francisco Pereira and José Francisco Pedroso at numbers 33 and 34, respectively, while Manuel da Piedade, an enslaved man from northern Portugal who used his bolsa to escape beatings from his enslaver, was number 36 in line (fig. 7).[47] For the many mandinga-users in Lisbon at the time, seeing these men march in an auto-da-fé, or at least hearing of their punishment, must have been a sobering event. Though each gained fame for producing objects that could protect from public violations like this one, the confiscation of their bolsas was likely tragic for them and their clientele. And yet, the Inquisition's public parade of the mandingas' power created new forms of engagement for the amulets. By incorporating a piece of the auto-da-fé list, the maker of António de Sousa's bolsa deftly seized a bit of the Inquisition's authority to engage in these grand public spectacles of violation while also, potentially, preserving some of the authority mandinga-makers possessed.

Fleeing the Archive: Manuel de Barros and João da Silva, 1742

Sitting before the Lisbon Inquisition accused of "sorcery and recourse to fetishes" in 1752, João da Silva, an enslaved "*natural* of Angola," testified as to how he came to possess the mandinga pouch that resulted in his arrest.[48] While enslaved in Bahia (northeastern Brazil) ten years prior, João asserted, he encountered Manuel de Barros, an African-born fugitive making his way toward Salvador, the capital port city. As a token of thanks for providing him with food and assistance, Manuel gifted João a leather amulet, which Manuel said had the power to free João from enslavement, just as it had done for him. João, however, held the object in suspicion. After Manuel departed, he showed it to several white people, asking them if it was permissible to wear it around his neck. None seemed to have an opinion, save for a young woman named Teresa who informed the local vicar that João possessed a mandinga. Soon after, the vicar confiscated João's amulet and tore it open, revealing "a square-shaped rock, a piece of garlic, two pieces of lead, a piece of consecrated host," and the paper reproduced here (fig. 8).[49]

This amulet was one of the few with the attested ability to allow Africans to escape the visual surveillance of slavery. Another trial attests that in the early months of 1737, in Lisbon, an enslaved man named Domingos received from another enslaved man, João Angola, an object

Sam Marcos Evangelistas te Rogue ✠ Jezus Christo
Seja bande ✠ ho espirito Santo Se ou milde A minha Vontade
De ✠ as 3 pesoa da Santissima trindade ✠ te conjuro Meu Amor
querer ✠ Se tu Me vires ✠ Mira-me ✠ e se tu Me Não ✠
vires por Mim Suspira ✠ ostia consagrada ✠ em teu coração ✠
em carne viva ✠ esteia e More Moraes ✠ tu por Mim a Sim como
Meu Snr Jezus Christo ✠ Morreo na Aruele da vera crus ✠ e onde andares
Na caza te tisiara par✠ vos bejos Santinos ✠ ne tenhas couza alguã estas a Sima
te reiceraas ✠ contigo Deo✠ ger de o ✠ pode✠ de o✠ alethe saude tanto ger
a sim falara rei eu tudo canto eu quizer ✠

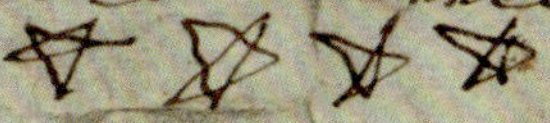

✠ ✠ ✠ ✠

Com arma de Sam gorgem ando armado Não Serei prezo nem tomado
e nem Meu Sangue derramado e nem Minha na tabera retratada
nem Meu Coração ✠ adontado, trilharei de dia de noute com m.ta
Alegria, A sim como Andou Meu Snr Jezus Christo nove Mes
No ventre da Virgem Maria Mãi Santissima

Valei-me ostia Sagrada Na testa valei-me Jezus Na boca
Vime de Cristus o Mim Meu Snr Jezus Christo Na olhada com
em cravado Valei me Jezus Na boca da virgem Maria aminha
eu voss se sinco pader 5 com sinco Ave Maria com sinco
goria na ter tos ferezido A morte paixam de Christo Snr
eu do pezo por aquela tua chaga em tre os te tomarei a Meu
corpo Na Sera Seri de Meu Maltratado de Meu inimigos e Meu
Sangue derramado no xam Siros e nem Meu inimigos tera mão para
Minca espingada Não tomara fogo A [...] para sua do-
Mora faga eu as pezo me diga no Sagrado e nem toques em
tram no meu Corpo tamim em de dia e de noute

✠ ✠ ✠

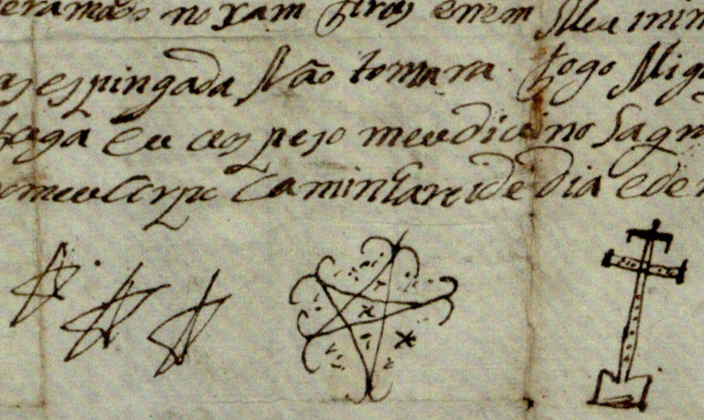

that allowed its owner to "not be hurt, and to be able to open [locked] doors without being detected . . . in order to run away from the house of his master."[50] Note how Domingos defined this object's powers not just as a way to escape enslavement, but to escape enslavement as a condition of bodily surveillance and restricted mobility. Both of these mandingas lack a known maker or origin, instead traded between enslaved people in mutual acknowledgment of their common predicament.

In allowing their enslaved users to escape surveillance and violence, the bolsas prefaced recent work by Saidiya Hartman and Krista Thompson, who define slavery as a contradictory visual condition, caught between "hypervisibility" (in that enslaved people are always under surveillance) and "invisibility" (in that enslaved people are socially invisible and, in a sense, absent from the archive).[51] The paper contained inside João's mandinga suggests its author used the pouch as a way out of this bind. Orations like these follow a structure relatively unchanged even in contemporary Brazil: the paper's top half, punctuated with small Latin crosses, reproduces the text of a prayer to Saint Mark, while the bottom half—the space typically reserved for personal petitions—refers to the Ave Maria and the Our Father, two other standard Catholic orations. But by the end, the writer asks for "sacred medicine," to "not have a sword enter into my body," and to be able to "walk day and night."

On one level, by petitioning for health, safety, and freedom of movement, these papers indicate that we should be careful not to mistake the paper's seeming Catholic imagery solely as evidence of its makers "conversion" to Catholicism.[52] An ocean away from the Inquisition's center, those who found themselves in Brazil constantly experimented and reinvented practices from central and western African religions, popular Catholicism, Islam, and Indigenous spiritual traditions. Africans in particular had to navigate not only this litany of new forces, but also the burdens of a social condition defined by their bodies and their skin. Recent excavations of an early nineteenth-century African burial ground in Rio de Janeiro attest to what one group of scholars characterize as Africans' "intensity of strategies for covering the skin"—the organ responsible for absorbing brutalities, for deflecting evils, and most closely tied to racial subjectivity.[53] A sparse but rich visual record left by eighteenth-century observers similarly testifies to Africans' frequent goal to "seal the body" from physical violence and malevolent spirits by using scarifications, jewelry, beads, medals, and mandingas. The Star of Solomon, a common talismanic and occult symbol used across Europe and West Africa for centuries, appears repeatedly on João's paper. This symbol also commonly appeared as a tattoo or in metal amulets worn by the enslaved. On João's paper, a series of four stars separate the text of Saint Mark's prayer from the personal petitions, while these symbols reemerge at the foot of the page: a group of three stars at left and, at center, another five-pointed star, this time accented and embellished (fig. 9). These stars are joined by another cross whose wide, shaded base and dotted accents suggest

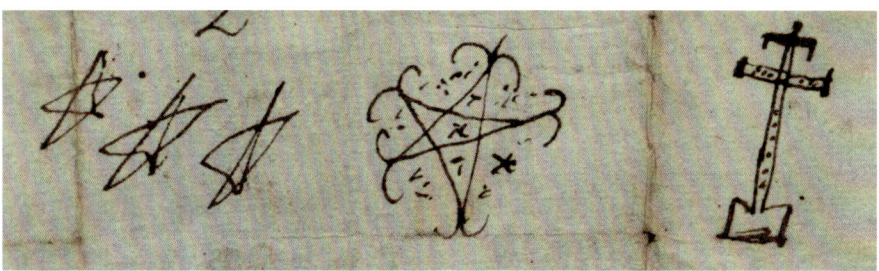

Fig. 9 Detail of paper once contained inside a pouch used by João da Silva, before 1742, Arquivo Nacional da Torre do Tombo, Lisbon

Courtesy of ANTT

it represents an architectural feature. Many Portuguese colonial cities featured large stone crosses like these at the center of public plazas or cemeteries where they functioned as markers of the Church's authority, but also as the locus of public devotions and petitions.

The addition of such empowering symbols to one's body was particularly charged and dangerous for fugitive Africans, as they likely tried to avoid any distinguishing characteristics during their ongoing flight from the oversight of their enslavers and the mercenaries they employed to return fugitives. Aldair Rodrigues, for example, located a series of descriptions of individuals from Savalou (present-day Republic of Benin) who were enslaved in Minas Gerais, in southeastern Brazil, in the 1740s and 1750s.[54] Descriptions of their heights, weights, facial features, and scarifications survive in local tax documents produced so their enslavers could identify them. Many of those described had fled into the mountains of Minas Gerais; accounts of their scarifications were used to confirm the fugitives' sale as well as to alert those charged with their recapture to their appearance. These records respond to Spillers's insistence on the blurred boundaries between the "marking and branding" of Black flesh that confirmed it as an owned commodity, and on the archival records created to codify Black violation. Here and elsewhere, the written markings on papers are not easily separable from markings and brandings; a dual-edged power that played out on fugitive Black bodies and the amulets they carried with them.

The papers contained inside João da Silva's mandinga, in sum, respond to the contested and competing roles of inscription in the early modern Black Atlantic world. This pouch's maker, like the others outlined above, sought to harness and control not only the spectacular power of the written word, but also an empowered range of corollary practices. Papers allowed mandinga-makers to transform and transport graphic writing systems, bodily scarifications, Catholic amulets, and the ephemerality of incantation. At the same time, writing inside mandingas may have also been a desperate effort to stave off the other, more malevolent uses of its power: to enslave and control African bodies, to ensure their complicity inside wider systems of surveillance, to regulate and define criminality, and to violently punish. With this perspective in mind, I conclude with some thoughts on the slavery archive that mandingas both depart from and help to constitute.

Conclusion

Produced by persons possessed of bodies and intellects continually under surveillance by nature of their racial inscription, mandinga pouches provide a series of striking interventions in Black and modernist art histories by critically demonstrating how the enslaved, from an early moment in the history of racial inscription, worked to disarticulate the aesthetics common to conceptions of modernity and the subjugation of Black life. Inside bolsas, the ritual specialists responsible for their creation first reconstructed the relationship between writing and literacy. In operating outside of presumed constructions of syntax and legibility, José Francisco, for example, reimagined a space to reckon with, and move beyond, practices of archival inscription and its power to dominate, subjugate, and disarticulate Black lives and livelihoods. The form of bolsas themselves expanded on this work. Small, often well-worn, visually banal objects that were habitually obscured from view under their users' clothes, bolsas like those of António de Sousa and those of Jacques Viegas appear in the archive as antimodels of the object, which—like their contents— often defied easy placement inside classificatory regimes. Bolsa-makers strategically engineered such a form in a seemingly desperate quest to reappropriate and disarticulate the visual culture of metropolitan imperial power, especially when contrasted with monumental edifices and public plazas used during the auto-da-fé, or the sumptuous churches that housed the riches of Portuguese Catholicism. By capturing, containing, and obscuring references to the ritual and political spectacles of these spaces, bolsa-makers also worked against presumed relationships between what Simone Browne articulates as conceptions of sovereign power reliant on optical forms of surveillance and its use of "acts of making the black body legible as property" in order to produce the figure of the enslaved person.[55] Ironically recorded and preserved inside the archives of slavery, bolsas thus show how enslaved subjects actively appropriated, reckoned with, and worked to deconstruct relations between writing and literacy, between spectacle and subjugation, and between archival markings and the originating metaphors of violation they perform. In working to de-inscribe the figure of the enslaved person and, thus, the modernist structures of power founded upon it, bolsa-makers used this strategic in-between space neither to confuse nor to force clarity, but rather to avoid both in a deliberate attempt to represent that which must escape systematization.

But returning to São Boaventura's letter, consider the paucity of information it contains concerning the accused. São Boaventura even apologizes for the letter's sparse contents. The unidentified Black man "said things to me daily," he wrote, but "I poorly understood" the words he said: "I do not now remember them in a form in which I can write them."[56] São Boaventura thus attests not just to the inviolability of the unnamed man's body because of the bolsa, but also renders his subject effectively inviolable by the Inquisition due to the confusion of his speech and his name. Indeed, I can find no record of this man ever being brought to trial, meaning that he, in a sense, possibly escaped the Inquisition's suppression as well as that of the archive. Even his speech, as São Boaventura alludes, was as difficult to interpret and as impossible to summarize as the unclear syntax used to empower mandinga pouches. Manuel de Barros, meanwhile, used his own mandinga not to simply escape enslavement, but also to escape from the archive. He entered it as quickly as he left: a ghostly specter that rushed in and out to deposit a fragment of history before once again disappearing. Fittingly, I have found no evidence that Manuel de Barros existed. João da Silva may have invented him during interrogations as a strategic explanation for how he came to possess the amulet in question. As such, Manuel de Barros—much like the unnamed man in São Boaventura's letter—has entered into a different kind of archival register that leaves no mark.

As Saidiya Hartman reminds us, the archive remains "a tomb."[57] "The raw numbers of the mortality account," she writes, "the strategic evasion and indirection of the captain's log, the florid and sentimental letters dispatched from slave ports by homesick merchants, the incantatory stories of *shocking* violence penned by abolitionists, the fascinated eyewitness reports of mercenary soldiers eager to divulge 'what decency forbids [them] to disclose,' and the rituals of torture, the beatings, hangings, and amputations enshrined as law" all inundate the archive of slavery with scandal and excess.[58] Yet in this context, she implores, narrating a counter-history of slavery necessitates we meditate on "the incomplete project of freedom" that continues through our work as scholars, a kind of reckoning with, and acknowledgment of, "the precarious life of the ex-slave, a condition defined by the vulnerability to premature death and to gratuitous acts of violence."[59] The pages that surround Jacques Viegas's pouch, José Francisco Pereira's drawings, and João da Silva's prayer petitions—the objects they may have trusted to protect them, the objects I argue are critical to their collective modernist counter-project—are those that violate them once again. Inside mandinga pouches, certain enslaved Africans desperately sought immediate responses to the violence around them, in some cases choosing to escape from their own bodies and the regulatory systems that sought to control them. In this framework, the existence of Portugal's Inquisitorial archive depends on its necessary incorporation of its assumed oppositions. Bolsas also played this game, actively seizing alternately empowered, unseen, ephemeral, and transgressive contents through the papers that constituted them. Perhaps, then, what is often framed as a form of "silence" of Black lives in the archive itself might in fact be the object of, rather than an obstacle to, a project of archival reckoning in the face of the presumed loss, a space that enslaved bolsa-users and makers created to reconceptualize the relationships between inscription, archival-corporeal violence, and the fugitive possibilities of personhood outside of, and in conversation with, the structures of imperial and religious authority in the modern world.

One of the surviving papers from José Francisco's mandingas stands out for its extensive text (fig. 10). Like his other orations, this paper is likely

Deus✝ vos✝ salve asucena de resplandesente e sempre mil Trindade
✝ Deos✝ vos calve✝ Roza florida eterna primavera Deos vos
salve exselentisima✝ Rainha✝ dos seos eleijos✝ de inumera
veis✝ estina soij e sorro gasiuas o virgem✝ santisima✝ da pen-
na✝ Bendita✝ soij entre as mulleres pois✝ de vos✝ quis tina ser
✝ entor✝ Jhs✝ Rei✝ dos seos✝ resplandor✝ da gloria, e ser alimenta-
do a vosos✝ peijto do vosos purisimo alimento✝ vos✝ S gloria zaolrin-
tes✝ cem us✝ os✝ amo vozos✝ Braços✝ o grou xestex✝ cainda✝ o fondos✝
p.ª✝ desua✝ Divina✝ magde✝ me al cansartes✝ os perdoam✝ inha
✝ asma✝ o minha✝ Singular advogada a nost vost rij✝ e ses✝ vos✝
✝ olios✝ mizirlor dizor✝ para✝ verde ast pitivos✝ alcansame
✝ o meij✝ de perado res✝ him✝ imteiro✝ perdão✝ domeus✝ peca-
dos✝ eu corasao✝ rinpo✝ henulde✝ ebenigno✝ ferido✝
com os✝ raios✝ do livino✝ ijme✝ devos✝ amado✝ fillotes
✝ daime✝ maij✝ ma✝ sr evva pas✝ de espirito✝ e luma✝ pure-
za✝ de comsiensia✝ pa✝ rez✝ devino✝ s✝ mor e minha
ar ma✝ ca sim✝ o virgem por a✝ vos✝ venera✝ evos✝ ser✝ vir✝
vos✝ asei tarez✝ esta✝ reza✝ do sabado✝ com✝ a vo sa✝ wn
gerkar✝ ra da inha✝ e mais✝ orasois de toda✝ es le ijio✝ vaso
✝ jinginka ara que lento rezado✝ e por elles✝ vos peso au✝
m✝ da✝ sm de igr✝ pas✝ e com✝ cordia✝ en des✝ os✝ prinse
pes✝ cri tão✝ a todo✝ os Bena✝ feitorez✝ amigos✝ os nimi-
gos✝ asim Come✝ com o✝ molleres✝ a todos✝ os vicis✝ Divos✝
e defundo✝ em grasa e pas✝ nos com servais✝ pª✝ senpre✝
o virgem prª✝ da pena✝ amen este q me serve tudo o tempo
q eu quizer me pode servir quero q qoalquer muller
ou mosa prinspie mos avida quer q me basa q o meu domin-
ador ou velo a q eu biever asução✝ por ajuda M ne me conte
da tudo oq eu quizer s eu Mames mo ne rey que por sua
ma mim por prio coerа nir q Brazil e quero q eu posa✝
vontade semeu gostar j isto nem emjene✝ a linha vi da✝
fazer oq eu quizer q seja d quero q qoal quer couza q eu
quero contentar a me quizer fazer o poder saber sem nta vido
asim q elegej minha vontade eq m eg d quer em dim quero
coando eu q zer a Brazil q me busu me basa com s Dias me
eu empidim quero q coando eu qzer a Brazil q me Busão
ahonde eu ganha o me via pª a Barzil quer mais abrir
algua porta sem ningem a honde meu cuida eu q ninguem
me sasa brei a saber o posa saber q uire eu coal quer oq
contentar quer couza q eu

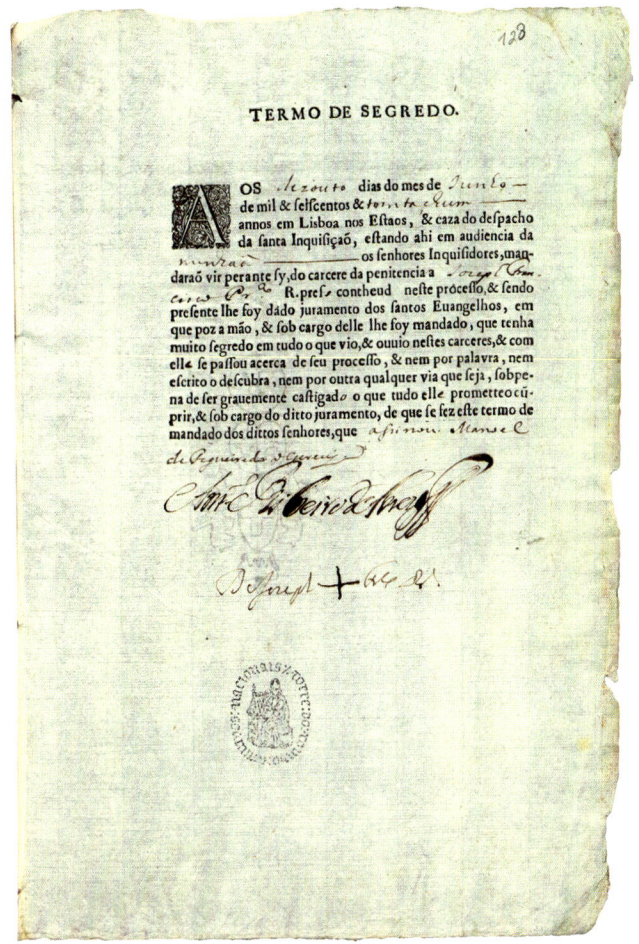

Fig. 10 Paper once contained inside a mandinga pouch made by José Francisco Pereira, c. 1730, Arquivo Nacional da Torre do Tombo, Lisbon

Courtesy of ANTT

Fig. 11 Page outlining the secrecy terms of the Lisbon Inquisition trial of José Francisco Pereira, 1731, Arquivo Nacional da Torre do Tombo, Lisbon

Courtesy of ANTT

António Guedes's transcription of José Francisco's own words. Repeated crosses, the common additions to the Christian orations with which he was so familiar, punctuate roughly written letters in the oration's top half, which reproduces a common prayer. In the bottom, through his trademark inventive spellings and obscure syntax, José Francisco's wishes shine through in brief moments of clarity. He implores God to let him do what he wants; to make what he wants; to have what he wants; to overcome any impediment; to open any door without anyone detecting him; and, in the final lines, to return to Brazil.

On June 18, 1731, the day after his public auto-da-fé, José Francisco sat before a document outlining the secrecy terms of his Inquisition trial (fig. 11). As he could not read it, he must have listened as printed words once again came alive before him. Ironically, they declared his silence. He "was to be very secret regarding everything seen, and heard," in his jail cell and during his trial, under penalty of "gratuitous punishment." After this statement was read, the presiding scribe wrote José Francisco's name at the bottom of the page. In between "José" and "Francisco," he traced the quill across the paper, using the same motion with which he had seen others empower Latin orations many times before: a shaky cross that sealed his fate.

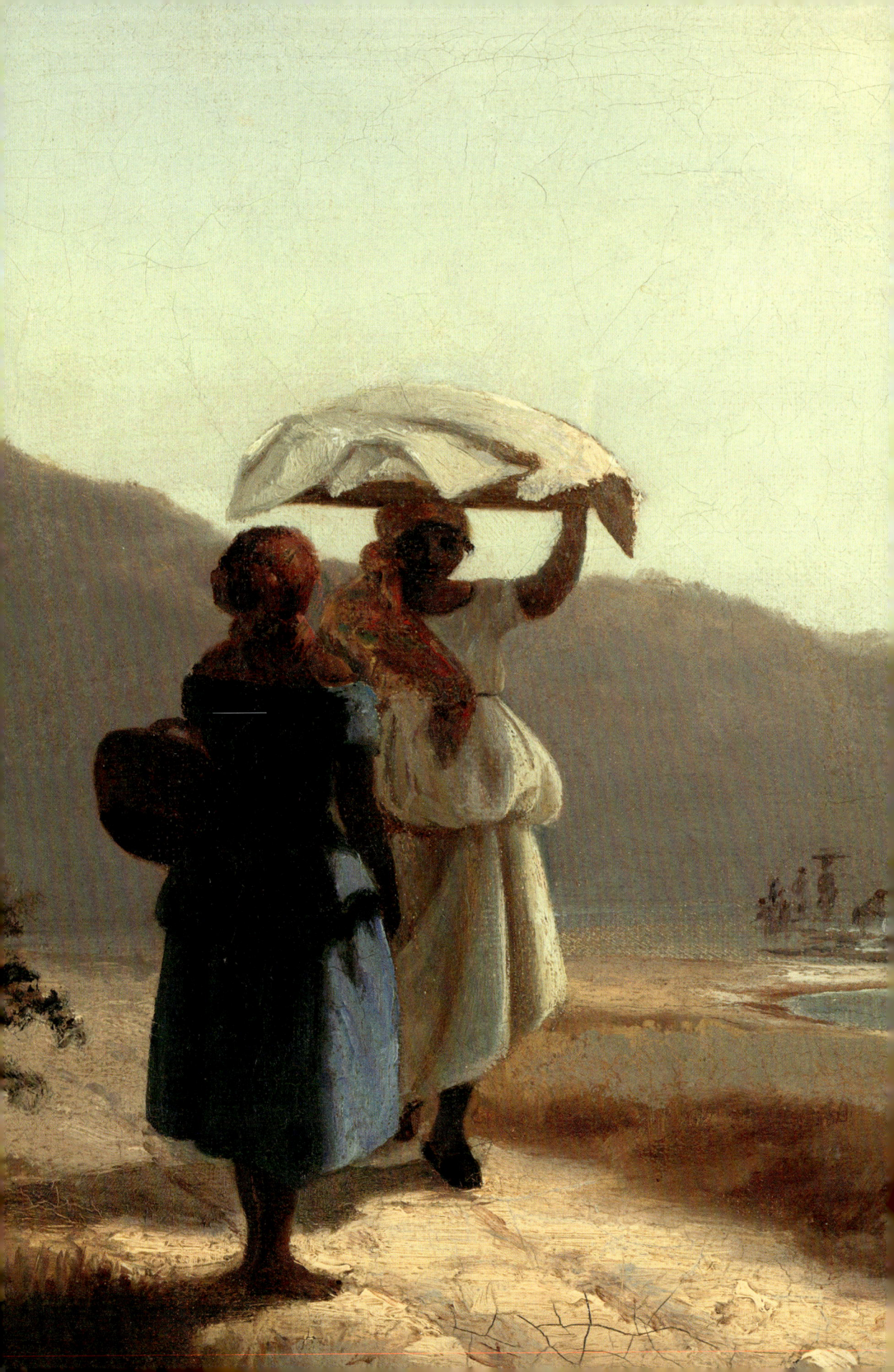

BARE FEET, OR, THE AMBIVALENCE OF EMANCIPATION: CAMILLE PISSARRO AND THE CARIBBEAN

C. C. MCKEE

In 1856, a young Camille Pissarro, who had arrived in Paris the previous year, painted a small canvas that captures two Black women who stop to chat on a seaside path outside of Charlotte Amalie, the capital city of the artist's natal isle of St. Thomas (fig. 1). St. Thomas and the neighboring islands of St. Croix and St. John constituted the Danish empire's colonial holding in the West Indies until the islands were sold to the United States in 1917; they, along with a number of smaller islands and atolls, form the US Virgin Islands. Pissarro's canvas, along with a corpus of his other paintings and drawings with Caribbean subjects, was executed in the wake of 1848, the year of slavery's abolition in the Danish West Indies. Despite this radical upheaval of colonial policies, it would seem that the artist's representation of Caribbean Blackness could obfuscate emancipation on the painting's surface. The possibility that this small canvas, which measures approximately ten by sixteen inches, could capture the fraught contradictions of Black freedom remains uncertain in the enigmatic intimacy of the depicted encounter. One woman faces the viewer, dressed in white with a patterned red kerchief spilling over her shoulder as she balances a load of thickly painted white fabric atop her head. Her companion turns her back to the viewer; a wicker basket in the crook of her arm, she wears a red headscarf similar to that of the woman in white and a sky-blue dress that rhymes with the bay before her.[1]

They form a pair that seems to converge in a brief moment of respite from their labor, with no overt signs of leisure. But the exact terms of this meeting are opaque. Are we to understand that this painting, made in the wake of emancipation, depicts Black women at rest in the tropical landscape—anathema to the recent memory of slavery's onerous conditions—while their momentary nonproductivity is simultaneously conjoined to the signs of their labor? Could the idle chatter ascribed to these women be characterized instead as withholding a conspiratorial air? Is freedom, from Pissarro's view, the ephemeral moment of rest that punctuates labor under conditions only nominally distinguishable from slavery? Who is to say that these women are free at all?

Black women, depicted beyond the confines of the plantation, are central figures in Pissarro's oeuvre of the 1850s and early 1860s. Their appearance—in his early drawings on St. Thomas, in Venezuela, and in paintings executed after moving to Paris—holds two conceptions of Black femininity in tension. On the one hand, Pissarro's representations of the Caribbean conform to a set of types that reduce the appearance of the Black woman to a fixture of the Caribbean landscape, one means of visually dissolving her potential agency during the continued struggle for emancipation and assertion of her personhood. Personhood, as deployed in this essay, stands distinct from subjectivity insofar as subjectivity speaks an impossible cohabitation of Blackness with full political agency in the post-emancipation era as a result of the subject's foundation in the onto-juridical recognition of the state. On the other hand, insisting on the uneasy modernity of Pissarro's images opens up the potential to read these works against themselves. Alternative and contradictory visions

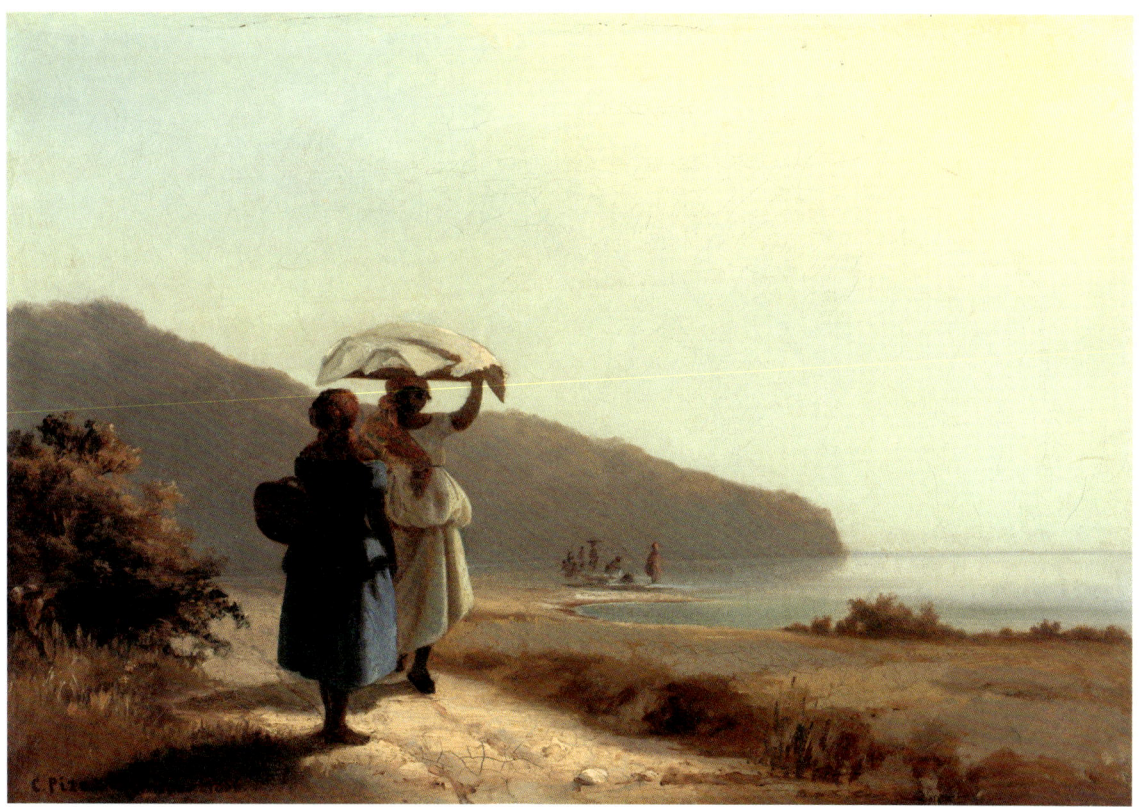

Fig. 1 Camille Pissarro, *Two Women Chatting by the Sea, St. Thomas*, 1856, oil on canvas, National Gallery of Art, Washington, Collection of Mr. and Mrs. Paul Mellon

of a post-emancipation modernism emerge if one traces the incongruities between the revolutionary leadership of Black women in the Danish West Indies during this period, and the history of representing laboring freedwomen as a symbol of erotic fantasy in the colony.

By attending to the appearance of Black women as less-than-free in this corpus conditioned by their racialized, sexed, and gendered labor, my analysis of Camille Pissarro's drawings and paintings puts pressure on his position in modernist art history as an avant-garde artist and political radical. In these accounts, freedom in a political and aesthetic sense becomes synonymous with the bearded father of impressionism. There are important corollaries between this Caribbean oeuvre and the discussion of Pissarro as a mature artist in the 1880s and 1890s, working in the trenches of the avant-garde for the sake of an anarchist vision. In art historian Linda Nochlin's formative essay "Camille Pissarro: The Unassuming Eye," she lauds his "particular unstrained and accepting modality of urban vision," which "had to do with a kind of freedom which he thought of as freedom of perception."[2] Nochlin's frank assessment of Pissarro's politicized vision presents an artist who used painting to aspire toward overthrowing the bourgeoisie. T. J. Clark similarly highlights Pissarro's naive anarchist politics of freedom in *Two Young Peasant Women* (1891–1892, fig. 2). In this painting of proletarian women who inhabit the leisure "available in the interstices of work," Clark describes how their indeterminate (in)action conveys anarchism's "central assertion in philosophical terms . . . that freedom and order are dialectical moments of one another, and that the

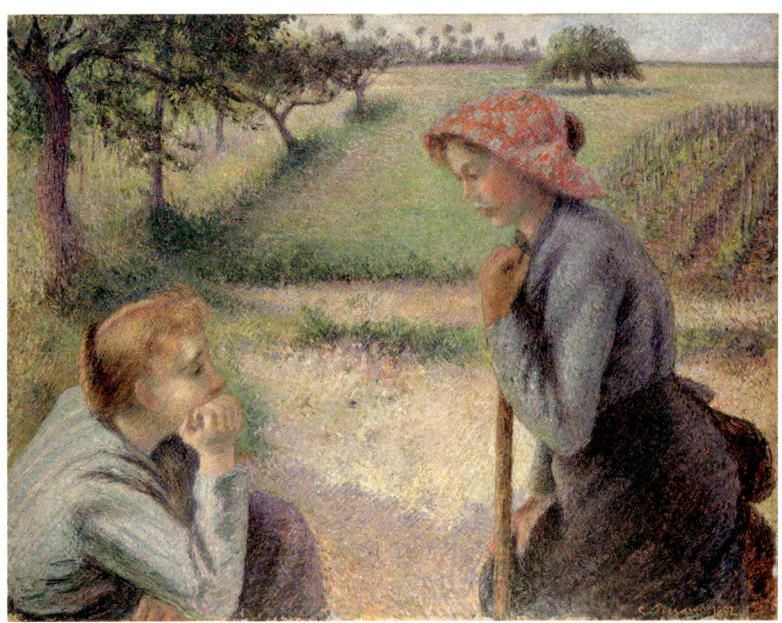

Fig. 2 Camille Pissarro, *Two Young Peasant Women*, 1891–1892, oil on canvas, Metropolitan Museum of Art, Gift of Mr. and Mrs. Charles Wrightsman

present horror of the forms assumed by each is due to that dialectic being broken."[3] He continues by inviting the spectator to "imagine a painter, then, who thought that pictures could be small epitomes of this repressed truth. In them order and freedom would be shown to be reconcilable—indeed not entities or qualities at all without one another."[4] Again freedom is made a central feature of Pissarro's painting through his political investments. Painting itself is lauded as the aesthetic conduit able to provide a truth of radical political freedom in late nineteenth-century France. Clark goes so far as to equate modernism with socialism, posing the question, "If they died together [in the late twentieth century] does that mean in some sense they lived together, in century-long co-dependency?"[5] For these art historians it was Pissarro's fin-de-siècle paintings that, in many ways, reinvigorated the confluence of socialist politics and modernist aesthetics advanced by Gustave Courbet's midcentury realism.

However, Black womanhood—and the racialized subjectivity proffered to freedwomen by emancipation—is a representational category central to Pissarro's modernism that goes overlooked and unmentioned by Clark, despite the fact that it is a pair of women, here white and French, who picture Pissarro's freedom as both anarchist and modernist. "The subject of *Two Young Peasant Women* is a form of sociability, and specifically of mental life, imagined as belonging to women. . . . Because the world of women could be imagined as standing just a little outside, or a little apart from, the struggle with the realm of necessity."[6] Clark's emphasis on the gendered dimension of this painting might seem to parallel the intersubjective dynamics of the earlier *Two Women Chatting by the Sea, St. Thomas*.[7] Yet, an attention to the enduring subjugation of Black women on the island colonies in the mid-nineteenth century reveals the limits of freedom and modernity's legibility for racialized subjects within extant forms of politics. Of Nochlin and Clark one may, or perhaps should, be compelled to ask:

To whom is the freedom in Pissarro's paintings extended? Knowing that Pissarro bore witness to the legislated freedom accompanying abolition in multiple national contexts, how far back in the artist's life do these arguments extend before they require revision? And, more capaciously, to what extent must histories of modernism continue to be revised if Blackness is brought squarely into the frame of analysis when attending to the contradictory politics of artists assigned the labels of "avant-garde," "socialist," or "radical," of which Pissarro was certainly one?[8]

Rather than retroactively apply Pissarro's later anarchism and impressionism, I read these works as instantiations of a *fantasied colonial memory* executed with a painterly realism that takes a pointedly ambivalent position toward the representation of laboring Black women and blurs the distinction between enslavement and freedom. When describing the artist's early career in Europe, Pissarro's son Ludovic-Rodo suggests, "Pissarro will have made small paintings at this time [circa 1855–1865], based on his memories of the Caribbean."[9] Therefore, these works are, foremost, *memory works*. They are paintings and drawings imbued with the entwined fact and fiction inherent to recollection, executed by a burgeoning artist and future political radical newly arrived in Paris and formed in the Tropics during the age of abolition. Psychoanalytic theory reminds us that memories have only an a posteriori facticity. Temporally fragmented and always conjoined to the present, a memory gains psychic value as a presumed anchor to the external world that is, in fact, a mutable amalgam of conscious and unconscious repressed content.[10] A Freudian approach to memory and fantasy furnishes a modernist vocabulary that elucidates the pictorial mechanisms of Black subjugation I locate in Pissarro's Caribbean oeuvre that exists at the juncture of slavery's immediate afterlife in the colonial Atlantic and nascent European modernism as an endeavor already exclusive to white men.[11]

Pissarro's corpus of Caribbean artworks does not attest to the realities of Black life in the Danish West Indies after emancipation. Rather, they retroact Black being toward bondage in freedom with a picturesque lens. Departing from a strictly Freudian perspective, Pissarro's fantasy of racial subjugation extends far beyond the artist himself; these verdant landscapes populated by Black figures were commercially attractive to a metropolitan audience with a taste for visions of an exotic elsewhere.[12] The exoticizing function of these paintings and drawings—their ability to materialize colonial territories as fully controlled—pushes Pissarro's memory into the realm of fantasy. Fantasy and memory are adjacent concepts in psychoanalysis, conjoined in their compulsion to mitigate psychic stress by achieving pleasure.[13] Distinct from the convincing "reality" of memory, fantasies are imaginary sequences predicated on the illusory fulfillment of a wish and are always, to a greater or lesser extent, distorted from the world toward which they strive.[14] In a given subject, particularly the neurotic in an analytic context, mentally conjuring a fantasy may replace reality, functioning analogously to the (always already distorted) memory.

Pissarro's Caribbean oeuvre as a whole, then, stands to contend with the psychic trauma of modernity as these artworks attempt to fill a gap in colonial memory. These are fantasized representations of the Tropics that tread the ambiguous waters of Black personhood after emancipation in pictorial terms that could equally be said to nostalgize slavery. For instance, the ostensible tranquility of *Two Women Chatting by the Sea, St. Thomas* recalls the distinct social relations between enslaved people and their oppressors in the Danish West Indies. Public corporeal punishments and domestic forms of injury maintained the fiction of colonial order in Caribbean plantation societies. However, unlike other colonial contexts in the region, Danish juridical procedure contained provisions wherein the enslaved could testify in their own defense, imbuing further nuance into the characterization of these people as speaking commodities.[15] Pissarro's representation of Black women in an indeterminate state between labor and rest produces a fantasy of racial subjugation that countervails emancipated Blackness and the specificity of slavery's history in the Danish Caribbean.

This memory gap is intentionally aporetic, a selective recollection that elides colonial violence in the service of affirming a legislated instantiation of freedom. Freud racialized the unconscious fantasy itself when he stated, one "may compare [fantasies] with individuals of mixed race who, taken all round, resemble white men, but who betray their coloured descent by some striking feature or other, and on that account are excluded from society and enjoy none of the privileges of white people." This prescient metaphor highlights the fact that fantasies, "in spite of their high degree of organization, remain repressed and therefore cannot become conscious."[16] When considered in relation to the integration of freedmen and freedwomen into an imperial polity, Freud's racialized discussion of fantasy reveals the extent to which it is impossible to read Pissarro's works from this period as securely representing a freed population.

These remembered scenes of the Caribbean trace what I identify as the profound ambivalence toward Black freedom and subjectivity in Pissarro's artistic practice during this period, an ambivalence intensified by the conjunction of race and gender in his visual lexicon. Look no further than the crucial asymmetry between the figures in *Two Women Chatting by the Sea, St. Thomas* that emerges against bright ochre soil and signals these women's politically ambivalent position that rests just beneath the painting's picturesque surface. At the base of their shadows, cast deep under the setting equatorial sun, the woman in white reveals a black shoe and stockinged foot as she steps forward to continue on her way. Her companion in blue stands firm, her bare feet planted on the path before her. Pissarro's class-based distinction between bare feet and shoes is representative of the ambivalence in this transatlantic body of work that precludes the secure ascription of Black freedom without foreclosing it entirely.

As a result of this distinguishing feature, the figure of the laboring Black woman in Pissarro's Caribbean oeuvre exists interstitially—or vestibularly, to modify Hortense J. Spillers's term. As was the case for Black women throughout the diaspora under the conditions of slavery, this figure "became the principal point of passage between the human and the nonhuman world."[17] We must remember that Pissarro's representations of Caribbean women came only a few decades after the death of Saartjie Baartman, or the "Hottentot Venus," who was paraded across Europe as a curiosity and eroticized as a para-human object to be devoured by leering white eyes.[18] The impossibility of securely representing a necessarily free Black subject in Pissarro's post-abolition oeuvre, I contend, demonstrates the extent to which, as Spillers reminds us, "Black is vestibular to culture" in the colonial Americas.[19] This vantage point requires that we look elsewhere for modes of Black personhood cultivated within and beyond the confines of colonial modernity.

Despite his proximity to Black life in the French, Danish, and Venezuelan contexts during the 1840s and 1850s, Camille Pissarro never publicly commented on the end of slavery. Only in a letter from 1878 did Pissarro recount his Caribbean adolescence in terms that aligned his upbringing with his political radicalism.[20] "Being a well-paid clerk in St. Thomas in [18]52," Pissarro averred that he "could no longer stand it there and without any further reflection I left everything and fled to Caracas [Venezuela], finally breaking the ties that bound me to the bourgeois life."[21] Pissarro constructs his youth in the Tropics as a fantasy of class imbued with his later anarcho-syndicalist politics lauded by art history; this epistle elides the fact that the artist lived alongside Black struggles for freedom that were inflected in his early artworks. Instead, he perpetuates their ambivalence by presenting his mobility as the source of a sustained political investment in representations of class devoid of race after his permanent move to France in 1856.

∎ ∎ ∎

But we have gotten ahead of ourselves; to elucidate the fixation with laboring Black women in Pissarro's oeuvre, it is necessary to understand his relationship to Danish colonialism in the Caribbean. The artist was born on the island of St. Thomas on July 10, 1830. St. Thomas was first colonized in 1671. Its small neighbor to the east, St. John, was acquired in 1717, and Denmark's colonial portfolio was completed with the purchase of the larger and most profitable St. Croix from the French in 1733. Of the three islands, the flat terrain and comparatively large size of St. Croix was best suited for the sugar plantations synonymous with the region. St. Thomas, by contrast, was a central commercial hub for the Caribbean and North and South America because of its open ports and international trade. At the peak of colonial slavery in 1835, the 19,876 enslaved people across the three islands constituted nearly 60 percent of the Danish West Indies' population.[22]

Pissarro was born to a Jewish merchant family with strong French Creole ties, and he was raised with enslaved persons in his home. Danish census records reveal that the Pissarro family enslaved people throughout his youth and young adulthood.[23] It would seem that his young adult infatuation with representations of Black women began at home. The 1841 census entry indicates that four of the five "unfree living in the house" were women: Catherine, Arabella, Rosa, Petronille, and Alexander. These enslaved members of the household came from across the archipelago—St. Thomas, Martinique, and St. Martin. They held divergent Catholic and Protestant faiths, and were of "good moral character," excepting Catherine, whose behavior was judged only "tolerable."[24] In 1841 he was sent to study at the Pension Savary in Passy, then a banlieue of Paris, where he was first trained in drawing.[25] After completing his studies in 1847, Pissarro returned to St. Thomas on the eve of emancipation in both the French and Danish empires. Did these women sit for a young Camille in the months or days preceding and following emancipation? Might they have participated in the uprising when, galvanized by the French proclamation of abolition on April 27, 1848, enslaved people in the Danish West Indies rejected the Crown's proposition of gradual emancipation from a decade earlier?[26]

Tensions between the white populations and people of color in the Danish West Indies erupted on St. Croix on the evening of Sunday, July 2, 1848, when the enslaved followed the precedent of other rebellions to broadcast their dissent by igniting fires, ringing estate bells, and blowing conch shells to signal the revolt. St. Croix's small size, measuring only 82 square miles, also facilitated organization. By the next morning some 8,000 enslaved people under the leadership of John Gotlieb (also spelled Gottlieb) Bordeaux (also spelled Bourdeaux), called General Buddhoe or Buddoe, converged at Frederiksfort on the western end of the island to stage a general strike and demand their immediate freedom.[27] To this point, the general strike against slavery in the Danish West Indies was distinctive for its nonviolence and the leaders' insistence on peaceful protest. Withholding labor and the refusal to continue being enslaved was protest enough to expedite the immediate abolition of slavery by Governor von Scholten that very day. Despite these efforts to maintain peace, insurrectionary violence erupted early the following morning when an outfit of Danish troops led by Colonel de Nully came across a "band of the now emancipated peasantry . . . and their leader armed with a musket (who was shot)."[28] For the following three days, the colonial leadership was thrown into turmoil as recently freedmen and women destroyed the materials that symbolized their slavery.

The revolution in the Danish West Indies was primarily articulated as symbolic property damage, an approach to protest distinct from the waves of murder that characterized the Haitian Revolution and other revolts by enslaved people in the Caribbean.[29] These iconoclastic acts represented a vicarious affront to white colonial authority through the desecration of its most potent symbols.[30] For freedmen and freedwomen in the Danish West Indies, these events can also be seen as symbolic acts of revolutionary creation flowing from the wellspring of freedom promised by emancipation. Uprooting the whipping post, defacing the prison that was the sick house, and desecrating the plantation signaled the inauguration of a life free from slavery's extra-juridical violence dependent on a racial hierarchy that precluded Blackness from full personhood.

In response to the ensuing chaos on St. Croix, Governor General von Scholten suffered a nervous breakdown on Thursday, July 6, abdicated control of the Danish islands, and fled to Denmark. The islands were placed under martial law by the newly arrived governor Peter Hansen, and Spanish troops summoned from Puerto Rico remained on St. Croix through November 26, 1848. On St. Thomas, movement was limited because the majority of freedmen and women simply left the plantations to find wage work in the commercial hub of Charlotte Amalie.

Despite the tumultuous social upheaval on the neighboring island of St. Croix, the young Pissarro, it appears, chose not to reflect on his proximity to the struggle for freedom in 1848 while he worked for his family's merchant business. Without textual documentation, we rely on a corpus of early sketches dominated by the figure of the laboring Black woman, a fascination apparent even in Pissarro's earliest sketches from St. Thomas. Take, for instance, the conjunction of race, gender, and labor in a drawing titled *Route de Bussy* signed "Camille Pizarro" and dated "13 avril 1852, St. T" (fig. 3).[31] A group of Black women stop before a copse and a walled compound that separate the sketchy beginnings of a colonial mansion

Fig. 3 Camille Pissarro, *Route de Bussy*, 1852, pencil on paper, Ashmolean Museum

© Ashmolean Museum, University of Oxford

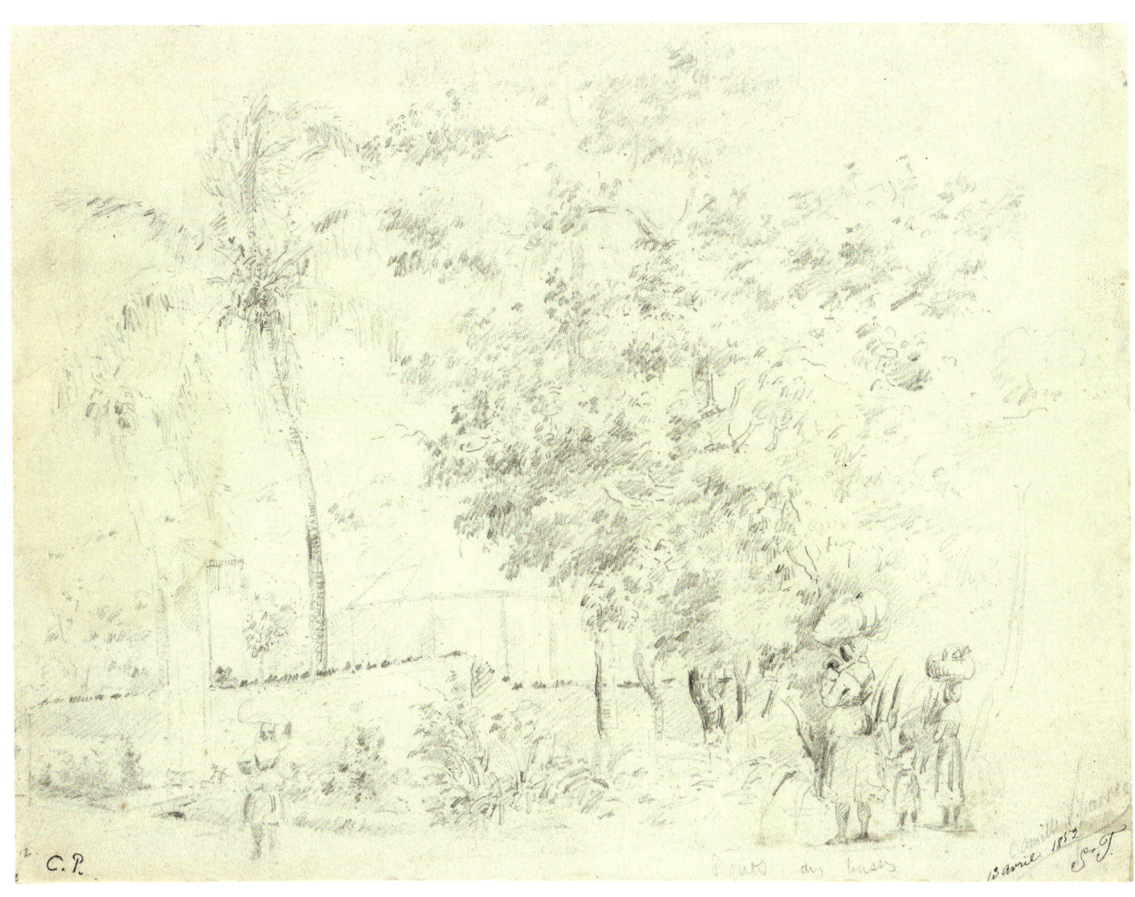

from the dirt road they travel. In the foreground the tallest female figure carries a load of clothing atop her head. She cradles a child in her left arm and holds the hand of a second child at her side. She is accompanied by a woman who also bears a tied bundle of washing. Another woman carrying laundry continues along the edge of the picture plane, presaging the similar trajectory of the faceless working women and girls in the foreground. Labor and its figuration as Black and female are not explicitly captured in this drawing, as they are in other sketches by Pissarro. Rather, the young artist's graphite mark-making naturalizes the ubiquity of Black women's labor as a near nonevent. As Saidiya Hartman attests, "It has proven difficult, if not impossible, to assimilate black women's domestic labors and reproductive capacities within narratives of the black worker, slave rebellion, maroonage, or black radicalism, even as this labor was critical to the creation of value, the realization of profit and the accumulation of capital."[32]

Route de Bussy is emblematic of the formal techniques Pissarro used to constrain race and gender to the act of labor. Paper and graphite materialize a play between positive and negative space, light and shadow. They posit stark divisions between race, gender, and class that indulge a fantasized colonial order in the act of its appearance, skirting resolution in an assertion of free Black subjectivity. Delicate graphite shading indicates both vegetation and black skin, and often the two are linked in this drawing. The heavy line of a crease in the central woman's skirt also signifies the shadowy depth of the trees in front of her. The bundle of white laundry creates a negative space that echoes the lack of graphite used to sketch the verdant branches. Both black skin and shadow are imbued with a distinctly visible and material character in this drawing.[33] The materiality of graphite on the surface of the drawing allows dark skin and the heavily shaded bark of a tree to take on an ameliorative, fantasized equivalence. These formal techniques highlight the broader exclusion of gendered Blackness from the colonial polity, here symbolized by the walled compound and suggestion of a mansion, through the ever-present intimation of labor.

In a sketch like *Route de Bussy*, Pissarro's ambivalent fascination with laboring women of color inadvertently furnishes a lens through which to understand the unique modernity of their personhood, however circumscribed, as instigators and leaders during the protest and revolution for emancipation in the Danish West Indies. Women of color are noted throughout the archival literature as having had a central role in securing the end of slavery in 1848. In response to women's leadership in a plot to burn a plantation on St. Croix, Governor-General von Scholten recounted:

> Among the black population, women play a role of great importance. They do the same work that the men do and their physical build and size render them formidable adversaries in the rough and tumble of a fight. Throughout the disturbances they were more aggressive, vengeful and altogether more violent in their passion than the men.[34]

While replete with the racial stereotypes used to un-gender Black women under slavery, von Scholten's comments underscore the powerful meaning ascribed to the violence and destruction enacted by women who would have been forced to work both in the fields and as domestics in the homes of plantation owners. There were recorded instances of women leaders during the revolution on St. Croix, one of whom was remembered for her "threats of murder and cutting people's heads off."[35] In addition, there were numerous accounts of Black women who destroyed or plundered the property of their former masters and mistresses. They severed the legs of pianos, chopped up cupboards and divans, and absconded with mattress covers when they could not remove the entire bed.[36] These women's acts of theft—though reclamation is perhaps more accurate—and symbolic destruction were, like the other acts of "vandalism" enacted during the protest for emancipation in the Danish West Indies, performances of freedom particularized by Black women's proximity to Creole wealth while working as domestics.[37] "The domestic space [of the planter's home], as much as the field," Hartman maintains, "defined [Black women's] experience of enslavement and the particular vulnerabilities of the captive body" to sexual violation in addition to bodily violence.[38] To wreck or claim their former masters' and mistresses' things asserted their own distance from thingliness as property, and embodied a social leveling required to upend colonial hierarchies.

Underscoring Black women's modes of emancipatory creation through revolutionary action in the Danish Caribbean elucidates the disjuncture between Black freedom and Pissarro's picturesque oeuvre. The genre of the picturesque—as a means of affirming colonial authority through stasis, aestheticization, and pacification—was ripe to assuage metropolitan and Creole anxieties surrounding the incorporation of a newly emancipated Black proletariat by conjoining a fantasy of Black femininity to scenes of productive labor. Both before and after emancipation the representational possibility of Black freedom was foreclosed by adaptations of the European picturesque to present a vision of harmonious colonial hierarchy in an idyllic tropical paradise.[39]

■ ■ ■

As a cosmopolitan commercial entrepôt, St. Thomas was by no means isolated from the European aesthetic tastes that proliferated throughout the mid-nineteenth-century Atlantic world. For example, the island's only newspaper, the *St. Tomæ Tidende*, stood as a barometer for colonial culture as it publicized events with an aspirational zeal and an eye transfixed by European taste imported to the Caribbean. On one occasion in the summer of 1847, the itinerant British artist and geologist James Gay Sawkins resided in Charlotte Amalie while working on a lithographic view of the city. Shortly after his arrival, the newspaper recounted a visit to his studio, concluding: "The delicacy and finish of his likenesses are in a style rarely seen in the West Indies," where there were few art academies and the

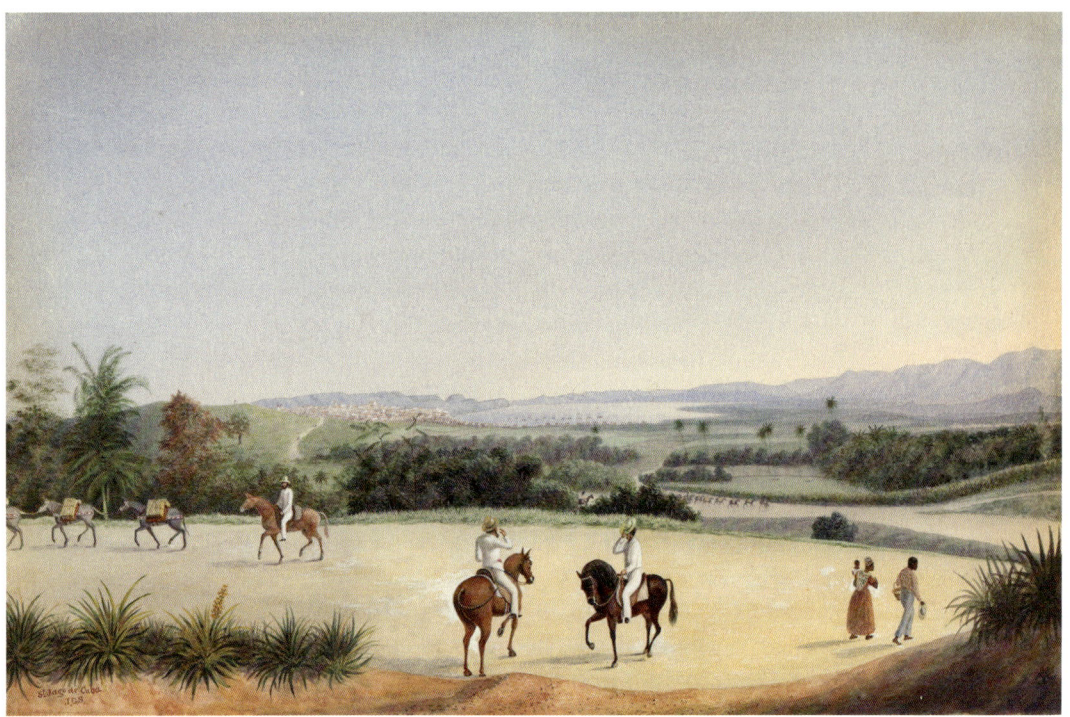

Fig. 4 James Gay Sawkins, *St. Jago de Cuba*, c. 1859, watercolor, National Library of Australia, Rex Nan Kivell Collection

artists were mostly local amateurs.[40] This record of an artistic milieu on St. Thomas also evinces how the newspaper functioned as the central public organ for defining the parameters of aesthetic taste emblematized by artists like Sawkins.

In his analysis of Pissarro's Caribbean pictures, Nicholas Mirzoeff homes in on Sawkins's practice as a precedent for Pissarro, contending that the British artist had a "careful anthropological style," which appeared to "concentrate on observation rather than moral commentary."[41] The assertion that anthropological observation is distinct from moral commentary adds up to the position that visual representation could lay claim to a detached objectivity in the colonial Caribbean. A surviving work by Sawkins from Santiago de Cuba demonstrates the extent to which Mirzoeff's claim belies reliance on the objectivity of sight, based in the science of the Enlightenment, that promised to reify colonial authority through the denigration of Blackness as a visual-material manifestation of human insufficiency (fig. 4). In the foreground of the watercolor a number of gentlemen are dressed in white linen suits, two of whom tip their hats in greeting as a third follows a train of donkeys transporting goods. To their right, Sawkins presents a group of figures, which could be read as a Black family, who make their way along the dirt road. Their modest clothing and bare feet stand in stark contrast to the dandified white suits of the Creole gentlemen. The scene opens onto a sweeping vista of the valley and bay beyond the shallow foreground populated with barely discernible Black laborers.

Sawkins's scene conforms to the tropes of the picturesque landscape that had defined the visual construction of the Caribbean since the eighteenth century. Because of the tension between idealization and social facticity inherent to the picturesque, the image reveals the conceit of its desired objectivity in the very act of its construction. Even in the ongoing struggle for abolition across the Atlantic world, Sawkins holds onto aesthetic genres developed to palliate the image of the tropical plantation and chattel slavery for metropolitan audiences.[42] It is true that the watercolor visualizes racial hierarchies that proliferated across the plantation zone with a minimum of implicit moral commentary: the white planter class acknowledges only its own kind; the status of the Black figures as enslaved or free is left ambiguous. Yet subtle visual techniques perpetuate the evacuation of possible Black subjectivities arguably inherent to the genre.[43] Although the foreground figures cast shadows of nearly the same length, indicating a similar position relative to recessionary space, the Black figures are notably smaller than the two Creole figures on horseback. Along with the almost imperceptible Black figures in the middle ground, it is apparent that Blackness remains a technique of staffage for Sawkins, a record of less-than-human agents in the Tropics that affirmed colonial power.

A drawing executed during Pissarro's Venezuelan period reveals the compositional and ideological affinities he may have gleaned from Sawkins (fig. 5).[44] The picturesque work of itinerant artists were precisely Pissarro's models when he met Frederik Georg (Fritz) Melbye—a young Danish marine painter just four years older than Pissarro—while he was sketching near the docks of Charlotte Amalie in 1852. The two artists developed a close relationship and traveled together from St. Thomas to Venezuela, arriving in the port of La Guaira on November 12, 1852. Pissarro and Melbye established a studio and worked in and around the capital of Caracas until the summer of 1854.[45]

In this drawing, Pissarro constructs a deftly abbreviated landscape of banana plants, palms, and hardwood trees populated by quickly rendered women of color laboring at the riverside. He includes or adapts a number of figural types developed in other drawings, including the foreground woman boiling clothes in a caldron and the group of women washing in the background.[46] Mirzoeff contends, "These observations were sketches for a *post-slavery imagination*, detailing the actions of those who might become either laborers or revolutionaries, such as washerwomen, coalers, and journeying traders of the town, as well as documenting the lush landscape that could provide alternative free means of subsistence."[47] This assertion boldly claims a work like the Venezuela sketch for the visual emergence of an emancipated Black subject.

However, Mirzoeff's claims do not encompass the full potential and contradictions of these early works on two counts. Taking the Venezuelan drawing as a point of analysis, Mirzoeff's argument elides the interwoven histories inherent to Pissarro's Caribbean oeuvre in favor of a clear-cut developmental narrative from slavery to abolition, even though he ultimately undercuts the affectively positive teleology that typically accompanies the historical shift from enslaved to free. First, Pissarro was not presenting "sketches for a post-slavery imagination," but constructing images freighted with a visual lexicon that still bound Blackness to slavery despite the ongoing echoes of emancipation across the region. Slavery was already abolished in the Danish West Indies when Pissarro executed his earliest known sketches from 1852. Venezuela, conversely, began the process of abolishing slavery under Simón Bolívar in solidarity with Haiti in 1815–1816. However, the institution was not fully abolished in Venezuela until March 24, 1854, during Pissarro's time in South America. To put it otherwise, Pissarro's drawings after 1848 do not propose a radical alternative to the picturesque; rather, they present the Caribbean as a space where the signifying power of the tropical was coextensive with the presentation of laboring Blackness (as enslaved). Second, in Mirzoeff's reading, the potential agencies of the women depicted in these works are constrained to a single category, an "either/or" opposition that segregates labor from revolutionary action. These refutations do not invalidate Mirzoeff's argument for the increasing acculturation of "the formerly enslaved to the disciplines of wage labor."[48] Nor do they claim some radical aesthetic foresight on the part of the young artist. Rather, my reading of this work insists upon the inherent contradictions of colonial modernity, with its imbricated histories and aesthetic strategies that could not necessarily align, but nonetheless coexisted on the page. Pissarro's corpus broadly gestures toward the tortuous and uneven path to freedom given flesh by Blackness across the Caribbean. But these are paths that never arrive in the young artist's work; his approach to vision remained dependent upon the discrepancy between the picturesque pacification of Blackness within the landscape and its coeval aspiration to provide a counter facticity.

Unlike Sawkins's finished watercolor, Pissarro's graphite sketch formally discloses the artist's ambivalence toward emancipated women's labor. While large banana leaves are abbreviated in two quick marks, the rapidly hatched strokes that depict the foreground trees and the peaks of the mountain beyond in delicately variant shades are also used to render racial difference, a technique similar to that employed in *Route de Bussy*. This formal continuity marks the foreground figures that would otherwise be indistinguishable. The pictorial conjunction of race and landscape in Pissarro's mark-making is reinforced compositionally. These women occupy a liminal space in the ever-deferred colonial politics of freedom. Unlike European colonial powers, Venezuela supported gradual or "free womb" abolition in the 1810s, a process by which the children of enslaved women were born free.[49] Working in Venezuela during the years directly preceding emancipation, the status of these Black women is indiscernible despite the fact that slavery dwindled in the nation during the first half of the nineteenth century. When abolition came to Venezuela in 1854, there were fewer than 24,000 enslaved people remaining.[50] This drawing offers one instantiation of the concatenation of gender, Blackness, and labor. Pissarro's representation is predicated on this ambivalent irresolution; perhaps these women are enslaved, perhaps they represent the enslaved mothers who would nonetheless birth free citizens, or perhaps

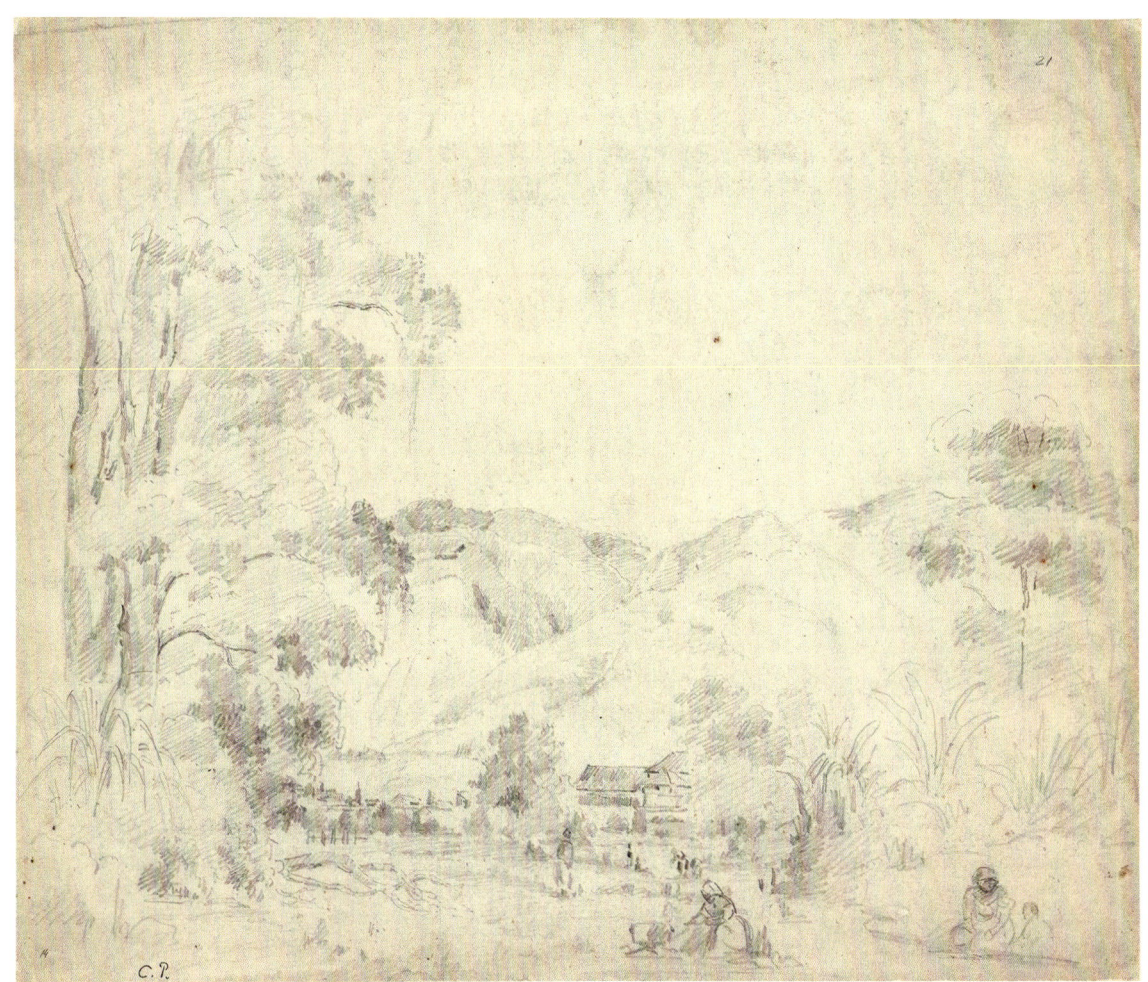

Fig. 5 Camille Pissarro, *Landscape with Female Figures Washing*, c. 1853–1854, pencil on paper, Ashmolean Museum

© Ashmolean Museum, University of Oxford

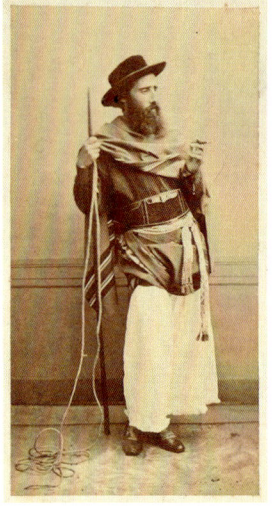
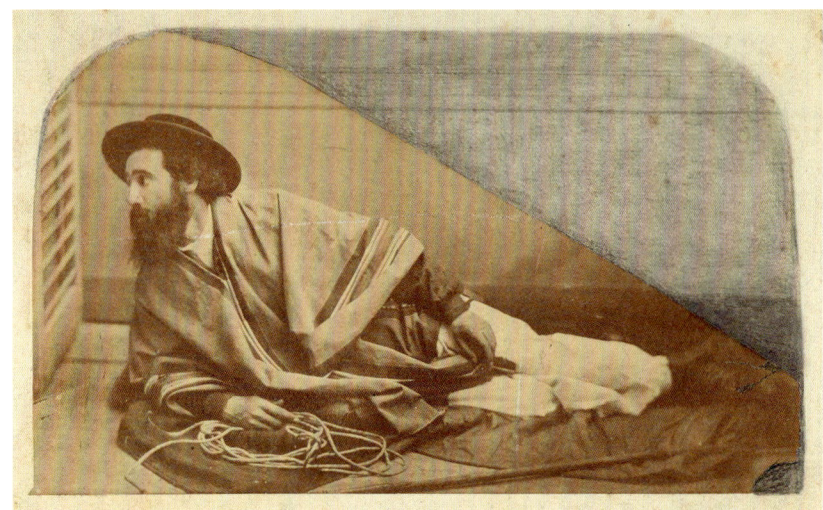

Fig. 6 Artist unknown, *Camille Pissarro in Llanero Costume*, c. 1855, calotype photograph, Ashmolean Museum

© Ashmolean Museum, University of Oxford

Fig. 7 Artist unknown, *Camille Pissarro in Llanero Costume*, c. 1855, calotype photograph, Ashmolean Museum

© Ashmolean Museum, University of Oxford

they represent the free Black proletariat. What seems clearer is that the conjunction of femininity and Blackness in the space of the Tropics makes their personhood, as opposed to legislated subjecthood, a representational site of continued subjugation at the moment of liberation.

Pissarro's early sketches evoke these gendered colonial discourses of labor while ambiguously representing work as a retrojected condition of slavery that thereby constrains the figure of the Black woman to capital. In these sketches Blackness and gender could only be represented as the fantasy of productive labor evacuated of the revolutionary catalyst that precipitated emancipation in the Danish West Indies. These conditions are also visible in a painting like *Two Women Chatting by the Sea, St. Thomas*, where rest is a temporal marker bracketed by labor. Even in a painting that begins to consider class—with the differential relationship to the land signaled by the distinction between feet bare and shod—its racialized and gendered subjects were nonetheless conscripted into modes of labor still tied to slavery. Memory and fantasy are sutured together so as to become nearly indistinguishable, interleaving free Black women's revolutionary action in the Danish West Indies with the picturesque retrojection of Blackness into servitude.

■ ■ ■

To this point, the fantasy of Pissarro's Caribbean period has been largely discussed as a psychoanalytic term applied to historical, cultural, and aesthetic formations that conditioned the foreclosed appearance of emancipated Blackness. However, two photographs in the collection of the Ashmolean Museum, Oxford, draw out the concurrent expressions of fantasy—spanning the erotic, cultural, and political—that structured the artist's depiction of Blackness in the Caribbean (figs. 6, 7). Brought to Pissarro in Paris by his brother Alfred, these are the first known photographs of the artist.[51] In both photographs, a young Camille Pissarro wears loose *pantalon bombacha*, a peasant blouse cinched at the waist with a

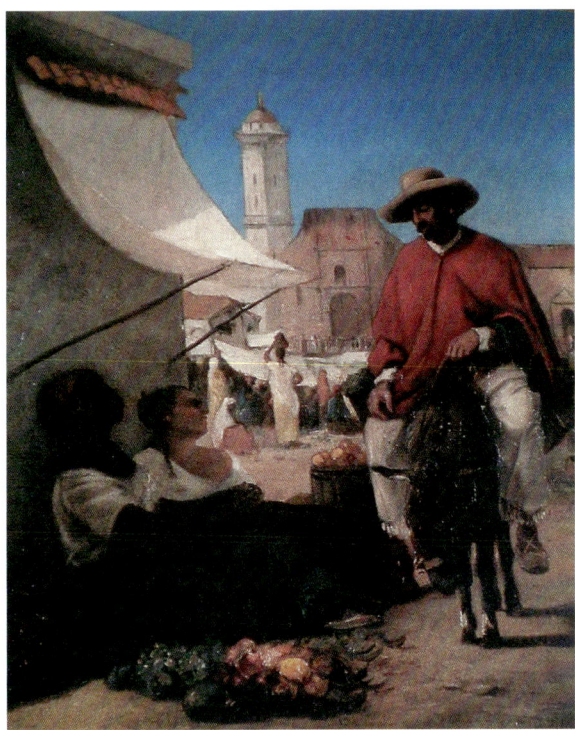

Fig. 8 Camille Pissarro, *Plaza Mayor de Caracas*, 1862, oil on canvas, La Casona Presidential Palace

cloth belt, a poncho, and a wide-brimmed hat—the traditional costume of a llanero, a herder and skilled horseman from the Llanos grasslands and symbol of Venezuelan national identity. The first photo presents him striking a sinuous contrapposto pose as he leans against a goad wound in rope while holding a cigar in his raised left hand. In the second, Pissarro props himself up on his right elbow as he reclines on a blanket; he holds a lasso in his right hand and gazes out of the frame, his face in profile.

Together, these staged images present Pissarro's fantasy of Venezuelan self-fashioning as it unfolded in 1853 and 1854, a fabrication that does not entirely align with the retrospective assertion of class struggle in his 1878 letter. In contrast, this identification with Venezuelan culture fulfilled Pissarro's projective wish to escape for the South American continent even after establishing himself in Europe. Distorted as these images are by Pissarro's awkward approximation of a llanero machismo and the presence of the studio in the frame, these photographs are visual and material manifestations of the fantasized ambivalence traced throughout this essay.

In one of Pissarro's last Caribbean memory paintings, executed in Paris in 1862, the artist took up the Venezuelan market in a work that enfolds the artist in an erotic fantasy of commercial exchange (fig. 8). In the foreground, two women of color recline in the shade of a makeshift fabric awning as they display a multitude of tropical fruits for sale on the Plaza Mayor in the capital of Caracas. A llanero riding a donkey looms above the two women, peering down from his elevated vantage point. This was a scene Pissarro would have known intimately because the apartment he rented with Melbye was located on the plaza and was the subject of many sketches.[52] The composition presents a nuanced interplay of displaced erotic fantasy in the guise of a genre painting. Painted in thick strokes, the fruit laid out in the sun provides a focal point, a grouping that serves to justify the llanero's gaze while also implying its erotic potential by proxy. The proximity of these women of color to, and their financial reliance upon, tropical produce makes fluid the distinction between possible transactions in Pissarro's treatment of the scene. Alongside their vegetable wares, they are ostensibly on display for the masculine onlooker, although they languorously turn a head or shut eyes, a refusal of the tropical heat and perhaps their interested customer.

This intimate work from memory epitomizes the fraught ambivalence with which Pissarro fantasized a connection to Venezuelan culture vis-à-vis the desire for women of color. This fantasy was explicitly cultivated after arriving in France in 1855, as both his brushed remembrance and studio photographs attest. That is to say, it is possible to map this embodied expression of his fantasy across the Atlantic onto the painting he executed almost a decade after arriving in France. The performed masculine nonchalance of his standing portrait echoes the ease with which the llanero sidles up to the market women. The penetrating stare of his reclining portrait can be loosely transposed onto the divergent power relations of sight in *Plaza Mayor de Caracas* enacted by the pointed gaze of the llanero, and its deferral by the two women onto the fruit before them. These women's capacity to rest, or otherwise exist outside of labor, is a political assertion of Black personhood latent in Pissarro's fantasized optical access to their bodies on the Plaza Mayor. T. J. Clark has elucidated the importance of idleness to modern subjectivity in Pissarro's *Two Young Peasant Women*. "Idleness," Clark asserts, "is ultimately a political matter. Pastoral is a dream of time—of leisure sewn into exertion, snatched from it easily, threaded through the rhythms of labor and insinuating other tempos and imperatives into the working day."[53] In a work from the Caribbean perhaps these peasant women's "dream of time" becomes an imperial fantasy in the Tropics, and it is necessarily multiple. *Plaza Mayor de Caracas* is tinged with a material fantasy, a cultivated memory of masculine domination. Retrospectively, Pissarro contradicts his own later claims to an investment in class struggle by positioning the herdsman against a passive, blind femininity.

A preliminary drawing for the painting, titled *Young Seated Negress*, attests to Pissarro's enduring fantasy that sought to tie femininity and Blackness together through labor or its absence (fig. 9). Also executed in Paris, this charcoal and chalk sketch captures another instance of modernity's uneven temporalities when we "take their measure from the Negress," as Huey Copeland conceptualizes the Black woman's categorical double exclusion from modernity on the basis of race and gender. "Negress," as an appellation of nonhumanity first applied to enslaved women in the seventeenth century, "underlines both the recursiveness and ubiquity of Western culture's profoundest misrecognitions of the 'other,' as well as the expansive capacities of countervailing raced, sexed, and gendered performances of self."[54] She is depicted in profile, her hands resting on her

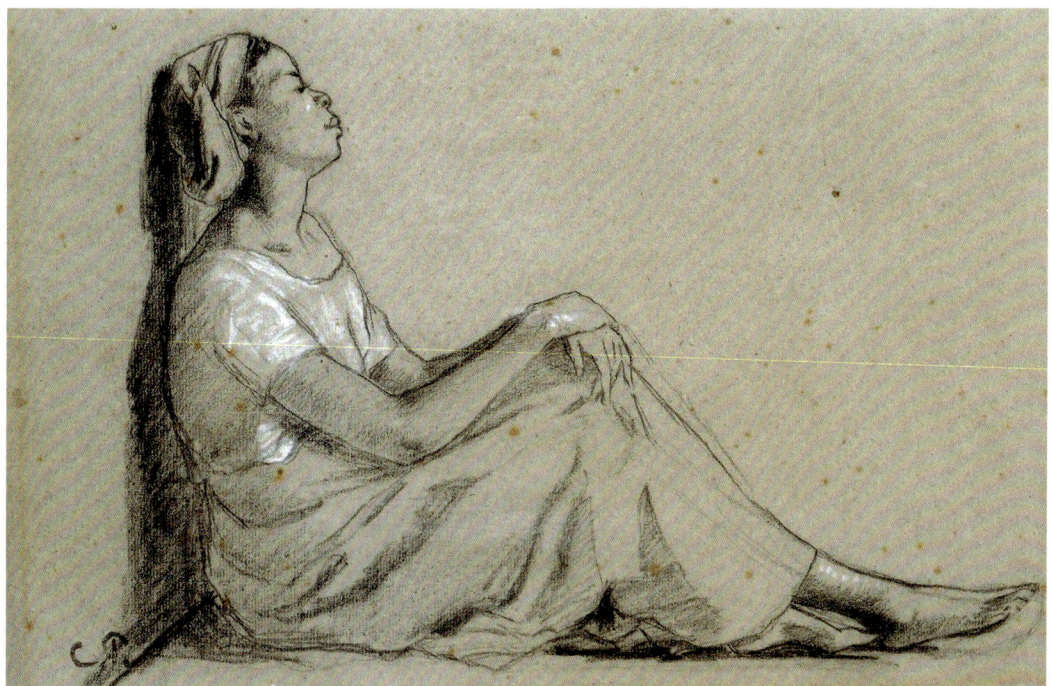

Fig. 9 Camille Pissarro, *Young Seated Negress*, c. 1855–1857, charcoal and white chalk on paper, private collection

© Christie's Images / Bridgeman Images

skirt as her bare feet emerge from beneath her dress; her eyes are closed, and her head is turned away from the bright light source that emanates from the right side of the sketch and casts her shadow, animating the wall on which she rests. In this fantasized detail, as with all his Caribbean paintings in Paris, Pissarro traverses the Atlantic through his desirous representation of Black womanhood. Formally, the thick strokes of charcoal that convey the negative space of shadow and epidermal darkness imbue the drawing with an erotic sensibility that obfuscates her "performance of self" through the decision to rest. Her bare feet—attentively rendered in black charcoal and white chalk—bespeak the long history of enslaved labor upon which Pissarro relies, and they stand at the crux of this modernist colonial fantasy. The relationship between sketch, photograph, and final painting emblematizes the erotic fantasy of the Tropics that emerges from the relationship between the artist and the representation of Blackness for which freedom is held in abeyance.

As we have seen in *Two Women Chatting by the Sea, St. Thomas* and *Young Seated Negress*, the relationship between women's bare or shod feet encapsulates the concatenated articulations of Blackness that exist interstitially between rest and activity, between freedom and servitude, between legislated subjectivity and personhood beyond the state yet relegated to the island. Pissarro's Caribbean oeuvre presents for the white European spectator an ambivalent fantasy of race in which Black women are erotic ciphers to affirm the security of colonial authority in a moment of flux.

To provide one means of concluding an investigation into the armature of colonial fantasy that undergirds modernism, it is important to note that Pissarro was not the only artist attuned to the political and potentially erotic relationship between bare feet and race in the nineteenth-century Atlantic world. Charles Baudelaire's prose poem "La Belle Dorothée," published posthumously as part of the collected *Le spleen de Paris* (1867), fetishizes the foot of a free Black woman as a marker of her subjugated race and gender difference that persist despite her nominal incorporation into an imperial subjectivity after abolition.[55] At the start of the poem, Dorothée's Blackness is constituted by the space of the Tropics. Dorothée, "strong and proud like the sun," walks alone down a street at dawn, her presence creating "a dazzling and black spot on the light" that surrounds her.[56] The poet's description of Dorothée is strikingly visual—a "moving tableau" as T. Denean Sharpley-Whiting characterizes it[57]—that denies interiority to this woman of color, who the reader is led to presume is also a sex worker. Her waist is thin, her hips large, her breasts pointed. Only her enormous head of hair, so black it is nearly blue, gives any indication of psychology, because it gives her "a triumphant and indolent air."[58] The eroticized description of Dorothée's body comes to a head in the description of her foot:

> And her foot, like the feet of the marble goddesses that Europe shuts away in its museums, faithfully imprints its form on the fine sand. Dorothée is so prodigiously coquettish, that the pleasure of being admired outweighs the pride of the freedwoman [*l'affranchi*], so even though she is free, she walks without shoes.[59]

To colonial eyes, Dorothée's bare feet become the site of her beauty, licentious and perverse in the distance between white marble and Blackness. She is for sale, free in name only for "some young officer who, on far away shores, heard talk from his comrades of the famous Dorothée."[60] Sharpley-Whiting argues "Dorothée's systemic and systematic denegation has reduced her to a state of sheer mimicry, where being freed, wearing shoes, is eschewed for bare feet, which in the colonies are paradoxically a marker of racial/sexual domination—that is, slavery."[61]

Dorothée's nominal freedom is circumscribed by the myriad ways in which this hypothetical john may own her. Bare feet appear again when the narrator fantasizes that Dorothée would beg to go to the opera "with bare feet, like the Sunday dances."[62] With this naive demand, Baudelaire evokes a tradition developed under slavery to further compound the extent to which the erotic consumption of Dorothée's bare feet render her enslaved even in her freedom. Dorothée does not speak, and she is excluded from freedom through the subjugation of her Black womanhood to white male consumption. Perhaps if she did, her bare feet could have another meaning, a rejection of colonial propriety that affirms her free identity in the Tropics rather than finding new chains with which to bind her to it.

The picturesque ambivalence of Pissarro's *Two Women Chatting by the Sea, St. Thomas* opens up possibilities beyond Baudelaire's exotic eroticism and devours Dorothée beneath a linguistic sheath of denigrated Blackness. These women who fleetingly pause their work to talk, perhaps of love, persistence, or rebellion, elicit an interrogation about Black feminine implacability drawn from Hartman: "What is the text of her insurgency and the genre of her refusal? What visions of the future world encourage her to run, or propel her flight? Or is she, as Spillers observes, a subject still awaiting her verb?" Although the two women Pissarro represented on the road to Charlotte Amalie are confined to emergent post-emancipation racial capitalism, they "are not reducible to or exhausted by it." As Hartman articulates: "These labors cannot be assimilated to the template or grid of the Black worker, but instead nourish the latent text of the fugitive."[63] This is not to say that Pissarro's women speak, but their formal treatment holds the various complexities of an emancipated Black proletariat together in the colonial Tropics. Even under the rubric of a modernity constituted by colonial exploitation, emancipated Black women found means of performing their personhood despite a colonized landscape pictured to render Blackness incompatible with freedom.

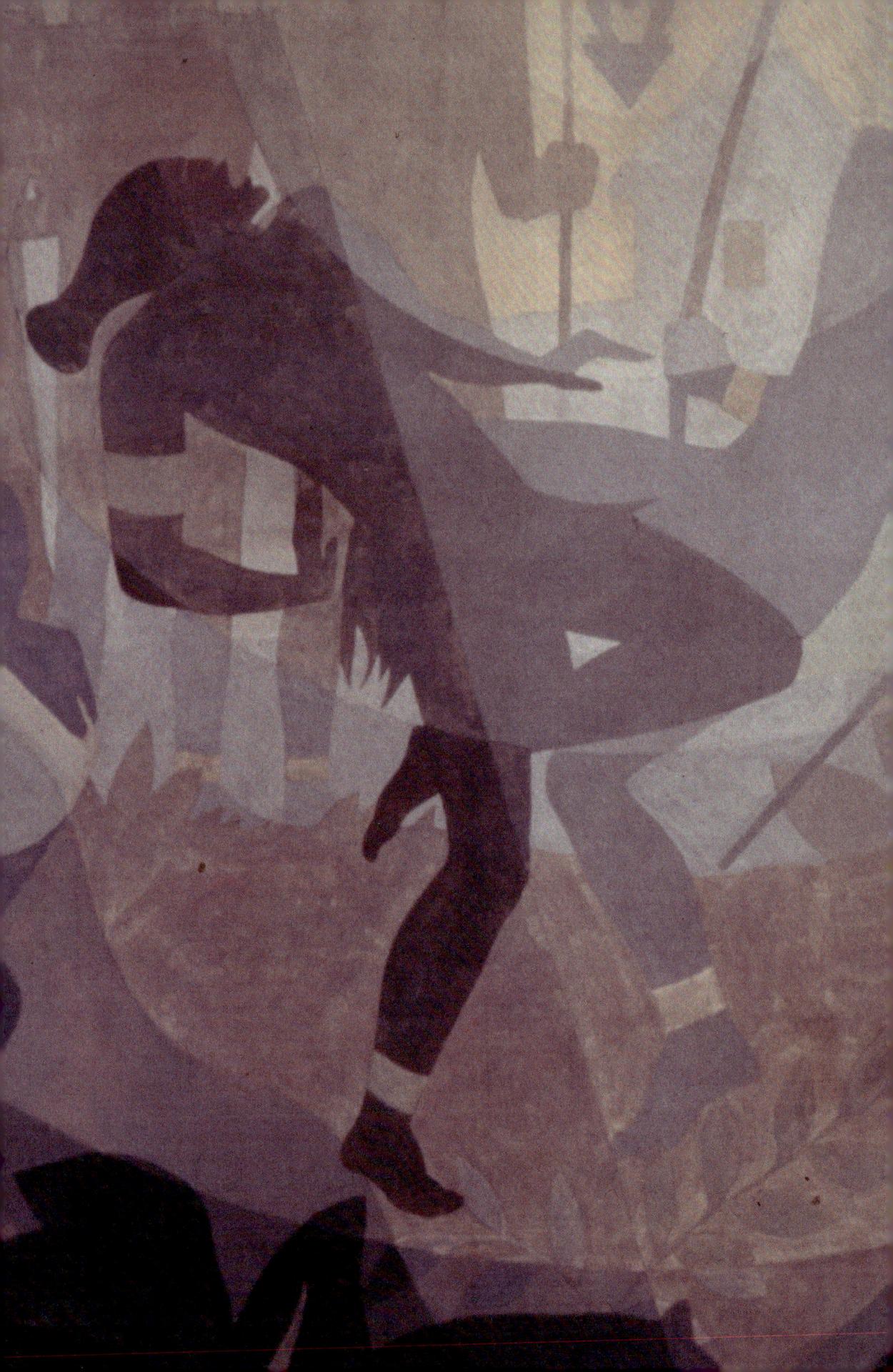

ON EUROPEAN MODERNISM AND BLACK BEING

SIMON GIKANDI

It is hard to tell when European modernism fell in love with Blackness. It could have been around 1863 when Édouard Manet painted *La Négresse (The Negress)* or in 1865 when Manet's *Olympia* was exhibited in the Paris Salon, or it could have been around 1899 when Joseph Conrad, having journeyed up the Congo River, decided to turn his African experience into his novella *Heart of Darkness*, a sensorium of modernity gone wild. Whatever the beginning point, modernism and Blackness have had an intimate but troubled relationship—intimate because it is hard to imagine a modernism without Blackness, troubled because modernism's engagement with the world of its Black "others" constantly raises the suspicion that when modernists turned to Black objects or subjects they were doing so not out of pure altruism, but as part of an aesthetic instrumentality. Modernism was underwritten by an aesthetic ideology driven by conflicting intentions regarding matters of race: modernists needed Blackness as a mechanism for maintaining and sustaining the new style of art as a counterpoint to realism and thus needed conceptual and stylistic resources ostensibly located in spaces of alterity.[1] At the same time, modernists rarely seemed to be interested in Black cultural life itself, and their Africanisms often functioned as an aesthetic resource divorced from the lived conditions of Black people.

Of course there is no singular form of modernism. Rubén Darío's *modernismo* in Spanish America is as distinct from Pablo Picasso's cubism as it is from the aesthetic project of the postcolonial Senegalese state. D. H. Lawrence's Mexican "primitive" is not the same as Paul Gauguin's Polynesian "native." But this diversity should not conceal the fact that from its very beginnings, modernism was motivated by a desire to generate an aesthetic that could be juxtaposed against the systems of art that had preceded it—romance and realism.[2] European modernism needed to assert its singularity as the force of its oppositional capacity, and it could not do so effectively without the invention of a uniform Blackness, one in which, through colonialist discourses and representation, the diverse peoples, cultures, and aesthetic traditions of Africa, the Caribbean, and the Black Americas were reduced into a uniform mass. Similarly, from the modernism of so-called folk artists in Africa and the Caribbean, to the self-conscious, European-influenced work of Negritude painters and poets, Black modernism would come in different shapes and forms. And yet, the shared experience of being dominated and repressed in the modern world demanded—by necessity if not intention—a unified aesthetic response. This aesthetic, which now goes by the name "Black modernism," went hand in hand with the contemporary political projects of Pan-Africanism, the New African, and the New Negro.

Arguably, the violence of modernity provided the unifying context for the varieties of Black modernism that emerged in the first decades of the twentieth century. And if there is one great irony in the history of modern art, it is that the period in which Black artists began to adopt the language of European modernism was one in which the lived condition of Blackness had come to be characterized by unimaginable brutality.[3]

European modernism was clearly generated by the violence of nineteenth-century modernity, but in most instances, this violence was seen as a consequence of a progressive history, of economic rationalization, and of civilization and its discontents.[4] The violence that surrounded Black subjects was, however, of a different kind: it was the outcome of deliberate policies intended to coerce Black people into bonded labor (as was the case in the majority of Europe's African colonies) or a systematic campaign to degrade or destroy them altogether (exemplified by lynching in the United States).

Focusing primarily on late nineteenth- and twentieth-century African American artists, I will consider here the specific context in which the aesthetic ideology and practices of European modernism became available to Black artists amid unimaginable violence. Coming to terms with this context is an essential condition for understanding Blackness as part of the primal scene of modernism. To do so, we must, as Judith Wilson has insisted, "look beyond questions of mere formal innovation to the more complex problem of merging specific ideological goals with an appropriate visual language."[5] Reflecting on the relation between Black bodies and the violence of modernity is also a recognition of the pressures brought to bear on those Black writers and artists who, at the dawn of the twentieth century, set out to adopt the vocabularies of modernism and redirect them toward the collective project of Black emancipation. Three critical questions thus emerge: Where did Black modernism come from? Why did Black artists come to see modernism as the form that could best help them affirm their humanity? And how did they separate the negative aspects of European modernism—its racism and ethnocentrism—from its usable qualities?

Modernism may have restored a measure of aesthetic value to Blackness, but this return did not obviate racial violence as the point of contact between the white and Black worlds. In fact, it is hard to escape the conjecture between key moments in high modernism and racial violence in the Americas and European colonies in Africa and the Caribbean. Consider these examples: The 1860s, the decade when Édouard Manet painted *Olympia* and poets such as Charles Baudelaire celebrated the flaneur in *The Painter of Modern Life*, was also the period of the American Civil War (1861–1865). During this time, slavery still reigned in Brazil, Cuba, and Spanish territories in Latin America, and the partition of Africa was well under way as European powers carved out chunks of the continent for themselves. The end of slavery in the United States was also the beginning of Reconstruction, a period that would witness the reversal of Black rights and the advent of Jim Crow. During this period, the freedom promised by the Emancipation Proclamation of 1863 and the Thirteenth Amendment of 1865 made no difference in the lives of the formerly enslaved. In 1903, a half century later, W. E. B. Du Bois noted in *The Souls of Black Folk*, "despite compromise, war, and struggle, the Negro is not free. . . . In the most cultured sections and cities of the South the Negroes are a segregated servile caste, with restricted rights and privileges."[6]

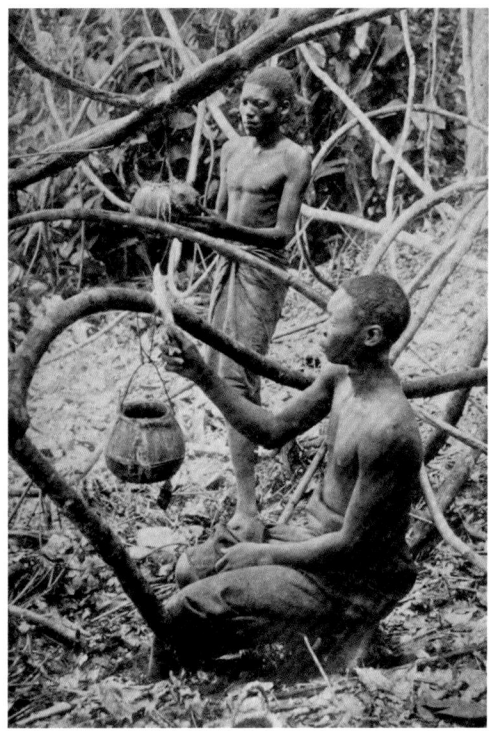

Fig. 1 Forced labor in the Congo, from Henry Wellington Wack, *The Story of the Congo Free State: Social, Political, and Economic Aspects of the Belgian System of Government in Central Africa* (New York, 1905)

One could point to other examples of the strange birth of modernism in the bowels of what Jean Franco has called "cruel modernity."[7] As Conrad was writing *Heart of Darkness*, first published in 1899, King Leopold II's agents in the Congo were involved in some of the worst atrocities of the modern period, including forced labor, amputations, and killings (fig. 1). In 1907, as Picasso was completing *Les Demoiselles d'Avignon (The Ladies of Avignon)* in his Paris studio, General Lothar von Trotha of Germany was putting the final touches on an "Extermination Decree" intended to wipe out the Herero and Nama of Namibia.[8] In the early 1920s, as T. S. Eliot's poem *The Waste Land* was being celebrated for having established a new language for poetry, Black bodies were hanging from trees in much of the American South, and citizens were burning the cross of white supremacy in the poet's natal Midwest (fig. 2). If one is looking for a scandal in modernism, it is not to be found where we usually expect to find it—in the eroticism and exoticism of Josephine Baker in the French cabaret or the influence of African fetishism in cubism—but in the institutional context where aesthetic effects were considered more important than the destruction of Black bodies.[9]

From Romance to Modernism

The best place to start is perhaps the last decade of the nineteenth century, for it is here that the early adoption of European modernism could be detected in what Walter Benjamin described as "a dialectical rising and falling in the lawmaking and law-preserving formations of violence."[10] By the 1890s, Black artists who wanted to be modern found themselves in a

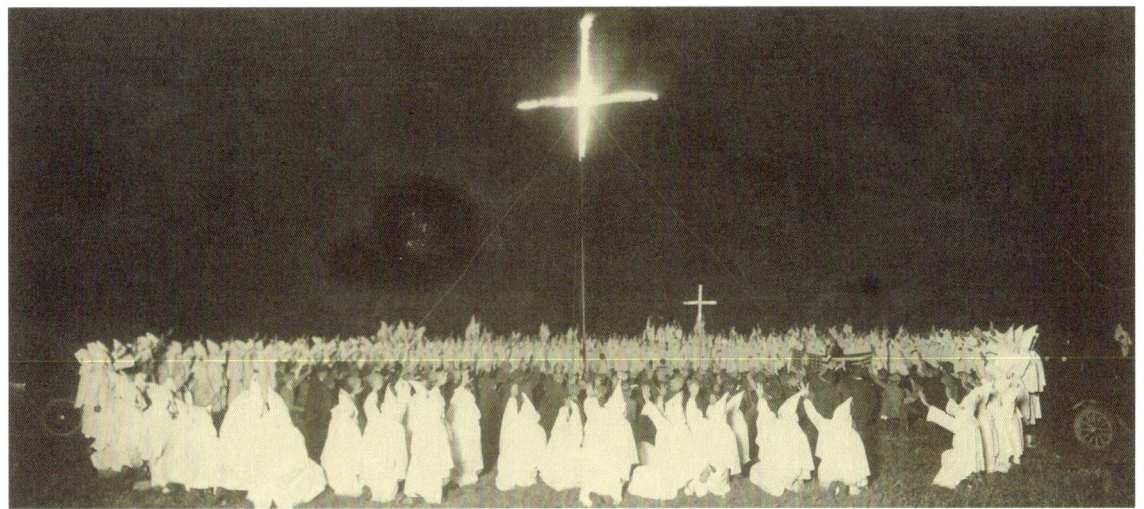

Fig. 2 Members of the Ku Klux Klan burning a cross in Topeka, between 1920 and 1929, Kansas State Historical Society

cauldron: if they wanted to break away from the folkloric space assigned to them by the institutions of interpretation, they needed to follow the example of Henry Ossawa Tanner and move to France, where Blackness had already entered the orbit of European modernism, but to be an expatriate meant being cut off from Black life and community.[11] This is the paradox that surrounded the production of Tanner's 1893 painting *The Banjo Lesson* (fig. 3), which stood out for its ability to reflect an identity that was far removed from the violence of Jim Crow, melding blue and light yellow colors to simultaneously, as Sharon F. Patton argues, create "a realistic image and evoke a romantic mood."[12] In its careful representation of an intimate Black space, Tanner's painting aspired to be realistic, but it was an aspiration to a realism enabled by discernible romantic effects—the deployment of the banjo (the quintessential instrument of Black new-world identity) as the point of contact between the teacher and the pupil; the spontaneous nature of the lesson denoted by the hat on the floor; and, of course, the intimacy of the pose of the teacher and the pupil. All these were subtle signals of the existence of an autonomous Black world beyond the reach of the violence that might have lurked just outside the cabin. More significantly, these romantic effects stand out as a direct refutation of the representational politics of Jim Crow circulating in the form of caricatures in the popular press and works such as Thomas Dixon Jr.'s novel *The Clansman: A Historical Romance of the Ku Klux Klan* (1905) and its film adaptation, D. W. Griffith's *The Birth of a Nation* (1915). Paradoxically, it was only in France that Tanner could have painted *The Banjo Lesson*. It was here, we are told by James A. Porter, that he would come to enjoy "a greater sense of freedom, a sense of expanded manhood, and a consciousness of responsibility" that would feed his "ambition and energy."[13]

But if *The Banjo Lesson* is a work of an American life recollected in tranquility in the vein of the Romanticists, it raises two difficult issues for scholars seeking the origins of Black modernism.[14] The first issue revolves around Tanner's relation to his mentor, Thomas Eakins. As Porter noted, Tanner had gone to France to find freedom and an expanded sense of

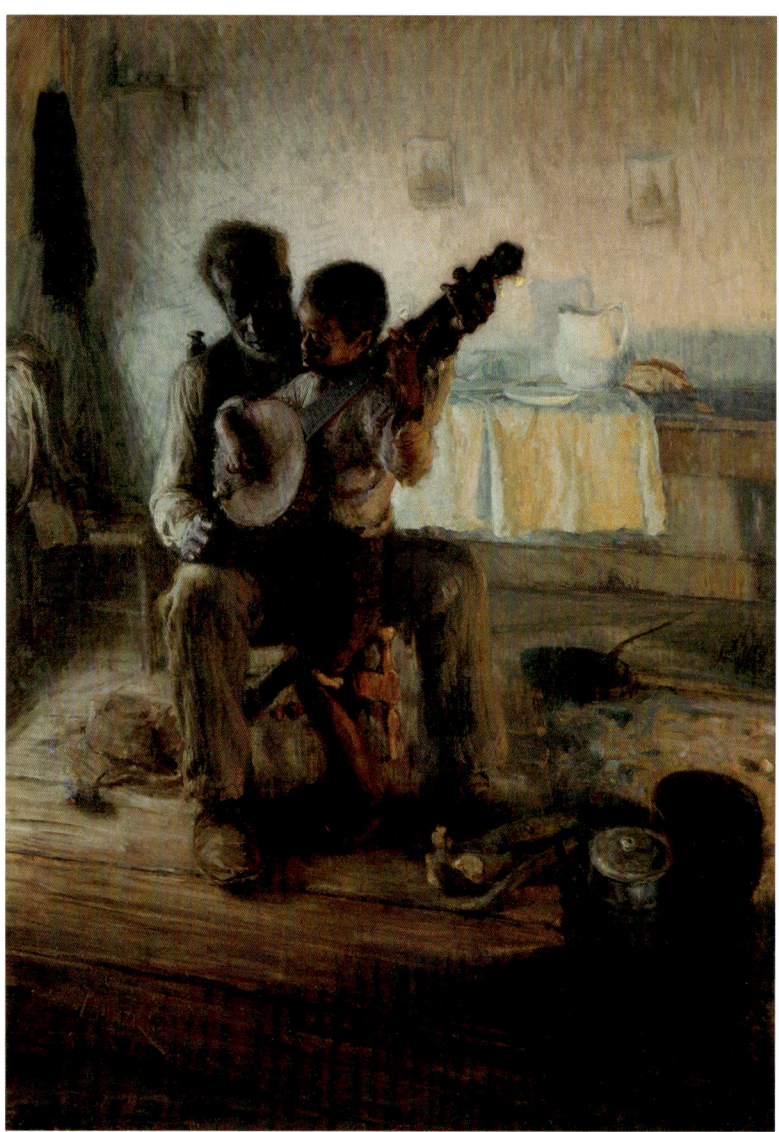

Fig. 3 Henry Ossawa Tanner, *The Banjo Lesson*, 1893, oil on canvas, Collection of the Hampton University Museum, Hampton, VA

selfhood, yet during his summers in Brittany his work differed little from "what he produced in America."[15] Why was Tanner, by all measures a most original artist, seemingly unable to escape the shadow of his mentor?[16] The second issue concerns Tanner's relation to the modern style emerging in France during his residency in the country: Why, in spite of his possible exposure to these new styles, was Tanner still attached to romance and genre painting? This issue has been framed well by Theresa Leininger-Miller in the broader context of African American artists in France: "Why does so much of their art seem conservative, even retrograde, compared to the contemporary French scene, especially at the end of the nineteenth century and the beginning of the twentieth?"[17] There is, however, a different framing of the question by way of David Scott: Why did Tanner consider romance as the ideal "problem space"—"a discursive context, a context for language"—in which Black life could be reimagined in art?[18] Or, to put it another way, what work was romance being asked to perform?

84

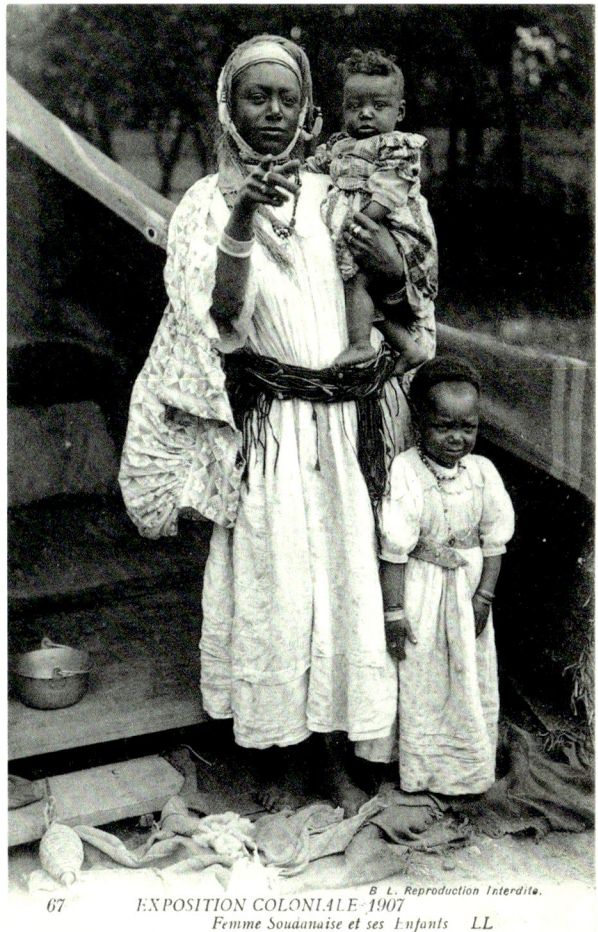

Fig. 4 *Femme Soudanaise et ses Enfants* (*Woman of Sudan and Her Children*), 1907, postcard, Colonial Exposition, Collection of Clemens Radauer

If we keep in mind the dialectic of violence as the condition of possibility of Black modernism, it is not hard to see why Black American artists could not easily dismiss romance from their aesthetic repertoire. For even when they were attuned to developments in art practices in Europe, their artistic projects were still informed by American concerns, more specifically the connection between violence and the representation of Blackness in Jim Crow art.[19] Confronted with the aesthetic ideology of Jim Crow, or with highly visible images of Africans and Afro-Caribbean peoples exhibited in zoos or world's fairs (fig. 4), the artist's preference for an allegory of Black intimacy—what Richard J. Powell has called "the paragons of positivism . . . in the welter of cultural stereotyping and ridicule"[20]—would become an imperative. For the same reason, the pioneering Black novels of this period, including W. E. B. Du Bois's *The Quest of the Silver Fleece* and Joseph Ephraim Casely Hayford's *Ethiopia Unbound* (both published in 1911) were conceived as romances.

Given the preponderance of romance in the aesthetic spaces where one would have expected to see modernist experimentation, it is important for critics to stop thinking of romantic tropes as a reflection of aesthetic failure or backwardness; instead, these devices should be recognized as significant starting points for Black art in the long twentieth century.

And rather than seeing Tanner as the symbol of Black artistic belatedness—a figure trapped in what Alain Locke conceived to be "the academic mould and the cosmopolitan outlook"[21]—we should perhaps see him as part of a generational attempt to make romance serviceable for Black subjects in a state of abjection. Here, romance should be read as both the symptom and the cure for the peculiar condition of Blackness in late nineteenth- and early twentieth-century modernity—a people asserting their rights as free autonomous subjects yet constantly barred from the house of modern culture.

In these circumstances, the subjected had to confront the dilemma inherent in an aesthetic of decolonization—how to secure and fashion an image of oneself that was powerful and positive enough to counter social and racial prejudice while at the same time inscribing the realities of racism, prejudice, and repression.[22] Indeed, if there is a common theme running through the writings and cultural practices of the Afro-Victorians, it is an insistence on their mastery of modern culture as evidence of their humanity and as a conduit for racial upliftment.[23] At the same time, however, this desire to represent Black people as modern subjects—indeed the whole romance of the New Negro for a New Century—could not escape the psychic violence that had come to define Black lives, a situation so dire that it bordered on what Julia Kristeva, writing in a different context, has described as a chain of an "infinite number of misfortunes" and a "devitalized existence."[24] For Black elites, the most obvious symptom of the depressive condition was what Du Bois called "double consciousness"—the Black American's longing "to attain self-conscious manhood, to merge his double self into a better and truer self."[25] Art and culture were to be embraced as alternative spaces of Black being—sites of "amatory idealization."[26] This idealization would find one of its primary forms in the symbol of the Sphinx as the guardian spirit of Blackness and the allegory of Ethiopia as the site of Black redemption.

These two figures—the Sphinx and Ethiopia—were perhaps brought together for the first time in Edward Wilmot Blyden's sermon "Ethiopia Stretching Out Her Hands unto God," delivered to a congregation in the United States in 1880:

> If we are to gather an analogy to Africa from ancient fable, the Sphinx supplies us with a truer symbol. The Sphinx was said to sit in the road side, and put riddles to every passenger. If the man could not answer, she swallowed him alive. If he could solve the riddle, the Sphinx was slain. Has not Africa been, through the ages, sitting on the highway of the world? Here she is, south of Europe, with but a lake between, joined on to Asia, with the most frequented oceans on the east and west of her—accessible to all the races, and yet her secret is unknown. She has swallowed up her thousands. The Sphinx must solve her own riddle at last. The opening up of Africa is to be the work of Africans.[27]

The image was taken up by Anna Julia Cooper in 1892:

> In the clash and clatter of our American Conflict, it has been said that the South remains Silent. Like the Sphinx she inspires vociferous disputation, but herself takes little part in the noisy controversy. One muffled strain in the Silent South, a jarring chord and a vague and uncomprehended cadenza has been and still is the Negro. And of that muffled chord, the one mute and voiceless note has been the sadly expectant Black Woman.[28]

It was then picked up by Du Bois in 1903:

> The shadow of a mighty Negro past flits through the tale of Ethiopia the Shadowy and of Egypt the Sphinx. Throughout history, the powers of single black men flash here and there like falling stars, and die sometimes before the world has rightly gauged their brightness. Here in America, in the few days since Emancipation, the black man's turning hither and thither in hesitant and doubtful striving has often made his very strength to lose effectiveness, to seem like absence of power, like weakness. And yet it is not weakness, but rather the contradiction of double aims.[29]

Ethiopia would become the sign of Black moral awakening and purpose in Hayford's *Ethiopia Unbound*:

> In the self-same era a god descended upon earth to teach the Ethiopians anew the way of life. He came not in thunder, or with great sound, but in the garb of a humble teacher, a John the Baptist among his brethren, preaching racial and national salvation. From land to land, and from shore to shore, his message was the self-same one, which, interpreted in the language of the Christ, was: What shall it profit a race if it shall gain the whole world and lose its own soul?[30]

And it would find its most famous artistic expression in Meta Vaux Warrick Fuller's *Ethiopia Awakening* (1921, fig. 5).

Ethiopia would henceforth be idealized as the fulcrum of Pan-Africanist ideologies across the Black Atlantic. But more than its politics, Ethiopianism generated an aesthetic ideology that would create another context for the adoption of modernism through the invocation of the romantic.[31] Three issues were involved in this process: The first one was the obvious invocation of both Egypt and Ethiopia as integral to Blackness. Conceived as part of a classical background, Egyptian and Ethiopic motifs could come to replace the Greek and Roman figures that had functioned as a resource for nineteenth-century Black artists, most notably Edmonia

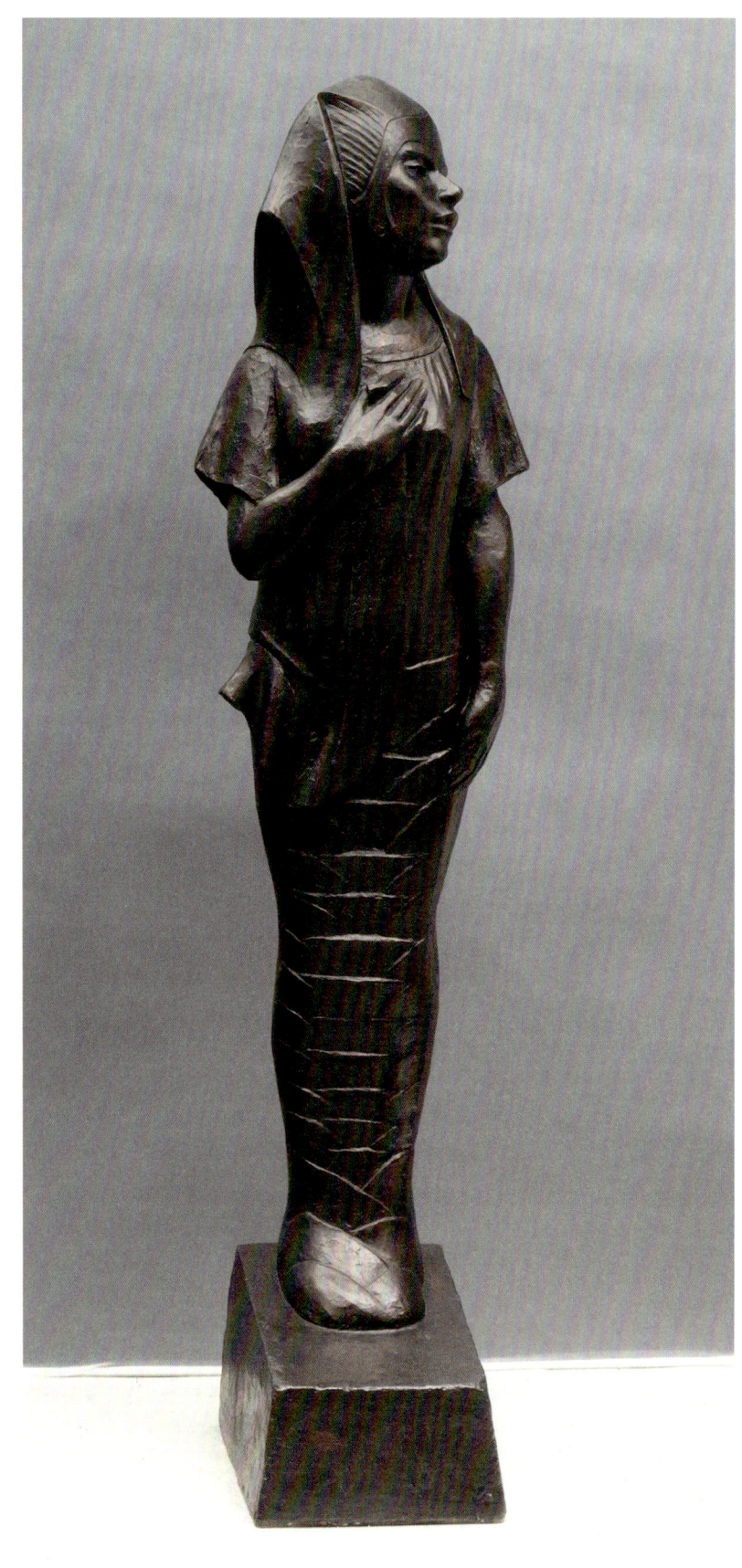

Fig. 5 Meta Vaux Warrick Fuller, *Ethiopia Awakening*, 1921, bronze, Art and Artifacts Division, Schomburg Center for Research in Black Culture, New York Public Library

Lewis. The second process was the use of an allegorical double—the Sphinx and the Ethiopic—one representing the riddle or mystery of Blackness, the other the inevitable emergence of repressed energies. Here the lesson was that Blackness, rather than being imprisoned in the violence of European modernity, had roots and potential located elsewhere, out of reach. Finally, the turn to Egypt and Ethiopia signaled the emergence of Black internationalism as the marker of a space in which Blackness could be imagined outside the constraints of the nation state.[32] More than any other work of art in its time, Fuller's *Ethiopia Awakening* would signal the passage from the Old to the New Negro, the movement from romance into a nascent Black modernism.

Now, making a claim for Fuller's modernism might appear strange. After all, her art is informed by deep allegory: rather than an object or experience, the dominant reading of her work assumes that the allegorical sign refers to a preceding one.[33] Renée Ater has noted how Fuller reimagined the figure of Cleopatra to create "an allegorical female form that articulates an imagined concept of Egypt rather than a literal archeological reference to Egyptian statuary or to a specific person."[34] Crucially, Fuller turned to allegory as the trope of newness: it was in its allegorical form that Ethiopia would arise from its mummified state to claim its place in the world. This choice is crucial because in the standard figurative readings of European modernism, it was irony, rather than allegory, that would be privileged as the trope of newness in the world and of the subject's alienation from its world. What was innovative in Fuller's work, then, was not just her bending of allegory to serve the temporal ends that we usually associate with irony—the clearance of a space for "a future recovery … a future happiness"[35]—but also her affirmation of romance as the self's search for what Northrop Frye calls "a fulfilment that will deliver it from the anxieties of reality" and a medium for sensing, in Fredric Jameson's formulation, "other historical rhythms."[36]

But Fuller departed from traditional theories of romance in at least one significant way: her sculpture does not contain any signs of the abject reality that surrounded Black lives. Her goal, as she put it in a 1921 letter, was to depict a group of people "who had once made history and now after a long sleep was awaking, gradually unwinding the bandage of its mummified past and looking out on life again, expectant but unafraid and at least a graceful gesture."[37] Ethiopia, despite Italian imperial ambitions in the Horn of Africa at the time, existed for African Americans to be loved somewhere and somehow in the future, and allegory would enable the viewers' identification with the sculpture and its promise. Furthermore, beyond the politics and poetics of Pan-Africanism, Fuller's work was pointing to a different aesthetic direction, something akin to what Clement Greenberg, discussing the Pre-Raphaelites, called proto-modernism: "They acted on a dissatisfaction with painting as practiced in their time, holding that its realism wasn't truthful enough."[38] Similarly, we could argue that beneath its amatory quality, Fuller's sculpture was indirectly expressing her dissatisfaction with the reality, realism, and genre painting that preceded her and

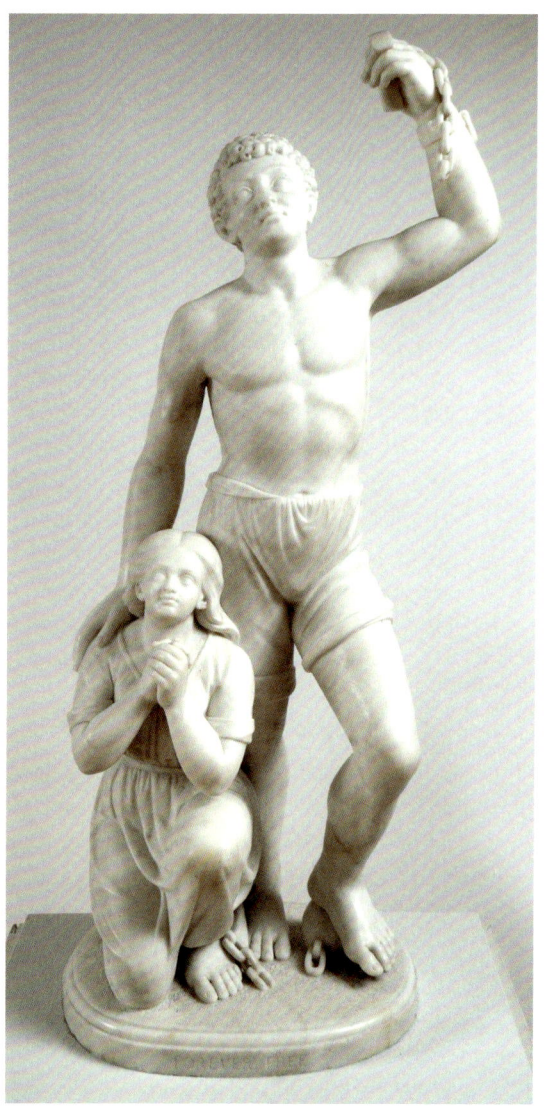

Fig. 6 Edmonia Lewis, *Forever Free*, 1867, marble, Howard University Gallery of Art

Photo by Gregory R. Staley. Licensed by Art Resource, NY

creating a new space that, while certainly not real, was truthful enough. Reality and realism were to be rejected through omission; romance was to be calibrated through a kind of aesthetic rerouting, which would take the viewer from Edmonia Lewis's *Forever Free* (1867), which had drawn its resources from Roman and Greek figures (fig. 6), and point us to Lois Mailou Jones's *The Ascent of Ethiopia* (1932), a much more abstract take on the same subject (fig. 7). Within that long trajectory, between the 1910s and 1930s, Black modernism would find its rhythm and idiom. However, this development did not mean that the Black artist had found a home in the world.

Dwelling in Modernism

It is no secret that one of the motivations for Black internationalism in the first half of the twentieth century was a collective sense that wherever they were in the world, people of African descent did not have a home

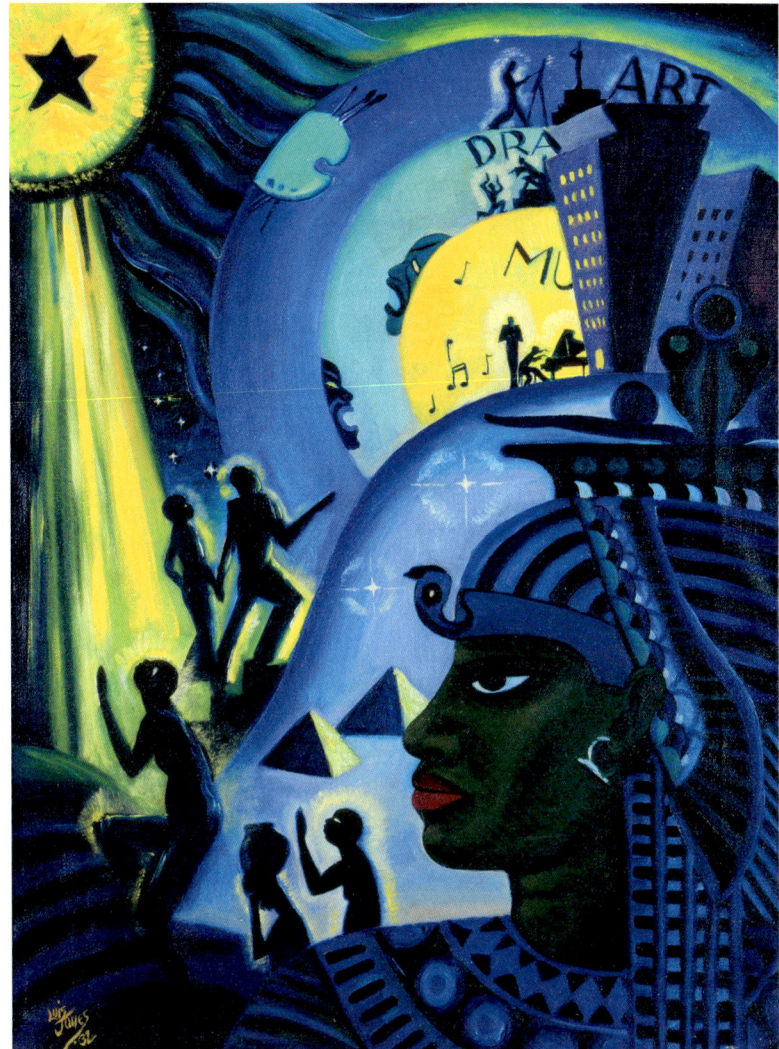

Fig. 7 Lois Mailou Jones, *The Ascent of Ethiopia*, 1932, oil on canvas, Milwaukee Art Museum, Purchase, African American Art Acquisition Fund, matching funds from Suzanne and Richard Pieper, with additional support from Arthur and Dorothy Nelle Sanders

Photo by John R. Glembin

they could call their own. The idea of Black homelessness was summed up by Aaron Douglas in a 1936 essay:

> Our chief concern has been to establish and maintain recognition of our essential humanity, in other words, complete social and political equality. This has been a difficult fight as we have been the constant object of attack by all manner of propaganda from nursery rhymes to false scientific racial theories. In this struggle the rest of the proletariat almost invariably has been arrayed against us. Some of us understand why this is so. But the Negro artist, unlike the white artist, has never known the big house.[39]

African American artists, like their diasporic brethren, seemed to understand that one of the main characteristics of modern identity and its art forms was the need for a space of emplacement, a room of their own as Virginia Woolf might have put it.[40] They understood how dwelling pervaded the whole range of being and that the fundamental characteristic of the human consisted "in dwelling... in the sense of the stay of mortals on the earth."[41] Unlike their European counterparts, however, Black subjects could not take their dwelling for granted; consequently, the period in which Black modernism emerged was one in which both real and existential homelessness defined what it meant to be excluded from the domain of the modern and the necessity of art as an accounting, if not a cure, for this homelessness.

As the new Black aesthetic began to cohere and to reconfigure European modernism between 1914 and 1940, it seemed driven by the need to produce forms of art that would be seen as agents of newness and transformation in a historical context that changed at the material level but remained ontologically the same. The Great Migration—Black Americans' departure from the South and their embrace of northern cities as sites of new identities—was the most visible sign of ongoing historical and spatial transformations. What had not changed were racial attitudes and racial violence; Black aspirations for freedom were constantly blocked either by the force of law or custom; and Black selfhood was put into doubt by racial theories and practices. In this context, one couldn't make serious claims for the autonomy of art without extending the imaginative capacity of Black subjects themselves. This in essence was the aesthetic project of the Harlem Renaissance as it was laid out by Alain Locke in *The New Negro* and in *The Negro in Art*.[42] What was taking place in Harlem—or at least what Locke assumed was taking place in the new Black metropolis—is the key to understanding the consolidation of modernism as part of Black self-fashioning.

But there is something curious about the common association of modernism and the Harlem Renaissance. For while the term "modernism" was in full bloom in both academic and popular articles and treatises when Locke produced his manifestos on the art of the New Negro, and he had a broad sense of artistic developments in the first two or three decades of the twentieth century, he was cautious in his use of the term, and he did not see the new Black art as bound to European aesthetic transformation. On the contrary, Locke assumed—and made the strong case—that the new Black art was intractably tied to a modernistic Black thinking about the self and its relation to the world. Thinking of themselves outside the narrow confines of national culture, Black subjects had become active agents in "the laboratory of a great race-welding" within a global and cosmopolitan world:

> In Harlem, Negro life is seizing upon its first chances for group expression and self-determination. It is—or promises at least to be—a race capital. That is why our comparison is taken with those nascent centers of folk-expression and self-determination which are playing a creative part in the world to-day. Without pretense to their political significance, Harlem has the same role to play for the New Negro as Dublin has had for the New Ireland or Prague for the New Czechoslovakia.[43]

Harlem—not the United States, not New York—was the space of a new way of being in the world, a creative agency associated with freedom and mobility. And for Locke, the images coming out of Harlem would independently affirm what T. J. Clark would consider to be two of the great wishes of modernism—one leading the audience "toward a recognition of the social reality of the sign" and the other returning "the sign back to a bedrock of World / Nature / Sensation / Subjectivity."[44]

Despite Locke's knowledge of European modernism and his understanding of the fundamental role African art had in its making, he was not promoting an alternative modernism, but rather a Black modernism without antecedents. Locke assumed that because the New Negro was a self-generated subject, the new art forms emerging in the Black metropolis would also be self-engendered. Once a Black subject had emerged, it seemed almost logical that new forms of art would emerge to express newness and to make it visible:

> For the younger generation is vibrant with a new psychology; the new spirit is awake in the masses, and under the very eyes of the professional observers is transforming what has been a perennial problem into the progressive phases of contemporary Negro life.[45]

For Locke, the project of a modernist form of Black art would be driven by a double imperative—the presentation of a hitherto repressed Black subjectivity through the self-assertion of the New Negro as a transcendental figure, one freed from the ugliness of everyday life. The art of the New Negro would be located in a realm of sensuous experience that would come to be known as soul. Or, as Archibald John Motley Jr. put it, the new Black art would be made of "nothing borrowed, nothing copied, just an unraveling of the soul."[46] The soul—that deep interior space within Black selves—was an attractive ontological category because it referred to a realm of the Black experience that had not been damaged by the violence of European modernity. The idea of art as immanent would inform the art of emerging practitioners such as Aaron Douglas, whose drawings framed the essays and creative works collected in *The New Negro*.

Looking at a Douglas illustration such as *Invincible Music: The Spirit of Africa* (1926, fig. 8), the murals that make up *Aspects of Negro Life* (figs. 9, 10), or the iconic illustration *The Crucifixion* (fig. 11), we can see why Locke singled him out as the "pioneering Africanist."[47] His use of Africanist elements—the Egyptian motifs, for example—and their abstraction pointed to an entirely new way of imaging the Black subject, one that can be compared to the sensory impression of the fiction of Jean Toomer, Zora Neale Hurston, and Eric D. Walrond, who were also represented in Locke's anthology. Individually and collectively, these works set out to wrench the Black subject away from the American tradition of portraiture and genre, to liberate it from white condescension, and to capture its soul, as it were. Here, what art historians have come to describe as the "Egyptian"

Fig. 8 Aaron Douglas, *Invincible Music: The Spirit of Africa*, illustration from *The Crisis: A Record of the Darker Races*, February 1926, 169, Jean Blackwell Hutson Research and Reference Division, Schomburg Center for Research in Black Culture, New York Public Library

© 2023 Heirs of Aaron Douglas / Licensed by VAGA at Artists Rights Society (ARS), New York

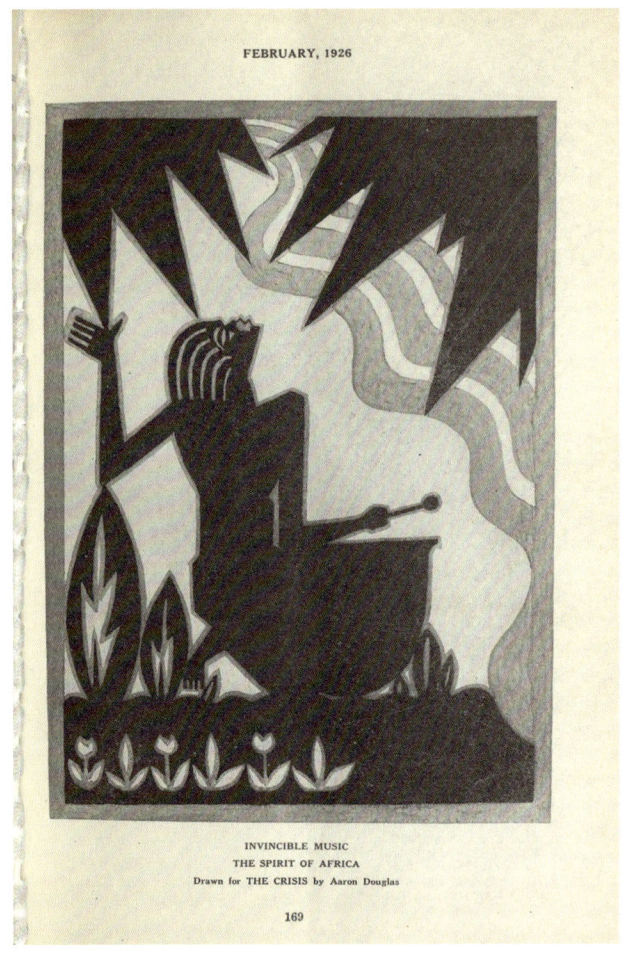

Fig. 9 Aaron Douglas, *Aspects of Negro Life: From Slavery Through Reconstruction*, 1934, oil on canvas, Art and Artifacts Division, Schomburg Center for Research in Black Culture, New York Public Library

© 2023 Heirs of Aaron Douglas / Licensed by VAGA at Artists Rights Society (ARS), New York

Fig. 10 Aaron Douglas, *Aspects of Negro Life: The Negro in an African Setting*, 1934, oil on canvas, Art and Artifacts Division, Schomburg Center for Research in Black Culture, New York Public Library

© 2023 Heirs of Aaron Douglas / Licensed by VAGA at Artists Rights Society (ARS), New York

form in Douglas's painting—the silhouetted figures, the tomb frescos, and the ethereal light—was intended to be nothing less than a redirection of artistic energies from the ugly outside to a treasured inside.[48] Similarly, abstraction would denote interiority and enact a transfiguration that would point to the other, immaterial world, in which a Black presence would be made visible. This inward turn implied that in a world where reality no longer constituted what the literary critic Georg Lukács called "a favorable soil for art" or satisfied the subject's longing for form, then it is to the interior, rather than the exterior world, that art must seek another world for its objects and motivation, affirm a form of life independent of the empirical world—"an essence that is divorced from life can crown itself with its own existence."[49] Strategically disconnected from the world, the work of art would be turned into "an intuitive, premonitory comprehension of the unattained and therefore inexpressible meaning of life—the innermost core of all action made manifest."[50]

This shift does not mean that the materiality of Black life was uninteresting to the project of Black modernism in its moment of emergence. Indeed, the context in which newness was being claimed—the search for the New Negro in the Black Atlantic—was intimately connected to a sense of displacement. If the idea of transcendental homelessness now seems

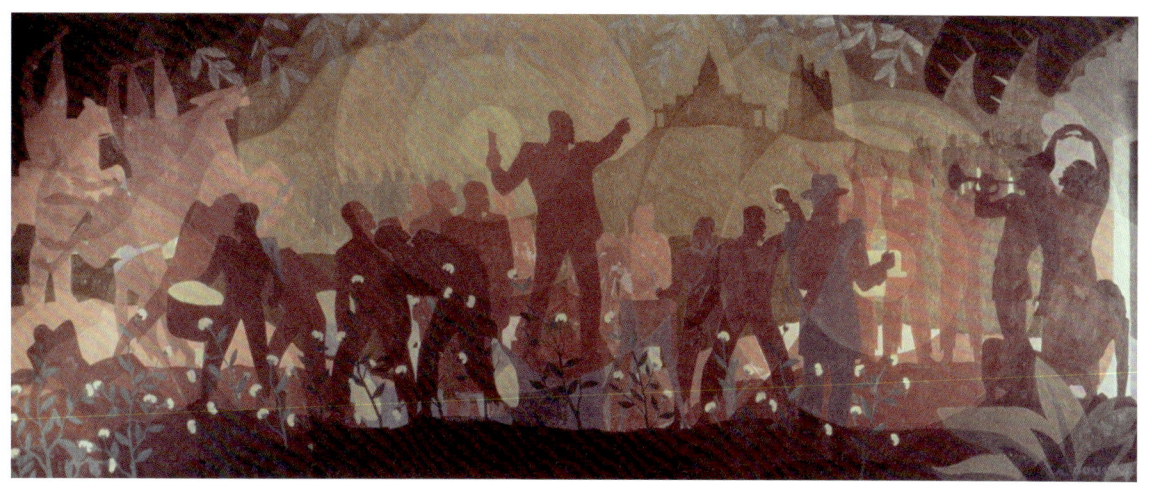

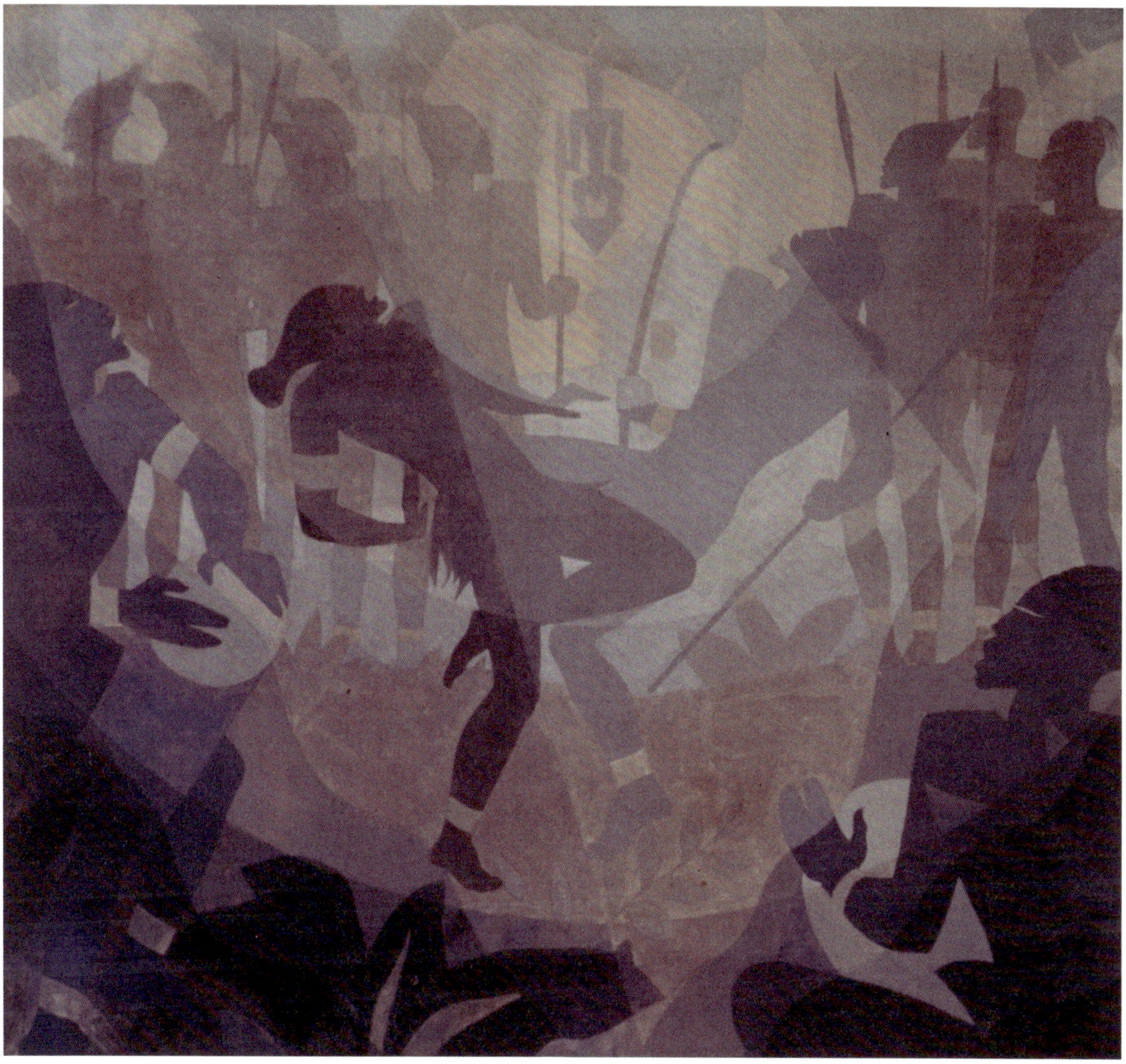

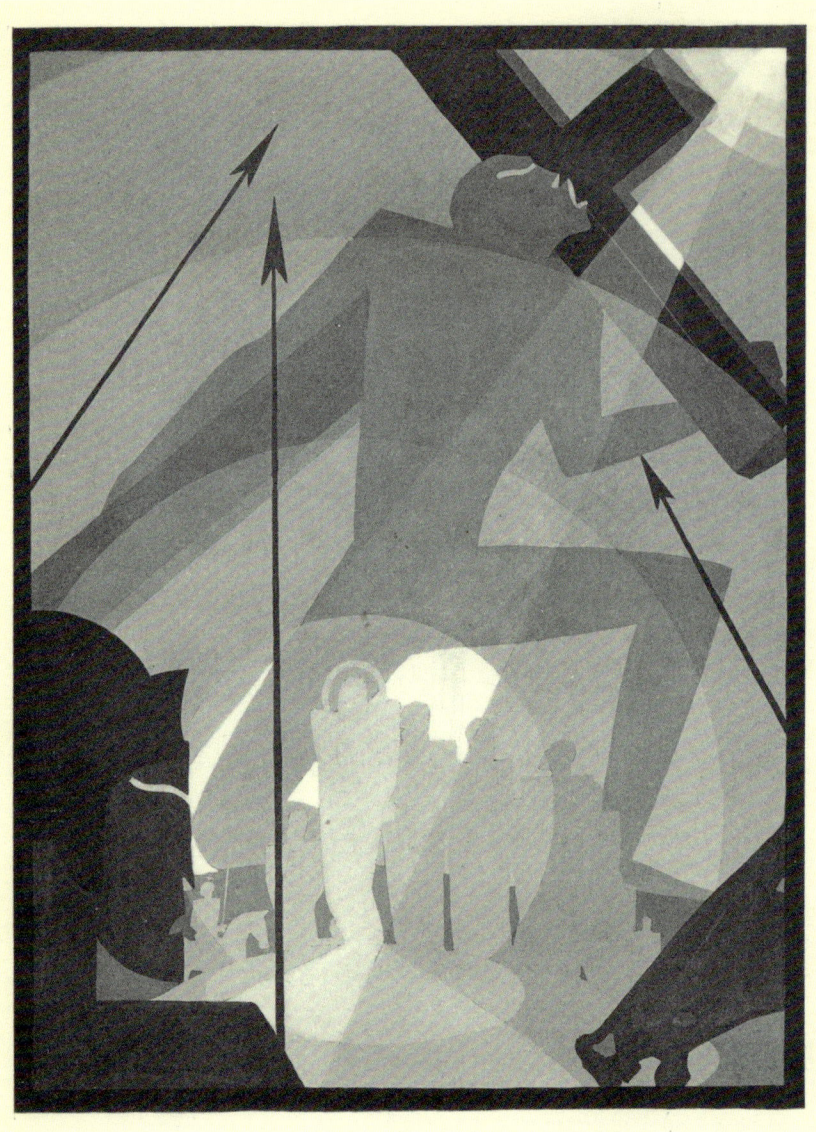

Fig. 11 Aaron Douglas, *The Crucifixion*, illustration from James Weldon Johnson, *God's Trombones* (New York, 1927), 38

© 2023 Heirs of Aaron Douglas / Licensed by VAGA at Artists Rights Society (ARS), New York

to have been one of the strongest impulses running through the emerging varieties of Black modernism in the first three decades of the twentieth century, it is because one of the consequences of late modernity was the continuous—and often collective—displacement of Black people and the perennial sense that they had no place of dwelling.[51] At the same time, to be homeless was also to be free. This was the point affirmed at the end of Aimé Césaire's *Cahier d'un retour au pays natal* (*Journal of a Homecoming*) published in 1939:

> monte lécheur de ciel
> et le grand trou noir où je voulais me noyer l'autre lune
> c'est là que je veux pêcher maintenant la langue maléfique de la nuit en
> son immobile verrition!

> ascend to lick the sky
> and the great black hole where a moon ago I longed to drown
> that's where I now long to fish out the night's malicious tongue in
> its sweeping stillness!⁵²

Out in the world, in the streets of the city or even in de-territorialized spaces such as the sea, art could unfetter life from the violence of late modernity. As the following example from Claude McKay's 1929 novel, *Banjo*, illustrates, "vagabondage" could denote a measure of freedom:

> Banjo was a great vagabond of lowly life. He was a child of the Cotton Belt, but he had wandered all over America. His life was a dream of vagabondage that he was perpetually pursuing and realizing in odd ways, always incomplete but never unsatisfactory. He had worked at all the easily-picked-up jobs—longshoreman, porter, factory worker, farm hand, seaman.⁵³

For McKay, the precondition for a new Black subjectivity was what Édouard Glissant would later describe as errantry—a frontal challenge to, and rejection of, the universal.⁵⁴ The techniques of modernism were indispensable in the representation of Black errantry.

The Sins of Modernism

Still, making a claim for the usefulness of European modernism to Black self-conception in the culture of modernity brings us face-to-face with a central conceptual and structural problem: Was it possible for Black artists to borrow the techniques of modernism and dispense with the baggage that was a constitutive element of its ideology—its sexism, ethnocentrism, and its powerful colonizing impulses?⁵⁵ Could Black artists avoid the "triumphal masculinism" of modernism and what Marianne Dekoven has called its "irresolvable ambivalence toward powerful femininity that itself forged many of Modernism's most characteristic formal innovations"?⁵⁶ And what could Black artists do with the African exoticism that modernism had marshaled as an indispensable part of its theories of difference? If all modernisms were predicted on a theory of difference, and if Black peoples and geographies were assumed to be the depositories of the so-called primitive, then the larger issue was not whether a Black modernism could find a detour around difference, but where its version of difference could be located. What would be the place of Josephine Baker, a Baule mask, or a Congolese fetish in the aesthetic project of Black modernism?⁵⁷

My argument is that rather than try to escape the tropes of difference that modernism had come to privilege, early Black modernists developed a discourse and practice in which primitivism and exoticism could be made serviceable to the project of Black freedom and self-expression. So, in an ironical twist, exoticism was itself turned into an eroticism with cultural value. While exoticism implied distance from the object of longing, eroticism would be celebrated for its representation of intimacy and connection. Where high modernism had located Black exoticism in a remote past, Black modernism would make eroticism a defining signature of the Black subject's claim to belong to the modern world.[58] Taking the erotic form, what appeared to be exotic and distant would be relocated into a space—the Black street—where it came to signify freedom and Black desire. Claude McKay's "The Harlem Dancer" (1922) is one of the earliest examples of this rerouting of desire:

> Applauding youths laughed with young prostitutes
> And watched her perfect, half-clothed body sway;
> Her voice was like the sound of blended flutes
> Blown by black players upon a picnic day.
> She sang and danced on gracefully and calm,
> The light gauze hanging loose about her form;
> To me she seemed a proudly-swaying palm
> Grown lovelier for passing through a storm.[59]

Black eroticism would also become an important trope in the painting and poetry of Negritude exemplified here by Léopold Sédar Senghor's tribute to Harlem in "À New York" ("To New York," 1956):

> J'ai vu dans Harlem bourdonnant de bruits de couleurs solennelles et d'odeurs flamboyantes
> —C'est l'heure du thé chez le livreur-en-produits-pharmaceutiques
> J'ai vu se préparer la fête de la Nuit à la fuite du jour.
> C'est l'heure pure où dans les rues, Dieu fait germer la vie d'avant mémoire
> Tous les éléments amphibies rayonnants comme des soleils.
> Harlem Harlem! voici ce que j'ai vu Harlem Harlem!
>
> I saw Harlem teeming with sounds and ritual colors
> And outrageous smells—
> At teatime in the home of the drugstore-deliveryman
> I saw the festival of Night begin at the retreat of day.
> And I proclaim Night more truthful than the day.
> It is the pure hour when God brings forth
> Life immemorial in the streets,
> All the amphibious elements shinning like suns.
> Harlem, Harlem! Now I've seen Harlem, Harlem![60]

As an aesthetic project underwritten by a longing for spaces of belonging, Black modernism deployed women—and asserted a barely disguised masculinism—in perhaps the same way as their European counterparts. But unlike European artists who used their masculinist aesthetic to escape what they saw as the nightmare of history or the curse of nationalism, Black intellectuals were attracted to masculinist projects as part

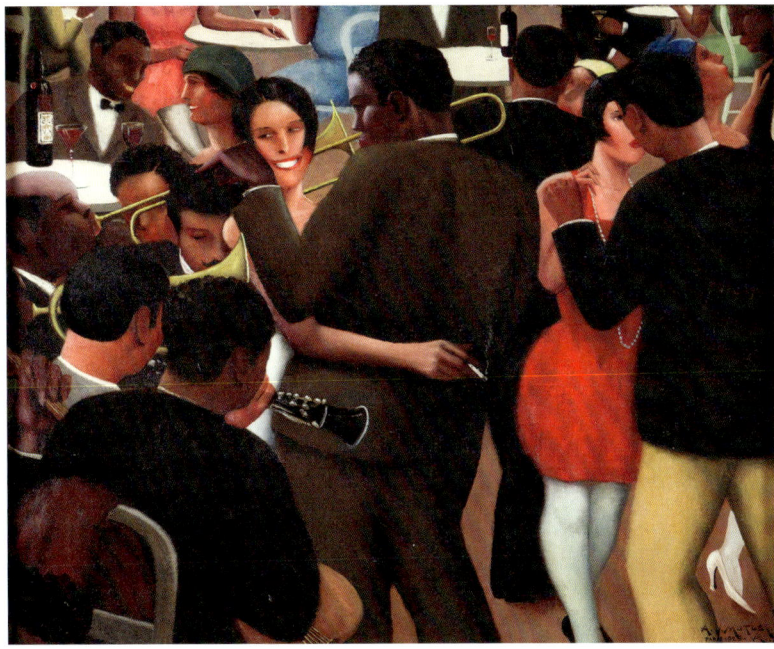

Fig. 12 Archibald John Motley Jr., *Blues*, 1929, oil on canvas, Collection of Mara Motley, MD, and Valerie Gerrard Browne

Image © Valerie Gerrard Browne, courtesy of Chicago History Museum

of what Michelle Ann Stephens has called "their desire to claim for black subjects the entitlements of nationality and citizenship."[61] Exoticism, then, was not merely an exhibition of Black difference; it was motivated by the need to find territories "that existed in temporalities outside of modernity,"[62] a world unmediated by the machinery of capital. This longing is most visible in paintings of Black dancers and musicians by artists such as Motley (fig. 12), but it also runs through most Black writing from the Harlem Renaissance to Negritude. Sometimes, as in works by the Afro-Cubans Nicolás Guillén and Wifredo Lam, Black modernists could use their writings and paintings to mock the now dominant European ideologies of Blackness, throwing the exotic back at those who had invented it. Here is what Guillén did to the ideology of Afro-Cubanismo in "Canto Negro":

> ¡Yambambó, yambambé!
> Repica el congo solongo,
> repica el negro bien negro;
> congo solongo del Songo
> baila yambó sobre un pie
>
> Yambambó, yambambé!
> The congo solongo is ringing,
> the real black man is ringing;
> congo solongo from the Songo
> is dancing the yambó on one foot[63]

Wifredo Lam's *The Awakening, I* (1938, fig. 13) worked with Picasso but against him, adopting the primitivist motif represented by the figure of the woman and the African mask but shifting its angles to represent what

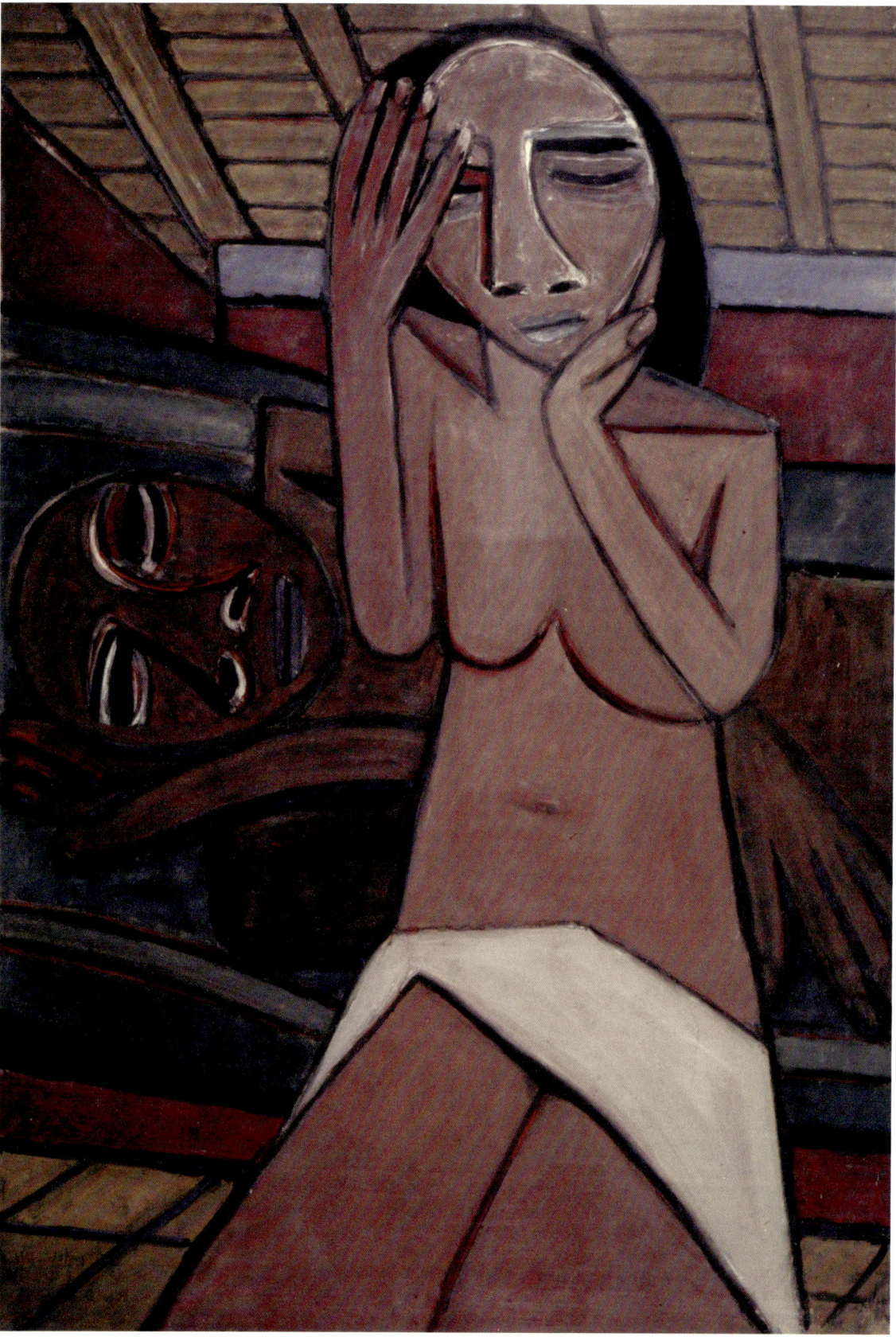

Lam himself described as "black cultural objects in terms of their own landscape and in relation to their own world."[64]

From all these examples, we can conclude that modernism was in effect the answer to the question that had troubled Black subjects since the beginning of the twentieth century: What did it mean to be Black in the violent culture of modernity? How, indeed, could one be Black and modern? By questioning the foundations of European thinking on a whole range of matters—the subject/object relationship, verisimilitude, and even consciousness—modernism had created doubt in the European project of conquest and rule. By privileging techniques of abstraction, flatness, fragmentation, and rupture, modernism had short-circuited the dominant narrative of modernity and in the process created a space in which Black artists could express their yearning to belong in the world.[65]

And there is perhaps no better expression of this claim and longing in early Black modernism than that scene in McKay's collection of itinerants, all drawn from all corners of the Black world, as they rollick to a "West African song," sung by a Senegalese called Taloufa:

> Taloufa had a voluptuous voice, richly colored like the sound of water lapping against a bank. And he chanted as he strummed the guitar:
>
> "Stay, Carolina, stay . . . "
>
> The whole song—the words of it, the lilt, the pattern, the color of it—seemed to be built up from that one word, Stay! When Taloufa sang, "Stay," his eyes grew bigger and whiter in his charmingly carnal countenance, the sound came from his mouth like a caressing, appealing command and reminded one of a beautiful, rearing young filly of the pasture that a trainer is breaking in. Stay![66]

Like the proverbial ring dance, as is the case in the works of the artists explored above, Taloufa's song creates a new way of being Black in the world—"a unique ring, doing the same simple thing, startlingly fresh in that atmosphere, with clicking of heels on the floor"[67]—in what might once have appeared to be a diaspora of loss.

Fig. 13 Wifredo Lam, *The Awakening, I*, 1938, gouache on paper, private collection

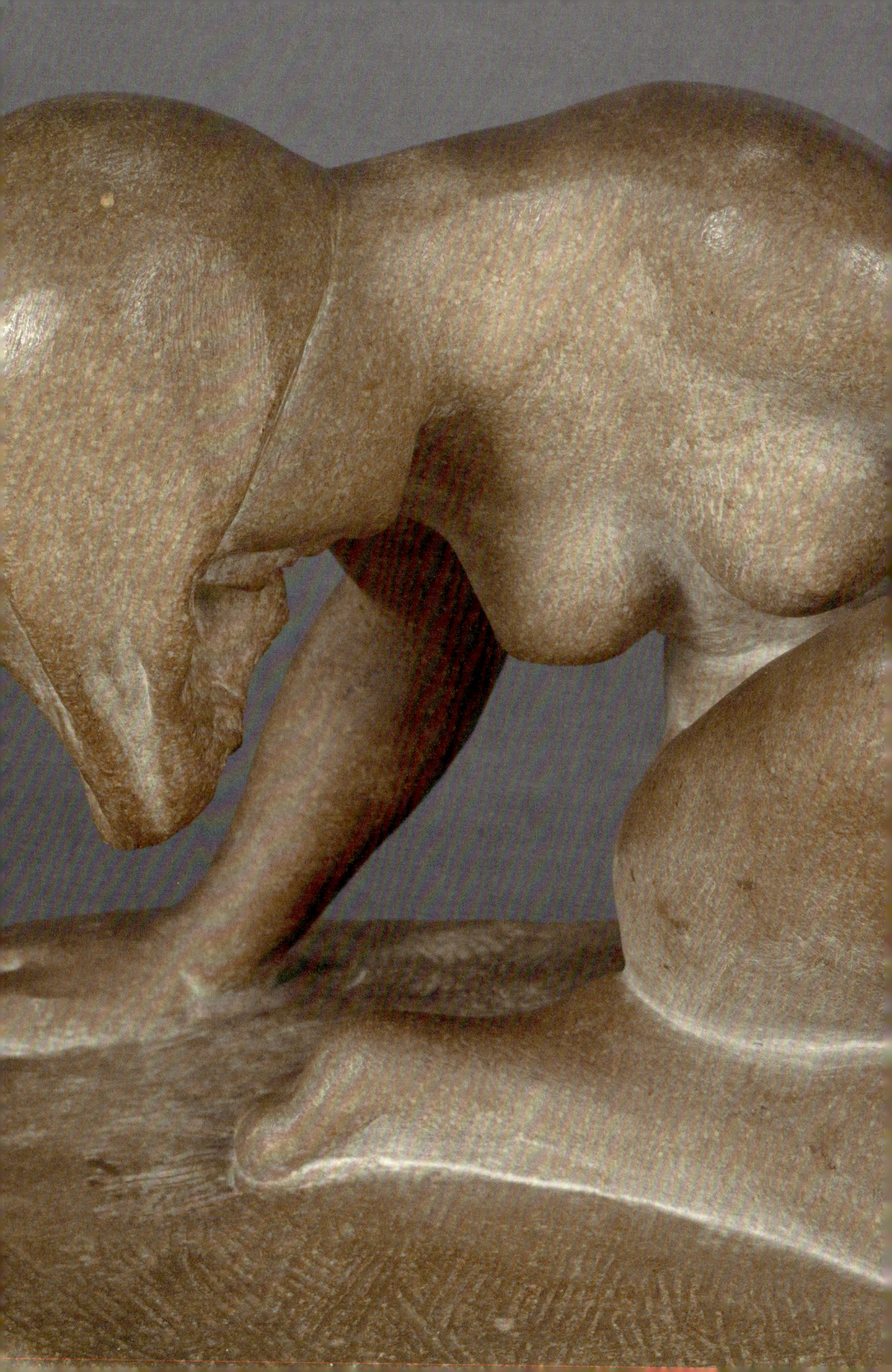

NANCY ELIZABETH PROPHET AND AUGUSTA SAVAGE: SCULPTURAL HABITS OF BLACK MODERNISM

KELLIE JONES

Thinking about Black women in the nineteenth and twentieth centuries and their intellectual and cultural production, scholar Brittney Cooper insists that the best way to honor them is not simply to admire and revere them but also to dive into and sit with their work. And while we may not always agree with these figures, we need to *trust* them and take their theoretical imaginations seriously.[1]

Cooper advances the idea of "embodied discourse," Black women centering the experiences of Black (primarily working-class) women as the basis of social thought and intersecting identities (of gender and Blackness), not as a burden but as energizing forces that open up possibilities for greater social and public responsibility and engagement—and hope.[2]

In one anecdote encapsulating the rationale for an embodied Black feminist discourse, activist and author Anna Julia Cooper (1858–1964) searches for a restroom in a train station, only to be confronted by two signs, one for "ladies," the other for "colored," presenting two inadequate options for her own comfort. In this moment she finds herself effectively erased from the public realm, a place that reveals itself as "designed not only to render Black bodies as inferior, but Black female bodies as unrecognizable and unknowable in civic terms."[3] Anna Julia Cooper's work, particularly her book *A Voice from the South* (1892), thus serves as "a symbolic representation of the body of the African-American woman of letters newly created in the public sphere."[4]

I want to bring Brittney Cooper's framing—of trust, of sitting with the work, and Black creative women newly visible in the public sphere—to two important African American artists of the early twentieth century: Nancy Elizabeth Prophet (1890–1960, b. Providence, Rhode Island) and Augusta Savage (1892–1962, b. Green Cove Springs, Florida). Prophet and Savage were significant figures in their time, the early twentieth-century moment that defined Black modernism. Their most productive period spanned the cultural effluence of the Harlem / New Negro Renaissance of the 1920s and 1930s. They received a certain amount of recognition in their lifetimes as well as in the art historical record. However, their shared role in developing languages of modern African American art making deserves greater discussion. In particular, it is the way their work inscribed the Black body in slavery's wake as an emblem of the modern, made in Harlem, in the diaspora, in migration, and celebrated in Paris and New York, in cabarets and on Broadway, as well as in literature and art, that merits greater emphasis.

Prophet and Savage trained at world-class institutions in the United States, at Rhode Island School of Design (Prophet) and the Cooper Union (Savage), as well as in France at École de Beaux-Arts (Prophet) and Académie de la Grande Chaumière (Savage). They challenged art world discrimination. Prophet pulled her work from a salon in her hometown of Providence, where she was able to exhibit but was asked not to attend. Savage's rejection by the Fontainebleau School of Paris (with the argument that white colleagues from the southern United States would be uncomfortable with her presence) was widely reported in the press of the early 1920s and became a site of activism on both sides of the Atlantic. To even become artists both Prophet and Savage had to first face down family in pursuit of their dreams. They paid their way through art school and for study and travel abroad. And to do all this they worked as domestics beginning in their teenage years—watching children, cleaning homes, cooking in kitchens, taking in laundry. Both moved in and out of such service industry work as their artistic fortunes ebbed and flowed.[5]

We know Prophet and Savage primarily through specific iconic pieces. Prophet's *Congolais* (1931, fig. 1) is an exquisitely detailed head of an African. Hewn from cherry wood while Prophet was working in Paris, it contrasts smooth handling of the face and meditative features with a textured headpiece and the rawness of the rougher, heavier marks of the base below. Embodying both serenity and power, the sculpture is intriguing as a Pan-African portrait, mixing the adornments of Maasai warriors of East Africa (Kenya and Tanzania) with a title that identifies a person from the Congo region of Central Africa (Republic of the Congo and Democratic

Fig. 1 Nancy Elizabeth Prophet, *Congolais*, 1931, cherry, Whitney Museum of American Art

Image © Whitney Museum of American Art / Licensed by Scala / Art Resource, NY

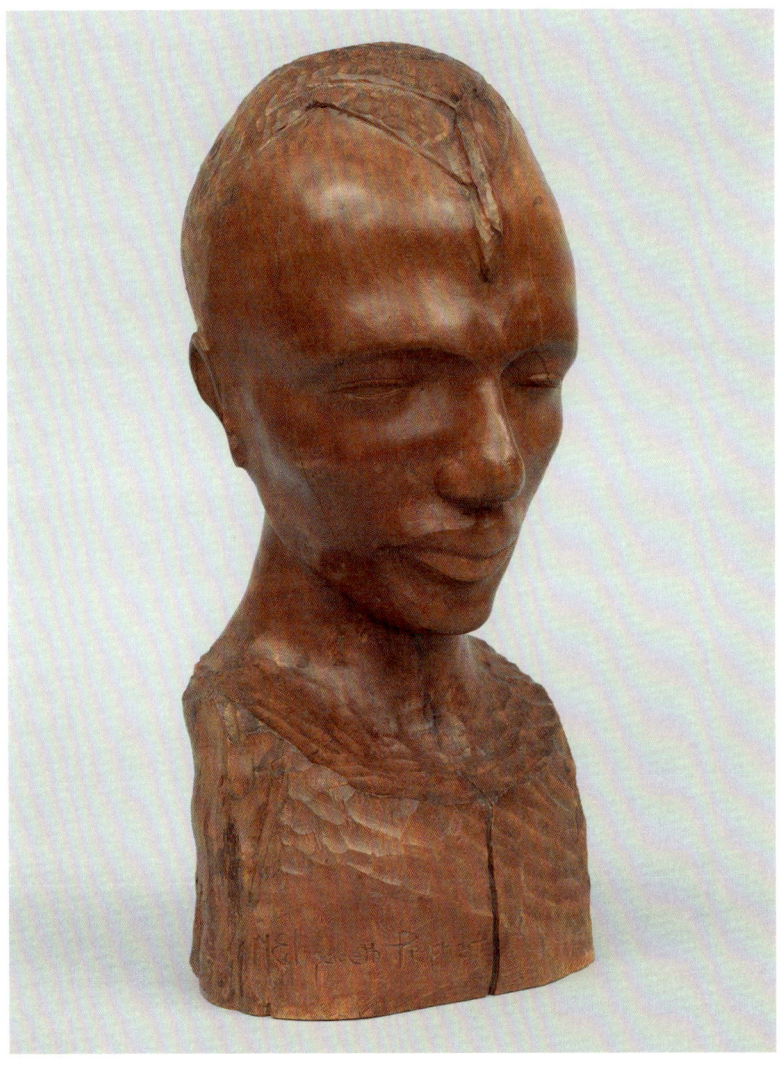

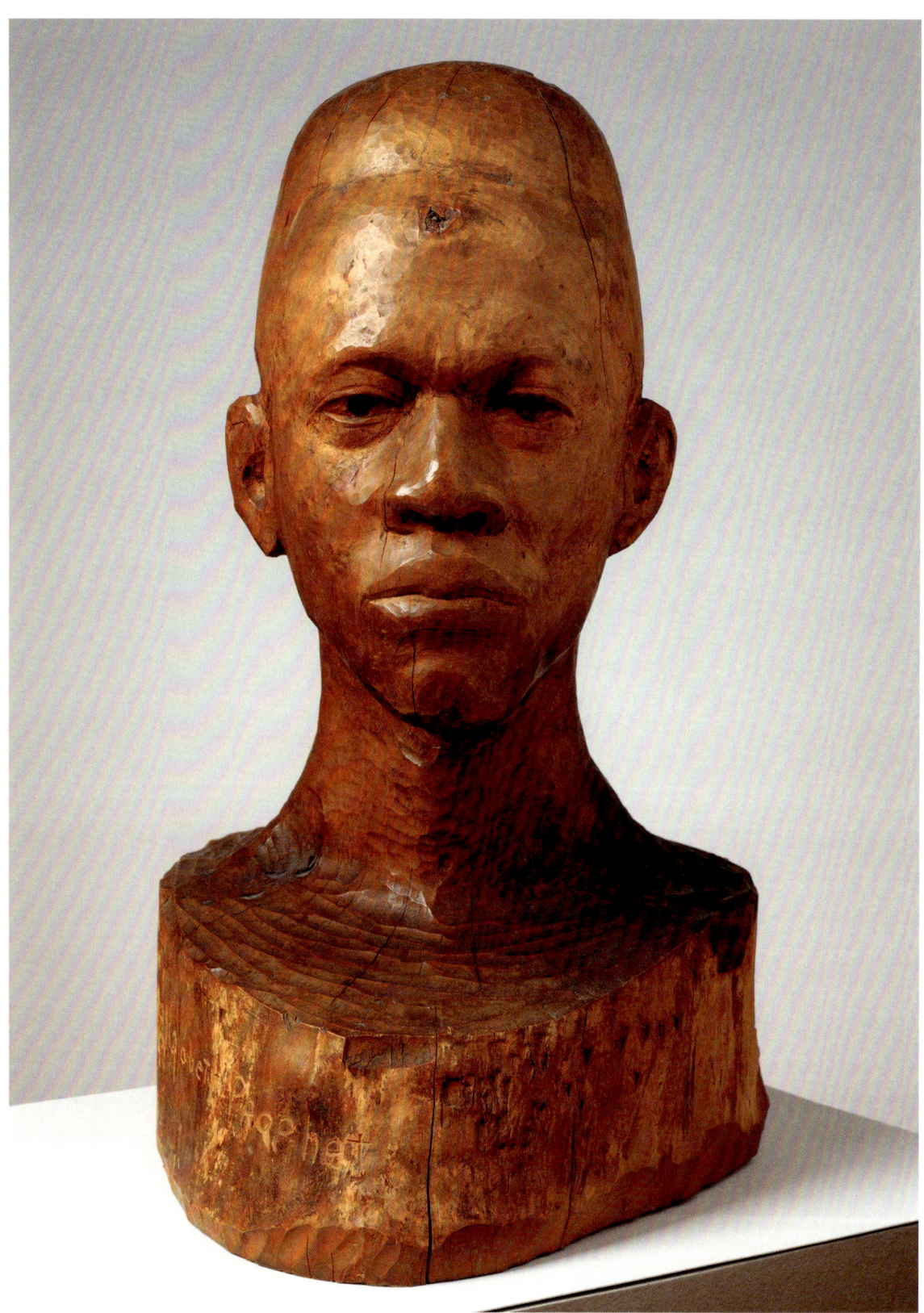

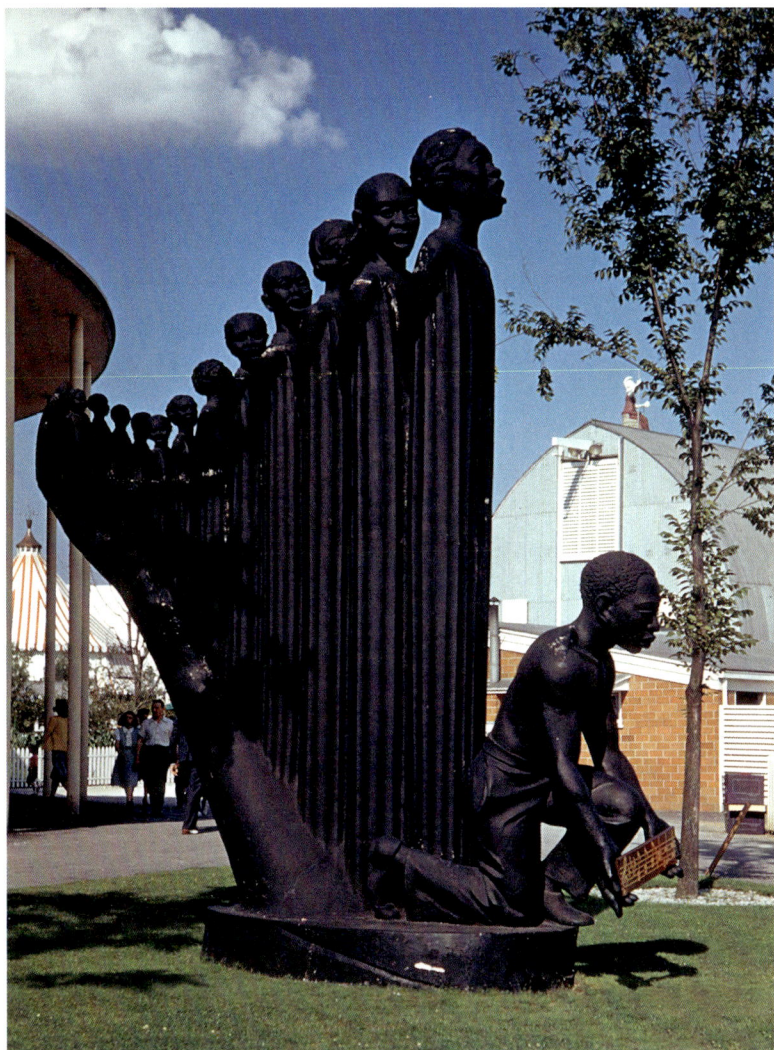

Fig. 2 Nancy Elizabeth Prophet, *Head of a Negro*, before 1927, wood, RISD Museum, Gift of Miss Eleanor B. Green

Courtesy of RISD Museum, Providence, RI

Fig. 3 Augusta Savage, *The Harp*, 1939, at the 1939 New York World's Fair

Sherman Oaks Antique Mall / Getty Images

Republic of the Congo). In many ways *Congolais* is a meditation on Black internationalism and the cosmopolitan context that Prophet encountered in interwar France. Like modern art (and dance) of the early twentieth century, her work found inspiration in global culture, one also wrought from structures of empire and imperialism.[6]

As Theresa Leininger-Miller reminds us, both Prophet and Savage worked in what can be considered relatively new materials in the hands of African American artists: wood and bronze. The cherry, pear, teak, and ebony favored by Prophet were the opposite of the white marble preferred in an earlier period by the likes of Edmonia Lewis and her nineteenth-century cohort. This difference allowed her to think about and imagine the chroma of dark skin. In this modern era works by Prophet such as *Head of a Negro* (before 1927, fig. 2) and *Congolais* were celebrated and sold easily.[7]

Like Prophet's *Congolais*, Savage's *The Harp* (1939, fig. 3) was admired in its day. Commissioned in 1937 by the committee for the 1939 New York World's Fair, it was purportedly one of the most popular pieces among fairgoers. The instrument stands 16 feet tall, and its strings become the bodies of an immense choir; a massive arm cradles the figures and takes the place of the instrument's soundbox. Interestingly, the mechanics of any harp are rendered as body parts: there is a neck, a shoulder or knee, a foot, and even a midrib. Kneeling below the chorus a youth offers a plaque with a snippet of a music chart. It holds the alternate title of the work, *Lift Every Voice and Sing*, a song penned by James Weldon Johnson and his brother J. Rosamond Johnson, and known as the Negro National Anthem. Through music, arguably African America's most recognizable gift to the world, Savage has imagined the modern national body.[8]

Both artists used the structures of romantic sculpture, embracing the lyricism and dynamism of classical form and meshing them with expanding contemporary realist frameworks. Like so many others, Prophet and Savage were drawn to Europe in the 1920s and 1930s because of the excitement in visual art that was happening there (in cubism, expressionism, and the rest), and because it was the art world that mattered in the opening decades of the twentieth century. Other African American artists of their generation who sojourned to Paris absorbed such modernist innovations in more visible ways—think of Archibald John Motley Jr. and his painting *Blues* (1929), for instance. By those standards Prophet's and Savage's sculptures of the era seem *retardataire*.

However, the growth of African diasporic themes in art of the early twentieth century was global, representing the articulation of modernity spurred by migration, colonialism, and new sociabilities. Visual modernism was not just a move toward greater "mental and technical possibilities" represented by abstraction but also understood via fresh subject matter, such as new Black protagonists who were self-possessed, activist, and uncompromising, described through a keen and more accurate portraiture.[9] Taking up the figures of Prophet and Savage, and as Erica Moiah James suggests, I want to think about how we might decolonize time, and move away from understandings of such work as impure, anachronistic, and lacking originality. As James writes, "To decolonize time means to completely disaggregate the value of art objects from the tyranny of temporally bound notions of art history that make creolized portraits like these extremely hard to see."[10]

Similarly, curator Meg Onli has interrogated the notion of Colored People's Time (CPT) in a series of recent exhibitions. Onli sees CPT as a device people of color use "to navigate their own temporality within and against the construct of Western time," a way that "people who are marginalized can shift their relationship to temporality" that is "living, liberatory."[11]

For Prophet and Savage the turn to more comprehensive work with the Black body was inspired by their time in Paris, where they had access to both models and the breadth of the African diasporic community. Early twentieth-century Paris has been theorized as a place of empowerment and activism for women who engaged in "cultural production in new ways."[12] The city nexus offered autonomy coupled with networks and spaces where one could articulate fresh sociabilities and desires. In uncovering the lives of African American women, T. Denean Sharpley-Whiting argues that these figures thrived in the ebullient culture of salons, soirées, ateliers, brasseries, cafés, and jazz revues, experiencing an expanded sense of "personal freedom and creativity."[13] France was absent the "violent racial animus" that plagued the United States, though there was still an "incongruous relationship" to empire, paternalism, and exoticism.[14] Within the Black diasporic community there could be found one centered on women. Or as Brent Hayes Edwards puts it, "Black internationalism in Paris has a historical origin among migrant communities of women of African descent."[15]

Interwar Paris was also relatively inexpensive, a boon for Black women creators who lived with financial precariousness. Their white counterparts were usually more affluent with an ability to dedicate themselves to their craft. Joanne Winning has discussed a broadly feminist or sapphic modernism, centered on the community created among the lesbian booksellers Adrienne Monnier of La Maison des Amis de Livres and Sylvia Beach of Shakespeare and Company, along with Natalie Barney, partner to painter Romaine Brooks, who hosted a woman-focused salon into the 1960s. However, as Sharpley-Whiting points out, there was only superficial interaction between African American and white women at best (perhaps especially Americans).[16]

With Paris regarded as "a meeting place for the black diaspora"[17] in the first part of the twentieth century, Prophet and Savage shared social pleasures with the likes of African American artists Palmer Hayden and Hale Woodruff, and poet Countee Cullen. This too was a creative modernist community with its own disregard for fixed notions of gender and sexuality. A good game of cards was often on the agenda, a fact corroborated in Parisian paintings by Woodruff and Hayden (fig. 4). Cullen was

Fig. 4 Hale Woodruff, *The Card Players*, 1930, oil on canvas, Metropolitan Museum of Art, George A. Hearn Fund, 2015

© 2020 Estate of Hale Woodruff / Licensed by VAGA at Artists Rights Society (ARS), New York. Image © Metropolitan Museum of Art / Art Resource, NY

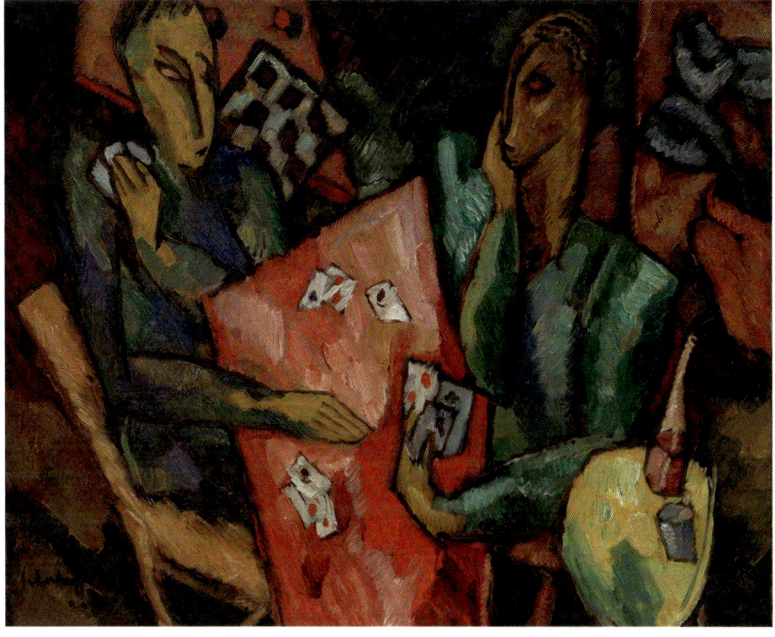

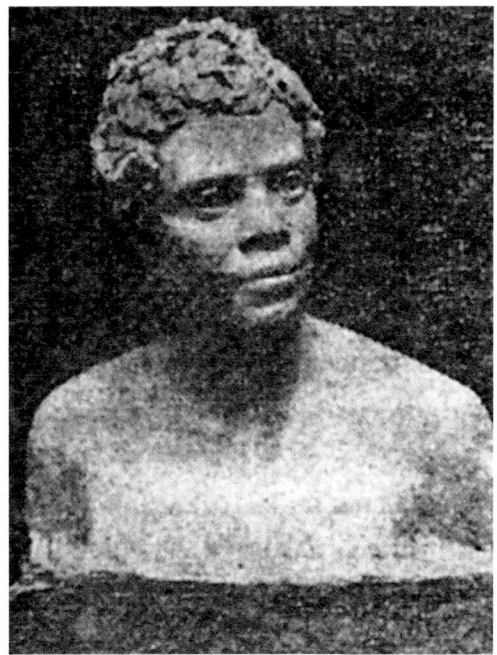
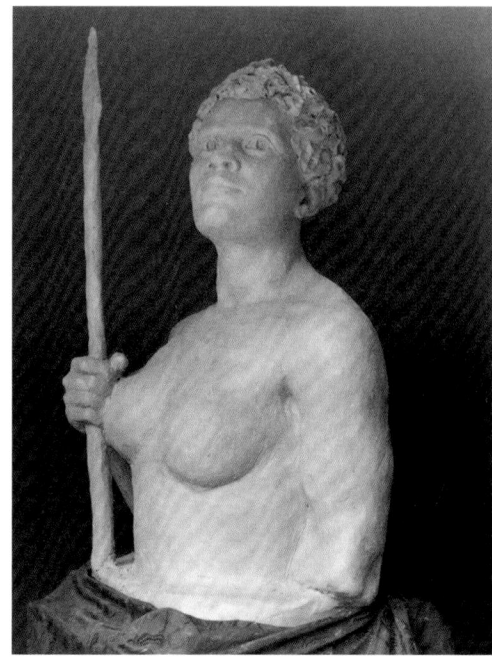

Fig. 5 Augusta Savage, *Tête de Jeune Fille*, c. 1930, from Theresa Leininger-Miller, *New Negro Artists in Paris: African American Painters and Sculptors in the City of Light, 1922–1934* (New Brunswick, NJ, 2001), 186

Fig. 6 Augusta Savage, *The Amazon*, c. 1930, clay, Fisk University Library, Rosenwald Collection

Courtesy of Fisk University Library

also known for his love of the pastime whether at home in Harlem or abroad. As one guest would report, "There was a whole small crowd of rather nice gay blacks around Countee Cullen. They used to meet practically every evening . . . and sit by the hour playing cards."[18]

While one part of the Black women's cultural community in interwar Paris was anchored by African American expatriate cabaret owner Ada "Bricktop" Smith, another aspect comprised the gatherings, magazine work, and cultural criticism of sisters Jane and Paulette Nardal, Martiniquais intellectuals and key figures in the developments of Black internationalism and the emergence of Negritude. Theirs was a multifaceted Black diasporic feminist network that revolved around the independent journals *La Dépêche africaine* and *Le Revue du monde noir*, the latter cofounded by Paulette Nardal. She hosted a salon in her home that became a point of convergence for a broad array of Black artists and thinkers from around the globe. Edwards has argued that hers were not the typical bourgeois gatherings but what Nardal termed *cercle d'amis* (circle of friends) and represented a "new migrant black communal space in Paris" whose profile was an always unexpected mix of luminaries, and characterized by the reciprocity of an earlier era, when "salons were the property of women."[19] It might be close to what Elizabeth Alexander has nominated "the black interior," a hopeful dream space, but one that is also a "presentational" and public physical location, a place where one can "see black imagination made visual."[20] Nardal's cercle d'amis *was* feminist practice and among what Edwards calls "the innovative dialogic spaces assembled by black women [that] played an often underappreciated role in transnational cultural circuits during the interwar period."[21]

In August 1930 Paulette Nardal published an article on Augusta Savage in *La Dépêche africaine*. Recounting a visit to the artist's studio,

Fig. 7 Augusta Savage, *Mourning Victory*, c. 1930, clay, Fisk University Library, Rosenwald Collection

Courtesy of Fisk University Library

it is one of the few detailed primary accounts of what Savage created in Europe, much of it now lost. Among the sculptures illustrating the article is *Tête de Jeune Fille* (c. 1930, fig. 5), one of three using the same Martiniquais model, a group that Nardal and others nominated as Amazons.[22] The series moves from modest portrait to full-scale rendering. *Tête de Jeune Fille* is a simple bust, a place for Savage to work out countenance and mood and the condition of the textured crown. *The Amazon* (c. 1930, fig. 6), in clay, enlarges the figure to torso length and has her holding fast to a spear. A third sculpture, *Mourning Victory* (c. 1930, fig. 7), also in clay, finally brings us to the body in full. Arms at her sides (the spear has gone missing), the figure casts her gaze downward to a severed head lying at her feet.

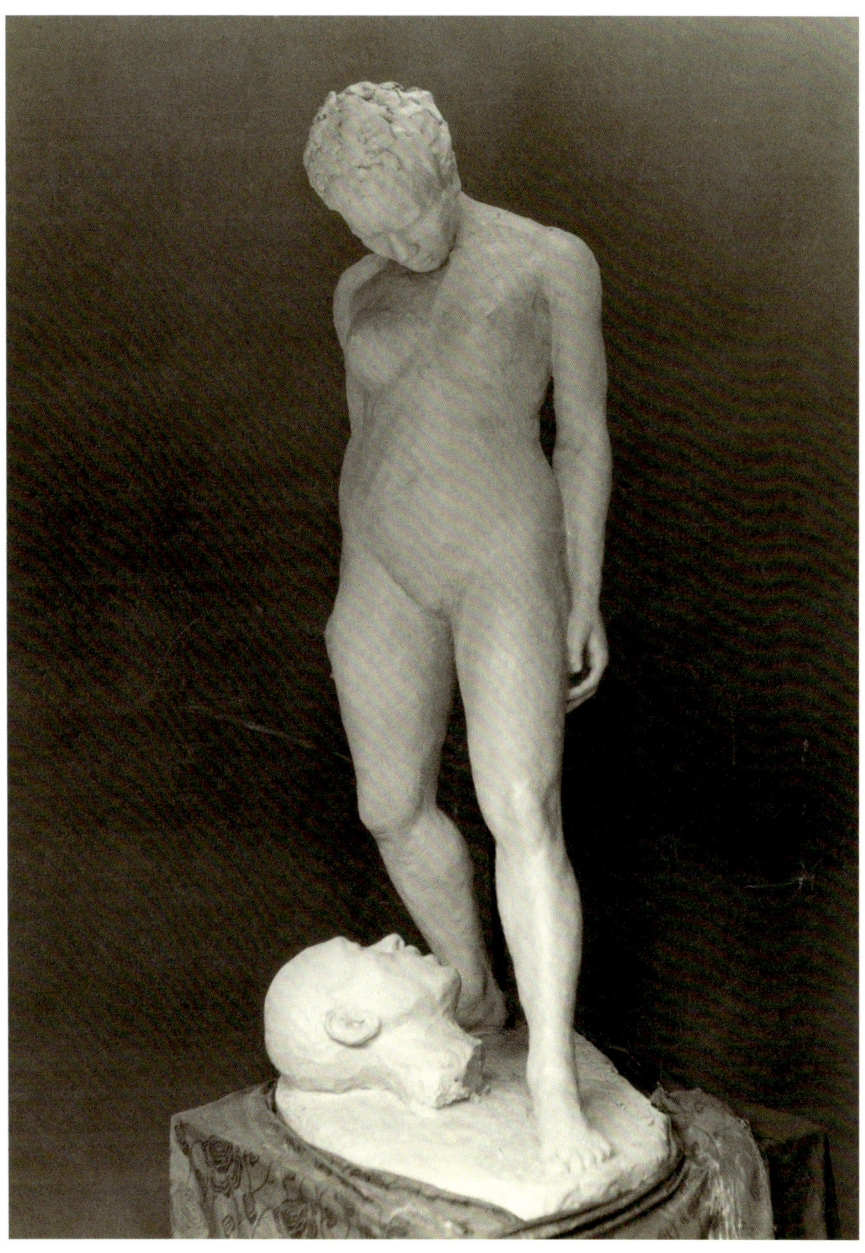

After Nardal, scholars have considered Greek and Dahomean sources for Savage's sculptures.[23] We find these legendary female combatants as early as the fifth century BCE in the metopes of the Parthenon Frieze, where virtuous Athenians battle centaurs, giants, and Amazons. The conflict with the Amazons warns against real (Persian) rivals, but also presents a cautionary tale against the breach of gender roles.[24] The storied women warriors of eighteenth- and nineteenth-century Dahomey, also known as Amazons, were fabled in colonial clashes. Later they formed part of French expositions and world's fairs that attempted to rationalize the colonial enterprise. In this context Savage's *Mourning Victory* might be a paean to the destruction of colonialism.[25]

While the Amazon series is lost, a recent retrospective of Savage's oeuvre affords us the opportunity to think about the dynamics of the figure and its relationship to changing conceptions of the Black body; moreover, it shines light on the nude.[26] The unclothed body appears rarely in art by African Americans in the pre–World War II period, due to a cultivated Victorian sensibility in slavery's aftermath, and a need to redefine personhood against dominant Western narratives of unbridled and violent sexuality attributed to Black people. Yet a politics of respectability was also integral to the early twentieth century. Growing urbanization of Black women through migration caused "moral panics" throughout the United States. Female migrants were characterized as "sexually degenerate" and "socially dangerous," and in need of the trappings of social respectability that would restore a "moral social order."[27] Such perceptions were just as much if not more responsible for the suppression of Western art's classic nude in African American art making, a growing practice that found itself caught between clashing modes of cultural representations, what Hazel Carby noted as that of "an emergent black bourgeoisie" and another of the "emerging urban black working class."[28]

Prophet crafted an artistic presence that fit such an unruly profile by at least 1922, the year she embarked on what would become a dozen years in Paris.[29] Emblematic of her commitment to a creative life, in what Kai M. Green calls a subversive act of "self-reclamation," she changed her name from the given Profitt to Prophet while in Paris.[30] She also buoyantly documented her existence with bodies of photographs, many of them professional studio shots, not only focusing on her sculpture but also centering her own fashionable presence. A Paris series follows her on board the SS *La France* in 1922 (fig. 8), with classmates at the École des Beaux-Arts in 1924, and in Parisian fashion, circa 1925–1929. Countee Cullen was among those impressed by Prophet's style, writing of his first encounter with her at Henry Ossawa Tanner's Paris studio in 1929, "She swept into Tanner's studio wearing, with an éclat that I have not seen equaled elsewhere, a flowing black cape and a broad, black felt hat."[31]

Prophet's sexual freedom was also quite contemporary. Her marriage to hometown sweetheart Francis Ford for well over a decade was apparently an open one, with him tolerating her numerous extramarital affairs and living at a distance. Saidiya Hartman's writing enables us to

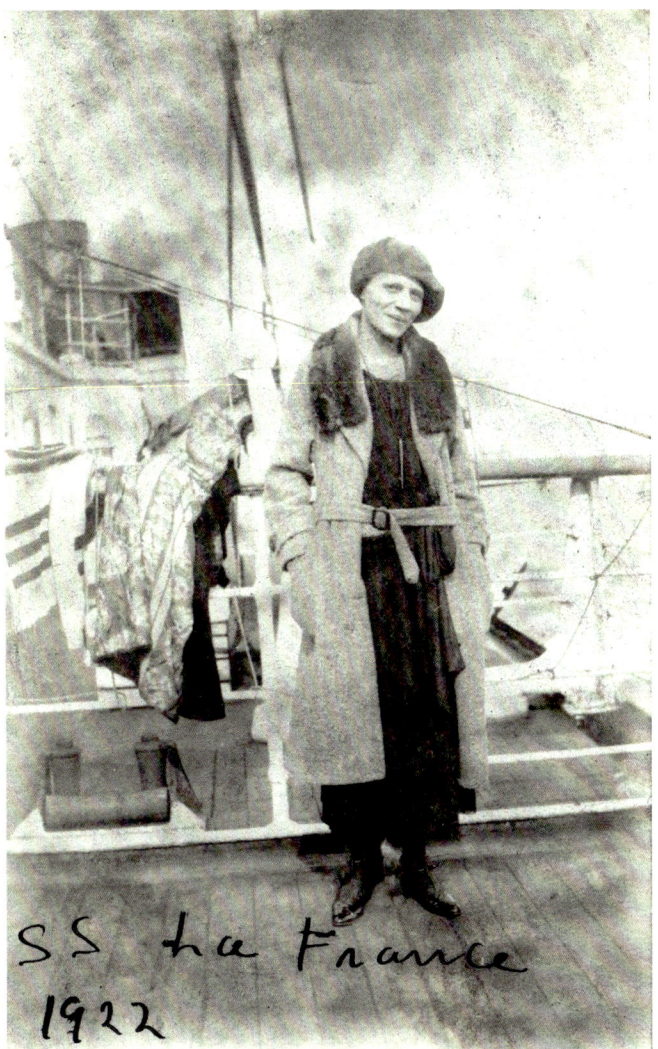

Fig. 8 Nancy Elizabeth Prophet on the SS *La France*, 1922, Nancy Elizabeth Prophet Collection, James P. Adams Library, Rhode Island College

pry apart the archive and rethink previous scholarship on an artist like Prophet, imagining things instead from inside the minds of young Black women remaking the world from their own imaginations. Hartman helps us foreground the will to beauty and adornment with extravagant clothing, and the expansive notions of coupling and sexuality in setting out to live the life one desired. She writes, "Few, then or now, recognized young black women as sexual modernists, free lovers, radicals, and anarchists, or realized that the flapper was a pale imitation of the ghetto girl."[32]

One space of urban degeneracy according to social reformers was the dance hall or cabaret, a place where the modern moved in bodies and in popular dance styles. For some, Black women blues singers embodied such sites and the fears associated with them. But such figures also chronicled African Americans' Great Migration and a reinvention of citizenship in the twentieth century. They were a modernizing force in (Black) American life that created an altogether new subject in the wake of centuries of enslavement, not only through the performing body but also with the glamour and sexuality of Black female corporeality. As Carby theorizes:

Fig. 9 Augusta Savage, *La Citadelle (Freedom)*, 1930, bronze, Howard University Gallery of Art

Photo by Gregory R. Staley

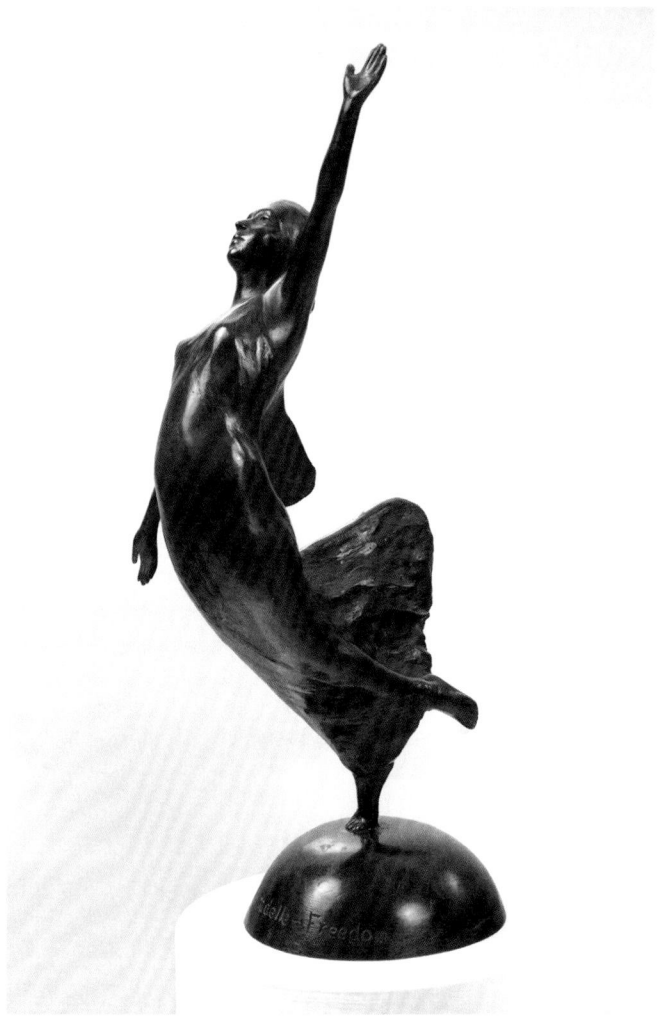

Fig. 10 Augusta Savage, *Terpsichore (or Reclining Nude)* (front), c. 1932, marble, Schomburg Center for Research in Black Culture, New York Public Library

Fig. 11 Augusta Savage, *Terpsichore (or Reclining Nude)* (back), c. 1932, marble, Schomburg Center for Research in Black Culture, New York Public Library

Their physical presence was a crucial aspect of their power; the visual display of spangled dresses, of furs, of gold teeth, of diamonds, of all the sumptuous and desirable aspects of their body, reclaimed female sexuality from being an objectification of male desire to a representation of female desire.[33]

Such images of popular performance captivated visual artists as well. We find it not only in Prophet's self-fashioning but also in Motley's painting *Blues*, capturing Paris; Richmond Barthé's sculpture *Rugcutters (Lindy Hoppers or Lindy Hop)* (1930), the artist's celebration of Harlem's raucous dance competitions; and Savage's prized statuettes *Susie Q* and *Truckin'*.[34]

A number of Savage's sculptures from this period also take concert dance as their theme. In *La Citadelle (Freedom)* (1930, fig. 9), a figure in bronze glides through the air propelled by wide-flung arms and a flowing frock and only just held to the ground by the toes of her right foot. In *Terpsichore (or Reclining Nude)* (c. 1932, figs. 10, 11), a nude seated on the ground strikes a pose that is at once a modern dance gesture and a meditation on the Greek goddess of dance. Though created in the same period,

114

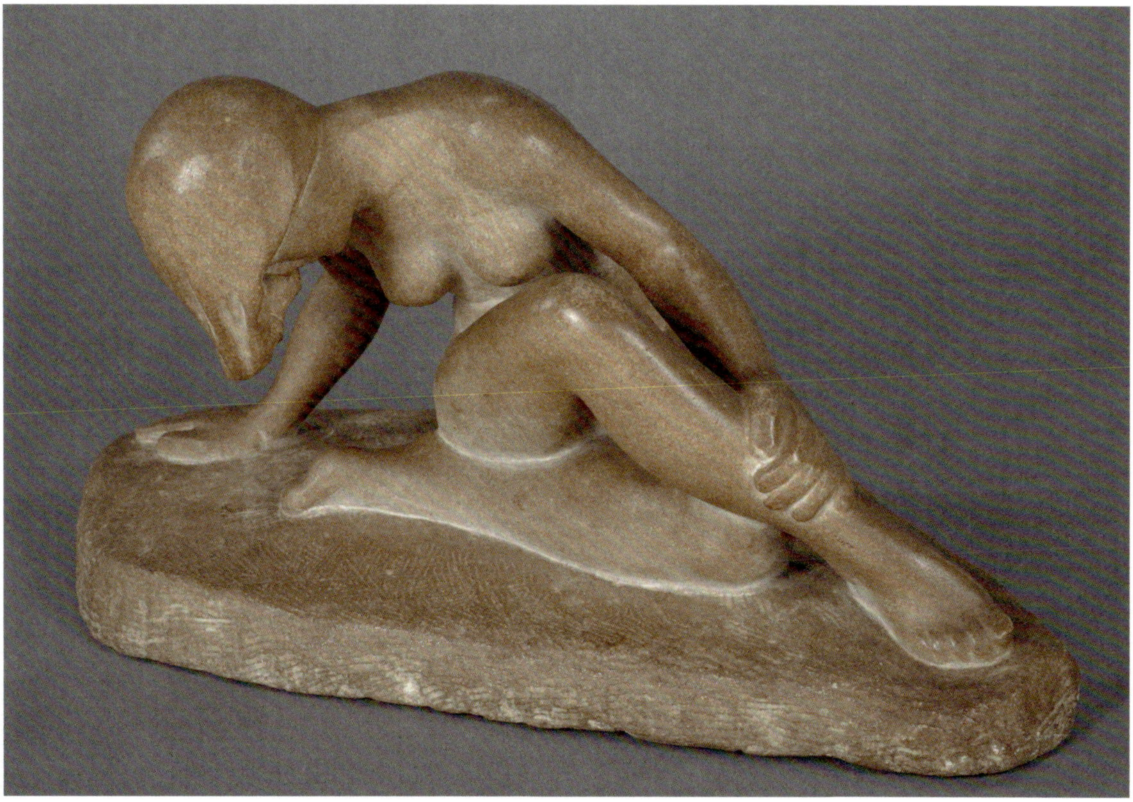

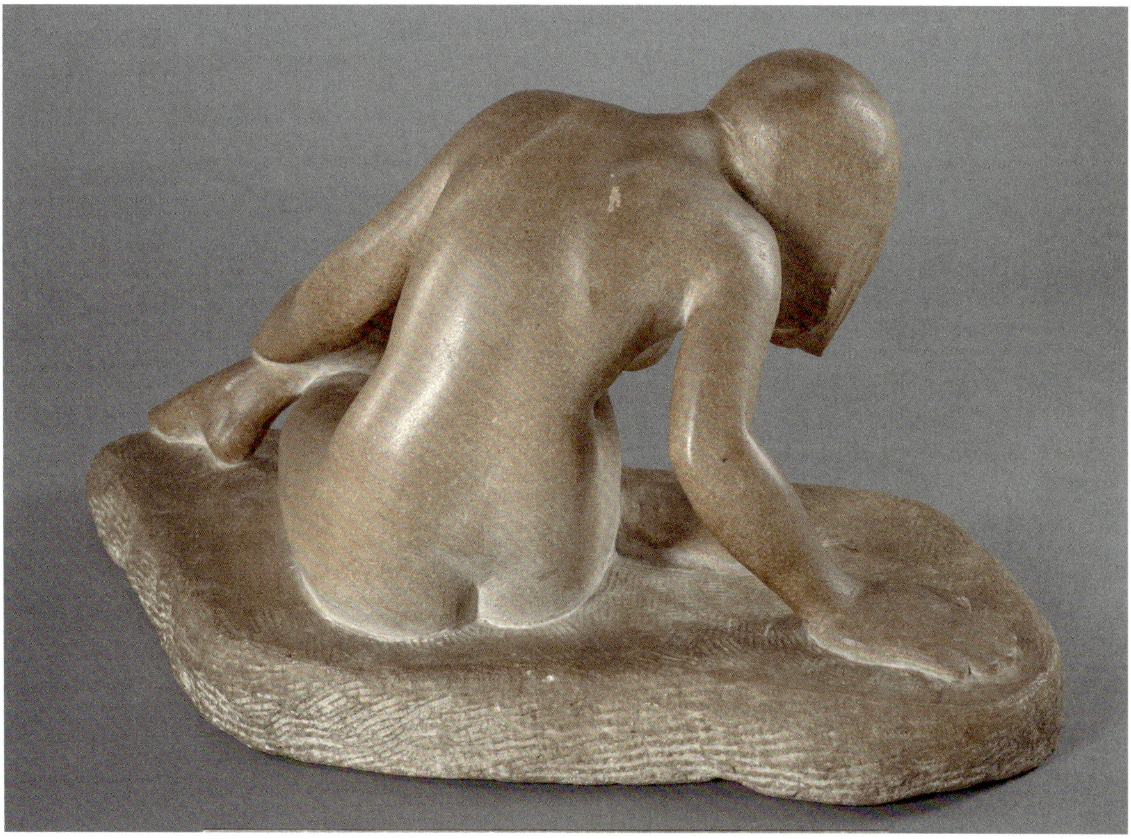

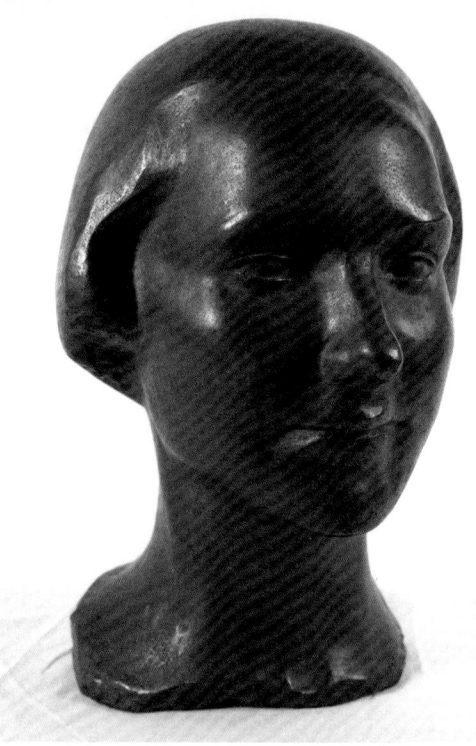

Fig. 12 Nancy Elizabeth Prophet, *Silence*, before 1930, bronze, Nancy Elizabeth Prophet Collection, James P. Adams Library, Rhode Island College

such works by Savage seem radically different from those of the Amazon series, in part due to their apparent eschewal of "African" features. Here we note evidence of nineteenth-century aesthetic frameworks privileging "European" attributes, as in the neoclassical marbles of Edmonia Lewis. We see a similar aesthetic in Prophet's robed figure *Le Pelerin* (The pilgrim) (c. 1922–1929) or the marble head *Silence*, made before 1930 (fig. 12).

In such works highlighting performance Savage seems to take a cue from emerging modern dance styles popularized by Isadora Duncan and Maud Allan, what Judith R. Walkowitz sees as an idiom routed in "a solitary, autonomous, unfettered, mobile, weighted, and scantily clad female body whose movements delineated emotional interiority, shifting states of consciousness, and autoeroticism."[35] Duncan's and Allan's athletic profiles, bare feet, and anti-ballet sensibilities intersected with a body beautiful movement, as well as a "war on corsets."[36] Much of this early twentieth-century practice was inspired by classical gesture based on Greek statuary, painting, and mythology, what one observer described as a "Grecian frieze form of movement," part of an "avant-garde passion for all things Greek."[37] As Allan herself described it, "I have sought all my attitudes and movement in the art galleries of Europe, on Etruscan vases and Assyrian tablets."[38]

The seemingly more academic approaches that characterized the sculpture of Prophet and Savage could also have been driven by the examples of sculptors Émile Antoine Bourdelle and Auguste Rodin, whom the women took as starting points for their own imaginings. Another inspiration might have been Henry Ossawa Tanner, a painter of biblical themes whose imagery played with the idea of the allegorical rather than the recognizable Black figure. Works by Prophet and Savage insist that we not get caught up in renderings of beautiful, sympathetic, non-caricatured Black bodies but stay in the place of concept, technique, and materials. In a sense these works, with their ambivalent templates, might function as abstract works do in the practices of other Black artists, occupying that space defined by T. J. Clark as "a distinctive patterning of mental and technical possibilities."[39] We can read openness, non-fixity, and the freedom not to adhere to a single standard, in which every figure must subscribe to certain ideas of Blackness or Black modernism. Margaret Rose Vendryes understands such examples as sites where the "border" of race is continually crossed. As she notes of sculptor Richmond Barthé, he "was comfortable in his brown skin, but not bound by it."[40]

Another way to consider the trajectory of Prophet and Savage and the slippery role of "race" in their production is to look at the place of sexuality and gender in their oeuvres and the appearance of the androgynous body. For Hartman, "Refusing the gender script was a frontal assault on the color line."[41] This characterizes Prophet's probing study of expressive countenance, *Discontent* (1925–1929, fig. 13), or even her remarkable *Congolais*, sometimes referred to by the feminine declension *Congolaise*. *Discontent* is ostensibly a work Prophet based on her own figure, lacking funds to pay models; at the same time, it erases any notion of a proper self-portrait or the markings of gender. Barthé was also his own most affordable model at certain moments, and the ambiguity of his female studies is often attributed to this (fig. 14). We might, however, see such sculptures as adopting a transgender method in which they reimagine accepted categories and subjectivities, challenging controlling images of gender and pleasure. Addressing the purported lack of dynamism as well as the masculine cast of Barthé's imagery of women, Vendryes suggests, "The sexual attraction that inspired his male nudes is missing in the females."[42]

Such ambiguous sculptural gestures that are not wholly nonobjective or nonbinary intersect with other types of modernist paradigms. As Laura Doan and Jane Garrity remind us, androgyny was the "prototype for the new woman"[43] in early twentieth-century Europe, the same period as Prophet's and Savage's residences there. Female masculinity was in vogue, particularly in the 1920s. Looking at London fashion of the period, Doan takes note of hair styled in the short Eton crop, along with "boyish or mannish attire."[44] These were signs of sexual fluidity and rebelliousness that also signaled a break from heterosexist power. As she proffers, the mannish look also afforded lesbians a cloak of invisibility under the sign of the ultramodern. Such aesthetics might account for the lithe and "boyish" figures of Prophet's *Le Pelerin*, *Discontent*, and others, or Savage's *Terpsichore*, identified by Leininger-Miller as portraying *la garçonne* (the female boy), the self-assured, contemporary woman.[45]

If Josephine Baker brought power to this image in Europe, with her eternally bobbed and pomaded hair, sometimes joined by a top hat and tuxedo, in the United States Gladys Bentley invented a proudly cross-dressing

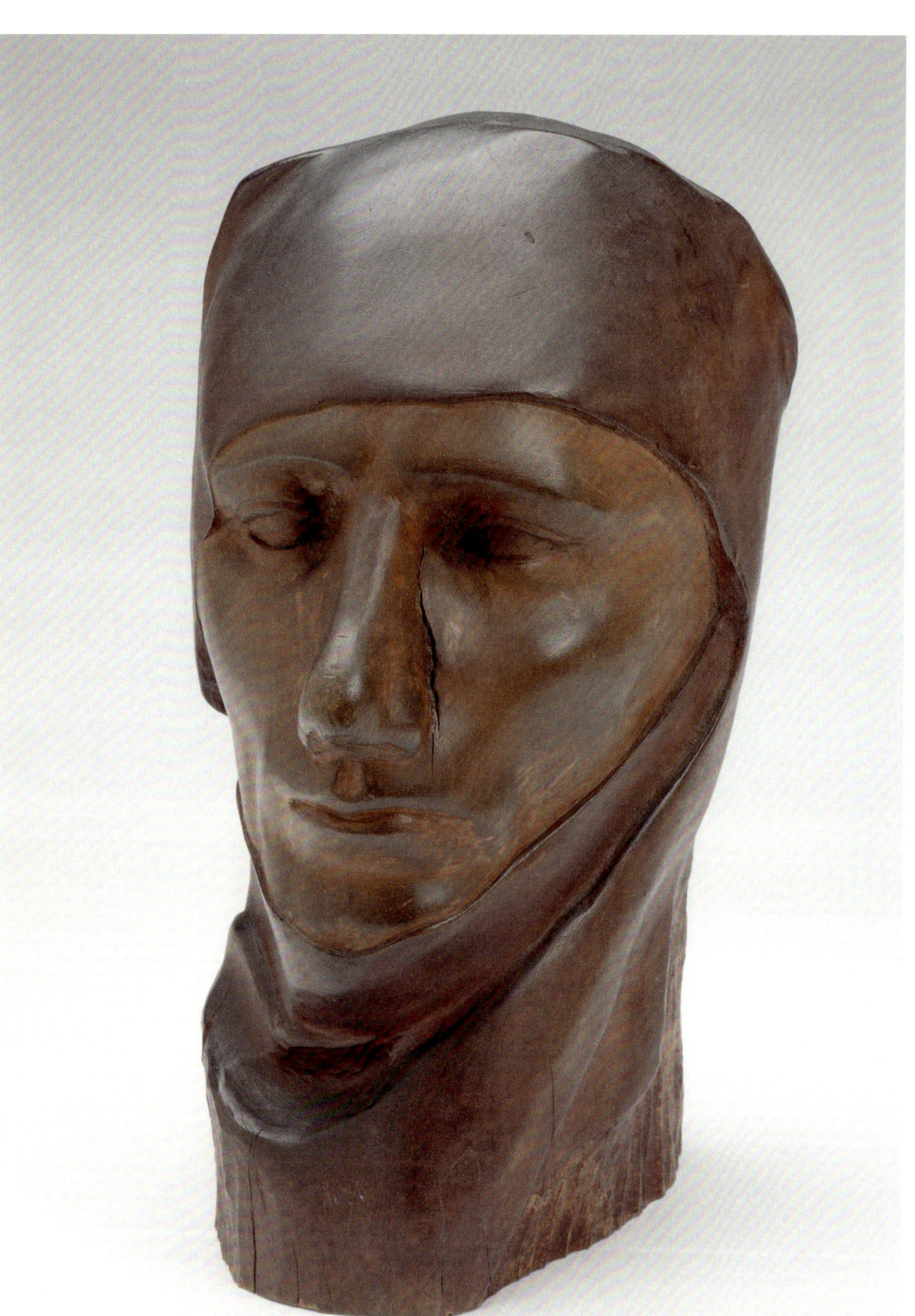

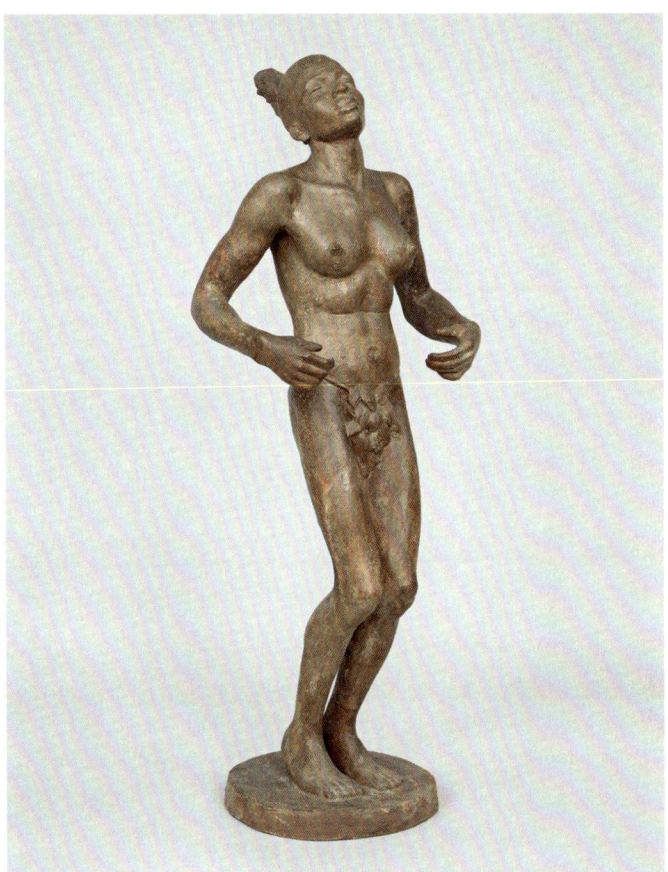

Fig. 13 Nancy Elizabeth Prophet, *Discontent*, 1925–1929, wood, RISD Museum, Gift of Miss Eleanor Green and Miss Ellen D. Sharpe

Courtesy of the RISD Museum, Providence, RI

Fig. 14 Richmond Barthé, *African Dancer*, 1933, plaster, Whitney Museum of American Art, New York

Image © Whitney Museum of American Art / Licensed by Scala / Art Resource, NY

lesbian persona, one that did not occlude sexuality but instead made it spectacular. Not the lithe and light chorine but ample, brown, and resplendent in a white tux, the popular entertainer was a blues-singing piano player known for the lewdness and innuendo of her performances. Accompanied by a "chorus of pansies" or sailors in her larger floor shows, she played king to effeminate queens. Strolling Harlem draped in masculine attire and beautiful women, Bentley exploded "socially concretized demarcations between gender, race, and class."[46] As the 1920s became the 1930s, censorship and violence sought to contain aspects of the modern in new women, new Negroes, queers, artists, and other outliers who celebrated and embodied these "multiple ways of being."[47]

In Krista Thompson's reading, Savage's *La Citadelle* traces such global modern parameters of the era. The work's title comes from the name of the mountaintop fortress commissioned by Henri Christophe (who later designated himself king) and built by Haitians in the early nineteenth century to defend their revolutionary Black republic. Thompson sees Savage's sculpture as embodying "black male leadership and emancipation," an idea of male power sited within the female form.[48] In this sense Savage's work also thinks broadly about African diasporic freedoms and reflects the connections the artist made with West Indian and African intellectuals during her time in Paris. Yet, it is not necessarily a monument that proclaims this visibly.

JONES

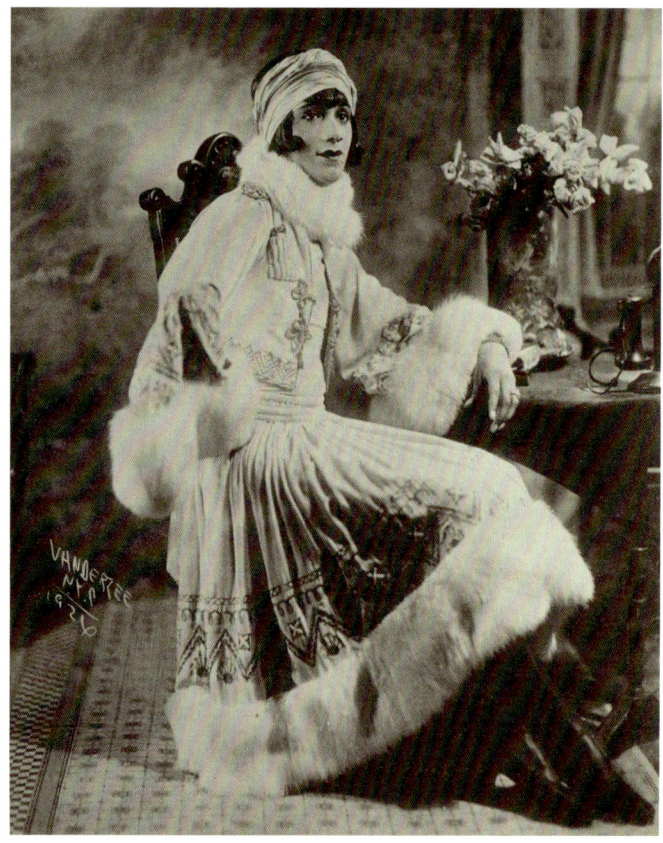

Fig. 15 James Van Der Zee, *Beau of the Ball*, 1926, gelatin silver print, James Van Der Zee photographs circa 1908–1935, David M. Rubenstein Rare Book and Manuscript Library, Duke University

© Donna Mussenden Van Der Zee

Along with scholars such as Vendryes and Jafari Allen, we can value the representational oscillation of Prophet's and Savage's sculptures as queer in their suppleness, intertextuality, and alternate "epistemological pleasure[s]" that go beyond heteronormativity.[49] After José Esteban Muñoz we can also recognize the practices of these artists as disidentification, which "proceeds to use [the code of the majority] as raw material for representing a disempowered politics or positionality that has been rendered unthinkable by the dominant culture."[50]

We should also think about Prophet's and Savage's sculpture in the context of what George Chauncey calls "Gay New York" during the early part of the century, when "multiple sexual cultures co-existed" and "hetero-homosexual binarism did not have the same power."[51] Or we can imagine the queer pageantry of Harlem then, chronicled in the Black press and crowned by the world-renowned Hamilton Lodge Ball (fig. 15). Chauncey's considerations of gender fluidity in the ball scene provide a way for us to think through what these artists might have been up to, as "the balls became a site for the projection and inversion of racial as well as gender identities."[52]

What was seen in the spaces of performance was also seen on the page. The storied Harlem Renaissance, Henry Louis Gates Jr. famously reminds us, "was surely as gay as it was black, not that it was exclusively either of these."[53] The era provided sanctuary for queer Black lives and the effluence of the "discontinuities and affinities" of their cultural expressions.[54] Indeed, one cannot consider the writing of the time without the implications of gay and lesbian perspectives, found in sublimated leitmotifs and coded language. Green sees a "fullness embedded in the silence and gaps" used to evade censors, one that also expansively signals the transgender in language and creativity.[55]

Using Manthia Diawara's sense of "the camouflage of expressive forms," Vendryes has suggested that "nudes based on classical models made the articulation of [Barthé's] homosexuality possible, while also preserving the protected heterosexual public identity Barthé advanced throughout his life."[56] Such evocations of ancient beauty stood in for the "homoeroticism of classical Greece."[57] Describing the work of Mary Butts, a British writer of the period, Jane Garrity sees "a modernist who consistently filtered her homoerotic preoccupations through a classical lens."[58] This was the aesthetic preference among the writer's circle that included lesbian writer Bryher, an important patron of Barthé.[59] In a 1936 interview with the *Pittsburgh Courier*, Augusta Savage touted her own training in the academic tradition and with Greek casts. In retrospect we might understand this as a means for Savage to align herself with a certain aesthetic (and patronage). With this perspective in mind, it is easier to recognize Savage's monumental *The Harp* as a succession of Greek columns. Solid and stalwart, the singing bodies become a Doric colonnade. Or, as topped by their spectacular open mouths in song, the crowning heads take the place of the more ornate foliage of a Corinthian order.[60]

The queer New Negro Renaissance in visual art has largely gone unremarked.[61] However, through figures like Barthé, Prophet, and Savage, we can begin to trace it. A review of a 1928 solo exhibition by Savage notes guests such as Bessye Bearden (New York editor of the *Chicago Defender* and mother of Romare), photographer James Latimer Allen, and gay writer and artist Richard Bruce Nugent (fig. 16) among the numerous guests.[62] The show was held in Savage's own studio/home at 284 West 137th Street, revealing not only her very centrality to Harlem as place, but also her proximity to its nightlife, queer-friendly clubs, and speakeasies.[63] She appears as a character in Nugent's "Smoke, Lilies and Jade," his groundbreaking homoerotic text of 1926.

If academic formula was one métier through which artists expressed the modern Black body, the arena of dance and, specifically, modern dance provided another significant outlet for same-sex narratives and sensibilities. Nugent, one of the few openly gay men of the New Negro movement, was also important to the development of Black concert dance into the 1940s. Savage was similarly involved with the world of Black dance, listed as a patron for some productions, and hosting discussions with troupes at the 138th Street YWCA, including Edna Guy's all-female company as well as Hemsley Winfield's ensemble.[64] As Nugent biographer Thomas Wirth notes, "Winfield achieved a measure of celebrity when he danced the role of Salome in drag with his troupe, the New Negro Art Theater, at the Cherry Lane Theater in 1929."[65] *Salome*, a play penned by Oscar Wilde in 1891 and banned in Great Britain for decades, was a notorious queer text. In the same period as Winfield, Nugent would create a series of watercolors called the *Salome* series. Given Savage's connections to Winfield, Nugent, and queer modern Harlem, let us return to her Amazon series. To analyses based on warriors challenging gender roles and colonialism, we can add another that centers sexuality.

In the late nineteenth century Wilde transformed the minor New Testament figure of Salome into an "exotic [princess] bent on manipulating [her] sexuality for political ends, and by shamelessly engaging in self-promotion as a mobile, serpentine, modern woman."[66] Salome becomes what Sarah Ahmed might call a "willful subject," breaking strictures and whose performance is as much about her own pleasure.[67] Wilde's play found numerous followers in its wake, developing into the craze of Salomania. In Europe performers from Sarah Bernhardt to Maud Allan took it on. For Mme. Acté, the star of a 1910 opera version at Covent Garden, the role was "essentially a modern part, and . . . there is more than a piece of Salome in every modern woman . . . a heart to feel and passion to let loose like floods."[68] The protagonist also became identified with militant feminism and the suffrage movement. At the same time Salome became a popular name for transvestites and female impersonators. She was also the protagonist's muse in "Smoke, Lilies and Jade."[69]

Fig. 16 Richard Bruce Nugent, *Salome Dancing*, c. 1925–1930, ink over graphite on paper, Brooklyn Museum, Gift of Dr. Thomas H. Wirth, gift of Frederick J. Adler, by exchange, bequest of Richard J. Kempe, by exchange, and gift of Abraham Walkowitz, by exchange

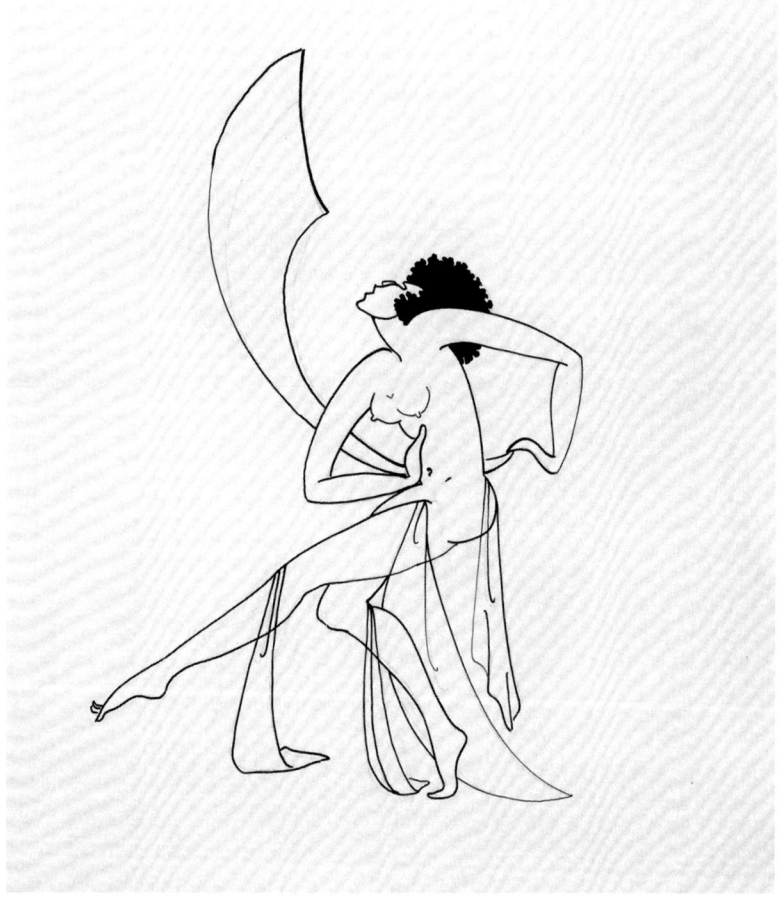

In her Amazon series, Savage progressively enshrines a portrait of disobedient, unruly, uncompromising modern womanhood, one whose nudity also offers "black erotic knowledge as a valuable resource."[70] *Tête de Jeune Fille* meets our gaze confidently. In *The Amazon*, the figure also holds a spear, perhaps used to behead John the Baptist, an aspect of the Salome narrative. In Savage's *Mourning Victory*, the presence of the severed head at her feet certainly links the work to portrayals of Salome. The body's contrapposto gesture is active, suggesting the modern dance postures of *Terpsichore* and *La Citadelle*. And, as Walkowitz reminds us, "However domesticated the female dancer had become, she remained a disorderly manifestation of sexual modernism, of cultural hybridity, and of disloyalty to the disciplined body politic."[71] Though not the bob or Eton crop, the close-cut coiffures of the Amazon series—Afro style—could certainly be a nod to gender nonconformity circa 1930; here hair parades its own freedom, without chemicals or pomade. Rather than occlusion of lesbian embodiment under the cover of a mannish *femme moderne*, we can instead imagine the oscillation between queer bodies and African warriors.

As scholars have pointed out, things changed for Black French subjects with the Empire's second abolition of slavery in 1848. Things also shifted for (white) women as they rejected gender roles and constrictions of the domestic sphere.[72] By the late nineteenth-century writers such as Charles Baudelaire and Wilde championed the sapphic figure as an "evocative symbol of feminized modernity,"[73] as a perverse sign, motivated by women's mobility, and also representing "modern forms of desire."[74] In that moment the elite horsewoman, as well as her outfit, became known as Amazon. As Helen Burnham notes, the Amazon and her ensemble represented "contradictory worlds: traditional and modern, masculine and feminine, stable and rapidly changing,"[75] and the clothing and its attendant roles could, in fact, be taken up by any number of people. "Bohemians, lesbians, and other progressive or transgressive women . . . adopted the costume and the moniker, taking on the mantle of the woman warrior as artistic pioneers or social deviants. . . . The riding dress, moreover, constituted something of a disguise, allowing the wearer to overstep the bounds of her own personal identity."[76] In the following century in interwar Europe, ambitious and accomplished modern women were identified as Amazons or viragos, whose implications of aberration and sexuality became attached to feminism as well.[77]

In the United States, Prophet and Savage were members of a broad cohort, along with Romare Bearden, Aaron Douglas, Langston Hughes, Richard Bruce Nugent, and others, who were intent on creating something that spoke to the new horizons of *their* early twentieth-century moment. Jeffrey Stewart understands this as a "generational revolution" by those intent on finding ways to finance their livelihood beyond the limited patronage schemes to which African American artists had access. Support of Black creators in this era to a large degree fell to the Harmon Foundation and its guiding light, philosopher Alain Locke, recognized as one of the architects of the Harlem Renaissance.[78]

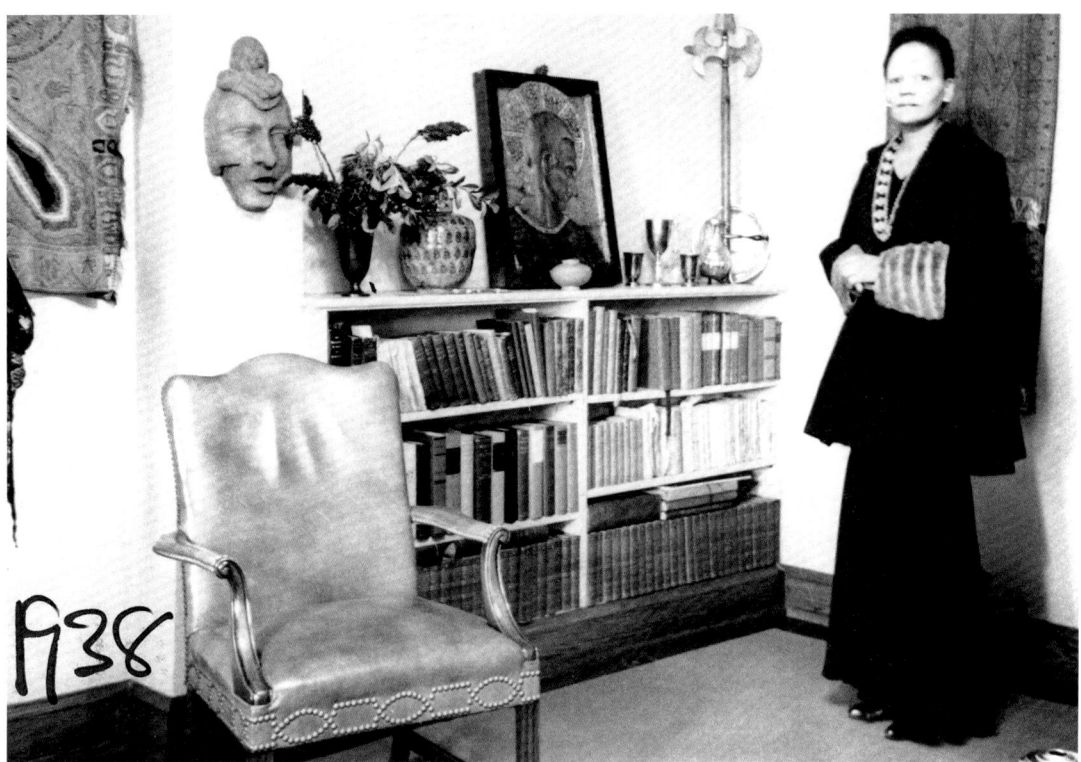

Fig. 17 Nancy Elizabeth Prophet in Atlanta, 1938, Nancy Elizabeth Prophet Collection, James P. Adams Library, Rhode Island College

As evidenced by essays like Hughes's "The Negro Artist and the Racial Mountain" (1926), Bearden's "The Negro Artist and Modern Art" (1934), and Prophet's "Art and Life" (1940), these artists felt increasingly stifled by narrow definitions of "Negro Art" and aesthetics.[79] By the 1930s, themes of social justice, Black nationalism, and a more prominent "Black gay spirit" (like Nugent's) were increasingly in evidence.[80] Prophet and Savage also found restrictions because they were modern women, driven, independent, and seen as obstreperous. The misogyny of this era is often remarked upon, including that of male moderns seeking to continually "protect their prerogatives."[81] Locke was a significant collector and promoter of artists. Yet, his aid was often limited to a coterie of young, beautiful, and (like him) respectably closeted gay men, a club that was open to Barthé, but not Prophet or Savage.[82]

When Prophet sailed from France for the final time her destination was Spelman College in Atlanta (fig. 17). There, in 1934, she joined painter Hale Woodruff to set up a formal art program that would include three-dimensional training as well as two-dimensional study and design. It was only the second such program at a historically Black college or university. In the late 1930s, while serving the Atlanta University complex (Spelman and Morehouse Colleges, Atlanta University professional schools), Prophet hosted shows of works by students along with her own at the converted power plant that served as her studio and classroom.[83]

The 1920s and 1930s saw an explosion of art education for African Americans. Sharif Bey identifies two veins of educational development: the support found in Historically Black Colleges and Universities, and that

124

which was part of a Community Art Center model. If Prophet's role in advancing art studies fell under the former rubric, then Savage pioneered the latter.[84] Savage began teaching at Harlem's Utopia Children's House in the late 1920s. Upon her return from Paris in the early 1930s she established the Savage Studios of Arts and Crafts at 163 West 143rd Street. From then on Savage was part of the leadership of numerous independent efforts begun by Black artists that eventually received funding in the New Deal era.[85]

It is interesting to consider the types of exhibition opportunities Prophet and Savage were afforded in their lifetimes. In Paris both participated in the Société des Artistes Français and Salon d'Automne. For the 1927 iteration of the latter Prophet is listed as a man (Eli), a tactic employed by legions of women artists as a way to access systems of distribution, display, and audience.[86] While the experience of personal freedom may have felt different in Paris, the prospects for securing outlets for their work seemed better in New York. The Harmon Foundation exhibited their sculpture.[87] Another source of support was American Art Association-Anderson Galleries, the precursor to Sotheby's auction house, where both participated in the Salons of America. Savage was represented for a time by Argent Galleries, while Prophet was able to place her work at 56th Street Galleries and Milch Galleries, and in New England at Boston Society of Independent Artists and Rhode Island School of Design, her alma mater.[88]

Savage's commission for the 1939 New York World's Fair looms large in this regard in terms of the access and audience she gained from the sculpture's popularity. This success was surely significant for Savage and her community of artists given their struggles for visibility, materials, and support in the US and global art scene. It was a major victory that Savage's *The Harp* was sited at the Contemporary Art Building at the fair rather than in a space designated for crafts or for works by Negroes. Yet she would still exhibit the following year at Chicago's American Negro Exposition, along with artists of a younger generation, including Elizabeth Catlett and Charles White.[89]

Savage also shaped her own exhibition opportunities. As we have seen, she hosted at least one show in her home/studio in 1928. A decade later in 1939 she opened the short-lived Salon of Contemporary Negro Art, a platform for her own work and legions of others. In formulating a gallery and her own corporation (Savage Studios Inc.) she was part of a cadre of African American artists who made their own opportunities instead of waiting a lifetime for recognition from the mainstream; these creators included Savage's student Norman Lewis, who cofounded Cinque Gallery in 1969 to continue to support artists of African descent.[90]

In 1942 Hale Woodruff launched the Atlanta University Annual exhibitions, which provided a showcase for African American artists until 1970. Prophet would never participate, even though it was one of the few outlets of the era that displayed the work of these practitioners on a regular basis. She would leave Atlanta by 1944, her spirit stifled by Southern mores, her

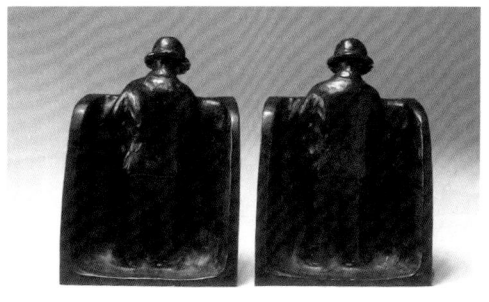
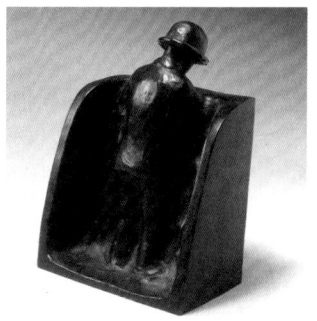

Fig. 18 Augusta Savage, *Untitled (bookends)* (front), 1930–1931, bronze, Collection of the Hampton University Museum, Hampton, VA

Fig. 19 Augusta Savage, *Untitled (bookends)* (side), 1930–1931, bronze, Collection of the Hampton University Museum, Hampton, VA

teaching duties a deterrent to her sculptural production. Indeed, it would seem Prophet incrementally moved away from listing herself as a Negro in later years. Perhaps, as Hartman suggests, "She had grown weary of being a Negro woman in all the ways expected of her. She wanted more than this."[91] Prophet's example points to a creative remaking of categories of woman, desire, and subjectivity as things multiple, malleable, and in flux. Following a transgender studies methodology, Prophet's art and life suggest "that we be more attuned to difference rather than sameness, understanding and declaring that our sameness will not protect us."[92]

In her theory of embodied discourse, Brittney Cooper frames alternate approaches to "creative and procreative possibilities," where Black women are able to produce "citizens not slaves."[93] She magnifies generative function as service to civic life, and beyond that originally imagined for Black women: producing labor for slavery's economic machine.[94] A parallel consideration comes from Omise'eke Natasha Tinsley. Writing on queer African diasporic relationships wrought by the Middle Passage, in which same-sex loving connection informs capacious human configurations, and motivations to live, she writes:

> Queer not in the sense of "gay" or same-sex loving identity waiting to be excavated from the ocean floor but as a practice of resistance. Queer in the sense of making disruption to the violence of the normative order and powerfully so. . . . loving your own kind when your kind was supposed to cease to exist.[95]

We might visualize such concepts in the work of these artists through a gift Savage made for Countee Cullen in 1930–1931: a pair of bronze bookends of men at a urinal (figs. 18, 19). In a reprise of Anna Julia Cooper's confrontation with her own body in the public sphere, Savage brings us back to the restroom. That we are in a communal or shared space is indicated by the figures draped in hats and overcoats and standing in partitioned alcoves. In place of Cooper's misrecognition, Savage substitutes recognition and acknowledgment, of such locales as sites of other kinds of encounters, those of clandestine same-sex intimacy, the forbidden love of the written texts that sometimes also crossed the color line.[96]

Nancy Elizabeth Prophet and Augusta Savage refused subservient roles in any and all ways possible. They rejected, in Hartman's words, "all that kept [them] fixed in place, stuck at the laundry, chained to an ironing board, suffocating and without any possibility of change."[97] The focus on performance, sexuality, and nonbinary modes illuminates the desire to remake the self tout court. Theirs was a redesigning of the body for an era to come, jettisoning stock categories of Negro womanhood as artists and as humans, creating their own scripts, based in "structures of feeling" that moved beyond "rote representational practices."[98] Dreaming and thinking was the work they wanted and needed to do, as Prophet would suggest in 1940:

> Americans, like other civilized peoples, have come to realize that there must be some aesthetic expression for their people, that the artist's place in the community is not only that of the useless dreamer—dreaming may precede thinking. The great dreamer may become a great thinker and from there a great man of action.[99]

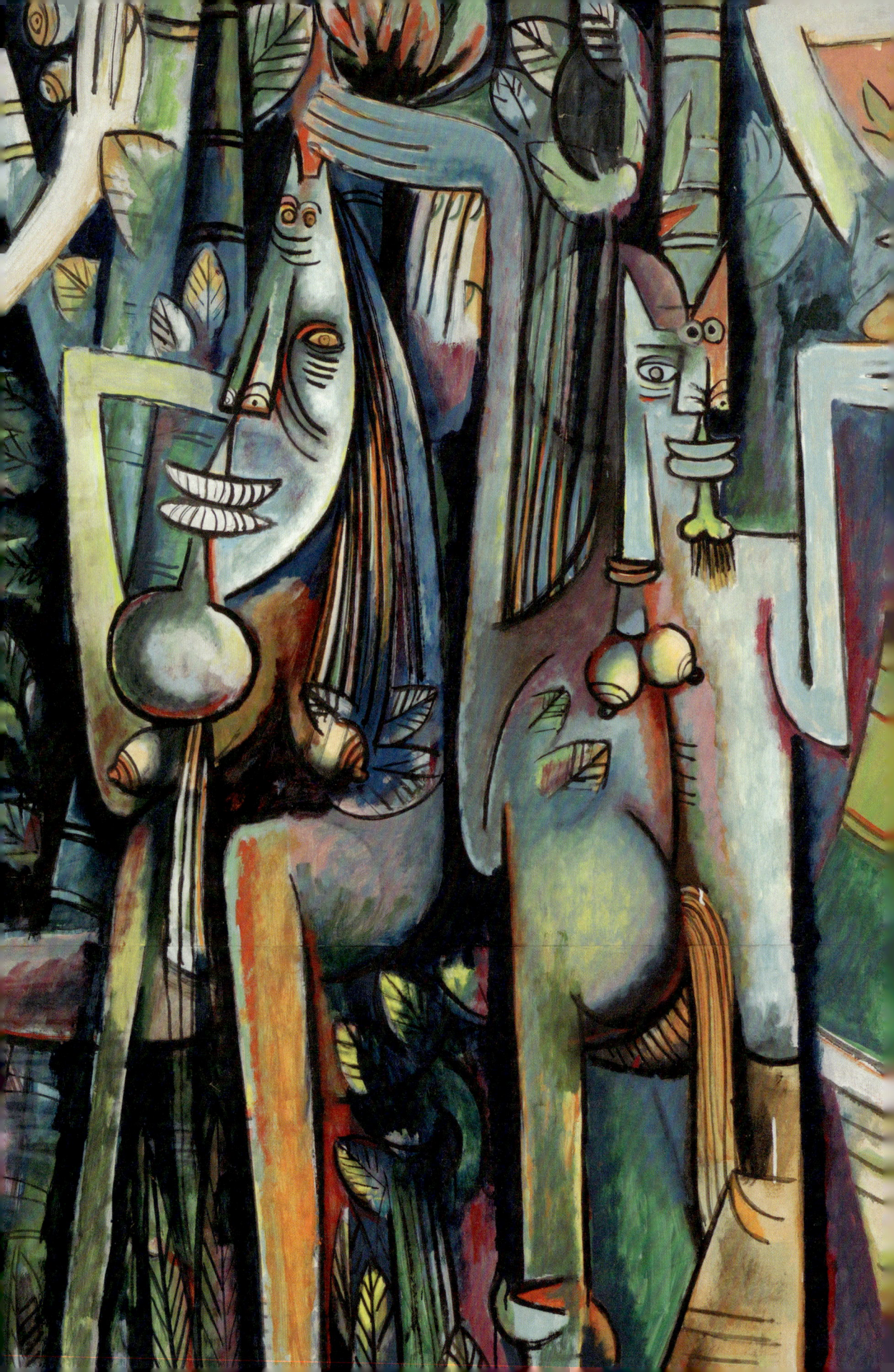

NUMINOUS AFFECT IN BLACK ATLANTIC MODERNISMS

SYLVESTER OKWUNODU OGBECHIE

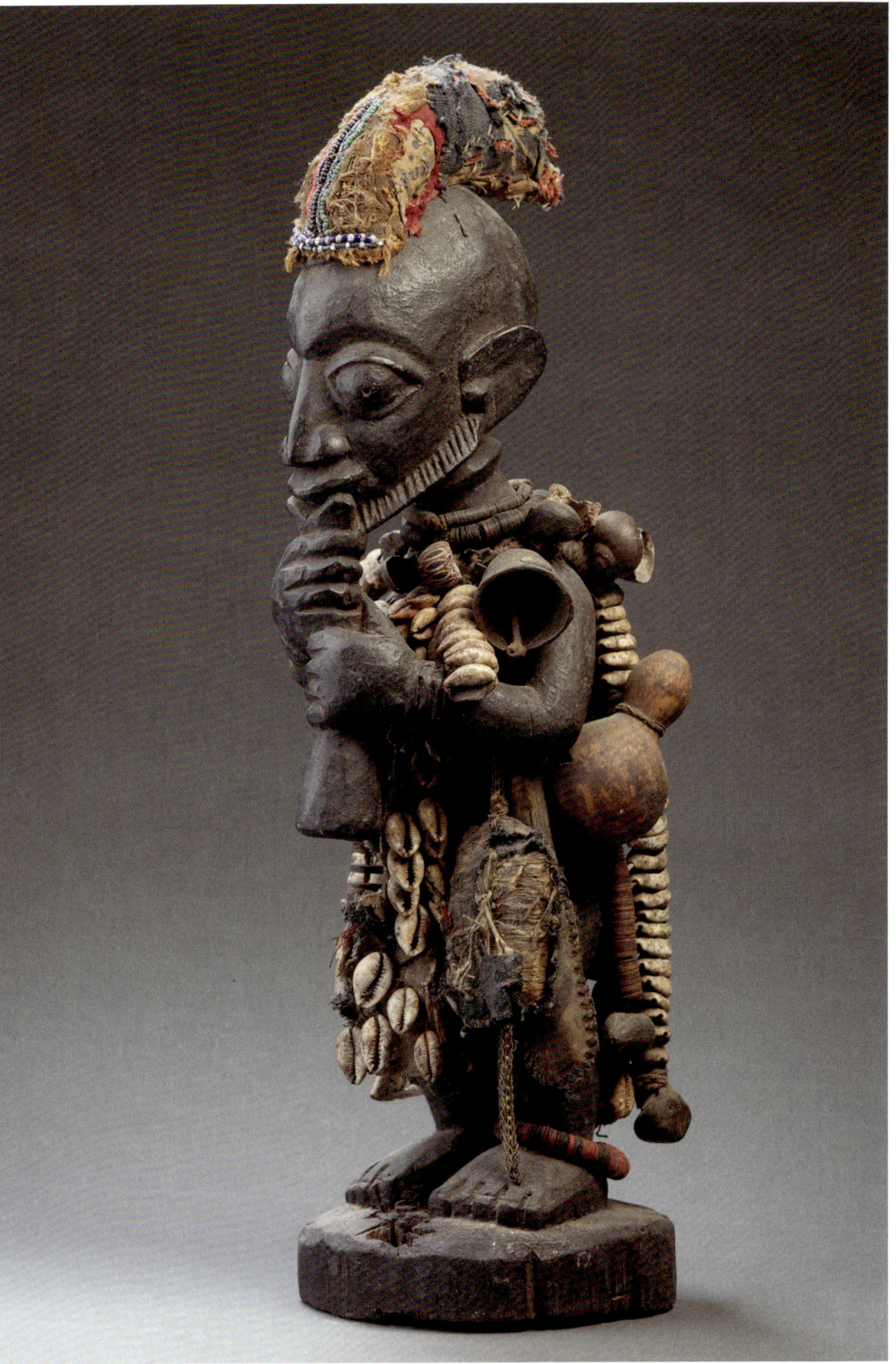

> Where there is no vision, the people perish.
> Proverbs 29:18

Eṣu, the divine trickster figure that originated among Yoruba and Fon peoples of West Africa, recurs with startling frequency in the mythologies of African diaspora populations (fig. 1). Eṣu (pronounced Eshu) is lord of the crossroads, who regulates interactions between the material and metaphysical worlds. The deity is sometimes represented as a figure with two faces, one gazing upon the world of the living while the other, hidden at the back of his elongated head, casts a mordant gaze into the invisible world of the spirits. Henry Louis Gates Jr. describes Eṣu in the African diaspora as "a sign of the disrupted wholeness of an African system of meaning and belief preserved by oral tradition, improvised upon in ritual—especially in the rituals of the repeated oral narrative—and willed to subsequent generations as sealed and encoded charts of cultural descent."[1] Eṣu is thus a repository of numinous affect and a preeminent topos in African and African diaspora religions and discourses. How, then, can the numinous affect of Eṣu be deployed for analysis of Black Atlantic modernisms, working from the modernist idea of the spiritual in art? A *numen* is a spirit or divine force, believed to inhabit a particular object that calls forth a reaction of awe and reverence. Numinous affect describes a holistic uniting of intellect and emotion, a direct link to the tangible and symbolic nature of the object, and an intensely profound connection with the past, self, and spirit.[2] I use this concept to evaluate how shared interest in the spiritual implications of contemporary artistic practice provides an interpretation of Black Atlantic modernism that centers African cultural registers.

I argue that Wifredo Lam of Cuba (1902–1982), Nigerian modernist Ben Enwonwu (1917–1994),[3] and the African American visionary artist James Hampton (1909–1964) all relied on numinous affect to frame their engagements with modern art. Lam interacted with key European modernists such as Pablo Picasso and the surrealists before creating a style of modern art that fused cubism and surrealism with African-inflected forms. For Lam, Eṣu (Elegguá) and other Santería deities gave his artworks complex meanings, though non-Cuban critics often ignore his Afro-Cuban engagements.[4] Enwonwu's international career as an African modernist plumbed numinous imagery of powerful Igbo-African masquerades across divergent modernist contexts and discourses. Embodied, imposing paintings and sculptures of masquerades pervade Enwonwu's sixty-year oeuvre. The numinous affect of these works is palpable in a contemporary Nigerian culture that still perceives masquerades as affective entities that were used to encode Indigenous knowledge and domesticate newness. James Hampton's *The Throne of the Third Heaven of the Nations' Millennium General Assembly* (c. 1950–1964) is a masterpiece of numinous affect that makes visible secret African knowledge systems that Black Atlantic populations used to contest their subjugation during and after the period of slavery. Hampton's magnificent installation has been overshadowed by its interpretation as a Christian construct, ignoring the Kongo-African

Fig. 1 Yoruba peoples, Nigeria, *Eṣu*, twentieth century, wood, cloth, leather strips, cowrie shells, iron bell, beads, and gourd, Femi Akinsanya African Art Collection, Lagos, Nigeria

© Femi Akinsanya African Art Collection, Lagos, Nigeria

spiritual registers that infuse the work. His fundamentalist Christianity, filtered through Baptist protocols of worship, should give us pause since African American Baptist practices encode African religious elements. The entertainment of the holy spirit, shaking, and speaking in tongues that characterize Baptist forms of worship derive directly from African ritual protocols. Lam, Enwonwu, and Hampton thus illustrate how African and African diaspora artists developed unique approaches to modernist representation through shared exploration of numinous affect. My analysis of these artists is a search for a genealogy of modernism that centers African cultural registers.

On the Spiritual in Black Atlantic Art

I posit Eṣu, which Gates discusses as an iterative divine figure across the African diaspora, as a discursive framework for interpreting Black Atlantic modernisms and countering their marginalization in art history.[5] A powerful Yoruba god in origin, Eṣu became a transnational deity that spread with other elements of the Orișa (pronounced Orisha; gods/goddesses in Yoruba/Fon religions) to the African diaspora, reaching such places as Brazil, Cuba, Haiti, Jamaica, Puerto Rico, Trinidad and Tobago, the United Kingdom, and the United States. As Eṣu spread, he acquired distinctive identities and became variously known as Eṣu-Elegbara (Yoruba/Fon), Eleda, Exú (in the Brazilian Orișa religion), Cxu Eleggua/Echu-Eleggua (in Cuban Santería), Cxu Elegbara, and Papa Legba (pronounced La-Bas) in the lwa pantheon of Haitian vodou. Eṣu is thus central to Black Atlantic religions, omnipresent and part of every offering. He is friend and foe, and a sign of multiplicity. He is also the sign of double vision and ruler of interpretations. Although referred to as masculine in most discourses, Eṣu is not restricted to human binaries of gender or sex.[6] Despite the different forms taken by Eṣu as a result of cross-cultural fertilization, narratives about the deity express "an unbroken arc of metaphysical presupposition and a pattern of figuration."[7] If the canonical narrative of modernism represents a closed arc, Eṣu's hermeneutics ruptures its teleology.[8]

Gates's contention that "signifyin(g) is black double-voicedness; because it always entails formal revision and an intertextual relation, and because of Eṣu's double-voiced representation in art,"[9] is exemplified in how African diaspora peoples cloaked iconic African deities in the visage of European saints. It is vital for us to reach beyond this visible order of syncretism to recover the spiritual vision encoded in the radical imaginary of African modernist visualities. Gates defines Eṣu as the "ultimate copula" or connective tissue between African and diasporic cultures, the symbolic and discursive core of Afro-Atlantic narratives and artistic traditions. Eṣu represents agentic power that enables multiplicity and intercultural spiritual connections between Africa and its diaspora. However, despite his centrality to Black Atlantic discourse and religion, Eṣu is absent from contemporary interpretations and analysis of African and African diaspora art. Black Atlantic artists are excluded from the canonical narrative of modernism for their reliance on African spiritual visualities, an absence that echoes the contemporary tendency to excise religion and spirituality from narratives of modern art. The invocations of African spiritualities by Lam, Enwonwu, and Hampton require us to reevaluate art history's teleological narrative of modernism. We must read these artists within their logics of visuality, using the same concept of numinous affect through which they formulated new interpretations of modern art.

Masquerades and Metamorphosis: Ben Enwonwu

In his original Yoruba-African context, Eṣu is represented in sculptures and celebrated in masquerade performances that highlight the malleable nature of his supernatural interventions. In this regard, masquerades represent the highest levels of Indigenous knowledge in most African cultures. Masquerades are considered liminal beings that exist between the worlds of the living and the spirits, metaphysical entities endowed with multiple meanings across sacred and secular contexts. Masquerades also narrate cultural cosmologies and serve as repositories of numinous affect that socializes their mostly male inductees as guardians of cultural knowledge.

Masquerades and themes of metamorphosis suffuse the oeuvre of Nigerian sculptor and painter Benedict Chukwukadibia Enwonwu, arguably the most significant modern African artist of the twentieth century. Internationally acclaimed during his lifetime, Enwonwu's art presented a unique form of African modernism, "a third space whose nature and parameters are at variance with art history's exclusionary narratives of modernity and its inscription of the modern artist-subject as a white, Western European male."[10] Although he readily accepted the label of avant-garde artist, Enwonwu rejected the Euro-modernist notion of art for art's sake, deploying instead a deeply entrenched focus on Igbo cultural symbolism within modernist conventions of representation. His expression of African aesthetics, which included artistic elements from numerous Nigerian ethnicities, gave his oeuvre a cultural and political impact in the context of British colonial occupation and the postcolonial era. As a transnational African modernist, Enwonwu harnessed his multicultural heritage to produce an artistic synthesis focused mainly on the imagery of masquerades, through which he sought metaphorical passage into the numinous realm of the great spirits by embodying the roles of artist and ritual expert. Enwonwu's use of masquerade imagery can therefore be interpreted as a quasi-religious exploration focused on Igbo masking systems. In this regard, his multiple identities in colonial and postcolonial culture and his search for agency in various contexts of practice were themselves sophisticated forms of masking.

During his childhood, Enwonwu was embedded in Igbo cultural practices, and images of masquerades appeared quite early in his oeuvre, beginning in 1936. They reappeared in his artworks for several decades and became preeminent in 1987 when, as he mourned the death of his brother Francis and contemplated his own mortality, the painter turned to masquerades as his principal subject matter. The Igbo pantheon of masquerades is called *Mmonwu* (spirits), and, among Enwonwu's Onitsha-Igbo people, masquerade performances bridge the vast gulfs between the living, gods, and spirits of dead ancestors through structured rituals. As the titular head of his family's patrilineage, Enwonwu was inspired by the graceful dance of Mmonwu Ogonogo and the death-defying acrobatics of Ogolo, both from the Ogulugu masquerade pantheon of Onitsha, during the funeral ceremonies for his elder brother. Enwonwu stated: "I saw the Ogolo among a host of other masquerades during my brother's funeral and it impressed me a lot. [In my subsequent artworks] I have focused on the Ogolo masked form.... It is a part of my recent important works [and has] generated a steady flow of thought and development. I find it extremely beautiful."[11] Various Igbo masquerades such as Agbogho Mmo, Ayolugbe, Mmonwu Ogonogo, and Mgbedike appear in Enwonwu's oeuvre. However, after his brother's funeral, Enwonwu focused almost exclusively on the Ogolo masquerade, distinguished by its white-faced masks; he represented it in frontal poses, as solitary figures, and in larger masquerade ensembles. In the most notable of these paintings, *Ogolo* (1989, fig. 2), a spectral presence surges forth from a tumultuous dark-blue background that merges sky and earth into a mordant mass. Enwonwu contoured the masquerade figure with multiple black outlines that destabilized its form, thus illustrating its enrapturing yet unknowable nature. A white mask emerges as the focus of the painting, eliciting awe. For Enwonwu, the mask and the physical visage of the masquerade represent the material manifestation of a spiritual being at a sacred site of ritual.[12]

Enwonwu's repeated focus on masquerades recalls Gates's assertion that "repetition and revision are fundamental to black artistic forms."[13] Through repetition, Enwonwu sought to capture the transcendence inherent in the masquerade's transits between material and metaphysical realms. British critics such as Eric Newton failed to understand Enwonwu's interrogation of numinous affect and saw his formal decisions—notably his rendering of figures in unstable pictorial spaces—as unfruitful experiments by an African artist venturing too far from his Indigenous cultural heritage.[14] Such criticism failed to comprehend that Enwonwu's artworks were not mere emulations of Indigenous African art, but rather a unique African interpretation of and contribution to modern art. Misinterpretations of Enwonwu's art arise from a fundamental misunderstanding of the numinous affect of African masquerade performances. As a member of the Onitsha-Igbo culture and an initiate into its higher orders of Indigenous knowledge, Enwonwu had developed a capacity to apprehend numinous visions.[15] In most African societies that use them, masquerades provide context-specific interpretations of reality that no single system of knowledge can decipher and no standard interpretation of material or visual culture can account for. In African contexts of belief, the convergence between the material and the metaphysical worlds is ineffable, and the encounter between physical and spiritual forces unfolds within an energy

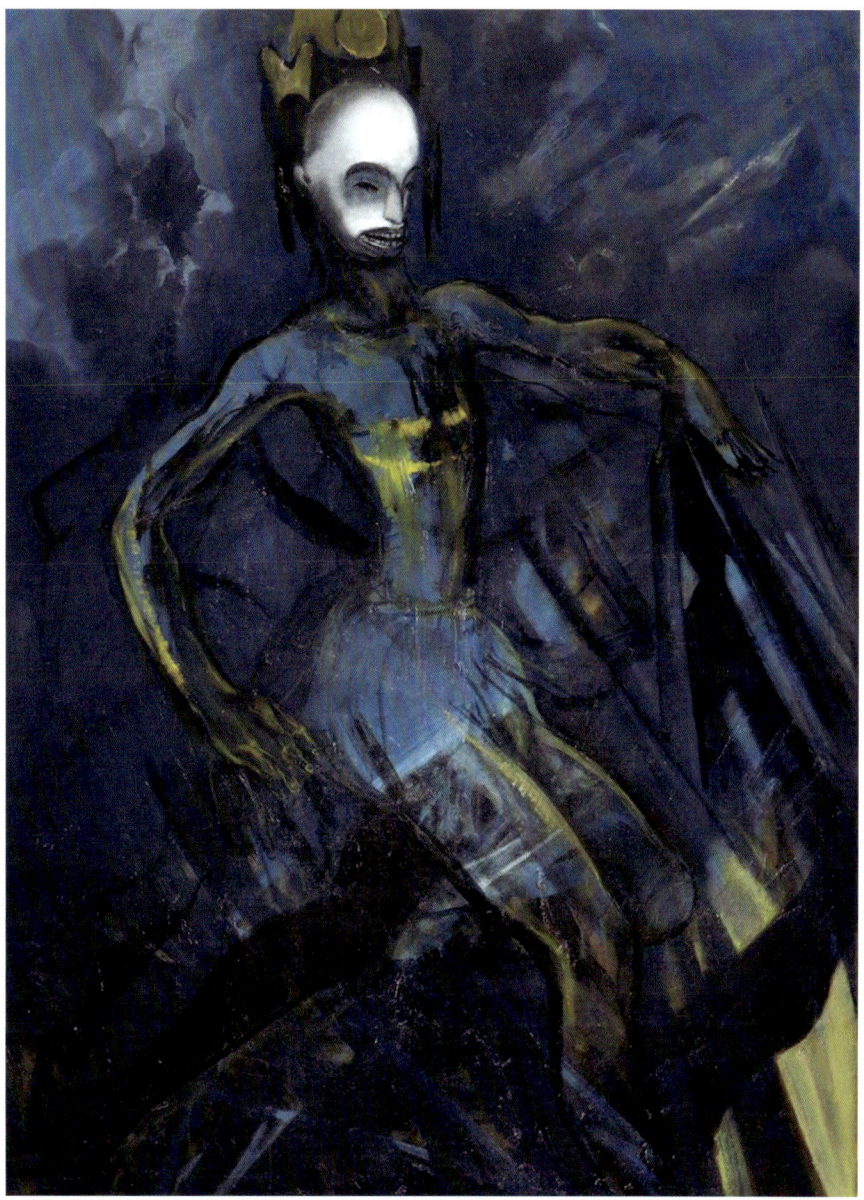

Fig. 2 Ben Enwonwu, *Ogolo*, 1989, oil on canvas

Courtesy of Ben Enwonwu Foundation

field, sustained by strict ritual protocols, which produces affective multimedia and multisensory experiences.

More than components of Indigenous cultural mythologies, masquerades are also a modern phenomenon that challenged colonial oppression. As cultural weapons, they disrupted power relations by reversing the notion of masks as objects that conceal; rather, they made the colonial subject visible.[16] In fact, the twentieth-century forms of most African masquerades served as discursive platforms through which Africans domesticated the newness of modernity and resisted colonial domination.

Masquerade imagery and performances were not just dynamic and emotionally charged, they also provided a framework for Enwonwu's engagement with modernism across multiple cultural, social, and religious registers. Moreover, Enwonwu's art challenges our definitions of diaspora.[17] Too often, we view the Africa diaspora solely in terms of movement of Africans outward from the continent, disregarding internal movements of populations within Africa itself.[18] Enwonwu's Onitsha people are part of the Ezechime clan, a group of nine towns west and east of the River Niger who claim origins in the Benin Kingdom. Enwonwu's art reflects the intersection of distinct systems of representation: African sculpture, European easel painting, his Onitsha-Igbo heritage, and the unique forms of visual representation in the art from the Edo Kingdom of Benin, also African but mediated by centuries-long engagements with global trade. In the fifteenth and sixteenth centuries, this interaction produced the so-called Afro-Portuguese ivories, whose integration of African and European systems of representation can be arguably defined as the earliest examples of modern African art. Enwonwu's art is thus rooted in Western, Igbo, and Edo-Benin visualities and mostly explored how the numinous affect of masquerade performances encoded highly structured forms of Indigenous knowledge (fig. 3). Although Enwonwu received his formal artistic training in London, he actively sought to learn the traditions

Fig. 3 Ben Enwonwu, *Agbogho Mmo*, 1949, oil on canvas

Courtesy of Bonhams

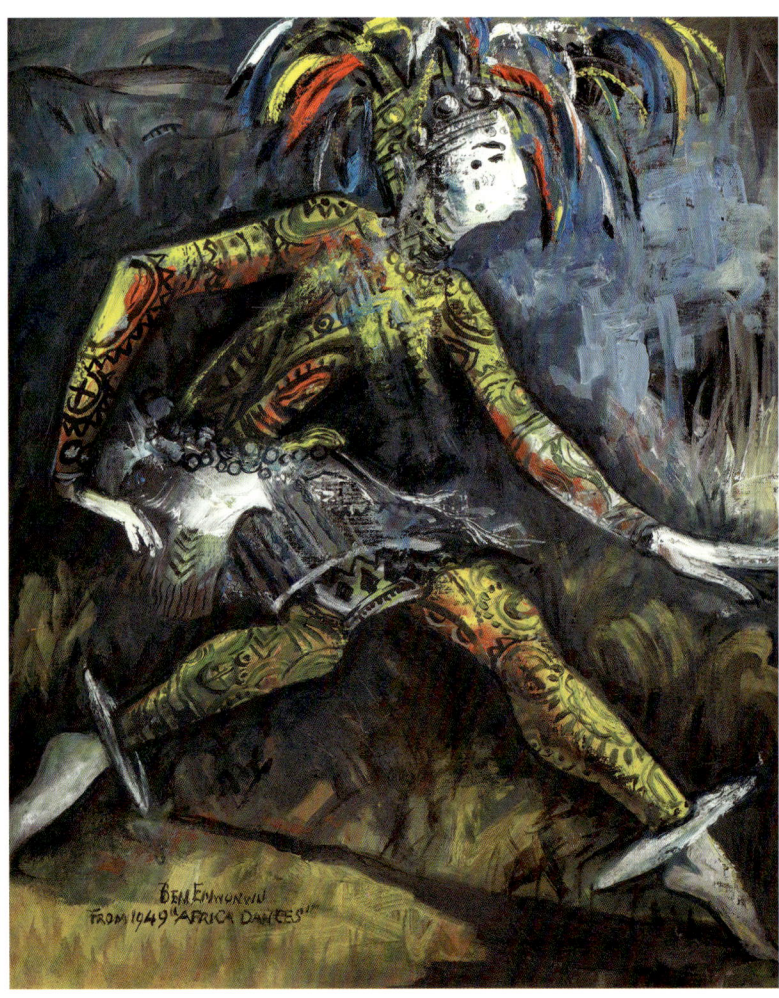

of Edo-Benin art through apprenticeships with master sculptors of the *Igbesanmwan* (ivory sculptor) and *Igun Eronmwon* (bronze caster) royal guilds. He created paintings suffused with Benin cultural imagery and painted portraits of the guardians of various important royal shrines.[19]

After receiving his art degree at the Slade School of Fine Arts in 1946 and a postgraduate degree at the University of London in 1948, Enwonwu once again deployed Igbo cultural registers as a conceptual framework for his art. He evaluated how Indigenous and modern art were each defined in secular and sacred contexts and how a colonial culture circumscribed by European cultural prescriptions constrained his art. In Igbo societies, "an art object was validated by a conceptual framework that subsumed aesthetics to the symbolic charge produced in the context of its use. The art object, however alluring its physical form, really becomes beautiful when it fulfills the required ritual and functional obligations for which it was created."[20] Encounters with the numen of masquerades elicit awe and reverence for the supernatural energies of the masked spirit itself. Enwonwu's paintings of masquerades captured the affective energy of their numinous manifestation. He conveyed a sense of motion through multiple black outlines that vibrate within the pictorial frame, which echoes how Ogolo's energetic performance builds graceful movements into a tight coil of tension that explodes into a kaleidoscope of colors.

The persistence of masquerades in Enwonwu's oeuvre suggests he used Igbo aesthetics as a framework for his transnational engagements with modern art. Enwonwu's assertion of an African modernist identity and his strategic self-representation in international discourses of modern art pursued what the cultural theorist Paul Gilroy described as the struggle to have Black people perceived as agents, as people with cognitive capacities and an intellectual history, and not just as mimics of European knowledge.[21] It is equally important to reiterate that, as an Onitsha-Igbo person, Enwonwu belonged to an internal African diaspora in which his ethnic identity was frequently contested since the people of the Ezechime clan do not identify as Igbo. As a cosmopolitan artist living and working in Africa, Europe, and the United States at various points in his life, he negotiated multiple identities between his Onitsha homeland, Benin culture, and European/American sojourns. Enwonwu's modern art mediated his contested identities by merging Indigenous African techniques and Igbo/Benin aesthetics with European protocols of representation. This rupture between the imaginary of his clan's Edo-Benin origins, his family's Indigenous Onitsha-Igbo art traditions, and the European forms of representation he adopted produced a multivocal consciousness that integrated his global cultural referents into a unique form of modern art. Enwonwu's reconfiguration of modernism's conventions thus challenged colonial discourse by centering African cultural registers. Within this space, his appeal to numinous affect connected him firmly to his myriad identities and allowed him to construct a modernist practice circumscribed by Igbo-African spiritualities.

Modernism and the Black Atlantic: Wifredo Lam

African diaspora populations constructed cultures that cloaked African beliefs in European religious imagery, creating new forms and interpretations of Eṣu in the process. Nowhere is this development more evident than in the worship of Yoruba Oriṣa in Cuba's Santería religion.[22] Into this Antillean country characterized by the convergence of Latin America, Europe, Africa, and Asia, Wifredo Óscar de la Concepción Lam y Castilla (Lam Fei Lung) was born in the provincial town of Sagua La Grande in 1902 to a Chinese immigrant father and a mother descended from a Spanish conquistador and an enslaved African. Ma'Antonica Wilson, Lam's godmother, was a Santería priestess who introduced him to the spirits and divination practices of this religion. As a powerful and well-respected prophetess and healer, Wilson was often asked for advice and cures, which she provided by calling upon her tutelary Oriṣa—Ṣango—the Yoruba god of thunder.[23] Wilson wanted to groom Lam as her successor but Lam was intent on becoming an artist, and he showed such promise that his hometown provided him with a scholarship to study in Madrid.[24] After studying at the Havana School of Fine Art and the Royal Academy of Fine Arts of San Fernando in Madrid, Lam moved to Paris in 1938, where he worked alongside André Breton, Pablo Picasso, and the surrealists. Mark Hudson notes that when Lam arrived in Paris, "he appeared a dazzlingly exotic figure: a strikingly handsome, brilliantly talented Cuban painter of Chinese, Spanish, and Congolese-African ancestry" who the surrealists acclaimed as "the embodiment of the authentic 'primitive' artist, whose vision was untainted by bourgeois values and umbilically linked to the mysteries of Africa."[25] Lam was uncomfortable with the effort to characterize him as a "primitive" artist but he did gain an appreciation for African and modern art through his interactions with Picasso, as is evident in his paintings *Woman with Long Hair I* (1938, fig. 4) and *Composition* (1940), both of which draw on the structure, imagery, and color scheme of Picasso's *Girl before a Mirror* (1932, fig. 5). Lam's work during this period was immersive, as evidenced by the large size of his canvases. However, the strong relationship between both artists ultimately led to a perception of Lam as Picasso's protégé and imitator—the Cuban Picasso.

In 1940, with the German army closing in on the city, Lam fled Paris and in Marseilles boarded a boat for the United States, a vessel filled with French modernist artists, writers, and intellectuals, including Breton. Lam was the sole Black person on the boat and the only passenger denied entry into the United States. A year later, he decided to return to his own country. His voyage back to Cuba reinvigorated Lam's creativity and the former refugee became a veritable modern artist the moment he stepped off the boat in his native Havana. Here, the Western forms of representation Lam had appropriated were transformed and channeled toward his Cuban roots, conjuring Santería spirits and ceremonies in direct deviation from his surrealist and cubist peers. Lam thus pushed back against the primitivism beloved by artists such as André Masson, and the colonialist

Fig. 4 Wifredo Lam, *Woman with Long Hair I*, 1938, oil on paper laid down on canvas

Courtesy of Cernuda Arte. Photo © ADAGP, Paris, 2020

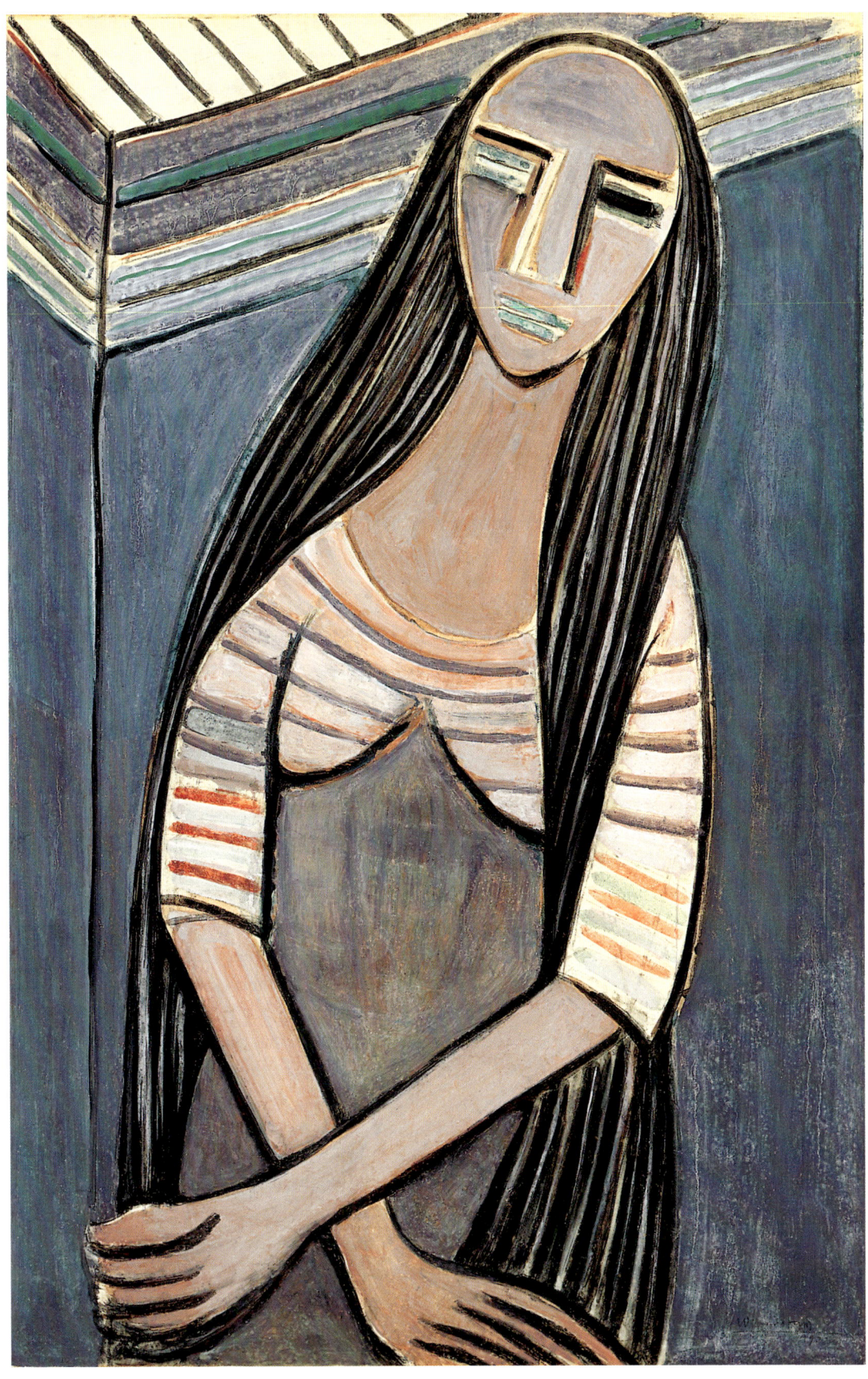

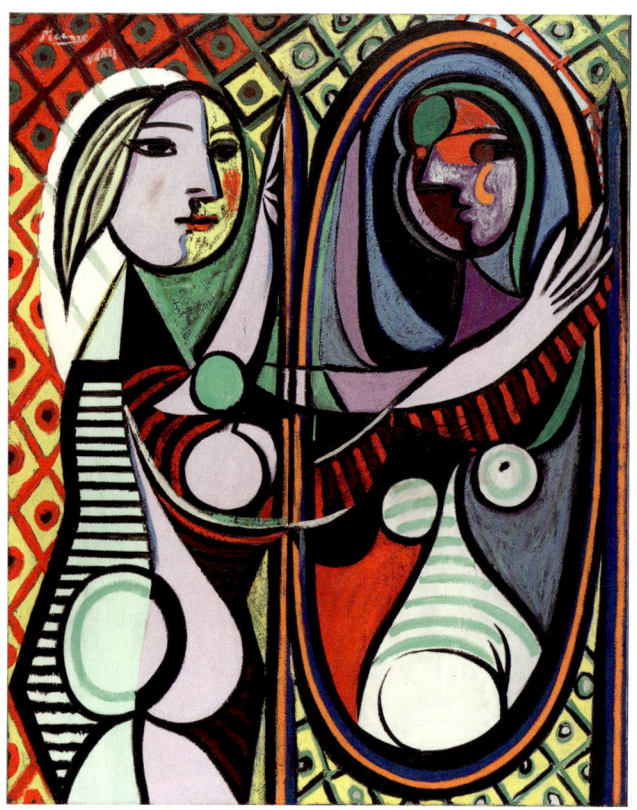

Fig. 5 Pablo Picasso, *Girl before a Mirror*, 1932, oil on canvas, Museum of Modern Art, New York, Gift of Mrs. Simon Guggenheim

© 2023 Estate of Pablo Picasso / Artists Rights Society (ARS), New York. Digital image © The Museum of Modern Art / Licensed by Scala / Art Resource, NY

fantasies of Paul Gauguin, to reimagine and recode the visual language of twentieth-century abstraction using African cultural registers. Lam's artwork upon returning to Cuba thus heavily reflected Afro-Cuban spirituality.²⁶ His godmother gifted him with the protection of divinities such as Ṣango/Chango, syncretically identified with Santa Bárbara, whose chief attribute is lightning and the symbolic color red, and "of Yemaja, goddess of the sea [identified with the Virgin of La Merced] . . . of Ogun-Ferraille, god of metal who gilded the sun every morning, always at the side of Olorun, the absolute god of creation."²⁷ These are all Afro-Cuban manifestations of iconic Yoruba deities (Oriṣa) celebrated in Santería ceremonies where "the supernatural merges with the natural world through masks, animals, or initiates who become possessed by a god. These ceremonies are moments of metamorphosis where a being is at once itself and otherworldly."²⁸ Their impact is comparable to the numinous affect of Enwonwu's Igbo masquerades.

Lam's newfound respect for Afro-Cuban culture greatly influenced his subsequent oeuvre. The first of Lam's artworks to refer to the Oriṣa was produced immediately after his return to Cuba in 1941. Henceforth we find increasing references to Santería deities in artworks such as *Ogue Orisa (Euggue Orissa, l'herbe des dieux)* (1943), *The Sombre Malembo: God of the Crossroads* (1943), and *Altar for Eleggua* (1944), the first literal invocation of the Yoruba deity Eṣu in Lam's art. Other paintings such as *Nude on Colored Background* (1942), *Figures with Shears* (1942), and *Light of the Forest* (1942) showed Lam amassing the visual vocabulary of his new Santería-influenced style, which showed a dazzling fusion of diverse influences.

It is relevant to note that Euro-modernist abstraction relied, in part, on African visual forms as we see in Picasso's appropriation of the architectonics of Fang masks. In this regard, Lam might be said to be treading a well-worn path. However, Lam lambasted nineteenth- and twentieth-century European artists for their exploitation of African and Oceanic artworks. He believed that merely painting their formal likeness stripped such artworks of their symbolic function and rendered them "pieces of exotica and sterile museum curiosities."[29] Lam wanted to be a kind of Trojan horse for Cuban culture in the Western world, a visionary who would "spew forth hallucinatory images with the power to surprise, to disturb the dreams of the exploiters."[30] The paintings he produced during the 1940s channeled this sentiment, reclaiming Afro-Cuban imagery and reinstating the numinous affect of Santería's religious symbolism. By referring directly to Eṣu in his art, Lam signaled a new modernism in which African cultural registers were paramount and radically differed from Euro-modernist forms.

Lam's new style coalesced in *La Jungla* (*The Jungle*) (1943, fig. 6), which exemplifies his break with European standards and his departure

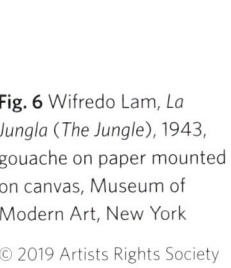

Fig. 6 Wifredo Lam, *La Jungla* (*The Jungle*), 1943, gouache on paper mounted on canvas, Museum of Modern Art, New York

© 2019 Artists Rights Society (ARS), New York / ADAGP, Paris. Digital image © The Museum of Modern Art / Licensed by Scala / Art Resource, NY

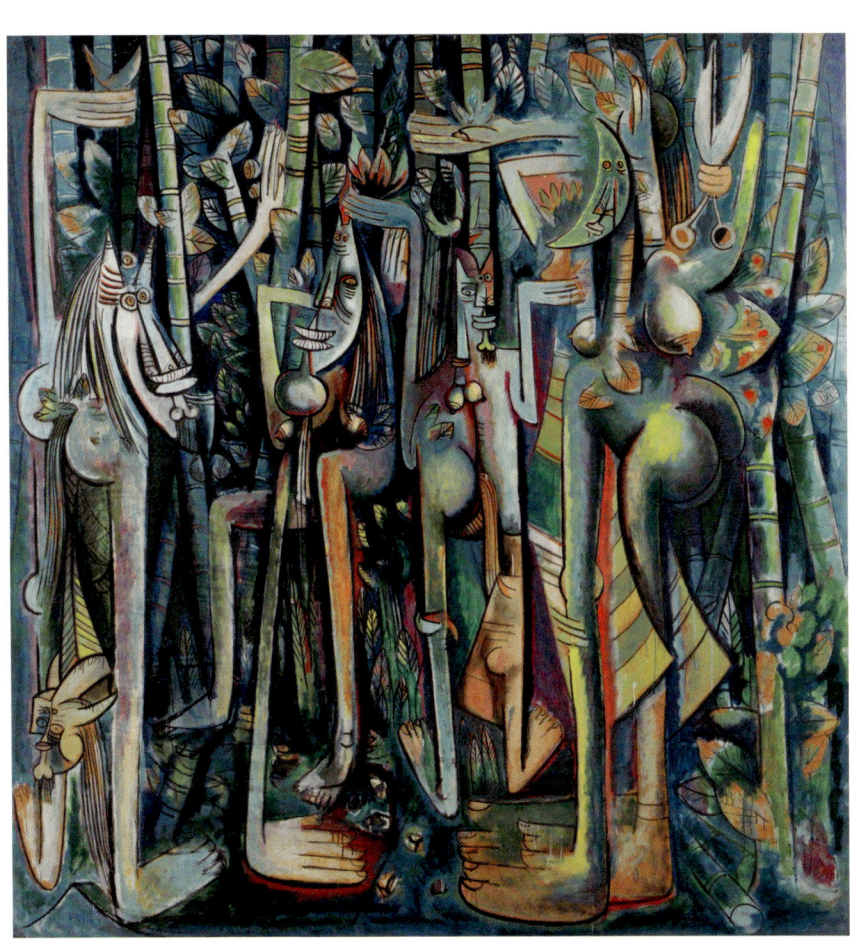

from the formal language of European modernists such as Picasso. It is widely considered his greatest work. *The Jungle* is a monumental painting depicting Afro-Cuban symbols that elaborate on Cuba's complex identities and tragic history of slavery. Like Enwonwu's Ogolo imagery, Lam's painting affords an encounter with the numinous affect of Santería divinities. Lam stated: "In *The Jungle* and in other works I have tried to relocate Black cultural objects in terms of their own landscape and in relation to their own world."[31] In the foreground of the painting, four figures are set against a background of tall bamboo—their long horizontal forms are almost equal in perceived height. Each figure wears a different mask. Bulbous forms emerge from these masked figures, indicating either breasts or buttocks. Read through the lens of Santería, Lam's references emerge. The disembodied head depicted in the lower left corner represents Eleggua (Eṣu), the Orișa tasked with protecting and opening the gate to the spirit world. Eleggua appears to be floating next to or partially connected to a horse-headed figure that stands with one foot planted firmly on the ground and the other raised skyward.[32] This stance is an iconic Kongo ritual pose. In Santería, a worshipper possessed by an Orișa is called the Orișa's horse (*caballo*); the horse-headed figure therefore visually describes, in Santería terminology, someone "ridden" or possessed by an Orișa.[33] On the far right, a tall figure, whose long cylindrical limbs almost mimic the surrounding bamboo, dons a crescent-moon mask. The figure refers to the Orișa Yemana (also Yemanja, from the Yoruba goddess of rivers, Yemoja), who is worshipped as goddess of the oceans in the African diaspora and often identified by celestial symbols such as the half-moon, and a hatchet.[34]

Lam wanted to paint the "drama of Cuba by thoroughly expressing the black spirit, the beauty of the plastic art of the blacks."[35] His focus on Eleggua/Eṣu reflects an ontological diversity in the ethnogenesis of new identities in the African diaspora. For Paula Sato, "Lam's Santería iconography was an important part of his Negritude—his desire to valorize Afro-Cuban cultural elements that were in danger of amputation."[36] However, museums are still reluctant to narrate Lam's reliance on numinous imagery as an essential element of his art. For example, the Museum of Modern Art (MoMA) in New York describes Lam's *The Jungle* by treating it as any other surrealist or cubist painting.[37] Regarding its imagery, MoMA writes: "With their fantastic appearance, they seem as if they could have sprung from the artist's dreams or possibly from his unconscious, the workings of the mind that especially interested the Surrealists."[38] Although it acknowledged his Afro-Cuban background, MoMA reinforced Eurocentric paradigms by narrating *The Jungle* through surrealism, thus effacing Lam's insistence on his art as an act of decolonization.[39] For Lam, "numinous affect" was not just about painting a picture of what decolonizing imagery would look like. It is *invocation*—a call for spiritual powers to affect material realities that challenges the Euro-modernist notion of art for art's sake.

Lam's artworks straddled multiple spaces and temporalities, and as Fernando Ortiz noted, the artist expanded their meanings beyond the

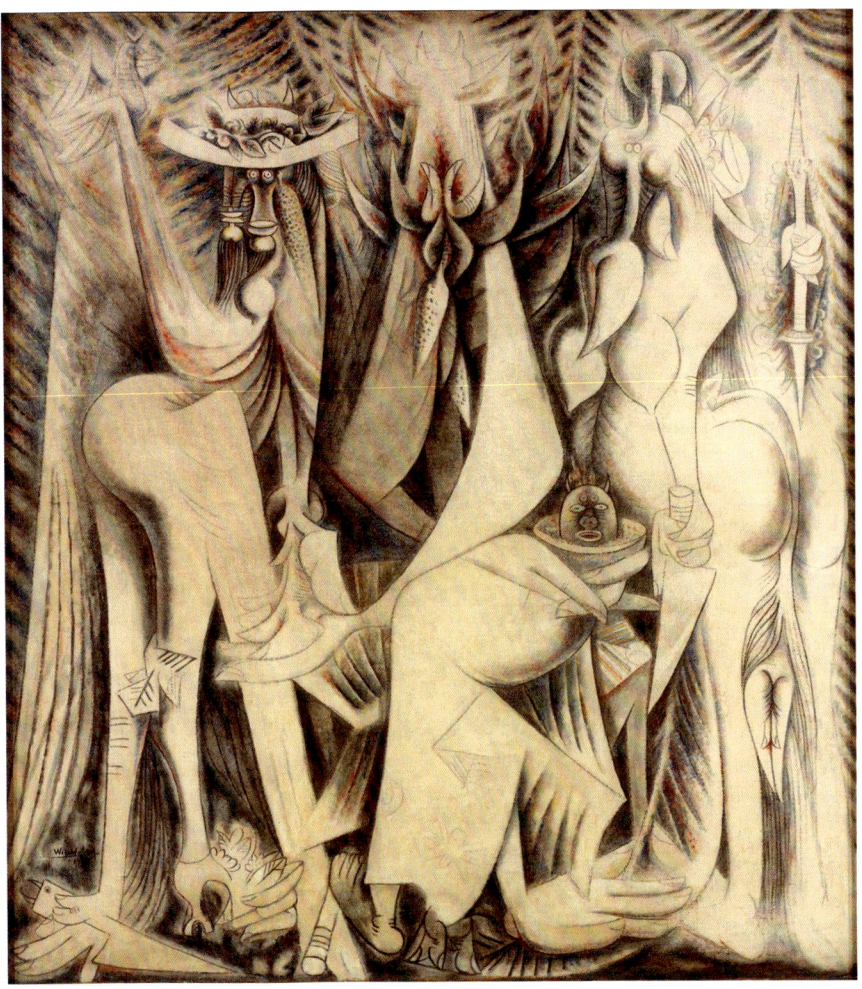

Fig. 7 Wifredo Lam, *Le Présent Éternel* (*The Eternal Present: Homage to Alejandro García Caturla*), 1944, oil on canvas, RISD Museum

© 2019 Artists Rights Society (ARS), New York / ADAGP, Paris

context of Afro-Cuban Santería into a universal pre-theistic aesthetic.[40] Ortiz's effort to tie Lam's paintings to the universal and pre-iconic are contested by Cuban theologian Roberto S. Goizueta, who notes that the universal cannot be made present without the particular. Strategies of interpretation around Lam's oeuvre, he asserts, should avoid the dichotomy between the particular and the universal. After all, it is "the Afro-Cuban iconography, grounded in the temporality and particularity of Lam's diverse conceptual sources, that gives expression to whatever pre-theistic forms are, or are not, present in his paintings."[41]

The interdependence between the particular and universal is brilliantly staged in *Le Présent Éternel* (*The Eternal Present: Homage to Alejandro García Caturla*, 1944, fig. 7), which brings a new understanding to Lam's Santería iconography but also speaks to his socialist political orientation. Alejandro García Caturla was a Cuban composer who, like Lam, championed Creolized Cuban themes. In the painting, according to Michel Leiris, two figures appear on either side of Nature, endowed with a lunar crescent and agricultural attributes. On the left is a double-faced woman with an ear of corn hanging near her eyes, wings sprouting from her rump, a parrot raised on her right hand, and a knife held in her toes. She is "the beast with two mouths . . . the prostitute, the legendary mulatto, the hybrid with disturbing and sophisticated charms, expressing not the union of races but colonial crossbreeding of the Occident and the Tropics."[42] On the right is Africa in the form of an equally fantastic creature armed with a large knife and Şango's scepter in the form of a lightning bolt. She holds another emblem—the sacred Eleggua—close to her body at the level of her bared womb. It is significant that Leiris uses the term "cross-breeding" to describe the mestiza figure on the left and the "mulatto" on the right. As Cuban Blacks, "mulattos" must negotiate between their African roots, represented by the thunderbolt in the upper right-hand corner—symbol of Şango—and the Western world, epitomized by the lure of money, within the twists and turns of their search for the bountiful life symbolized by the ear of corn. The presence of Eleggua, however, suggests a conflation of different dimensions of reality.[43] Here, and across Lam's oeuvre, Eleggua mediates the conjunction of diverse spaces and temporalities.[44] Graceful and dreadful, Eşu/Eleggua straddles the divide between the natural and supernatural worlds, bridges the particular and the universal, and gives presence and particularity to the eternal.

The universal experience of the numinous in Lam's art therefore stems from his reliance on Afro-Cuban religious symbolism. Even if Lam's religious symbols are only suggestive, they nevertheless mediate between the artist and his modernist engagements. As an artist of Afro-Cuban and Chinese descent, Lam's modernist practice is anchored by Black Atlantic spiritual visualities.[45] The spiritual underpinning of his art is often overlooked or deliberately marginalized in art historical analyses that mostly narrate Lam's artworks through his involvement with the New York School, and his relationship with Pablo Picasso and the School of Paris.[46] However, though some of Lam's paintings may appear visually similar to those of Picasso and the surrealists, Lam's work moves beyond such references through his invocation of African-derived forms and symbolism. In this manner, they reflect Eşu's double vision,[47] which in Lam's art merges his personal history and involvement with Santería spiritualities with his Euro-modernist engagements. Resituating Lam within his Afro-Cuban/Santería cultural symbolism reaffirms the numinous affect of his art. His paintings are numinous objects that recode the language of modernist abstraction by merging cubist architectonics with Afro-Cuban spiritual iconography.

Inscribing the Divine: James Hampton

The spectacular scenography of altars, according to Gerardo Mosquera, is perhaps the greatest African American aesthetic/ritual expression in art.[48] In this regard, James Hampton's *The Throne of the Third Heaven of the Nations' Millennium General Assembly* (c. 1950–1964) is a visionary art repository of numinous affect (fig. 8). Hampton's sculptural installation showcases "a unique fusion of Biblical and Afro-American traditional imagery,"[49] and was made from aluminum foil, cardboard boxes, light bulbs, wood scraps, jelly jars, and other items salvaged from trash bins and diverse sources.[50] Hampton assembled the structural and decorative elements of the installation with glue, upholstery tacks, nails, straight pins, and wrapped foil. At its center, he built a seven-foot-tall throne resting on an armchair and towering over the rest of the 180 objects in the ensemble, capped with the words "Fear Not." In the African American context, according to Grey Gundaker and Judith McWillie, "Stools, thrones, and specially constructed seats are associated with visionary experience and sight [that] remind visitors of unseen watchers [and serve as] earthly counterparts of the seats prepared for the faithful in Heaven, or are dedicated to Christ's return in the last days."[51] Hampton's *Throne* is the work to end all such works, a majestic and supernatural vision. The numinous affect of *Throne* is evident not only in the physical throne itself but also in Hampton's extensive written manuscripts, which use an undeciphered, symbol-based language that merges European and African antecedents.[52] Hampton devoted many years to building and assembling this artwork, compelled by his spiritual visions, insights into the biblical Book of Revelation, and his African American cultural heritage of Kongo *Nkisi* traditions in the New World.[53] After long night shifts as a janitor at the General Services Administration, Hampton diligently worked on his elaborate sculpture in a now-razed garage at 1133 N Street NW, in Washington, DC, which he began renting around 1950. It was here that the ensemble was discovered after his death and quickly hailed as a miracle that had emerged out of Hampton's deep isolation and personal connection with God.

Born in 1909 in Elloree, South Carolina, Hampton is frequently categorized as an "outsider" or "outlier" artist. He had no formal art training, and his education was centered on an intricate knowledge of biblical texts and the spiritual visions that he received throughout his life, which he diligently documented in a diary. These inscriptions provided Hampton with a context for making sense of his visions and their messages. The conjoined affect of Hampton's written and visual production helps to situate his practice within the larger context of the Black Atlantic. The characterization of Hampton's *Throne* as "outsider art" upon its reception exemplifies Eurocentric boundary markers that marginalize African and African diaspora artists. Grey Gundaker suggests we use the term "insider" when describing Hampton's important role as a visionary artist, as his artwork "simultaneously indexes African American social worlds and the performance orientation of black expressive culture."[54] Gundaker describes Hampton as a diasporic artist layering African and Western cultures to create installations suffused with spiritual symbolism. She argues that recontextualizing Hampton's writings as disruptive and visionary connects his communicative method with other scripts of African origin, Arabic occult scripts, West African syllabaries, and the Djuka script of Suriname.[55] She notes that "in all these cases, the personal aspect asserts a claim to deep knowledge, and the social asserts a changed world, whether apocalyptically altered or simply revised for the better."[56] When considered through the framework of double consciousness, double vision, and double

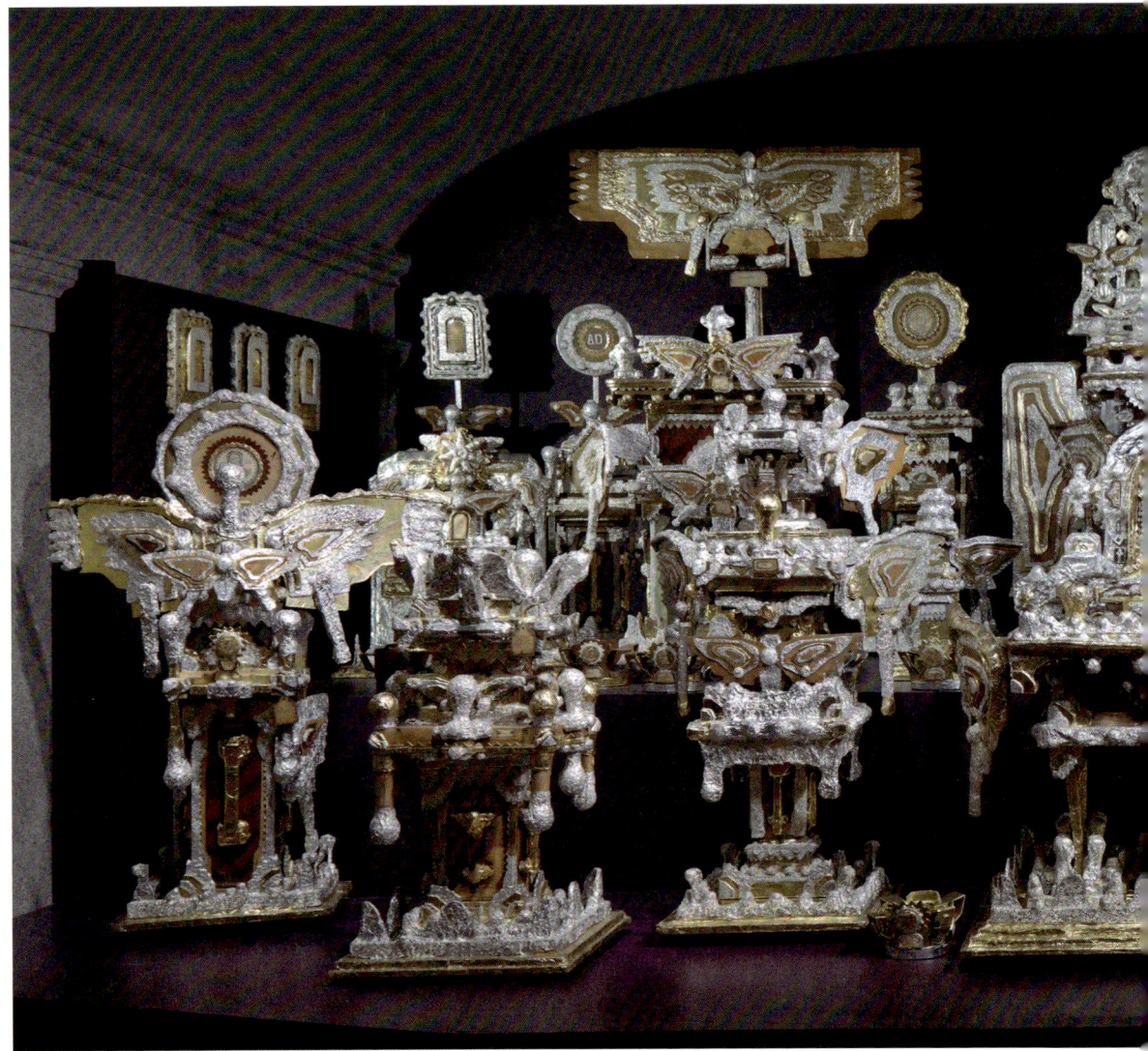

Fig. 8 James Hampton, *The Throne of the Third Heaven of the Nations' Millennium General Assembly*, c. 1950–1964, mixed media, Smithsonian American Art Museum, Gift of Anonymous Donors

voicing, Hampton's symbol-based writing system encodes Black Atlantic religious percepts that link material and metaphysical worlds (fig. 9). They reflect the unique temporalities of African American existence and affirm the art historical significance of the artist's subjective experience.

Hampton's *Throne* is too obviously interpreted as a work of Christian allegory but, if we take the notion of double vision seriously, we might ask what underlying vision of numinous affect the work represents. Hampton wanted to build a church, and it was in Black churches that the deepest heritage of African spiritual knowledge was preserved among African Americans. The protocols of ritual performance that invoked elements of African spirituality were masked by the liturgical order of Christianity. A similar ideal underlies the Santería protocol of masking African deities in the visage of Catholic saints, thus representing Şango, the Yoruba god of thunder, as Santa Bárbara. Several factors thus complicate any interpretation of Hampton's *Throne* as a straightforward allegory of Christian redemption. First, Hampton worked in isolation. He was deeply religious

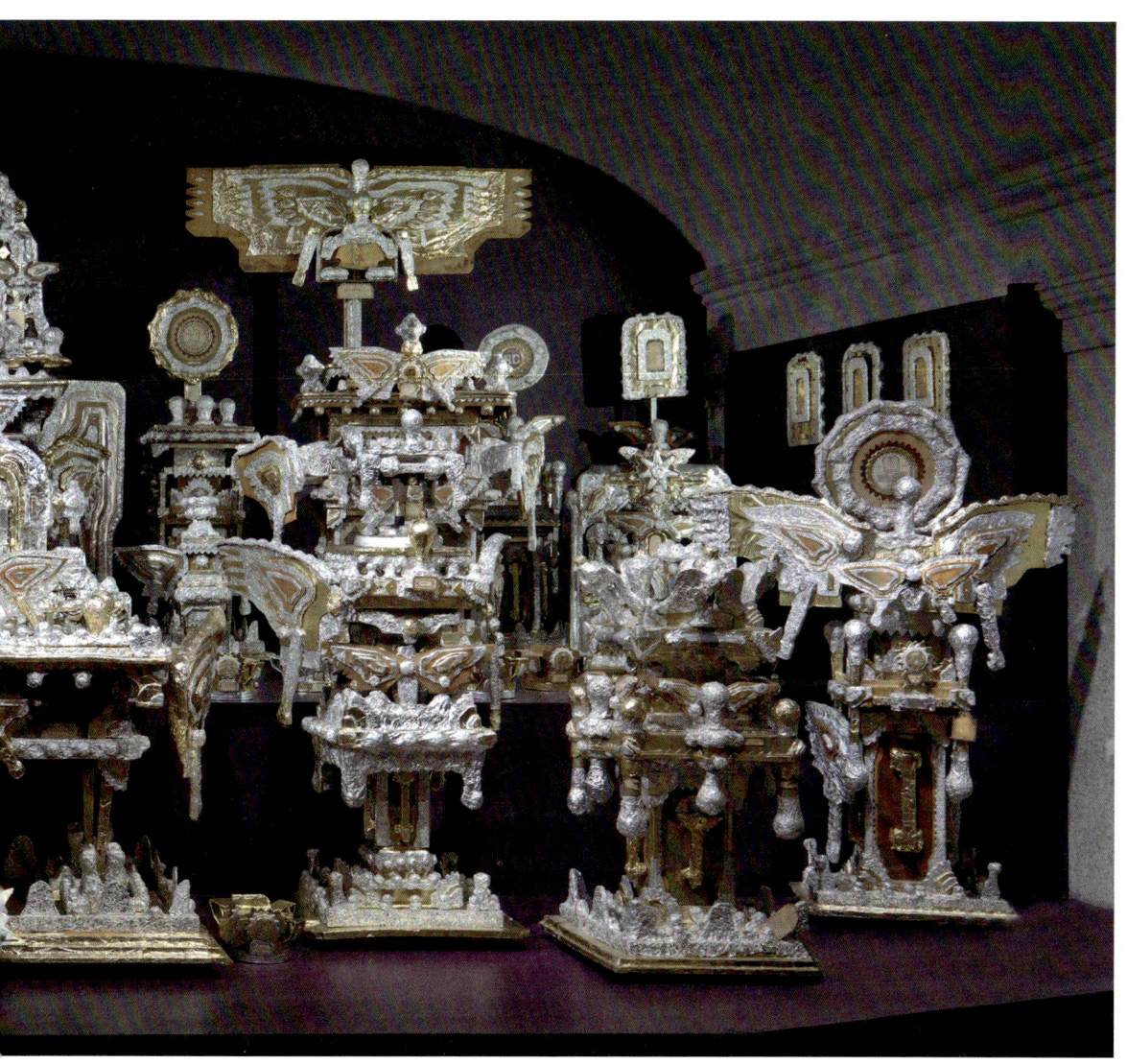

but almost never attended church. Instead, he wanted to use his personal and undecipherable script to create liturgy for a church he planned to build. Second, although produced in isolation, *Throne* has clear historical roots in contemporary African American religiosity. Hampton's move to Washington, DC, from his native South Carolina in 1931 was part of a mass movement of millions of African Americans from the rural American South to urban centers in the Northeast, Midwest, and West. This event, now known as the Great Migration, occurred over several decades from 1880 to 1950. For African Americans, the collective experience of migration was embedded in a larger metaphorical movement from Jim Crow segregation to increased civic participation. The large internal migration changed the demographics and dynamics of various cities as African Americans quickly created socially and culturally vibrant neighborhoods.

The centrality of religion to African American social life made an imprint on the cityscape of Washington, DC, in this period. Churches flourished all over the city, and Hampton drew inspiration from Black

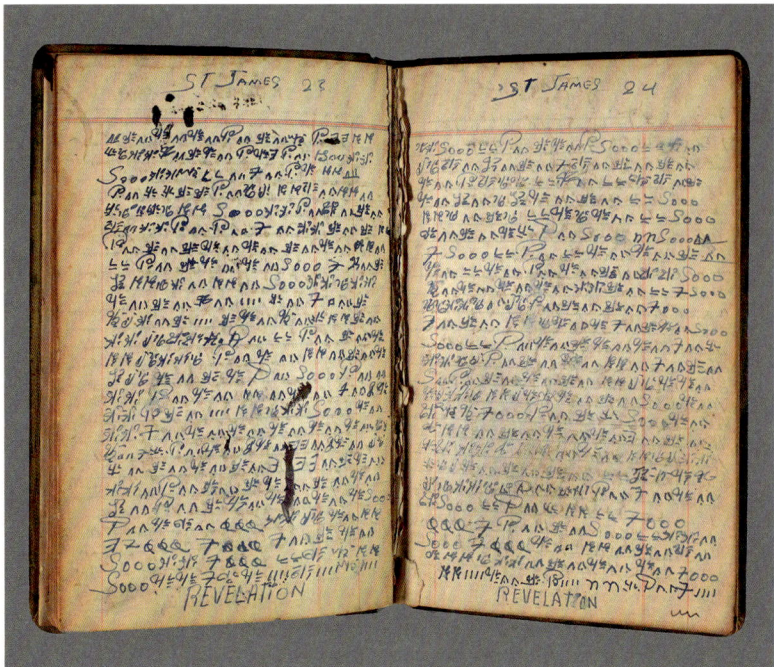

Fig. 9 James Hampton, *The Book of the 7 Dispensation*, c. 1945–1964, commercially printed ledger, cardboard, ink, and foil, Smithsonian American Art Museum, Gift of Harry Lowe

places of worship and the numerous churches of his neighborhood, most of them located in small and simple storefront dwellings. The most important feature of any church was its altar, which was usually fabricated by members of the congregation. In addition, churches would hang a calendar from their altar and place on it hand-lettered signs of warning or comfort, such as "God Is Love." This gesture is similar to the "Fear Not" text that crowns Hampton's ensemble.[57] Hampton also made calendars and signs for *Throne* announcing the return of Christ and communicating prophetic messages. Hampton was undoubtedly sensitive to the charismatic presence of Black religious leaders in Washington, DC, such as A. J. Tyler of the Mount Airy Baptist Church. Tyler's church had an electric sign that read: "Monument to Jesus."[58] Hampton not only inscribed the same phrase on his installation, but also wrote A. J. Tyler's name on it. Charles Manuel "Sweet Daddy" Grace, who had an estimated three million followers nationwide via satellite churches, worked blocks away from Hampton's garage and, most importantly, conducted his famous faith healings and ceremonies from a throne.

If Hampton's *Throne* recalls the interior decoration of Black churches, it also draws on the aesthetic of African American yard sales. More than an occasion to make money or buy goods for a cheap price, yard sales are cultural activities with deep spiritual bearings. According to art historian Robert Farris Thompson, "Icons in the yard may variously command the spirit to move, come in, be kept at bay, be entertained with a richness of images or be baffled with their density, savor sunlight flashing in a colored bottle or be arrested with the contours, and, above all, be healed or entertained by the order and beauty inherent in the improvised arrangement of icon and object."[59] The resemblance between Hampton's *Throne* and African American yards, where one encounters invocations of numinous affect, is striking. Hampton's use of discarded materials to build an altar to sacred divinities also recalls vodou altars. The practice of putting together ritually charged objects in vodou altars symbolizes the combination and assimilation of different beliefs and cultural lineages characterizing Creole identity. Such altars, according to Donald Cosentino, are "models of heaven."[60] Like African masquerades, vodou altars and Hampton's *Throne* shock worshippers into states of heightened awareness necessary for visionary encounter.[61] *Throne* thus reflects diasporic notions of the power of ever-present spirits and the liminal nature of supernatural encounters.

The numinous affect of Hampton's altar stems from the metaphysical identity of the throne, the sacred place where Jesus/the divine Spirit will sit when he/it descends to earth. Not incidentally, it is also the throne of judgment that speaks to African American preoccupation with the ability of divine power to deliver justice for their suffering under various forms of oppression. Christ's holy arrival is both an impalpable and corporeal spiritual experience that can only be apprehended through double vision. As a special power of spiritual comprehension, double vision crosses the boundaries between the material and metaphysical dimensions of reality. Double vision is also exemplified by Hampton's juxtaposition of English and Roman printing in his 108-page loose-leaf notebook titled *The Book of the 7 Dispensation* (fig. 9), as well as on his commandment-bearing tablets. Hampton's undecipherable writing can be understood through his identities as an artist and religious figure of the African diaspora. While some of his manuscripts contain Latin characters and include descriptions of his visions in addition to biblical references, it is possible that these various symbol-based texts, when read aloud, were used to activate the throne and invoke Christ. I use the word "activate" to imply a physical transformation of Hampton's throne from constructed assemblage to numinous object, which transforms Hampton's mysterious script into glossolalia. Through the sonic dimensions of affective speech, Hampton's throne allowed him to communicate with the divine.[62] Therefore, rather than defining Hampton's throne merely as a monument to Christ, we should consider it as an invocation of the divine, enunciated in a similar manner to bottle trees, yard artworks, and Santería shrines. Among African diaspora peoples, numinous inscription combined verbal and visual expression in gestural codes, ideographic renderings of words of power, intricate divination systems, and most importantly, invocations of spirits.[63] The repetitive symbols in Hampton's script can thus be seen as a form of visual chanting used to summon the Spirit. From the viewpoint of Kongo-African visualities, which are iconic in African diaspora religions, Hampton's throne is an *Nkisi*, a numinous object designed to generate and redirect the supernatural power of spiritual entities.[64]

The mystery surrounding Hampton's visionary inscriptions prevents any certitude. It is important to keep in mind, however, that mystery carries significant weight in African and African American cultures. Maintaining secret and esoteric knowledge allowed African diaspora peoples to survive the social death of slavery. Hampton interacted with such mysteries through his prophetic visions, through which he bridged the transitions between his physical reality and a spiritually revealed realm. He endeavored to capture the numinous affect of these transitions in *Throne*, which is best narrated as a pathway to heaven.

Numinous Affect and the Project(s) of Modernism

The concept of numinous affect, as enunciated in this essay, is double-voiced; it speaks not only to the impact of African religious imagery on Black Atlantic modernism but also to the pervasive role of spiritualism in modernism's emergence. The canonical narrative of modernism eschewed the religious or spiritual and framed abstraction as a secular protocol of artistic practice. This interpretation is increasingly untenable since it effaces the significance of earlier investigation of the spiritual in modern art, exemplified in the paintings of Hilma af Klint, and Wassily Kandinsky, whose seminal text—*Concerning the Spiritual in Art*—elucidates a theory of abstraction that centers spirituality as a key element.[65] Recently, scholars such as Thomas Crow have challenged the excision of religion/spirituality from analysis of modern art and argued for its reintegration.[66] I similarly argue that African spiritualities are essential to interpretations of Black Atlantic modernism. The concept of numinous affect enables new interpretations of works by Enwonwu, Lam, and Hampton; dismissing it from analysis forestalls their pursuit of difference and counter-hegemonic subjectivity and further marginalizes Black Atlantic artists that don't conform to, engage with, or otherwise rely on canonical Euro-modernist approaches to modernism. We don't need to wedge African and African diaspora modernists into exclusionary art historical narratives as secondary figures. Instead, we should attend to how they used African-derived forms and symbolism to articulate their modernist identities.

Modernism emerged within a transcultural context of mobility, circulation, networks, and connectivity of artworks, bodies, and ideologies. Its various iterations express notions of local history, spatiality, and temporality.[67] Modernity in this regard describes historical conditions of cultural transformations, and its various modernisms are best interpreted as culturally coded logics of seeing rather than a singular or normative protocol of representation. The canonical narrative of modernism, despite its appropriation of African, Asian, Oceanic, and Native American forms, is insular and dismissive of divergent forms and contexts. Eṣu hermeneutics ruptures such closed narratives. Its focus on indeterminacy, multiplicity, and double-voicedness asserts the agency of Black Atlantic artists and foregrounds how African spiritual registers frame their unique logic of modern art.

Artist and art historian Moyo Okediji suggests analyzing modernism as part of a larger hybrid global dialogue.[68] However, problems of definition plague our understanding of the spatiality and temporality of African and African diaspora modernism. Despite recent scholarship challenging established definitions of Blackness, we still don't have an agreed term to describe the artistic and cultural production of Black artists in the transatlantic world.⁶⁹ Scholarly interrogation of the category "Black" has also not produced a succinct definition.⁷⁰ Art history continues to marginalize the importance of numinous vision and African spiritual registers in interpretations of modern art. Sonal Khullar notes that over the past decade, art historians have enriched and expanded what we understand as modernism to include discourses and practices outside of the established narrative of developments in Paris and New York, such as those in Brazil, China, Eastern Europe, Iran, Japan, Mexico, Nigeria, Senegal, Pakistan, and Vietnam.⁷¹ However, these emergent discourses are often bogged down in questions of definition, and what Kobena Mercer has derided as the "the traditional art historical concern with primordiality—who did or said what first."⁷² According to Mercer, "Avoidance of close attention to modernist practices on the part of non-Western and minority artists throughout the twentieth century as a whole is reinforced by a predominant critique of Eurocentrism that endlessly returns the discussion to Western artists and institutions."⁷³ The great failing of recent work on the subject is therefore the continued marginalization of longstanding efforts to foreground the status of African and African diaspora subjects in the metaphysics of modernity.

The idea that we need to insert Black Atlantic artists into established narratives of modernism locates African and African diaspora subjects outside history and limits analysis to arguments about whether they can be included. I argue that Black Atlantic artists were foundational to the transcultural context of mobility, circulation, networks, and connectivity of artworks, bodies, and ideologies within which modernity, modernism, and all variants of modern art emerged. Paul Gilroy builds on this idea by positing a distinctively modern, transatlantic cultural-political space that is not specifically African, American, Caribbean, or British, but rather a hybrid mix of all these identities at once.⁷⁴ We will do well to interpret all participants in this transatlantic world as diasporic populations.

Conclusion

The oeuvres of Ben Enwonwu, Wifredo Lam, and James Hampton highlight convergent notions of numinous affect and the transactional nature of human/spirit interaction in African and African diaspora cultures. In these contexts, spirits are here and now, the worlds of ancestors and the living interact, and spiritual matters are enmeshed with purposeful, practical action. The three Black Atlantic artists discussed in this essay foregrounded African spiritual registers in their art. To fully understand and properly interpret their artworks, we must look to Mosquera's notion of metamorphosis, which posits that gods are not represented but embodied. Enwonwu's masquerades, Lam's Afro-Cuban Santería imagery, and the *Nkisi* altars of James Hampton channel the numinous affect of African spiritualities, encoded in Eṣu's double-voice. Understanding this code is vital to future interpretations of Black Atlantic modernism.

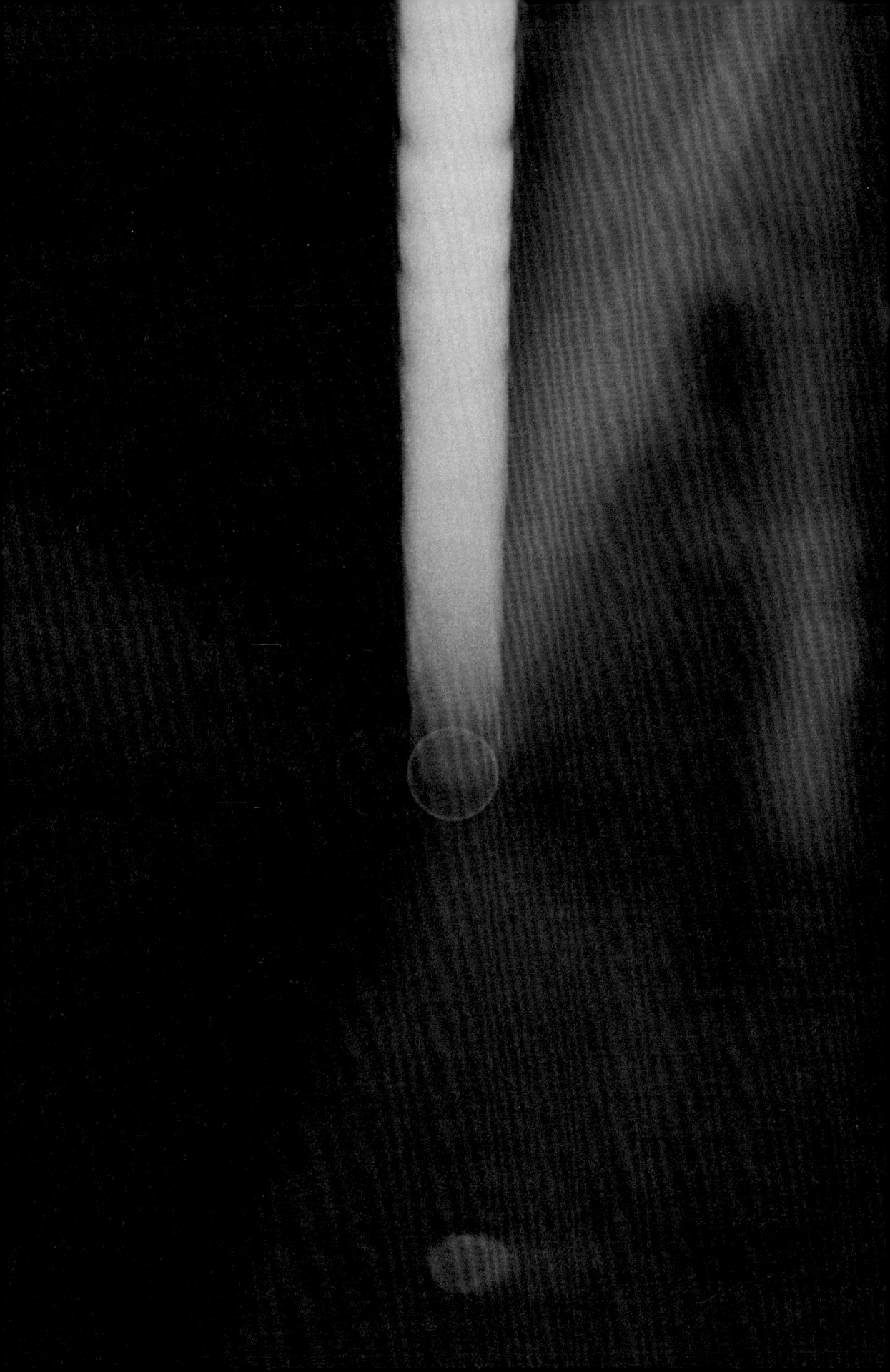

DARKNESS AND THE *UNVISIBLE*: NORMAN LEWIS, ROY DECARAVA, AND POSTWAR ABSTRACTION

KOBENA MERCER

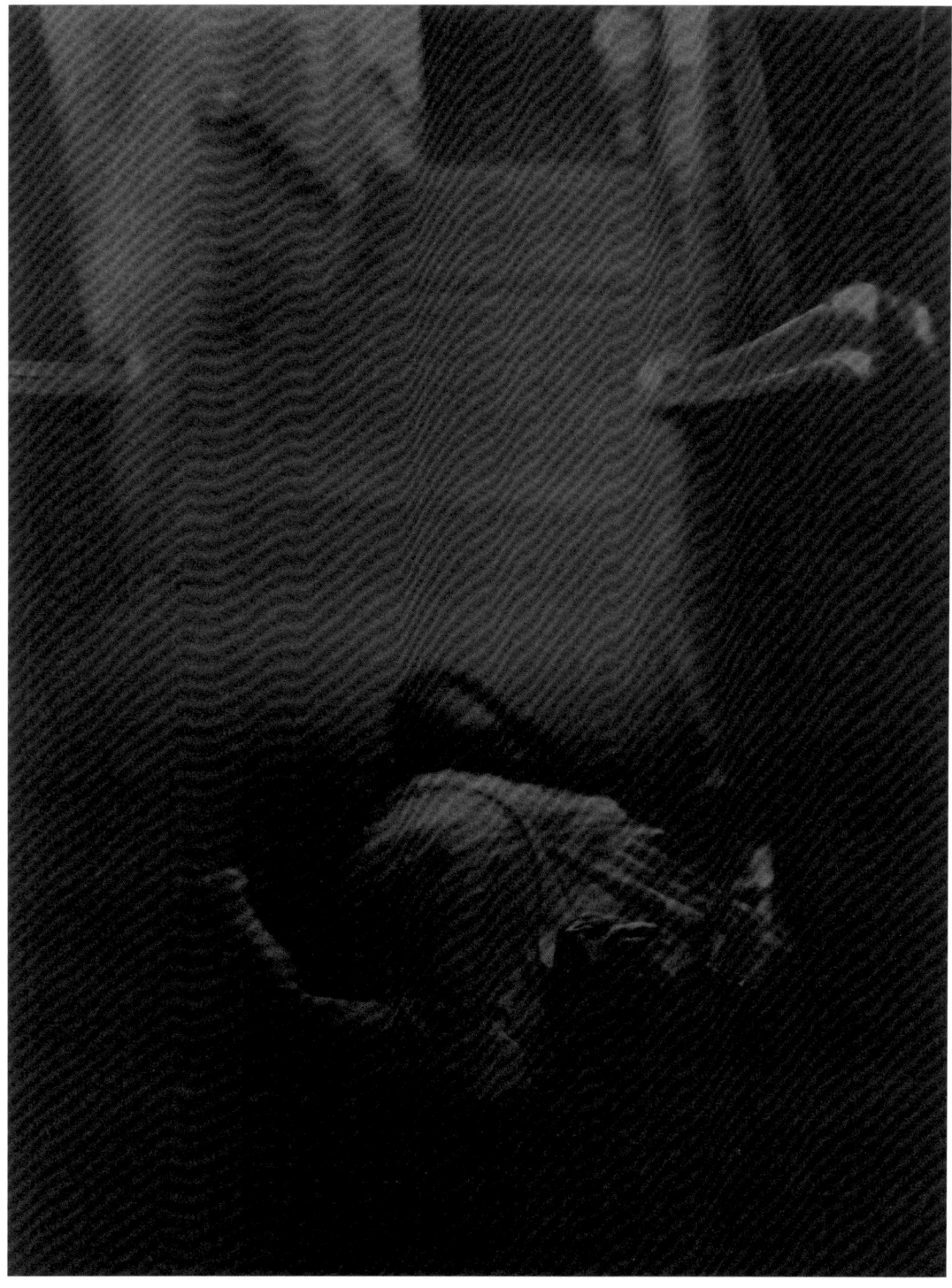

Fig. 1 Roy DeCarava, *Man lying down, subway steps*, 1965

© Sherry Turner DeCarava and the DeCarava Estate. Courtesy of the Roy and Sherry DeCarava Archives

The interplay of darkness and light was a defining concern that painter Norman Lewis (1909–1979) shared in common with photographer Roy DeCarava (1919–2009). Both artists mobilized abstraction to investigate blackness in ways that were inseparably aesthetic and political. But understanding why dark colors and shadowy tones pervade their work is too often circumscribed by a color symbolism approach that interprets a palette of black and white as automatically referring to raced identities. To come away from abstract art with a figurative reading is not only reductive, but also, when the quest to find a referent assumes black color can have only "one" possible meaning, such an approach shuts down the plurality of meanings put into play by blackness as a perceptual phenomenon. Shifting our interpretive standpoint a few degrees—with black and white now also considered as perceptual qualities of shadow and luminosity—allows for a fresh set of analytical moves that turn from a representationalist outlook toward a phenomenological one when we study Black modernist abstraction.

"I tend to work toward a softer tonality . . . I am not a contrasty printer," said DeCarava when asked why he chose available light, which often rendered his prints dark and at times made the subjects in his photographs difficult to see. Rejecting documentary photography's demand for the instant legibility of the "'perfect' information laden print," DeCarava's tendencies toward abstraction resist the assumption that Black life can be visually consumed in the blink of an eye. His investment in shadow—"Many times it comes out dark because I like the full tonality. The soft tonality reveals more," he said—makes us look closer.[1] Abstracting clear-cut geometric lines into floating tonal contours, *Man lying down, subway steps* (1965, fig. 1) decomposes the figure/ground differential to such an extent that one could overlook the Black man crumpled in the foreground. As glints of light bounce off railings that direct the eye to the dark patch at the top of the picture, which is a subway entrance, one realizes that the upside-down figure is no accidental snapshot, but a trope bearing witness to the ways Black life goes unrecognized. Lying prone "beneath" our gaze as diagonals orient our looking toward the rear, where an anthropomorphic shape emerges, the borderline legibility of this almost indecipherable figure makes us aware of what ordinarily goes unseen. To pair such a photograph with Lewis's *Orpheus* (1953, fig. 2), as both evoke subterranean realms, is to say the dark tonalities of Lewis's abstract painting also invite the beholder's perceptual immersion, urging attentiveness to an interplay of line, shape, and color that cannot be fully captured in a single glance.

The prevalence of black color in Lewis's oeuvre is widely noted, but when interpretation proceeds by asking what it symbolizes, the very notion of "symbolism" is at fault. It sets out to establish correspondences between form and content even though abstraction undermines any mimetic conception of meaning-making. In place of asking "What does blackness stand for?"—a representationalist question that assumes a dualism in which two unalike elements enter into one-to-one correspondence—the

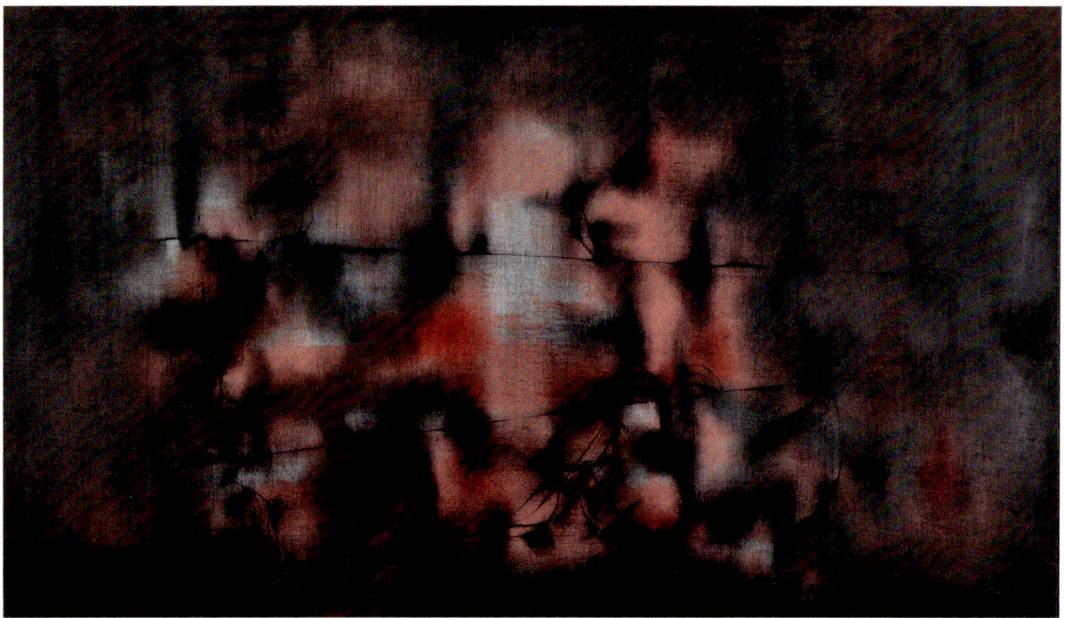

Fig. 2 Norman Lewis, *Orpheus*, 1953, oil on canvas

© Estate of Norman Lewis. Courtesy of Michael Rosenfeld Gallery LLC, New York, NY

phenomenological question that asks, "What does blackness do?" redirects our attention to the affective dimension of an artwork's sensory impact on embodied viewers. Insofar as Lewis and DeCarava used darkness to make us look closer, putting the beholder's vision under strain, to what extent did their Black modernist modes of abstraction question the epistemological privilege of sight in Western modernity? Did the paths taken by Lewis and DeCarava intersect with Ralph Ellison's *Invisible Man* (1952), whose narrator dwells in an underground realm as he also questions an ocular-centric worldview in which blackness signifies only negation? Ellison, Lewis, and DeCarava were close—abstract artist Jack Whitten "knew Ellison personally, through their mutual friends Norman Lewis and Roy DeCarava," writes one curator—but rather than biography it is their aesthetic commitment to the nexus of race, darkness, and vision that drives my inquiry.[2]

Where recent shifts toward phenomenological methods of inquiry have decentered the formalist emphasis on medium-specificity that rendered African American artists marginal to previous studies of postwar abstraction, curators have reset the interpretive context. Asking, "What is it that a black object does?" Pace Gallery's exhibition *Blackness in Abstraction* (2016) drew on the performative turn to foreground the materiality of the art object over questions of identity; it was followed by Tate Modern's *Soul of a Nation* (2017), whose pan-medium approach to "Black abstraction" placed DeCarava full square in a narrative arc that began with Lewis and reached forward to Mel Edwards, Howardena Pindell, and others in the 1960s and since.[3] As I pursue insights opened up by this paradigmatic shift I nonetheless want to sidestep a zero-sum view that regards the representational approach to art's production of meaning as now outmoded or superseded by the contemporary turn toward ontology. Whereas inquiry into an artwork's material conditions of existence in the world counteracts the view that meaning is solely a matter of cognition, I suggest that attending to the sensorial and affective dimension does not dispense with issues of representation, but rather deepens our understanding of how Black modernist practices of abstraction contested the ocular-centrism that saw blackness only as negation.

Taking Lewis's "lifelong dedication to exploring the relation of darkness and vision" as her guiding research question, Ann Eden Gibson showed that dominant meanings ascribed to blackness have been challenged and re-signified in counter-discourses articulated by W. E. B. Du Bois, as well as Theodor Adorno, Frantz Fanon, and Toni Morrison, among others. Interpreting Lewis's abstraction as a similar quest to unfix the semiotics of blackness from the discursive chains of equivalence and the codes of mimetic correspondence to which it had been historically bound, Gibson took this representationalist line of inquiry as far as it could go when she concluded that Lewis "succeeded in turning blackness[,] a trope of invisibility, of absence, into a presence. Lewis did not see the action of darkness as simply a cancellation, or as nothingness—the opposite of presence—but as the visual manifestation of situations full of presences unseen and coming into being."[4] Put another way: once blackness is no longer the opposite of anything, it becomes a site of multiplicity—where unforeseeable possibilities come into being—by virtue of being set loose from dualistic codes. But where some performative approaches often entail a presentism that de-historicizes the artwork in order to focus on perceptual encounter, two issues ask us to consider how we might combine the ontological turn with attention to the process of "coming into being" that Gibson underscores.

First, the nexus of race, darkness, and vision is period-specific in that calling the primacy of sight into question was a response to the lethal light emitted on August 6 and 9, 1945, when the United States military dropped atomic bombs on Hiroshima and Nagasaki, historic events that prompted responses from numerous abstract artists.[5] Second, to the extent that darkened spaces in Lewis's paintings and DeCarava's photographs are "vestibular spaces," in Hortense J. Spillers's sense of spaces of emergent possibility in an oppressive social and symbolic order, how do we account for the temporality whereby moments of Black modernist rupture hitherto ignored by formalist narratives have become intelligible only under contemporary conditions?[6] Looking first at the divergent meanings blackness held for Lewis and fellow abstract painter Ad Reinhardt (1913–1967), I provide a fresh interpretive context in which to see how darkness and luminosity in Lewis's signature abstract works connect with the shadowy tonal depths of DeCarava's photographs.

Blackness Taken in Contrary Directions

Lewis sat across the table from Reinhardt at the Artists' Sessions at Studio 35 in April 1950 (fig. 3). When Lewis raised the question of how abstract art reaches the public, Reinhardt was the only one to respond—both artists

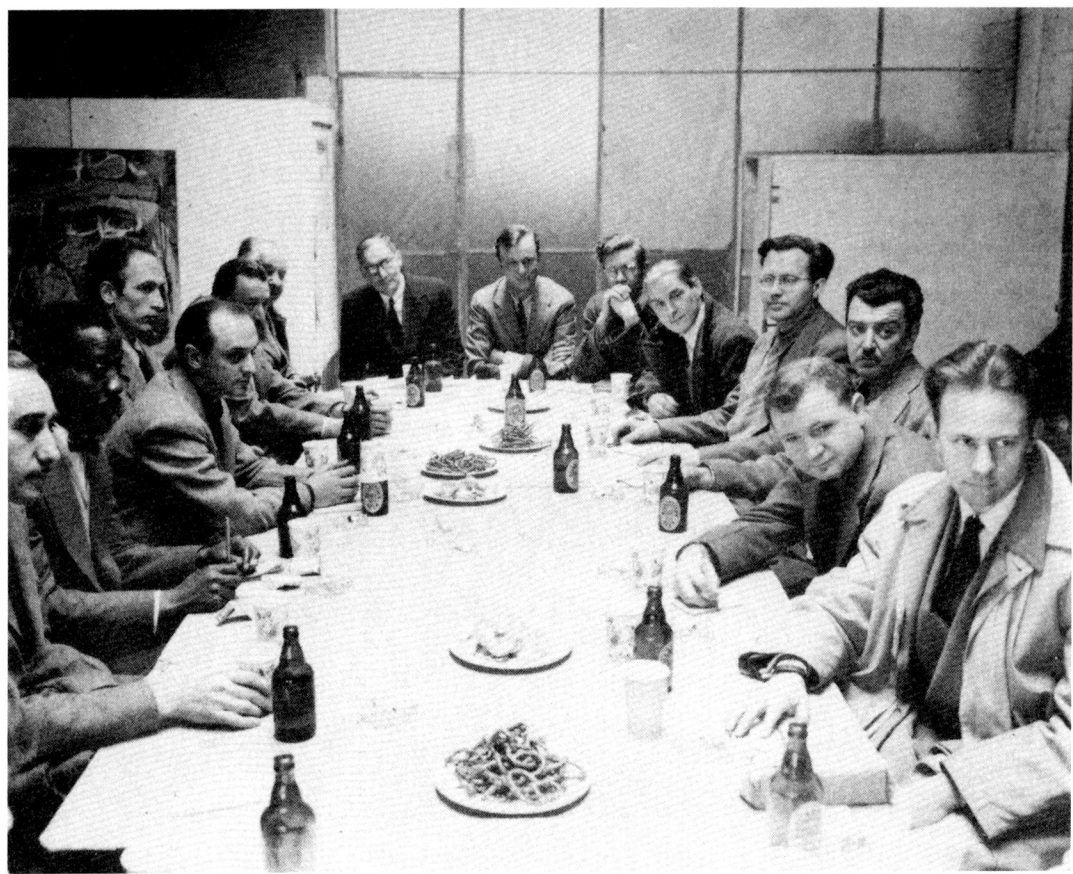

Fig. 3 Artists' Sessions at Studio 35, 1950, Museum of Modern Art Library, New York. Norman Lewis is second from the left, Ad Reinhardt is second from the right.

Courtesy of Wittenborn Art Books, San Francisco, www.art-books.com. Photo by Max Yavno. Digital image © The Museum of Modern Art / Licensed by Scala / Art Resource, NY

were at odds with the prevailing discourse on abstract art in the 1950s. Lewis evoked the Federal Art Project era when he voiced his concern:

> People no longer have this intimacy with the artists, so the public does not actually know what is going on, what is being done by the painter. I remember organizing for a union on the waterfront. People didn't know the function of a union, or what was good about it, but gradually they were made aware of it. . . . The same is true of our relationship with the people: in making them aware of what we are doing.

After Reinhardt reiterated, "Exactly what is our involvement, our relation to the outside world? I think everybody should be asked to say something about this," moderator Alfred Barr Jr. noted, "Apparently many people don't want to answer the question."[7]

Having met in the 1930s as members of the Artist's Union, the two next crossed paths in various art world settings, as well as when Lewis and Reinhardt both briefly taught at the Thomas Jefferson School of Social Science, an adult education center in New York City run by the Communist Party from 1944 to 1956. With Lewis having participated in the Harlem artist's group that met at 306 West 141st Street under the direction of Charles Alston, with Federal Art Project (FAP) support, many of his fellow

Black artists such as Gwendolyn Bennett, Elizabeth Catlett, and Charles White also taught at the Jefferson School in the 1940s.[8] Lewis's concurrent membership of the Civil Rights Congress, however, led to his investigation by the House Un-American Activities Committee, who saw the CRC as a front for the Communist Party. Lewis quit teaching at Jefferson in 1949, the same year he relocated his studio from 28th Street to 125th Street, which was also the year he joined Marian Willard's gallery. With six solo shows at Willard between 1949 and 1964, Lewis had a vocal presence in the 1950 Artists' Sessions that undercuts the simplistic historiographic view that Black artists were either included or excluded from the New York school of abstraction. The silence he encountered at the Artists' Sessions had everything to do with the Cold War climate in which any mention of 1930s activism was regarded not just as partisan, but as off-limits in discourse on abstract art that aspired to universality by avoiding topics—how art reaches the public, for instance—that might be contentious.

Lewis enjoyed success in the 1950s—exhibiting in *Abstract Painting and Sculpture in America* at the Museum of Modern Art, New York (MoMA), in 1951, and in *American Artists Paint the City*, a themed exhibition curated at the Art Institute of Chicago and shown at the 1956 Venice Biennale—yet the era's official discourse of color-blind universalism served to silence diversity.[9] The Artists' Sessions began in 1948 when Robert Motherwell, Mark Rothko, and others organized weekly talks on the "Subjects of the Artists" in a loft at 35 East 8th Street. Hale Woodruff, an African American painter, was one of three New York University professors (Robert Inglehart and Tony Smith were the others) to direct the 1949–1950 sessions, yet with no available discourse for cultural diversity, Black artists experienced conflicted conditions. Racial liberalism prevailed in an era when desegregation was on the agenda, but assimilation remained the unspoken expectation.

It is instructive to note Reinhardt's stance with regard to Black artists as differentiated from his painting's engagement with black color. His 1946 cartoon *How to Look at Modern Art in America* (fig. 4) visualizes modernism as a tree from whose trunk various branches sprouted on an "abstract" to "social-surrealist" continuum, with some weighed down by "business as art patron" above a field in which brands such as Pepsi-Cola signified mass culture as corny. With Lewis and Romare Bearden on the third branch from the left, plus Jacob Lawrence farther to the right in a leaf above which flies a bird named for Horace Pippin, African American artists were fully part of Reinhardt's left-leaning standpoint. Concerned that modernism's ability to critique the status quo was becoming compromised as a result of its uptake by the culture industries, Reinhardt's 1953 essay "Twelve Rules for a New Academy" castigated artists who accepted opportunities created by advertising and design industries that ingested abstract art as a mere "academic" style. On the one hand, his tongue was surely in cheek when Reinhardt's absurd rules declared "the fine art studio should be . . . twenty-five feet wide and thirty feet long . . . the fine artist need not sit cross-legged." But, on the other hand, when his black monochrome grids such as *Abstract Painting No. 5* (1962, fig. 5)

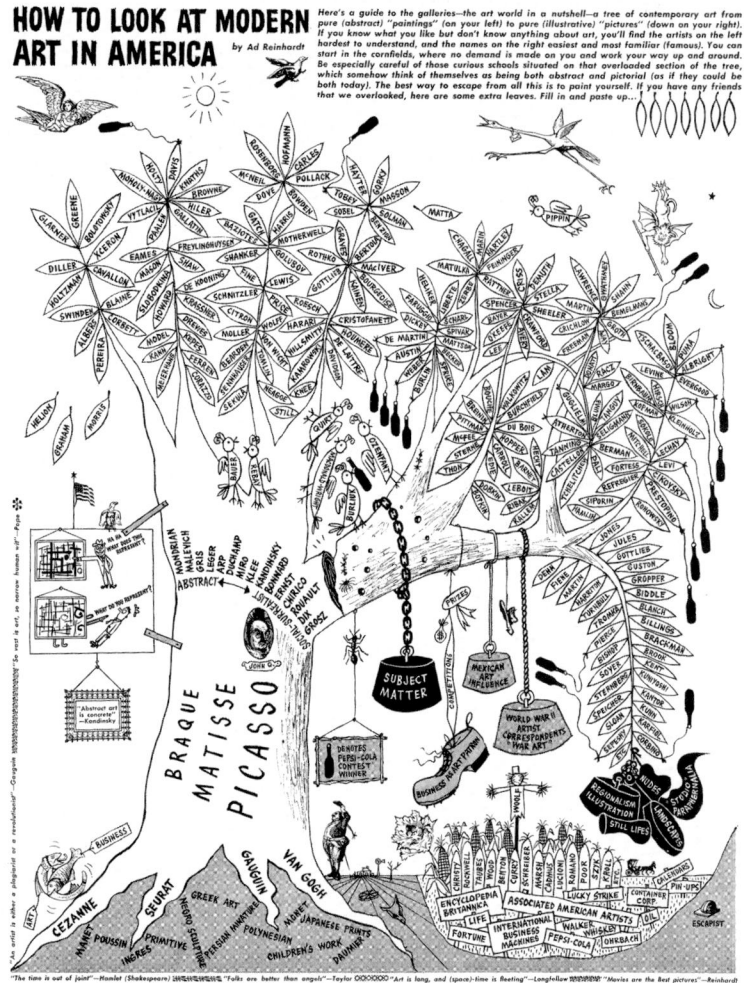

Fig. 4 Ad Reinhardt, *How to Look at Modern Art in America*, June 2, 1946

© 2019 Estate of Ad Reinhardt / Artists Rights Society (ARS), New York. Courtesy of David Zwirner

put the doctrine into practice—Reinhardt produced nothing else from 1957 to his death in 1967—his equation of blackness with negation ("no texture . . . no brushwork . . . no forms . . . no colors . . . no object, no subject, no matter") disclosed an all-or-nothing absolutism that bordered on the authoritarian.[10]

Claiming that "fine art can only be defined as exclusive, negative, absolute, and timeless," Reinhardt sought to leap into an ahistorical realm of pure autonomy in which art "is not . . . subservient to anything else."[11] There was draconian finality in Reinhardt's claim that "I'm merely making the last paintings anyone could make."[12] Yet in this scenario, where black color signified the death of painting, to equate blackness solely with negativity was to reproduce the logic of antiblackness within a practice of abstraction-as-endgame, whereas Lewis, for his part, used black color in ways more attuned to ambivalence than absolutism.

For Lewis 1949 marked several breaks. Unlike the semi-figurative work in his first solo show, Lewis's second Willard one-person exhibition in 1951 foregrounded his transition into full-blown abstraction. Indeed, in 1949 Lewis left his 28th Street studio after he "discovered that despite the fact

Fig. 5 Ad Reinhardt, *Abstract Painting No. 5*, 1962, oil on canvas, Tate, London, presented by Mrs. Rita Reinhardt through the American Federation of Arts 1972

© 2019 Estate of Ad Reinhardt / Artists Rights Society (ARS), New York. Photo © Tate, London 2019

that these were a bunch of left-wing artists . . . I was paying twice as much rent as they." These "left-wing artists" included "a very good friend of mine [who] just died, Ad Reinhardt" as well as "Jackson Pollock, Franz Kline, Barney Newman, Jackson Pollock's wife [Lee Krasner]." Lewis added, in this 1968 interview, that "their problems and mine never coincided despite the fact that we were fighting for, say, a better world . . . [as] I was constantly being investigated by the FBI."[13] At this turning point, in which Lewis realigned his positioning as a Black artist, his working methods also placed him at odds with the era's two influential paradigms of art criticism.

In contrast to Harold Rosenberg's notion of action painting, which led to a psychologizing interpretation of abstract art as the outpouring of an inner self, Lewis worked methodically in series.[14] Gibson distinguishes the Tenements, Geometrics, and Structures series of the 1940s and 1950s from the Rituals, Dark Vistas, and Atmospherics of the 1960s and 1970s.[15] Putting variations of line, color, shape, and texture through multiple combinations, Lewis was an abstract permutationalist more so than an abstract expressionist. His 1946 mission statement stressed combinatorial procedures, as he laid out his conception of art as "an activity of discovery

[that] seeks to find hitherto ignored or unknown combinations of forms, colors, and textures . . . and perhaps to cause new types of experience in the artist as well as the viewer."[16] Committed to experimentation, Lewis thus distanced himself from the eliminative drive toward purity that was paramount in Clement Greenberg's formalist criticism, in which art was to take art itself as its only subject matter in its quest to achieve medium-specific self-consciousness.[17] As an artist who did not regard social commitment and painterly experiment as either/or choices, and who did not treat abstract and figurative as mutually exclusive, Lewis was gradually eclipsed from art historical narratives based on the "rhetoric of purity."[18] Looking closely at how blackness features in his abstract painting, Lewis's combinational performance of autotelic mark-making with brushstrokes and patterns that are also referentially suggestive, is best described as a hybrid mode of abstraction that fits well with Jean-François Lyotard's concept of "the figural," defined as indeterminate inscriptions that generate affective intensities in the beholder by breaking down categorical codifications of sensory experience.[19]

Atomic Light: Abstraction at the Limits of Vision

Moving "a loaded stroke first in one direction, then another," white and black pigment activates a flickering luminosity in *Every Atom Glows: Electrons in Luminous Vibration* (1951, fig. 6). As angular vertical shapes pull forward from rear-ground amorphous swirls in a pattern "not unlike sewing," as Gibson notes, Lewis "stitches his forms together, cell by cell, atom by atom" to imply a cosmology in which such stitching is "analogous to the building blocks of the universe."[20] At one scale, the painting evokes the vast macrocosm of a galaxy punctuated by glowing stars. But the pulsating tonalities are also enlargements of the microscopic warp and weft of the canvas support. Picking up on Lewis's interest in science, Katy Siegel reads *Every Atom Glows* as answering the enigma of what makes stars shine—thermonuclear fusion, the same principle by which atomic energy is detonated. In the figural ambivalence by which it "linked the wondrous and the disastrous," a closer look reveals how Lewis was being socially responsive to the world-historical event of atomic power, while at the same time playing with painterly processes to produce perceptual effects of luminous shimmer.[21]

"We all loved Einstein," said Lewis's then partner, Joan Murray (later Weissman), "but we had a lot of trouble loving him and knowing he had discovered the thing that could cause this destruction."[22] Many shared the existential dread provoked by atomic energy's destructive powers, but in the repressive climate of McCarthyism that made such anxieties unspeakable, we need to notice the source for Lewis's title. It hints at a philosophical outlook that *Every Atom Glows* enacts in its very figurality. With titles of twelve of the seventeen works in his 1951 solo show taken from poems by Ralph Waldo Emerson, the closing lines of Emerson's "Nature"—"Spirit that lurks each form within / Beckons to spirit

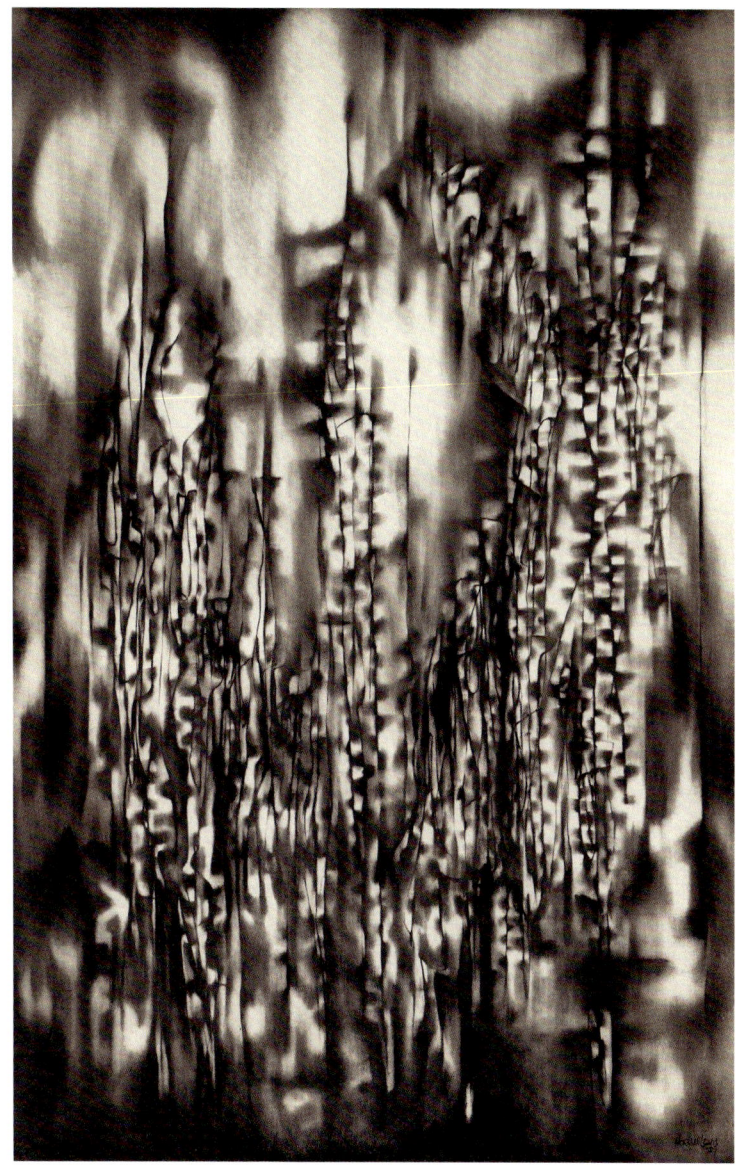

Fig. 6 Norman Lewis, *Every Atom Glows: Electrons in Luminous Vibration*, 1951, oil on canvas, Museum of Fine Arts, Boston, The John Axelrod Collection— Frank B. Bemis Fund, Charles H. Bayley Fund, and The Heritage Fund for a Diverse Collection

Photo © 2023 Museum of Fine Arts, Boston

of its kin / Self-kindled every atom glows / And hints the future which it owes"—distill a worldview in which spirit is immanent to nature rather than dwelling in a transcendental realm dualistically opposed to that of mortal humans.[23] Contrary to the view that interprets Lewis's full-blown abstraction, in 1951, as "a decision to divorce his political activities from his art," Emerson's worldview offered not a retreat into mysticism but a quest for an alternative to the dualistic mentality of the West's foundational dichotomies—Aristotle's form/matter, Plato's appearance/essence, Newton's energy/substance, Descartes's mind/body—in an era when atomic energy's capacity for total planetary extinction demanded new ways of envisioning future human survival.[24]

In December 1951 Einstein was a witness for the defense in the trial of W. E. B. Du Bois. As chair of the Peace Information Center, Du Bois circulated a petition against nuclear warfare, the Stockholm Appeal, which won

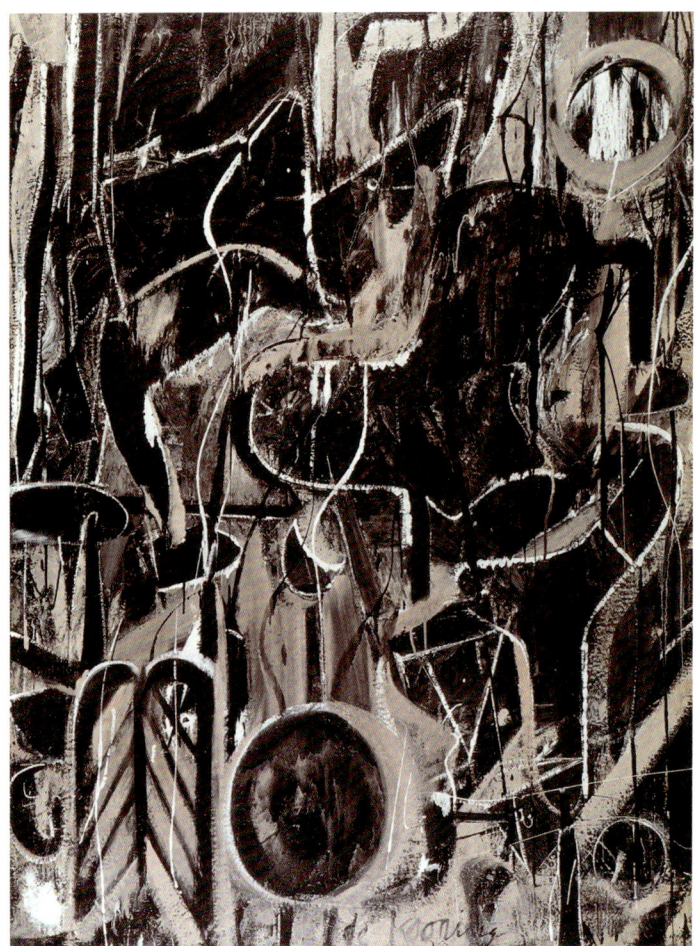

Fig. 7 Willem de Kooning, *Light in August*, 1946, oil on canvas, Museum of Contemporary Art, Tehran

© 2019 The Willem de Kooning Foundation / Artists Rights Society (ARS), New York. Image © akg-images / André Held

2.5 million American signatures. Such activism resulted in government charges of being a foreign agent and the seizure of his passport, although all charges were later dropped. "We have always thought of science as the emancipator," wrote Du Bois in 1945, but in the face of the atom bomb "we now see it as the enslaver of mankind," and Du Bois's standpoint was echoed when "Simple," Langston Hughes's journalistic persona in the *Chicago Defender*, pointed out the racialized character of the genocidal event that ended World War II—"They did not want to use them on white folks. Germans is white . . . Japs is colored."[25]

The splitting of the atom tore apart the Newtonian view that the atom was indivisible. However, voices in the Black public sphere, as Du Bois and Hughes indicate, took distinct emphases from mainstream responses, such as when Willem de Kooning linked race and atomic power in *Light in August* (1946, fig. 7). Borrowing his title from William Faulkner's 1932 novel, de Kooning's black and white shapes are not so much figural as jarringly expressive of conflicted feeling. Where Siegel shows that the threat of nuclear apocalypse revived Puritan traditions of prophetic thinking in post-1945 America, de Kooning (who was not himself religious) evoked the end-time moment of Rapture with both urgency and irony when, in a 1951 talk at MoMA, he said:

> Today, some people think that the light of the atom bomb will change the concept of painting once and for all. The eyes that actually saw the light melted out of sheer ecstasy. For one instant, everybody was the same color. It made angels out of everybody. A truly Christian light, painful but forgiving.[26]

Atomic light's destructive power was a source of redemptive suffering for such end-time absolutism, a blinding light creating raceless angels; whereas for Black modernists the issue of surviving a life-threatening catastrophe did not foretell a future apocalypse, but one that had already happened, at the very dawn of modernity, with the world-shattering Middle Passage that transported Black peoples into diaspora.

Unlike the antinuclear positions conveyed when the atom bomb's mushroom cloud was made into an icon—which implied that its destructive power could be tamed and contained by the representational frame of an image—Lewis did not adopt a straightforwardly oppositional stance of protest. Rather, figurality in *Every Atom Glows* opened a space in which relations among science, destruction, and modernization could be thought anew from a Black diasporic point of view. Lewis's painterly means of breaking through to such a space was *sfumato*, a quattrocento term for a mode of painting "without lines or borders" in which pigment seems "to evaporate like smoke."[27] Just as the electrons highlighted in the painting's subtitle allude to subatomic particles that cannot be seen by the eye, only detected by their radiating energy—in microcosmic counterpoint to the macrocosmic expansion of endlessly divisible matter in the darkness of an ever-expanding universe, equally out of reach to human sight—so Lewis recalibrated the technique of sfumato for the nuclear age, pushing further at the limits of the visible so as to question the common-sense, the *sensus communis*, of his era.

In *Blending* (1952, fig. 8) a crystalline network hovers above an evaporating tonal background. "The picture is a black picture," said Lewis in a 1973 interview with Bearden. Yet even as he denied a racial referent for blackness—"It has no social connotation to me"—Lewis's emphasis on hue variation within chromatic blackness carried far-reaching implications. He stated, "I wanted to see if I could get out of black the suggestion of other nuances of color, using it in such a way as to arouse other colors.... This was my becoming ... using color in such a way that it could become other things."[28] Seeking to generate "other nuances ... other things" out of chromatic blackness *signifies a condition of multiplicity*. In addition to such transformative capacities, Lewis's verb choice—*becoming*—is highly revealing. It applies not just to black color but to himself as well, his own artistic "becoming," which thus reinscribes the seemingly disavowed social connotations of blackness. In the multiple signifieds gathering beneath his assertion that *Blending* "is a black picture," Lewis discloses the multi-accentuality that makes blackness a floating signifier, generating a semiotic surplus that overflows dualistic codes that seek to fix one-to-one correspondences between painted marks and their potential meanings.

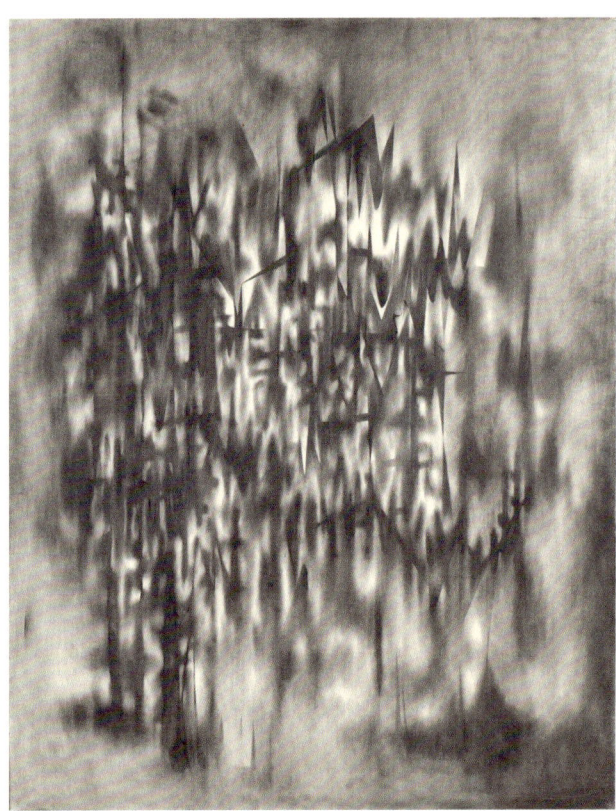

Fig. 8 Norman Lewis, *Blending*, 1952, oil and ink on canvas, Munson-Williams-Proctor Arts Institute, Museum Purchase

© Estate of Norman Lewis. Photo © Munson-Williams-Proctor Arts Institute / Art Resource, NY

In light of such semantic slippage, it is intriguing to note that when Bearden and Harry Henderson discuss *Blending* as "one of a series of black-and-white abstractions in which black shapes are defined primarily by white backlighting," their parenthetical remark, "(which has its own social meaning)," is not elaborated, yet "white backlighting" acquires added significance in the atomic context.[29] The backlighting Bearden and Henderson posit implies a rear-ground light source producing a luminous halo around blackened foreground figures, much as the *contra-jour* setup in photography goes "against the light" to create black silhouettes. Apropos *Blending*, we may thus speculate on a figural scenario in which, if the spiky shapes interposed between backlighting and beholder were to be removed, the beholder's eye would be blinded by such "white backlighting," unable to see by virtue of an overpowering radiance coming from the rear of the picture plane. Lewis's use of sfumato in *Blending* thereby rejoins the black and white palette of *Every Atom Glows* to further trouble the limits of vision, mobilizing abstraction to contest an ocular-centric worldview in which Western knowledge sought mastery of the world through sight.

On August 6 and 9, 1945, it was not just that densely populated cities were evaporated "like smoke," but that the shadows blasted onto concrete by the bomb's lethal light were white, not black. The death-bringing power of atomic light demanded an entire rethinking of the West's epistemological order, argues film scholar Akira Mizuta Lippit, for the privilege of vision established since the quattrocento, in which sight was the sense whereby Vitruvian Man took possession of the world and rendered it knowable, was thoroughly decentered by the "avisuality" of an event in which, in de Kooning's words, "the eyes that actually saw the light melted."[30]

To the extent that sfumato departs from the realm of Euclidean geometry—in which dualistic distinctions of near/far or surface/depth are delineated by clear-cut borders that separate the observing subject from the observable world—it unfixes either/or polarities in a haze of evanescent gradations. In the cognitive and affective space opened up by Lewis's sfumato, darkness can no longer be the opposite of luminosity. Indeed, it is the undoing of dualism that cuts an opening into the closed codes of representation, such as the Christian symbolism of darkness and light. Leonardo da Vinci posited a tenebrous continuum rather than an absolute binary when he wrote, "Between light and darkness there is infinite variation."[31] I see Lewis's use of sfumato tapping into and transforming this alternative to dualistic reasoning by bringing such "infinite variation" to bear on blackness not as sightless negation, but as a condition of unending multiplicity. It is relevant here to add that Lewis was fascinated by fog. Alone in a boat off Long Island, he said, "It was foggy and the sky and water catalyzed so that you could not see the point at which they fell together.... Fog, this ethereal filter, fascinated me."[32] Like smoke, fog has a purely phenomenal existence. It appears to the eye in the very same moment it disappears into invisibility. Whereas atmospheric phenomena such as fog and smoke often feature in Western pictorial traditions as elusive elements to be captured and mastered by the painter's eye, Lewis's interests point instead toward blackness as fugitive phenomenality, something that escapes capture within the visual codes of representational space.

Harlem Turns White (1955, fig. 9) has long been regarded as one of Lewis's most important works. But when interpretation leans on an anthropomorphic reading of its brushwork—in which white, cloud-like

Fig. 9 Norman Lewis, *Harlem Turns White*, 1955, oil on canvas, private collection

© Estate of Norman Lewis. Courtesy of Michael Rosenfeld Gallery LLC, New York, NY

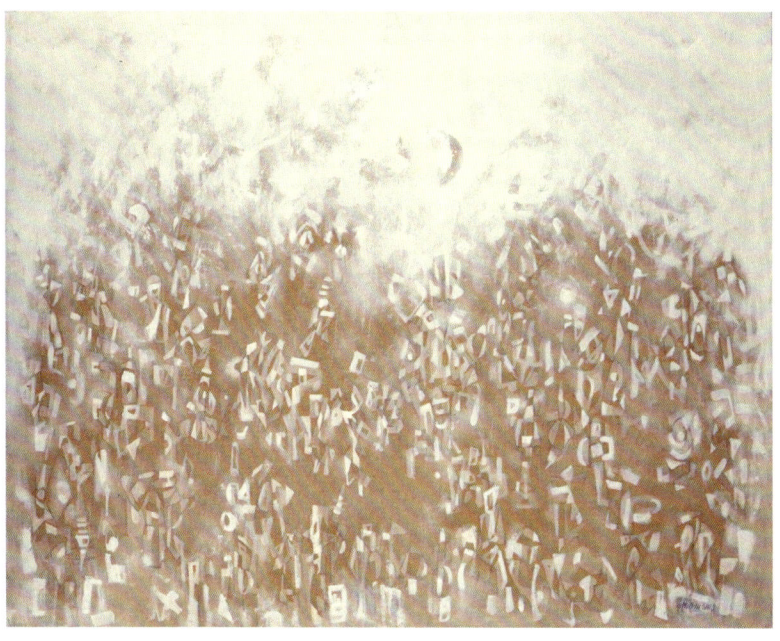

sfumato fills the upper portion while staccato rhomboids and triangles populate the rest of the canvas's muted tan ground—the affective dynamic of figural ambivalence is flattened by referential literalism. To see "an imaginary scene: the black community of Harlem transformed to reflect its earlier history as a white community," as Sharon Patton suggests, is to take up the socially committed side of Lewis's abstraction, but such a view diminishes the investigative depth of Lewis's Black modernist engagement with the apocalyptic scale of postwar dilemmas.[33] If we accept the painting's landscape orientation as suggesting an observable scene, the whiteout scenario of an atomic blast, with skeletal remains in its aftermath, strikes me as a more plausible way to grasp the emotional gravitas of an artwork that evokes "the presence of something which escapes presentation," as one commentator puts it when summing up Lyotard's concept of the figural.[34]

In view of Stuart Hall's point, "In art things get said in ways that cannot get said in any other domain," Lewis's use of the figural to open a space in which the unthinkable violence of total planetary destruction could be rendered thinkable reframes the postwar context in which to understand other critically Black responses to atomic light.[35] In his self-financed movie *The World, The Flesh and The Devil* (1959), Harry Belafonte is an engineer working underground who emerges into a postapocalyptic world as sole survivor of an atomic blast until he meets a white woman, with both then hunted down by a white man. Using the science-fiction genre to address fears and fantasies deemed socially unspeakable, Belafonte's intervention complements the suite of paintings Lewis produced in the 1950s and warrants further inquiry.

Going Underground—Vestibular Spaces

That the subterranean location of Ellison's narrator might serve as a shelter from nuclear fallout is as relevant as the fact that Ellison started writing his novel in August 1945. Collaborating with his friend Gordon Parks (1912–2006), Ellison authorized a three-page spread in *Life* magazine that visualized episodes from the narrative in the manner of film stills.[36] In the most striking image, Parks renders Ellison's narrator illuminated by 1,369 light bulbs as he dwells beneath the city, listening to multiple recordings of Louis Armstrong's "(What Did I Do to Be So) Black and Blue," his senses immersed in the music's syncopated breaks (fig. 10).

Where Ellison's chthonic lair is a site of both dark confinement and creative escape it intersects with the subway spaces that feature so frequently in DeCarava's oeuvre. Spillers describes "vestibular cultural formations" as both outcomes of antiblack violence, which ripped apart distinctions of subject/object, male/female, and person/property, and as also *sites of emergence* in which the dissolution of categorical boundaries generates a "patterning . . . of possibilities," in T. J. Clark's terms, with the potential to open up alternatives to capitalist modernization.[37] Following on from the figural agency of Lewis's abstraction, did the subterranean

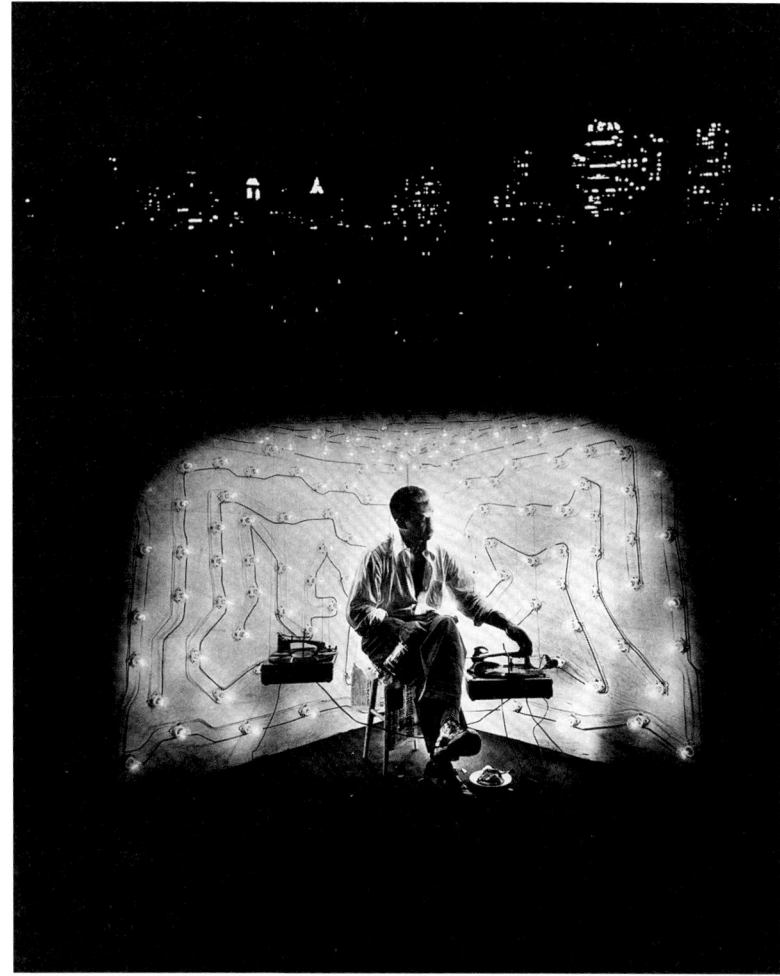

Fig. 10 Gordon Parks, *Invisible Man Retreat, Harlem, New York*, 1952

Courtesy of and © The Gordon Parks Foundation

darkness surrounding Ellison's narrator, and suffusing DeCarava's photographs, grant Black modernists the freedom to think of modern life independently of Vitruvian Man's ocular-centric episteme?

Sharply distinct from Walker Evans's furtive snapshots of transit passengers, DeCarava's *Mott Avenue* (1951) depicts a subway station devoid of people. Even his portraits in subway settings, such as *Woman on train* (1961), give blur and shadow a major role to play in creating an enigmatic mood. Where curator Mark Godfrey notices, "Many of DeCarava's most famous photographs were made on the subway," it is striking that DeCarava's more abstract works, as well as architectural studies such as *Subway ceiling, New York* (1965), often have an autotelic aspect, set loose from any referent, as in *Platform and Light* (1960, fig. 11). Godfrey suggests that in "'abstracting' the image … by throwing everything out of focus," DeCarava's modernist strategies of estrangement feature "everyday objects made unrecognizable through close cropping; scenes made unfamiliar through un-focusing," and "to call these 'abstract' is hardly controversial."[38] Nonetheless while DeCarava's abstraction is ignored when his work is interpreted solely as social documentary, the converse problem pervades Peter Galassi's view in DeCarava's 1996 MoMA retrospective.

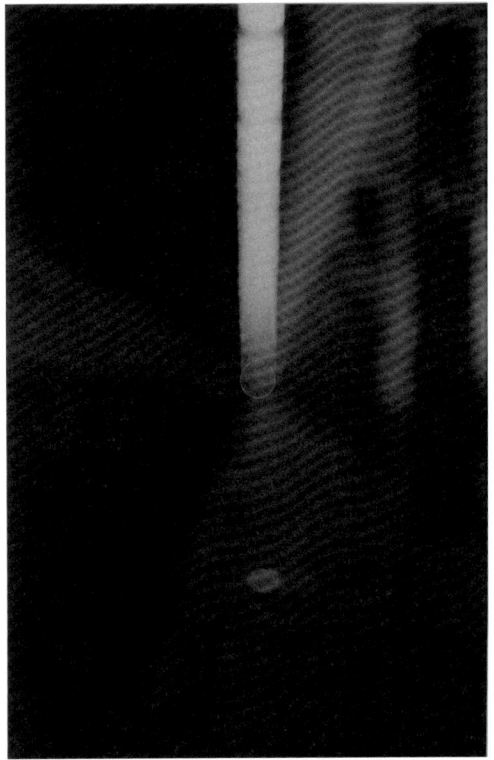
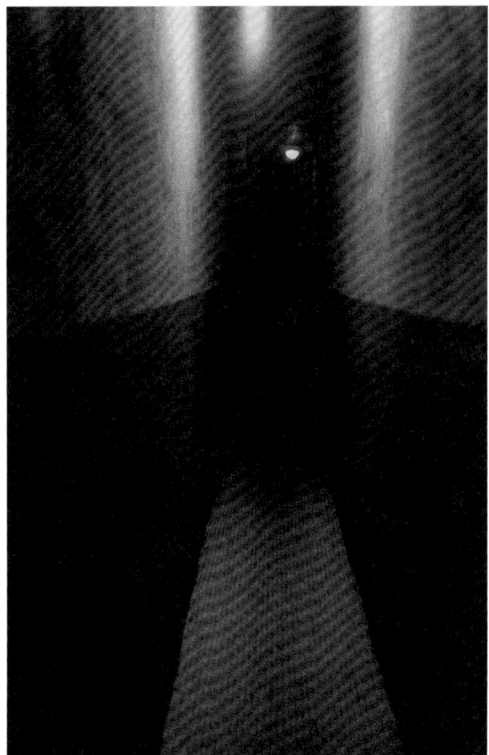

Fig. 11 Roy DeCarava, *Platform and Light*, 1960

© Sherry Turner DeCarava and the DeCarava Estate. Courtesy of the Roy and Sherry DeCarava Archives

Fig. 12 Roy DeCarava, *Hallway*, 1953

© Sherry Turner DeCarava and the DeCarava Estate. Courtesy of the Roy and Sherry DeCarava Archives

Here formalism had eyes only for hard-edge geometric patterns. Rarely, if at all, did it attend to the sfumato effects seen in *Traffic Light and Fog* (1950), or *Face Out of Focus* (1960), for example, which bring sight to the limits of the seeable.[39]

In *Hallway* (1953, fig. 12) DeCarava's Black modernist engagement with sfumato comes together with alluring tonal darkness, inviting the viewer to linger over a threshold. As it slows down our looking, the image grows more abstract before our eyes. What appears at first sight to be a dour inner-city scene gives way, thanks to the "soft tonality [that] reveals more," to the feeling that the endless vanishing point that disappears into darkness is teeming with "presences unseen and coming into being," as Gibson said of Lewis. "If I ever wanted to be marooned with one photograph," said DeCarava to Sherry Turner DeCarava, who organized his 1981 retrospective, "I would want to be marooned with *Hallway* because it was one of my first photographs to break through a kind of literalness." Describing the image's social referent—"it was all the hallways I grew up in. They were poor, poor tenements, badly lit and confining"—DeCarava highlights its affective power—"it was frightening, it was scary, it was spooky"—before he then immediately acknowledges his ambivalence when he adds, "And yet, here I am an adult, years and ages and ages later . . . finding it beautiful. . . . As beautiful as the photograph is, the subject is not beautiful in the sense of living in it."[40]

Maren Stange notes how much DeCarava's sensibility resonates with Lewis's ability to "forge a style at once individually expressive and

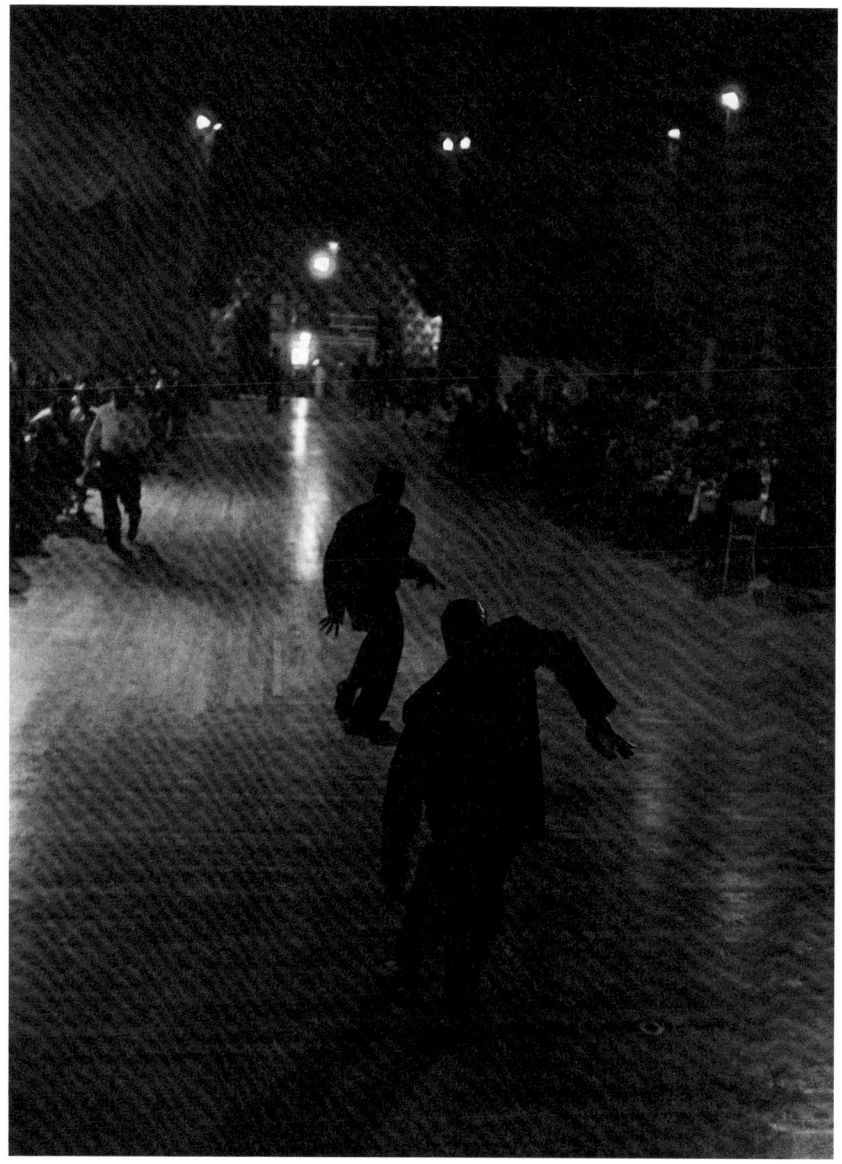

Fig. 13 Roy DeCarava, *Dancers*, 1953

© Sherry Turner DeCarava and the DeCarava Estate. Courtesy of the Roy and Sherry DeCarava Archives

socially significant."[41] As we consider how DeCarava used abstraction to put contradictory affects in play—keeping them in dynamic balance—we should also know that he stressed the phenomenology of shadow and light when he said, "The ambience, the light in the hallway was . . . so individual that any other kind of light would not have worked."[42] This observation speaks to his photographic handling of sfumato, whose figural agency we see intensified in another of DeCarava's canonical works, *Dancers* (1953, fig. 13).

The vestibular hallway, at once narrowly confining yet teeming with potential, is now a site of kinetic conjuration. DeCarava stated, "These two dancers represent a terrible torment for me in that I feel a great ambiguity about the image," when he said *Dancers* was taken at a dance of a social club at the 110th Street Manor at Fifth Avenue:

> It is the intermission ... and the entertainment was two dancers who danced ... in the manner of black vaudeville performers.... [They were] ... in an awkward position before the man, for the man, to demean themselves in order to survive.... And yet there is something in the figures not about that; something that is very real and very black in the finest sense of the word. So there is this duality, this ambiguity in the photograph that I find very hard to live with.... it is good because of those things and in spite of those things.[43]

On a floor tilted upward—such that the cavernous space of captivity seems walled-in—the dancing pair throw figural shapes that are hard to decipher in the *sfumato noir*. Yet it is precisely their fugitive legibility that imparts affective intensity to the photograph's dark tonalities, urging us to look closer, to look slower. In his underground dwelling, Ellison's narrator concludes *Invisible Man* by saying, "Who knows but that on the lower frequency, I speak for you."[44] Where Paul Gilroy, in turn, has understood Black culture's "politics of transfiguration" to exist "on a lower frequency where ... words will never be enough to communicate its unsayable claims to truth," the "unsayable" ambiguities DeCarava evoked in his 1981 commentary are made palpable in *Dancers* through a practice of Black modernist abstraction that reveals blackness not as a site of negation, but as a transfiguring locus of shape-shifting multiplicity.[45]

Conclusion: Modern or Contemporary?

Formalism's interpretive monopoly on postwar abstraction did not wither of its own accord. It was displaced by methods that opened the "internalist" priorities of Greenbergian criticism to a variety of recontextualizing approaches. The 1960s Black Arts Movement era has been a key site in which scholars such as Darby English, Kellie Jones, and others have initiated a long overdue reappraisal of Black abstraction, although in focusing on the postwar era my study points further back for a genealogy of Black modernisms that contested the forces of Western modernity.[46] English rightly stresses that racial Blackness is but one among multiple connotations contending for attention in David Hammons's *Concerto in Black and Blue* (2002, fig. 14), an installation in which darkened rooms are illuminated only by blue lights viewers pick up when entering the gallery. To argue that Lewis's *Seachange* (1975, fig. 15) is fully part of the genealogy in which Hammons performs his iteration of the nexus of darkness, race, and vision is to call for research that sets out to *historicize* this specific Black modernist line of inquiry. This pursuit means further dismantling the binary that opposes the limitations of Black representational space to the supposedly transcendental freedoms of abstraction, which is a Cold War dualism that lingers on.

The postwar African American efflorescence linking Lewis, Ellison, and DeCarava to bebop and other underground scenes gives us a fresh

Fig. 14 David Hammons, *Concerto in Black and Blue* (installation view), 2002

© David Hammons.
Courtesy of ACE Gallery

Fig. 15 Norman Lewis, *Seachange*, 1975, oil on canvas, Collection of Gerald Powers, MD

© Estate of Norman Lewis

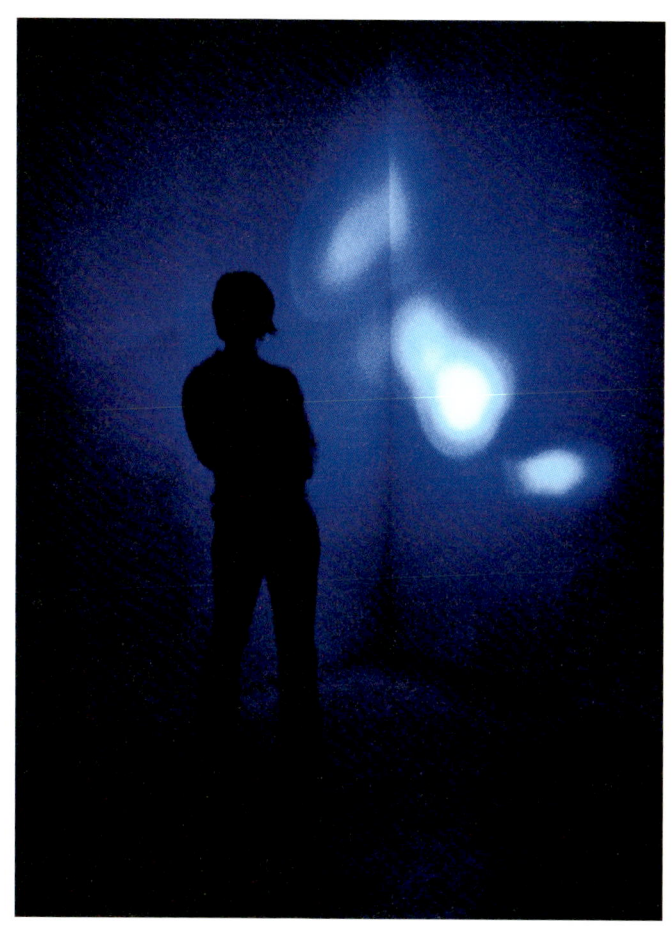
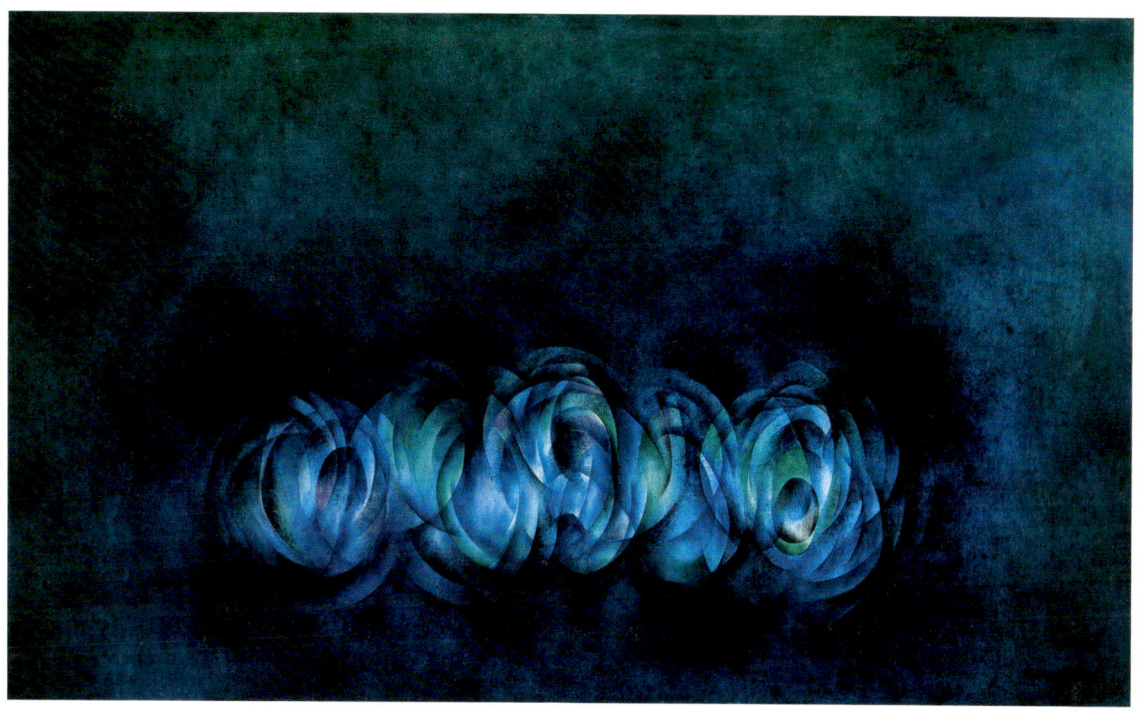

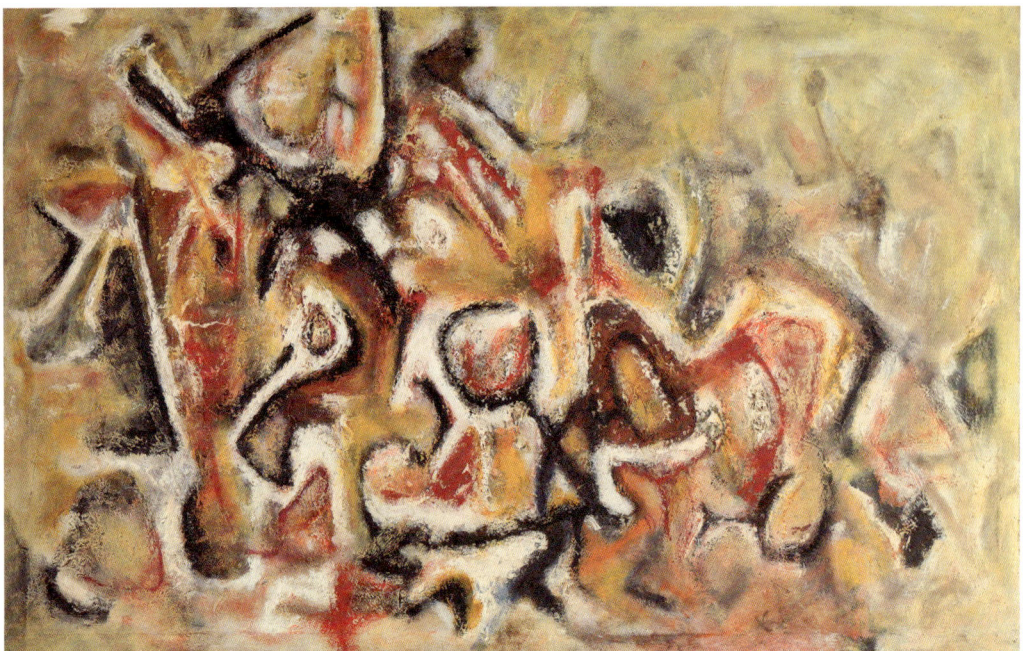

Fig. 16 Aubrey Williams, *Death and the Conquistador*, 1959, oil on canvas, Tate, London

© 2019 Artists Rights Society (ARS), New York / DACS, London. Photo © Tate, London 2019

view of the mid-twentieth-century crisis of humanism. This 1940s moment galvanized the "Double V for Victory" campaign, which called for racial democracy at home and overseas, and offered a glimpse of a post-West-centric future for anti-colonial and Black internationalist movements.[47] But where a "vestibular cultural formation . . . can be invaded at any given and arbitrary moment by the property relations," as Spillers says, the Eisenhower era of modernization shut down such emergent possibilities.[48] The resegregated urban planning of the 1950s, as well as delayed integration in education, and, we should add, formalism's drive to purification in art, were all developments that led to a hegemonic narrative of American abstraction as modern art's ultimate achievement—and this triumphalist narrative was only opened for critical reinterpretation as recently as the 1990s.

African American abstraction has often been analogized to jazz, which speaks to the liberating effects of being set loose from fixed codifications of sensorial affect, even if such approaches often reinforce a dualism of sound and vision.[49] Closely reading a 1967 radio debate that addressed the multiplicity of "Black as a special concept, symbol, paint quality; the social-political implications of black; black as stasis, negation, nothingness and black as change, impermanence and potentiality," theorist Fred Moten recalibrates the aural and the visual on a performative plane. He counterposes the joy with which musician Cecil Taylor embraced the "admixture" of the contending meanings of blackness with Ad Reinhardt's sullen fixity regarding the "negativeness of black."[50] As Moten invites us to contrast an *optical* discourse in which blackness is feared as apocalyptic negation, with an *ontological* discourse in which Blackness is recognized as an open-ended condition of pluripotentiality, his theoretical framework renders intelligible what was at stake for Lewis's and DeCarava's postwar investigations of race, darkness, and vision that had been, for more than half a century, unreadable under formalist eyes.

What are the art historical implications of claiming a Black modernist strategy of the 1950s—sfumato noir—becomes intelligible only today, thanks to ground-clearing moves instigated by contemporary thinking in the Black Radical Tradition that regards the critique of Western civilization as the defining aim of Black intellectual life?[51] When T. J. Clark argued that "Modernism is unintelligible now," as remote for him as an archeological ruin, he registered the epochal shift whereby the global conditions of "modernity," which from the 1550s to the 1960s organized capitalist accumulation under an imperial clock centered in the West, have today given way to conditions of "contemporaneity."[52] Terry Smith offers "contemporaneity" to describe the coexistence of multiple temporalities in a decentered world in which West-centric hegemony is constantly contested, even as worldwide capitalism establishes new regimes of social regulation in which racialized inequalities grow more entrenched.[53] Thus, whereas Clark's account of modernism and modernity remains centered in the West, the study of Black modernisms puts us in a converse situation in which multiple modernisms that were hitherto suppressed under Euro-American chronometry now become freshly intelligible *for the first time* as a result of the contemporaneity in which the copresence of disparate temporalities is acknowledged. From such a standpoint, curator Okwui Enwezor put forward his *Postwar* (2017) survey exhibition to illuminate the midcentury crisis of liberal humanist Man as the condition of emergence, after 1945, of artistic practices whose contestation of West-centrism paved the way for contemporaneity.[54]

This study has led to a question—Did atomic aftermath lead to the traumatic recognition that modernity began in violence?—that cannot be answered in a single essay. To conclude with a prospectus for further research, I suggest that a genealogy in a transnational frame would have to take in such works as *Death and the Conquistador* (1959, fig. 16) by Aubrey Williams, the Caribbean painter whose abstract works began in the 1950s by addressing the genocidal terror on which New World societies were built.[55] In the African American context, Jack Whitten is pivotal to understanding the transgenerational influence of Lewis's *Seachange* series, with Whitten's *April's Shark* (1974, fig. 17) as a fugitive mapping of post-Euclidean space that is at once astral and oceanic.[56] Equally necessary would be a trans-medium angle that brings in moving-image works such as Glenn Ligon's *The Death of Tom* (2008, fig. 18), in which illegible film footage is matched by the sonic figurality of a haunting aural score by Jason Moran. Also important is Sondra Perry's *Black/Cloud* (2010, fig.19), whose rhythmic alternation of abstract and nonabstract elements is flowingly figural. Above all, a genealogy of the nexus of race, darkness, and vision needs to conceptualize modernity anew in a way that asks whether the aesthetic and political conditions brought to light by Black modernism really do belong to the past, or whether they continue, in contemporaneity, in the afterlife of our unanswered questions.

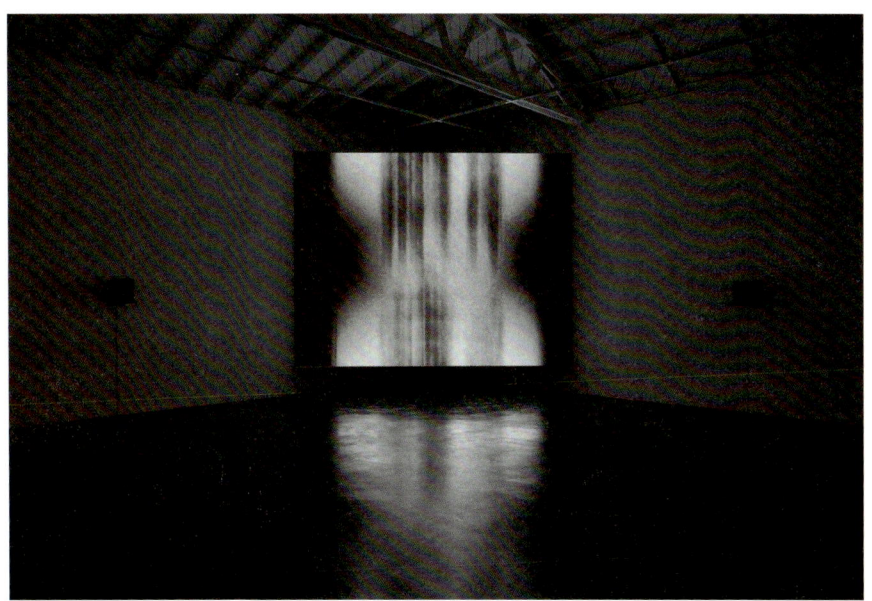

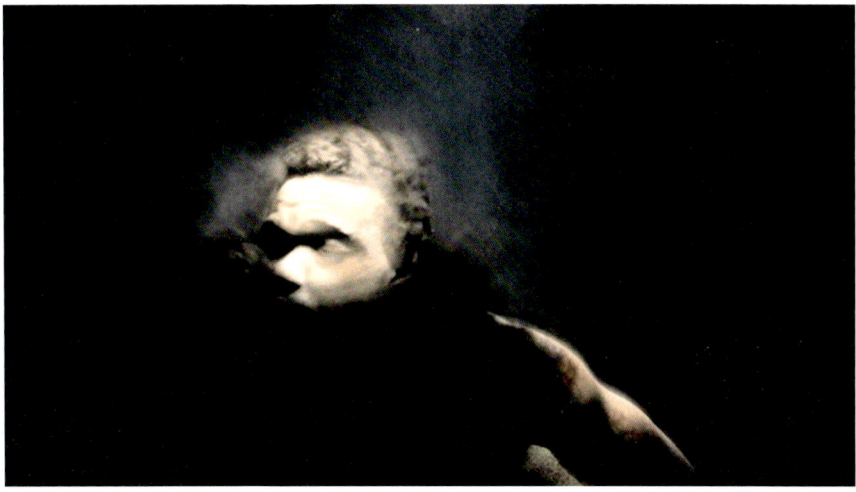

Fig. 17 Jack Whitten, *April's Shark*, 1974, acrylic on canvas

© Jack Whitten Estate. Courtesy of the Estate and Hauser & Wirth. Photo by Jeff McLane

Fig. 18 Glenn Ligon, *The Death of Tom* (installation view at Regen Projects, Los Angeles), 2008, 16 mm black-and-white film/video transfer, running time 23 min., edition of 3 and 1 AP, collection of Museum of Modern Art, New York; Los Angeles County Museum of Art

© Glenn Ligon; courtesy of the artist, Hauser & Wirth, New York, Regen Projects, Los Angeles, Thomas Dane Gallery, London, and Chantal Crousel, Paris

Fig. 19 Sondra Perry, *Black/Cloud* (film still), 2010, 1-channel installation, loop, color, silent, running time 30 min.

Courtesy of the artist, Bridget Donahue, NYC, and Electronic Arts Intermix (EAI), New York

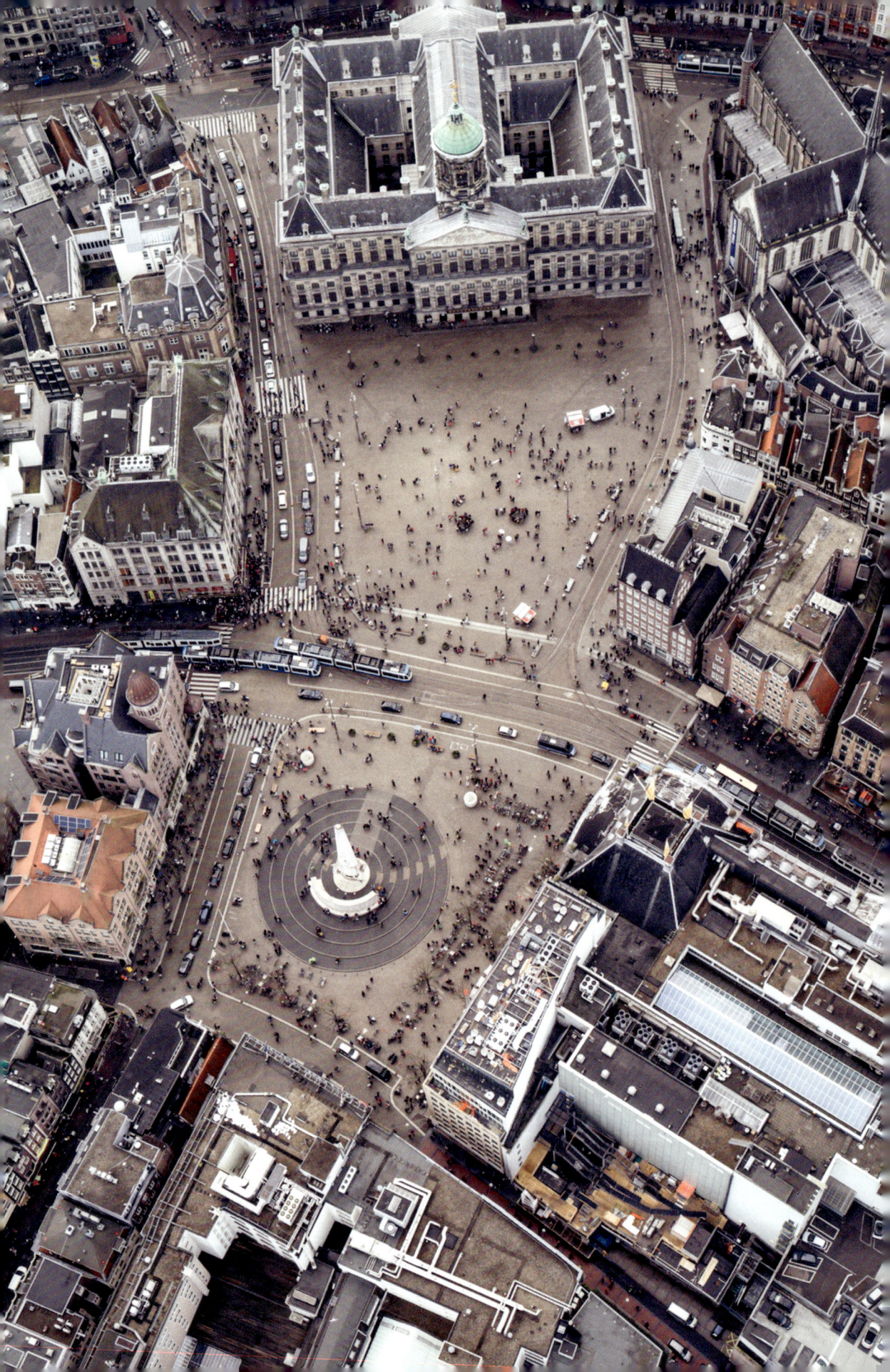

AT THE THRESHOLD OF WITHHOLDING: STANLEY BROUWN'S MODERNIST REPETITIONS

ADRIENNE EDWARDS

At the request of the artist, no bibliographical information is provided here.
Christophe Cherix

The *This Way Brouwn* drawing series involves the peripatetic artist Stanley Brouwn (1935–2017) strolling city streets and randomly approaching people, "ask[ing] anonymous passersby to draw on a sheet of paper directions to a particular unnamed location"; he would then apply to the drawing his eponymous stamp and later add his handwritten signature and the date.[1] Each *This Way Brouwn* drawing is a plane in oscillating fields of experience, operating between chance and discipline, historical moments and scenes. The square, the grid of the city and of public space, paradoxically provides a veil of latency, so that the ritual of the event fluctuates between the drawings and the "performance," while withholding from the viewer language exchanged, feelings shared, and a whole range of other sensory information summoned and conjoined in the realization of the work. For ultimately what is presented to us, the viewers, as the work of art is only partial, re-presented in two-dimensional form—a piece of paper—the support for that which could never be entirely captured. The cacophony of the public square is compressed into the most minimal of materials.

This Way Brouwn reroutes the modernist imperative of genre specificity and authorial role through methods of variation, repetition, and multiplicity. The work serves as a meaningful counterpoint to modernism's tendency to reflect the process and status of the genre and/or its form through a demonstration of such awareness.[2] We are redirected away from an "I"-centered referent to questioning the intentions of the "I" who stages the events. Thus, despite Brouwn's determination to withhold the "I" in the self-reflexive tradition of modernism, he proffers a way of thinking about Blackness's vexing affinity, the ways in which its resonance is not revealed representationally as an ideogram so much as felt—resemblance forsaken for semblance. Of course, imbricating Brouwn and Blackness risks a mislaid analysis precisely because he refused to acknowledge such indexical structures in his work, at least explicitly. Nevertheless, we can imagine an underlying sense constellated under the veil of Blackness.

As suspended in Brouwn's work, the qualities of Blackness illuminate the historical and social fashioning that resulted from the organizing systems of modernity; these systems include the concept of race and capitalism as well as the institutions and nation-states that sustain them—bodies as literal commodities subjugated into the service of imperialist and colonialist regimes. I argue that Brouwn's art provides a singular opportunity for contemplating how highly relevant strategies of abstract, opaque, conceptually driven works want to convey or complicate a particular kind of experiential knowledge of Blackness. His art navigates such terrain in the most oblique of ways by exploiting a minoritarian position from which modernism has always extracted its inspiration, now mirrored back to itself from "the outsider within" in a way Denise Ferreira da Silva might describe as a "fact beyond evidence."[3] In this formulation, modernism implies a metalanguage heretofore thought of as a constant, standard aesthetic measure, while "minor," following the Deleuzian and Guattarian formulation, describes that which is in fluctuation, necessitates a connection, ever betwixt, and of transition and variation.[4] Brouwn's representational refusal reminds us that there are inexplicable events and conditions that fueled modernity that are in fact beyond capture, devastations and dispersals that are unrepresentable. Such an understanding privileges the full range of feelings and affects that persist in the work over any modernist trope, school, and form or even the typical ways conceptual art is portrayed with its proclivity for data-driven information.

Brouwn makes his approach to such tendencies through a mode of displacement and destabilization—never solely explored through an "I" but always a "we"—which raises a range of questions. Precisely, what is possible to glean from a withholding? What could foster a desire for withholding, especially when such a withdrawal takes place as a spectacle of elaboration? Why *this* strategy? Because Brouwn's conceptualization of the work of art circumvents an authorial position for a nexus of relationality. What might he be querying about matters of authority in the social, political, and economic senses, and about the value of art *as* art in such a context? What might this insistence on relation have to say about matters of the world, and how the world comes to matter, which is as much a question of value as it is of material? What is meaningful is not the fact that Brouwn demonstrates a disciplinary disregard for the qualities associated with the modernist impulse, but rather the presence of variation, repetition, and pluralism within modernism itself, which reflects the very qualities and conditions of the postcolonial era and its aesthetics.

One of the most important conceptual artists working in Europe, Brouwn had his work presented in Documenta 5, 6, 7, and 11. He also represented the Netherlands at the 1976 Venice Biennale. Beginning in 1972, Brouwn did not permit reproductions of his art, give interviews, allow photographs, attend openings, or provide any biographical information. His seeming invisibility is often characterized by scholars as a desire for privacy, a concern for disappearance, and a form of nonexistence.[5] While our knowledge of Brouwn is minimal, the strict limitations he set around interpretations of his work demand some speculation, which can only be buttressed by a structural, information-driven framework, much like the work itself. Conjecture, as an analytical and temporal distancing, is also beneficial in coming to terms with the premise of Brouwn's art. To historicize his art requires working with and through an anachronistic relationality to consider his methods of opacity, his encounters, their context, and the profundity of the propositions he sets into motion.

A few coordinates are necessary: Brouwn was born in Paramaribo, Suriname, then a Dutch colony, and moved to Amsterdam in 1957, nearly twenty years before the small South American country, though culturally Caribbean, would become independent (fig. 1). Brouwn was active in the Dutch art scene from his arrival in Amsterdam, participating in or sharing affinities with: Fluxus, an interdisciplinary community of artists concerned

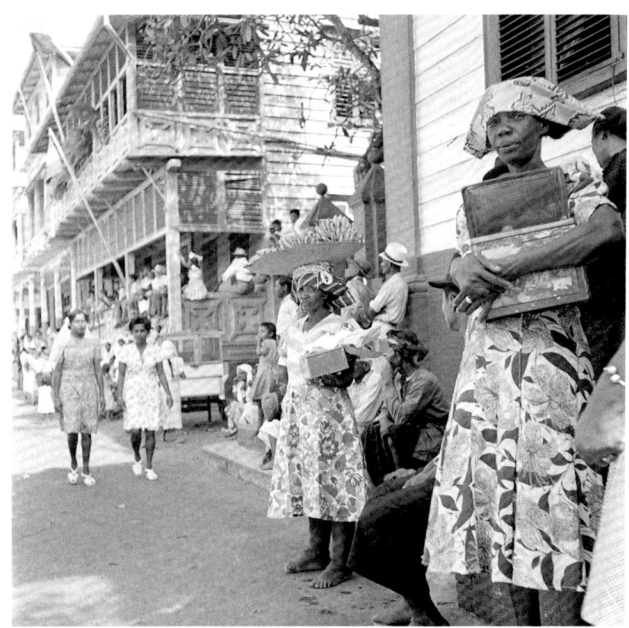

Fig. 1 Paramaribo, Suriname, April 1946

Photo by Earl Leaf. Courtesy of Michael Ochs Archives, Getty Images

with the artistic process, often through participatory and live artworks; the Nul group, a Dutch movement interested in modern reality–based art reflective of the times; and the ZERO group, a loose collective of artists founded in 1937 in Düsseldorf, Germany, whose works were preoccupied with perception, motion, monochromatic color, and light, often made with nontraditional materials.[6]

In step with such movements, *This Way Brouwn* illumines the function of repetition within a singular work that is nevertheless expansive because of the fathomless variations attendant to its formal system and its seriality. Coincident with the drawing series was a different series of actions: Brouwn threw blank sheets of white paper in the street, unsuspecting pedestrians marked them with their footprints, and then Brouwn collected them. In another of his perambulatory works, *Steps*, initiated a decade later on the occasion of his solo exhibition at the Stedelijk Museum, Amsterdam, in 1971, the artist traveled from the Netherlands through Belgium, France, Spain, Morocco, and Algeria, and back again. He sent daily transmissions of the total number of his steps to the museum; the data was written on index cards alongside the coordinates of date and country.[7] This series would go on to involve destinations to twenty-one widespread cities, including Addis Ababa, Bahia, Manila, Tokyo, Calcutta, and numerous European cities, represented entirely by the "number of footsteps taken in each location."[8] Brouwn also had a series of works in which he would use his body as an individualized unit of measure or would turn to archaic ones no longer in use such as the Egyptian cubit, Castilian *pié*, European ell, and Spanish *vara*. Often these works demonstrate a preoccupation with distance, being away from or approximate to something other than where one currently is. It also emphasizes the truth of fluctuation, irregularity, and variation as things to be valued against conformity and universalism.

182

...

When taken together and at a distance, we can observe how Brouwn's artwork is engaged in formal techniques and aesthetic operations that challenge legibility, rely upon opacity, and proceed by errantry. For Édouard Glissant, errantry discards and challenges the universal.[9] Accordingly, it matters when Brouwn arrived in Amsterdam, and so do the historical, social, economic, and political realities that existed there, as well as in Suriname at the time of his emigration from there to the Netherlands. Errantry does not concern a melancholic longing or seemingly unending agitation from a heartbreak of fundamental loss. Rather, errantry as an identity is extended through a relationship with another.[10] In public squares, on walks, Brouwn's wanderings are an attempt to locate himself—in place, in art, through questions as a poetics—an inside outsider embodied in the center of the city as much as imagined by others as an Other always on its periphery. His position is that of a remainder of society, its odds and ends, a figure possessed by a Western world convinced of its own primacy and superiority. Brouwn personalized art about and as errantry, voyaging to insist upon the particulars of somatic encounter, which resist generalities for the specificities marked by the hand of one in a fundamental relation to the other.[11] Such conditions and contexts require that errant ones like Brouwn instead find and ride the edge of their capacities, individually and collectively. Errant acts, if we think of them as improvised choreographies, are less about abandonment or disavowal than about the imaginative pursuit of what is possible in the aftermath of the catastrophe that is the modern era.

While the idea of errantry could be applied to anyone with an experience of migration, those of us who have an embodied knowledge of Blackness have a particular and peculiar relationship to this condition of being astray. Indeed, the longue durée of enslavement, colonialism, and capitalist extraction, in which the past is at times indistinguishable from the present or a desired future, have contoured Black life in ways that require manufactured dispositions to contend with the structural positions imposed upon us. This is to say, we have had to set new paths within incredible constraints. As Glissant suggests, "Identity is no longer completely within the root but also within Relation."[12] If the center (root, originary belonging) cannot hold, a constitutive response is to seek relation as a multiplicity within the multitude. In comparison to the colonialist "arrowlike nomadism,"[13] of conquest, manifest destiny, and universalism, errant ones subvert centrality in favor of anarchy, unsettled truth, skepticism, ambivalence, yet with a sense of overwhelming expansiveness, which is dispersed in every direction, a necessarily illegible, opaque, and thick cartography, aligning through relation as they must and as they desire. Ironically, such precarious arrangements have the capacity to reaffirm identity precisely because of movement, the negotiations attendant to it, and the performances that arise from it, which is certainly the case for Brouwn. It is because exile is very real that errancy requires what

Glissant describes as "an imaginary vision"[14] that must nevertheless be constantly reached for.

Migration—which singularly defined the work of Glissant and, I would argue, of Brouwn—characterizes the Caribbean reality, both within the archipelago and in the continental countries adjacent to it. In 1954, a few years before Brouwn arrived in the Netherlands, there were fewer than five thousand Surinamese and Dutch-speaking Antilleans living there, primarily in Amsterdam.[15] Despite the relatively small number of émigrés, there was a prevailing anxiety of the "dangers" presented by the presence of migrants in the late 1940s.[16] By 1958, the year after Brouwn's disembarkation, some members of the Dutch government were expressing angst over the perceived threat posed by the Surinamese, who were imagined as especially inclined toward criminal activity and external to Dutch culture.[17] A 1962 study composed by civil servants of the Dutch ministries focused on what they described as the issue of "the antisocial Surinamese in the metropolis" and concluded that the only solution was a more restrictive immigration policy for such an "unacceptable" and "undesirable situation."[18] At the time, there were only around eight thousand Surinamese in a population of more than eleven million people.[19] Over the ensuing twenty years, the Dutch would continue to grapple with the reality of Caribbean immigration, particularly given the historical colonial relationship that resulted in substantive structural differences in their respective economic prospects.[20]

In July 1971, during a Dutch government delegation's visit to the region, the Netherlands announced the likelihood of independence for Suriname and the Antillean islands within the next few years, after which migration to the Netherlands soared.[21] Around this time, the press often reported "alarming tensions" between "native" Dutch and the Caribbean émigrés in cities like Rotterdam and Amsterdam.[22] Full independence was ultimately declared in 1975; the negotiations sustained the right to citizenship for the populations of the now former colonies, heightening the national debate about migration in the Netherlands. For their parts, the Antilles and Suriname sought to retain their right of abode even after independence.[23] Indeed, free movement between the countries was one of the most important dimensions of Surinamese negotiations for independence, advocated by leaders of the nationalist movement such as Eddy Bruma, who would become minister of economic affairs in the administration of Henck Arron, the first prime minister of independent Suriname. The significance of the policy is reflected in this declaration by Surinamese revolutionary activist and anti-colonialist writer Anton de Kom: "Torture racks have been replaced by poverty, fear, and mental suffering. It is as if we have been taken out of the fire . . . and thrown into the ocean, even though we cannot swim. It is foolish to suppose that those who have been repressed for centuries . . . could truly live in freedom with no support, just a piece of land."[24]

From 1975 to 1980 a transitional period ensued, and the Surinamese had the option of choosing their nationality. Dutch Prime Minister Joop den

Uyl resisted strict immigration regulations aimed to discourage the influx of former colonial subjects.[25] Animating his principled position was "the fear that skin color would become the criterion for enforcement."[26] The immigration agreement between the Netherlands and Suriname required Surinamese immigrants to register their arrival. During the year of independence for a four-month period, three to four thousand Surinamese moved to the Netherlands, a dramatic increase over previous years.[27] The years of open movement from 1975 to 1980 saw thirty thousand Surinamese immigrate to the Netherlands and secure Dutch nationality.[28]

Class played a major role in the evolution of immigration to the Netherlands and in émigrés' experiences there. Prior to the 1970s, the majority of people moving to the Netherlands were of Afro-Surinamese descent from a range of economic positions, though mostly middle class; many were university students.[29] Following independence in 1975, the class profile became more diverse with poor and working-class people emigrating, instigated by an economic crisis in Suriname. They were met in the Netherlands, however, with an economic reality that was on the decline, buffeted by economic restructuring that eliminated many low-skilled jobs and increased unemployment, which disproportionately affected the new arrivals.[30] By 1979, 25 percent of Surinamese living in the Netherlands were unemployed, five times the rate of ethnic Dutch.[31] Of the Afro-Surinamese employed a decade prior to independence, observed during the 1964 census, 40 percent worked in civil service.[32]

Surinamese employment in the Dutch government has its antecedents in the nascent days of emancipation from enslavement. Following manumission in Suriname in 1863, a small number of Afro-Surinamese formed the core of administrators who became the custodians of the Dutch colonial bureaucracy.[33] In the years following their freedom, Black peasants, or *volkscreolen*, undertook a significant internal migration, leaving the rural areas in search for non-plantation opportunities in the capital city, Paramaribo, where "business and bureaucratic structures provided stronger possibilities for stable employment and educational environment for their children."[34] In 1876, when compulsory free education was made available, there was a "scramble among the lower middle-class Creoles for all kinds of diplomas and certificates . . . as important in their anticipated upward mobility as learned individuals in typing, bookkeeping, and other skills disassociated from agriculture and its tedious fieldwork. Their 'papers,' once acquired, promised a lifestyle beyond that of field laborers."[35] They would eventually become the small but burgeoning middle class fomented by a desire for social mobility, propelled by educational opportunities and work in civil service.

Such a survey of the intricacies of migration and colonial realities between Suriname and the Netherlands and the impetus for its recurring waves during the period in which Brouwn made his art remind us that although Karl Marx does not provide us with an aesthetic theory, we can deduce, from his economic concept of capitalism, that whether we produce widgets or art, we produce the very conditions of our lives. Art

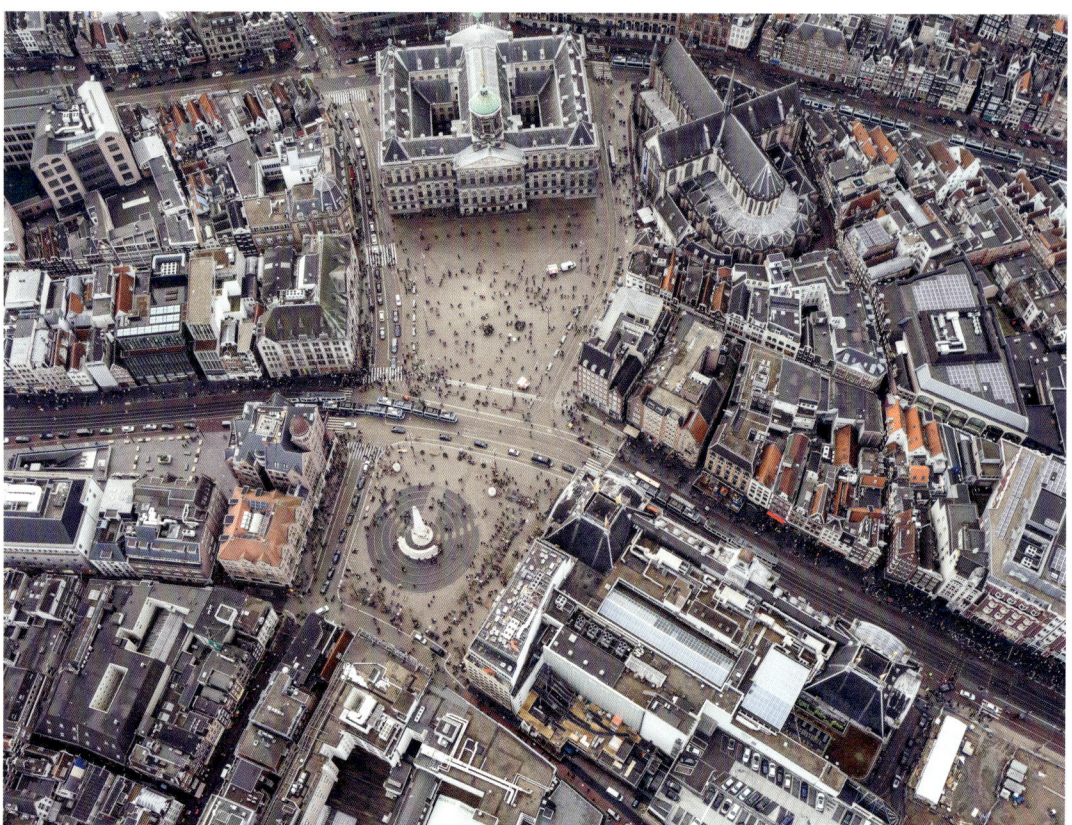

Fig. 2. Aerial view of Amsterdam Center over Dam Square, n.d.

Photo by Nisian Hughes. Courtesy of Getty Images

historian Eric de Bruyn describes Amsterdam in 1964 as "shifting and intersecting social networks of power . . . a highly dense force field that demonstrated its own complex set of transitions between striated and smooth spaces" (fig. 2).[36] Contemplating the sociological and political context in which Brouwn arrived lends a unique density to the forces possibly animating Brouwn's art. As Eve Meltzer points out, historical conceptual art reflected a world that was a network of systems, and the implications of being subjected to those systems informed the art being made in the 1960s and 1970s. The conventions with which Brouwn's aesthetics probe and play intervene into this world-system at the intersection of labor, management, production, circulation, and distribution, conflating the historic and the contemporary, from enslavement to postcolonial life. His art demonstrates a vernacular of bureaucratic power attendant to what art historian Benjamin Buchloh, in his defining essay on conceptualism, names an "administrative world" preoccupied with rigorous and relentless order, the "operating logic of late capitalism and its positivist instrumentality."[37]

Time is an inextricable factor in the administration of power in the world, particularly in capitalism's colonial scenes. The peculiarity of Brouwn's present in Amsterdam arrived sedimented through the historical as a cultural rationale, as conceptual and material referent in his art.[38] In this way, no moment in each of Brouwn's encounters that compose *This Way Brouwn* is original; each is a "moment of repetition, a moment in which the past returns to the present in expanded form, a moment in which present time finds stored and accumulated within itself a nonsynchronous array of past times," as Ian Baucom astutely insists.[39] Brouwn's work, like history itself, oscillates. The tendency we are tracing here lies between the ways in which finance capital itself performs and how it is emblematic in Brouwn's art, for, "time does not pass, it accumulates," and "time also repeats itself."[40] Repetition in Brouwn's art reflects the futility intrinsic to notions of progress. Indeed, only intensities matter, which can be extracted from the circulation of things, be they conditions of being or aesthetics. Our mandate is to seek out affinities between histories and Brouwn's art, between the artworks themselves, within bodies of work (as in a series) to which they belong and as correspondences among the series themselves, and in the wide arc of historical and contemporary visual representations of the Surinamese. To wit, *Narrative of a Five Years Expedition against the Revolted Negroes of Surinam* by John Gabriel Stedman (1744–1797), first published in 1796, and the 1976 film *Wan Pipel* (One people), directed by Pim de la Parra, offer two distinct approaches to visual representation of the encounter between the Dutch colonial project and the Surinamese, providing meaningful insight into the affinities and counterpoints between them and Brouwn.

■ ■ ■

The introduction to Stedman's travelogue, in which he is at times ethnographer and at others a hopeless romantic, of his years in a decadent world begotten and besotted by extreme violence opens with Voltaire's 1759 satire of slavery in the Americas and Caribbean with a narrative of Suriname:

> As they drew near the town they came upon a Negro lying on the ground wearing only half his clothes, that is to say a pair of blue cotton drawers; this poor man had no left leg and no right hand. "Good heavens!" said Candide to him in Dutch, "what are you doing there, my friend, in that horrible state?" "I am waiting for my master . . ." "Was it Monsieur Vanderdendur . . . who treated you this way?" "Yes, sir," said the Negro, "it is the custom."[41]

Stedman responded to a call for volunteers to the West Indies, arriving in Suriname in 1773 to stay for over four years.[42] The corps had been sent to the colony to buttress the military's efforts to cease the incessant waves of Maroon warfare, which were threatening the colony's economic viability.[43] Marronage in the Dutch colony was common at the time. Maroons—self-liberated former captives—freed the still enslaved, captured ammunition and military posts, and burned property, making them a vital force against the colonists and enslavers, which by the mid-eighteenth century had made Suriname "a theater of perpetual war."[44] The Maroons' guerilla techniques revolted against a particularly "crude philistine plantocracy," as Caribbean scholar Gordon K. Lewis described them, who owned sugar estates with on average 228 enslaved people, more than seventeen times as large as contemporary plantations in Virginia or Maryland.[45] Stedman captured this perplexing world in 106 watercolor drawings during his stay, including depictions of Indigenous and Black life in Suriname; the latter more often than not show the sorts of distended, fragmented bodies that Voltaire encountered. A selection of these drawings, eighty-one in total, was engraved to illustrate the book.[46] Most remarkable among them are the sixteen scenes of terror inflicted upon the enslaved, etched and signed by William Blake between 1792 and 1794 (fig. 3).[47] Their titles are as evocative in conveying the acts as the visual representations themselves: "A Negro hung alive by the ribs to a gallows," "Flagellation of a female Samboe slave," and "The Execution of Breaking on the Rack." Blake was deeply opposed to slavery, and his graphic portrayals of torture were also regularly reproduced in abolitionist media campaigns of the time.[48]

Strangely, the technique of etching, an act of inscription that is itself also an act of extraction performed in order to constitute form by repeatedly drawing lines into the metal material, captures the pathos of enslavement in Suriname. In other words, the form and methodology embody and enact the very subject they aim to represent. While Brouwn also selects others to make his inscriptions, his methodology and form operate differently inasmuch as his appropriated drawings are additive, lines applied to paper; they are also accumulations of individual works into a collective body, and like the function of colonialization, Blake's etchings are developed through the process of removal—one of derivation and deduction. Further, Blake's interpretation of Stedman's colored sketches is a process of translation, a mode of abstraction that performs the conditions of enslavement as literal cuts into the materials that make the work. Aesthetics come to produce the conditions of the lives the work aims to represent. That Stedman's drawings are already perceptions of what he experiences, imbued with personal desire and a perspective *colored* with and by cultural, societal, and political forces, neither Stedman's work nor Blake's can ever be understood as meticulous representations—liberties have been taken all along given the distinctively Romantic eighteenth-century European manner in which the works are styled. How are we to judge the felicity of the abstraction of violence in these works, which is to say the extent to which they compel us to feel what they aim to represent, their capacity as affective representations? Literary scholar Emily Senior has thought about the tropical colonial scene as a site of living death in which the integrity of the body is always undermined.[49] The body is fragile because it has been susceptible to an intense proximity to the colony, space/time in which the condition of fungibility metamorphoses a being into "a living body in a process of disintegration."[50]

This intense proximity is negotiated and read through the skin, which as "a marker of health and human difference was nowhere more evident than in the colonies, where it became the focus for medical and racial models of the body."[51] As Senior notes, "Skin is the motif through which

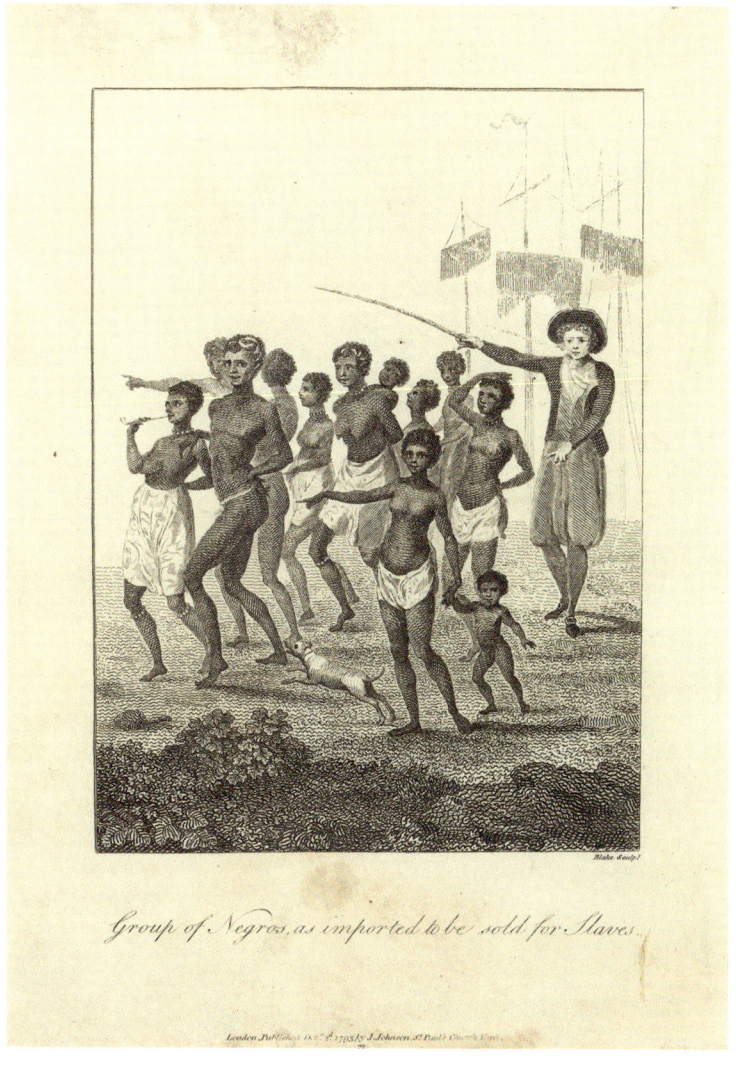

Fig. 3 William Blake after John Gabriel Stedman, *Group of Negros, as imported to be sold for Slaves*, 1793, engraving, National Gallery of Art, Washington, Rosenwald Collection

Stedman imagines the corruptive influence of the colonial environment."[52] Such a living body in Stedman's drawings and Blake's etchings is rendered in a state of metastasis, presented as "dismembered, dissected, rotting, and generally opened up and pieced apart."[53] In this context, Stedman's and Blake's skins are the sites of a range of entanglements—the locus of feeling and sympathy, the visual site of suffering for the violated enslaved and for the susceptible foreigner ailing from exposure.[54] Brouwn pursues these historical scenes in obscurity, an indirect acknowledgment or manifested unacknowledging (depending upon how you look at it) marking all that has led to these moments of encounter, of arrival. Difference need not be spoken but rather its parameters, edges, and sites of transgression are to be felt. For the skin has already been mapped/marked in the moments of arrival, in the coming to know its differentiation from then to now.

If Stedman's travelogue records the Maroon Rebellion as a set of conditions that contour and contextualize his arrival and life in Suriname—that is to say as an individual example of a general condition—then Surinamese filmmaker de la Parra's *Wan Pipel* is also fashioned at a critical moment instigated by a desire for freedom in the form of his country's independence from the Netherlands.[55] An allegory, the movie follows the character Roy Ferrol (Borger Breeveld), a Black Surinamese student living in the Netherlands who returns home as his mother is dying. Rife with symbolism, the film has a narrative axis formed around his interracial romantic entanglements with Karina (Willeke van Ammelrooy), a Dutch woman, and Rubia (Diana Gangaram Panday), a Hindu woman, as much as by the tensions between urban and rural life, modern and traditional ways of being. Rubia and Roy, who ultimately remain together, represent a unification of Black and brown peoples, and thereby, a doing away with colonial beliefs and historical fictions delineated by race, culture, and geography. With sexual and romantic liaisons as a leitmotif, *Wan Pipel* characterizes the dynamics of race, power, privilege, and sex in relationships between Dutch expats and the local population. Such thematic concerns are core to Stedman's accounts as well, most evident in his many descriptions of paid sexual affairs with enslaved women and particularly his "Surinamese marriage" to Joanna, an enslaved mixed-race woman who is represented in a single plate in the book, yet discussed at length in Stedman's recollections.[56] As makers of the first Surinamese feature film, de la Parra, along with screenwriters Rudi Kross and Lou Lichtveld, envisioned *Wan Pipel* as an explicit political statement concerning the colonial relationship between Suriname and the Netherlands.

"Each generation must discover its mission, fulfill it or betray it, in relative opacity," Frantz Fanon remarked in his formulation of "national culture" for colonized people.[57] His imperative articulates a meaningful distinction between de la Parra's project and Brouwn's, works of the same generation, in that the latter would turn away from the drive to express an idea of national culture, while the former, as we have seen, would constitute one by operating within a set of symbols meant to signify Suriname and its people. For Fanon, the "colonized intellectual" compares one's colonized culture in relation to the West at great risk. One becomes susceptible to the seduction of validation and thereby vulnerable to losing oneself, an unavoidable position when it is necessary to incessantly affirm one's humanity and culture in the long and ongoing aftermath of events as recorded in Stedman's journal. Accordingly, the desire for a national culture pursues the past, seeks its essence, situates itself as far away as possible from its current colonial reality. *Wan Pipel* enacts this as a kind of sentimentality for Suriname, especially in the scenes of Karina, Roy, and his father's visit to, as he put it, "the bush" with its long takes of a rushing river, thick descriptions of the surrounding flora and fauna of which, according to the father, "Roy knows nothing about." Karina, after a swim, says to Roy and his father, "I keep thinking Amsterdam is behind those trees," to which the father replies, "Amsterdam never existed, child," which Roy repeats and asks if his father is now a medicine man. The father replies that he's always wanted to raise his family in the interior of the country and indicates this is Roy's first time visiting this "ancestral" place. Following this scene is a dream sequence in which Roy throws Karina from a small rocky outcropping in the middle of the river, witnessed consecutively by his father and then Rubia, both accompanied by the same group of Indigenous people. Following Fanon, the colonized intellectual, like de la Parra, aims "to put his struggle on a legitimate footing, who is intent on providing proof and accepts to bare himself in order to better display the history of his body, is fated to journey deep into the very bowels of his people."[58] Here, signified by the rural landscape, ancestral plots, indigeneity, and the failure of memory, a literal journey unfolds, with a romanticism reminiscent of Stedman and an arrested recovery to which Brouwn's own peregrinations provide an exacting counterpoint.

Several scenes throughout the film reflect a style of exuberance that Fanon attributes to efforts toward what he proclaims as a national culture, "full of imagery . . . alive with rhythms bursting with life. A colorful style too, bronzed, bathed in sunlight and harsh," though they are full of "terribly sterile clichés" and a "banal quest for the exotic" (fig. 4).[59] Indeed, the veneer of exoticism was a constituent element in the development of visual art in Suriname, where professional education in such fields was not possible until the mid-twentieth century. Even then, arts education was limited to high-school courses and drawing lessons taught by Dutch artists living in Suriname, especially Nola Hatterman's classes.[60] Hatterman, who moved to Suriname in 1953, helped foster an art movement invested in developing an "authentic" folk culture recognizable for its distinct and recognizable figurative and thematic directness identifiable in people, flora, and fauna.[61] Fanon warned about such a concern for developing a visual language for the colonized: "The colonist experts do not recognize these new forms and rush to the rescue of indigenous traditions. It is the colonialists who become the defenders of indigenous style."[62]

Well after Brouwn moved to the Netherlands, the Surinamese Academy of Visual Arts was established in 1966. It is not known if Brouwn studied art in Suriname or what engagement he may have had with artists living there. However, K. Schippers, a Dutch artist and art critic of neo-Dadaist aesthetics who personally knew Brouwn, indicated in a 1965 text that Brouwn had long been occupied with doing actions and had already started doing so while living in Suriname.[63] Brouwn also wrote poetry in the 1950s, which was published in *Spiral* magazine, along with some of his drawings, and rife with symbolism and magical, even irrational poesy. Much of the language describes stunning exotic imagery of nature to a Dutch public, clearly referencing his native Suriname with mentions of swamps, snakes, reeds, and jaguars, and conveying a sense of existential angst and violence: "beauty beauty has burned her face," "sang a white snake holy," "larynxes encased under leopard," "field of the deadless people," "black pools river black," and so on.[64]

One cannot imagine that Brouwn would have thought of himself as a "colonized creator," however, our understanding of the evolution of his art is greatly enhanced by the theoretical framework Fanon has provided. Consider Fanon's analysis of visual art in the context of Brouwn's movements of withdrawal:

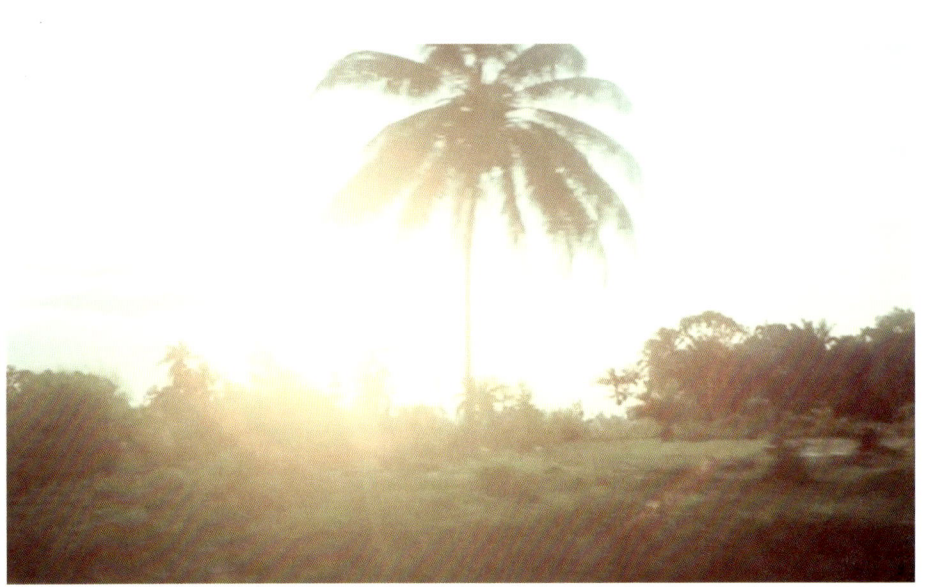
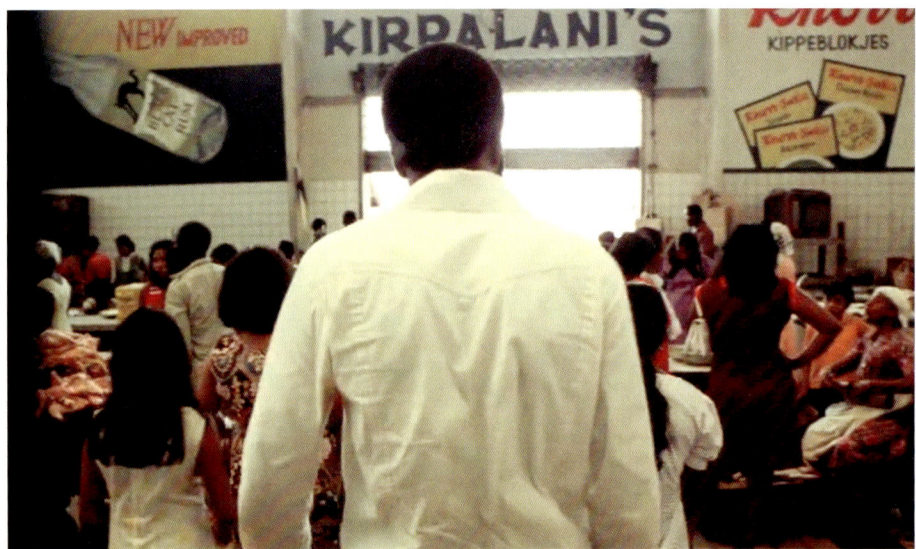
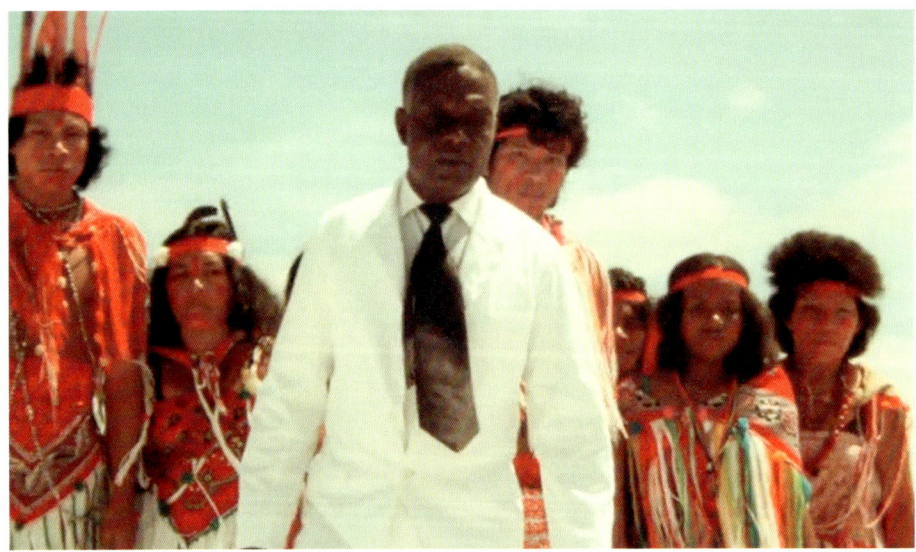

(He) confines himself to stereotyping details. These artists despite having been immersed in modern techniques and influenced by the major contemporary trends in painting and architecture, turn their backs on foreign culture, challenge it.... But these creators forget that modes of thought, diet, modern techniques of communication, language, and dress have dialectically reorganized the mind of the people and that the abiding features that acted as safeguards during the colonial period are in the process of undergoing enormous radical transformations.[65]

In other words, in order to fully respond to the circumstances that colonization presents, the artist cannot negate the transformations that have occurred in the wake of the encounter with the colonizer. While certain structural conceits have the potential to be redressed in terms of law, economics, and politics, the convolution of seismic cultural, emotional, and linguistic changes, to name just a few, resulting from the rupture having taken place and its aftermath can be neither negated nor neglected. An adequate response, which Brouwn seems to exemplify, is to create a language of reality and to exploit the uses of realism that can mobilize the entanglements of cultures, life, and society as—and through—creative endeavors.

Though Brouwn's early work, which he eventually disavowed, has a close semblance to exotic reminiscences of the Surinamese environment, he did quickly aim to surpass the literary symbolism explored in his poetry, evolving a technique of actions and objects within the context of the experimental visual art scene. His early forays in visual art and performance incubate a new language that abandons inherited ones. Brouwn would find himself between two disparate yet distinct aesthetics that seemed to forge ideas manifested in his later work. On the one hand there is the aforementioned shift in artistic discipline, from a poet to an artist concerned primarily with concept and process in art making. On the other hand is his coming to terms with aesthetics valued at the time in both Suriname, in the development of a folk visual art, and in the Netherlands, in the form of CoBrA (c. 1948–1951), an internationalist European-based experimental approach to art that sought a break from naturalism and abstraction in pursuit of an art influenced by improvisation, children's drawings, and Indigenous art from Africa, Oceania, and the Americas. Brouwn's transformation was a kind of protest, a rejection by complication of the stylistic proclivities of the time in Suriname and the Netherlands.

Instead Brouwn evolved an informal sensibility that shared elements with the international Fluxus, ZERO, and Concrete artists of the time, and though he knew and worked with some of them, he retained a kind of outsider stance. In the late 1950s and early 1960s, Brouwn not only presented himself as a transgressive figure, but also developed a transgressive language in his disavowed works that was seemingly conceptually absent in Suriname and materially unusual in the Netherlands (such as banana sculptures fabricated in brown cardboard, fly swatters, toy Indians, a

Fig. 4 Pim de la Parra, *Wan Pipel* (film stills), 1976, Eye Filmmuseum, Amsterdam

mutilated cat, plastic bags, a drawing with a woman's blouse as its support, a flashlight, and so on). In the mid-1960s, the artist began to annex works of art, or better, colored what he touched. Everything was *browned*. Alongside *This Way Brouwn*, he made other eponymous works presented as Brouwn books—*Cowboybrouwn* (1964), in which a supplied toy cowboy on a horse was to be placed on varying prestamped locations on a page; *Knipbrouwn* (1964), where pages were cut into pieces using scissors along a dotted line and placed into a plastic bag; and a book that was to be read with a hammer.[66]

Perhaps what is most important about Brouwn's adjacency to the art movements in the Netherlands of the time is a shared concern for the social developments and shifting ideas about the function of an artwork and its role in real life. Brouwn's sensibility registers as a transgressive imperative a step further than his colleagues in that he creates a new system of signs, a form of representation not dependent upon iconography, legibility, symbols, or even line for that matter, but on the signs of and remarks upon reality itself—the ways in which one lives a life. Accordingly, the mundane, the banal are rendered epic in the sense of scale and in the ubiquity and imposition of such elements. One's daily walk is epic. It is the lack of self-awareness, the givenness of the walk, that is essential.

In this sense, we can think of Brouwn's art of the 1960s and 1970s as what cultural theorist Homi K. Bhabha described in "Of Mimicry and Man" as "part-objects of presence."[67] As matter concerning experience and existence, thinking, feeling the work in the context of Bhabha's notion of mimicry reveals nuances of these walks as being a mode of critical engagement with colonialism. *This Way Brouwn* is a structure for uncertainty and fluctuation, and as such it "continually produce(s) its slippage, its excess, its difference."[68] The authority of the work operates from its position of indeterminacy. Within our understanding of the ways in which visual representation functions in art, Brouwn, in asking for directions to be inscribed, not only presents variation in the styles of mark-making among the drawings that comprise *This Way Brouwn*, but also engages his unwitting participants in imprinting their difference upon him and upon the others he engages in making the work. By interpolating these participants, each—Brouwn and them—also marks a position in relation to one another. This is necessarily a process of disavowal, one of distinction between you and another, a matter of proximity as much as intimacy. Therefore, each drawing is always a double vision, "a double articulation; a complex strategy of reform, regulation and discipline, which 'appropriates' the Other as it visualizes power."[69]

Appropriation is precisely a matter of closing the distance between space and intimacy such that they collapse upon one another and in so doing illumine that which extends beyond the boundaries they share. Thus mimicry, in its desire for shared space and close feelings, marks what is also inappropriate, thus necessitating the norms cultivated by colonial power and setting forth a disciplinary effort in the form of surveillance.[70] What is considered normal in a public interaction in which one party asks for directional assistance, for our purposes, is a literal demonstration of difference in citizenship and civility, as Bhabha puts it, "almost the same, *but not quite*." Brouwn, in asking for assistance, magnifies his difference, his Otherness, as a rupture within the social field because he has fixed himself as a "'partial' presence . . . both 'incomplete' and 'virtual.'"[71] In other words, in *This Way Brouwn* performances, the artist structures "some strategic limitation or prohibition" within the work itself. The request for directions, for example, is one such strategic limitation, since the instructions given are always already partial and incomplete, when, in order to be effective, they would need to be more authoritative than they could ever be, because the parameters of the work would never allow the directions to be more material than the work. The resulting maps are inherently what Bhabha calls "inappropriate objects" because their subjectivity "ensure[s their] strategic failure," making the work "at once resemblance and menace."[72] In so doing, between these performances of mimesis and mimicry out of which the drawing manifests "is a *writing*, a mode of representation, that marginalizes the monumentality of history, quite simply mocks its power to be a model, that power which supposedly makes it imitable."[73] Brouwn's minimal aesthetics form a partial presence in the work that operates through repetition rather than representation, because the breaks with cultural, racial, and historical difference (marked in each iteration of its performance) are the force that marks a break with colonial authority and asserts individual capacity, always not quite whole and somehow concealed, between the lines.

■ ■ ■

Such are the performances of the concept of Blackness in modernity and its modernisms, part and parcel of the capitalist system that gave it its form and through which apparatuses it circulates, arrives, and makes its presence known in the register of abstraction. It is important to restate that there is no record of Brouwn discussing Blackness in his work or otherwise. Nevertheless, a form of conceptualism perhaps resonated for Brouwn precisely because it is a formal and ideological interrogation of modernism and its conventions, functioning as an aesthetic of possibility within capitalism's systems of modernity that have instigated the conditions, affects, and contexts we describe as Blackness. For Blackness derives from modernity's concept of race yet is not limited by it. Therefore, Blackness is always already conceptual, assessed as a mode, means, and methodology neither situated in any singular historical narrative nor concerned with matters of ontology. Rather, we must approach Blackness as an animating force qua counterpoint to the ways in which the state or empire demonstrates its power through such structures as race, colonialism, capitalism, and the institutional and nation-state apparatuses. Blackness is a way of becoming abstract to deal with being of the world. Brouwn's opacity, his inclination to "show up to withhold"[74] in his art jettisons modernism's formalisms; instrumentalizes conceptual art's vocabulary; breaks with Stedman, Blake, and de la Parra's visual representations; performs Glissant's notions of relation and opacity; responds to Fanon's call for art aligned to the complex realities of colonialism; and enunciates and embodies mimicry as Bhabha proposes, to subvert through abstraction the established social, political, and formal systems, insisting that we linger at the complex threshold between a dematerialized identity and a historicized "body." We can comprehend Brouwn's refusal to share biographical data, photographs of himself, and reproductions of his art as a resistance to the fate of overwhelming visuality he would have well known as an Afro-Surinamese living in the Netherlands at the moment of heightened anxieties around immigration.

If, as art historian Lucy Lippard has described it, conceptual art is in part the dematerialization of the object, then perhaps for an artist such as Brouwn, entangled in Blackness and the colonial and capitalist systems from which it takes form, the act of dematerialization also resides elsewhere and as otherwise, which is to say not solely in regard to the physical matter of the work, but equally in the deconstruction of identity and representations of it. Brouwn's approach to conceptual art is somewhat classical given his adherence to qualities consistent with its production, namely a questioning of authorship, variations on ways to represent the body, and the visualization of information (text and data as art). Here I have explored the ways in which the parameters of Brouwn's art are determined by the social, political, and historical conditions in which conceptualism occurs, namely the structures, systems, and realities of colonialism and migration, thereby constituting a sensible tracing of them. One dimension concerns the embodiment of the colonial bureaucratic administration: the conceptualization, itemization, enumeration, and adherence to a set of tactics structured for the embodiment and therefore expression of operations, procedures, supervision, rules, regulation, control, and management within his works. For example, such a proclivity manifests as the stamp in *This Way Brouwn* or in the display of the cards included in the gray metal file cabinets of *The Total Number of My Steps*. Another distinct and recurring motif in his art is walking as a means of navigating urban space, instigating encounters with others, and tracing distances from home and difference as a being.

Brouwn stages occasions for relation through person-to-person exchange. His maneuvers, appearing at first transactional, belie the intimacy and care the artist elicits, even facilitates, in these encounters: it is not sufficient to merely describe how to get from one point to another; time and effort are requested to diagram the destination as well. Brouwn remarked, "People talk while sketching their explorations, and sometimes they talk more than they draw. On the sketches we can see what people explained. But we cannot see whatever they omitted, having some difficulty to realize that what they take for granted needs to be explained."[75] Herein lies the power of the work: subtle insistence on mutual recognition at a complex moment in Dutch and Surinamese history, taking an account of what is taken for granted, in which notions of motion, movement, and questions of belonging are necessitated and conjured by migration.

In both being toward abstraction and formulating a conceptual space within the real confines of the built environment, Brouwn disavows categorization, discipline, time, all the organizing structures of the modern world, as he finds himself existing within it. The work raises questions about the limits of freedom operating on at least two levels: the possibility that rules and austerity of materials enable infinitely more trajectories in his art, and the ability to negotiate and navigate space and time are experiments with and modes of questioning civic life and civilian subjectivity for a colonial subject living in the metropole. Systems and their structures (the grid of the city, the reliance upon language and diagrams, universal and peculiar measurements) put forth a constellation of relative simultaneity in which limits within escape routes, relationality within invisibility, and belonging within isolation are explored episodically, relationally, and diversely, revealing their intentional slippages and mergers.

While art history has attended to the formal qualities of Brouwn's practice as materialized in drawings, the interrelation between the gesture and the diagram and the implications of the embodied acts from which the objects (drawings and text as drawings) derive are but two elements in a constellation of encounters. For instance, in *This Way Brouwn*, lines on paper indicate moments along a trajectory of actions and exchanges ultimately occluded in the final manifestation of the work. The vector of opacity in which Brouwn exists and treasures above all else is analyzed as a productive withholding, which is vital to understanding such an inclination as a catalyst for dematerializing social structures at the level of the individual, which is to say to consciously actualize one's imperative in a process of testing, and thereby, coming to know oneself in the larger social schema. In sussing out the contours of his reality through the perception of others and his perception of them, the encounter is rendered as an outline—sheer surface, a veneer—of a place at a particular moment, suggestive of an auto portrait of the event as much as a comment on the impossibility of capturing the intimacy of the exchange. The remainder is a stark reminder of the unrepresentable, the indiscernible, all that is deficient at the level of the visible. The image of the event, as drawing or text as drawing, illuminates the productivity and possibility of imagination as sense escapes the grasp of being-made-object in deference to modes and methods of corporeal abstraction.

The scarcity of literature and critical engagement with the work—we know almost nothing of the artist's intentions—is precisely what makes an interpretation (historical or theoretical) of his art both necessary and entirely speculative. In some sense, Brouwn's reconfiguring of the visible, a minimal presence that is nevertheless dense and thick with the complexities and contradictions of modern history, has already set the terms for engagement, and we can only contend with his art through the very parameters he defines—that of one-on-one encounters, elusive cartographies, and pursuits of dead-ends—attending to its silences and abyss as much as to its strategies, devices, context, and contours.

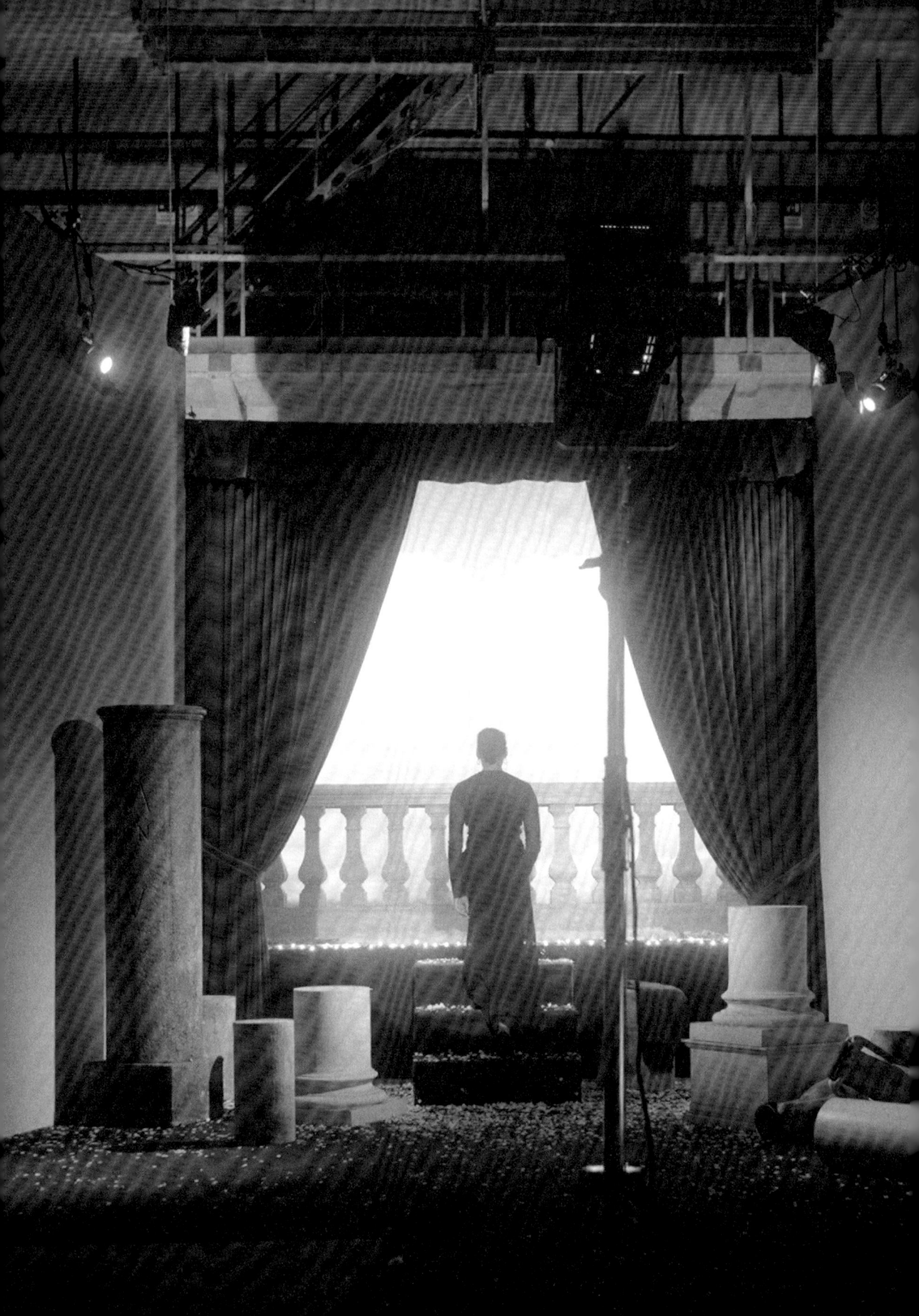

SPACES IN THE SHADOWS: ARCHIVES AND ARCHITECTURES IN THE WORK OF CARRIE MAE WEEMS

MABEL O. WILSON

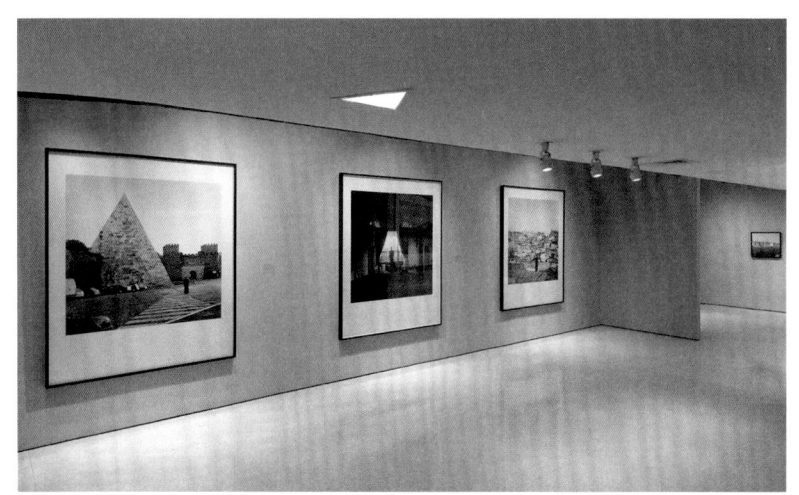

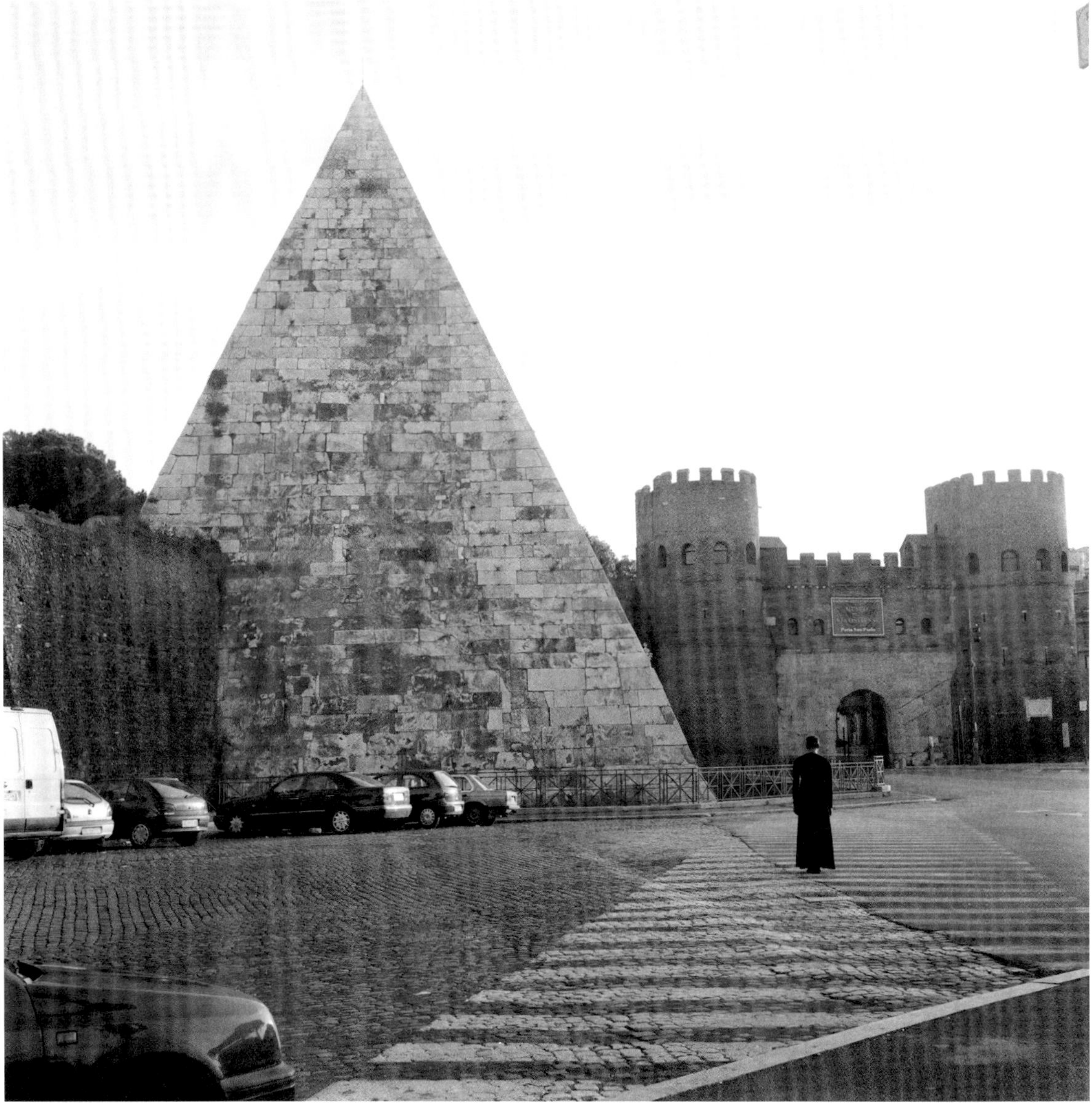

Only the BLACK WOMAN, can say "when and where I enter, in the quiet, undisputed dignity of my womanhood, without violence and without suing or special patronage, then and there the whole … race enters with me."
Anna Julia Cooper

Let's face it. I am a marked woman, but not everybody knows my name. "Peaches" and "Brown Sugar," "Sapphire" and "Earth Mother," "Aunty," "Granny," God's "Holy Fool," a "Miss Ebony First," or "Black Woman at the Podium": I describe a locus of confounded identities, a meeting ground of investments and privations in the national treasury of rhetorical wealth. My country needs me, and if I were not here, I would have to be invented.
Hortense J. Spillers

In a side gallery off the main spiral of New York City's Guggenheim Museum, I stood entranced by a large photograph that showed a woman sheathed in a long black dress with her back to the camera (figs. 1, 2). In the photograph, the Pyramid of Cestius, which dates to 18–12 BCE, overshadows the figure of the woman. The pyramid identifies the location as Rome—imperial capital of the Roman Empire, inspiration for the capital city of Washington, DC. Within Rome's historical landscape of ancient temples and theaters, the unusual pyramid, more common to upper Egypt, houses the tomb of Caius Cestius. A powerful magistrate, Cestius served as governor of the Roman Province of Egypt at a time when the Roman Empire ringed the Mediterranean. Today, the pyramid appears grafted into Rome's Aurelian walls, which were constructed around it in the third century. The woman, standing regally erect and perfectly still, turns toward the Porta San Paolo. Originally called the Porta Ostiensis, this imposing gateway flanked by two crenellated cylindrical towers marked a southern portal that connected ancient Rome to the port of Ostia on the Tyrrhenian Sea, where ships once embarked for and arrived from the Ptolemaic Kingdom.[1] The photograph's details revealed to me that this is not only ancient Rome, but also contemporary Rome. Parked cars and delivery vans nestle close to the tall brick Aurelian walls that once secured the city. The woman stands on asphalt that abuts the city's older cobblestone paving—both painted over by cross hatching to orchestrate passage through the intersection of the Piazzale Ostiense. I traveled with the woman in black, who is a Black woman like me, on a tour from Rome's "eternal past" to its present—a metric of how modernity defines temporality and constructs historicity through space, architecture, and the city. Where did she come from and where was she taking me? At this crossroads of time and space, a place where Africa had planted its monumental forms in Europe, what had she/we witnessed? Dressed in black, what was she, what were we mourning? As a Black woman in the streets of Rome was she "a marked woman"—was she a tourist, a tour guide, an artist, an expat,

Fig. 1 Carrie Mae Weems: Three Decades of Photography and Video exhibition, Solomon R. Guggenheim Museum, January 24–May 14, 2014

Photo by David Heald

Fig. 2 Carrie Mae Weems, Pyramids of Rome—Ancient Rome, from the series Roaming, 2006, photograph

Courtesy of the artist and Jack Shainman Gallery, New York, NY

a domestic worker, a nanny, a refugee, a sex worker, or could she be found in the lineup of stereotypes assembled by scholar Hortense J. Spillers: "'Peaches' and 'Brown Sugar,' 'Sapphire' and 'Earth Mother,' 'Aunty,' 'Granny,' God's 'Holy Fool,' a 'Miss Ebony First,' or 'Black Woman at the Podium'"?[2]

Pyramids of Rome—Ancient Rome appears in artist Carrie Mae Weems's homophonically titled series *Roaming* (2006), which she created while on a fellowship at the American Academy in Rome in 2005-2006. For architectural historian Manfredo Tafuri, referring to Piranesi's eclectic and fantastical *Campo Marzo*, Rome is a "colossal piece of bricolage," a city of fragments.[3] It is also a city whose imperial monuments provided models for the architecture of the Enlightenment's new republics birthed from revolution. In and around Rome, Weems photographed herself at several important ancient and modern sites. Always in her costume—a black gown—and standing with her back to the camera and to the viewer, Weems guides me through a series of views, "histories" of palimpsestic Roman vistas that juxtapose artifacts of antiquity alongside the conveyances and conveniences of everyday life in the European metropolis. Of *Roaming*'s enigmatic onlooker Weems explains, "This woman can stand in for me and for you; she leads you into history. She's a witness and guide."[4] Thus when I enter "into history" with her, into the West's temporal and spatial orders, what do we encounter?

Instead of traveling along the West's grand boulevard of Progress and Universal Knowledge, Weems roams time to rewrite and recast in her photographic series its signifiers of nationalism, culture, gender, and racial difference that mark history's unfolding and its hierarchies of power. For scholar Sarah Jane Cervenak the "spectacular opacity" of Weems's wandering indicates "a realm of phantasmatic movement inside an oppressive state; stillness and contemplation arguably disrupt the fetish of capitalist productivity at the heart of 'straight time.'"[5] Weems's roaming, however, isn't entirely aimless as the term "to wander" might suggest. She purposefully seeks to expose, attest, challenge, and recast institutions and structures—both discursive and material—by bearing witness. Her tour through Rome's civic, cultural, and religious monuments, its streets and backstreets, confronts the lineage of the West's political and cultural origins as defined by the canons of art and architecture and popularized in film and tour guidebooks. These encounters occur precisely because roaming the city as well as other sites in her oeuvre "marked" as a Black American woman—whose containment is necessary for definition and figuration of racialized human difference—unsettles the West's modern liberal subject's ability to know and thus situate himself in the metrics of time and the stable significations of space (political, cultural, and social) that Rome represents in the West.

Equally important in her travels is how Weems engages museums, their archives, and their collections as sites of power and regulation. Weems draws out the pervasive racialization of Black figures, especially women, in the archives central to the writing of art history and the cultural and spatial logics that categorize museums into different types:

art, history, and natural history. That the museum, like the monument, functions as a time machine, dividing culture into epochs and periods, is discernable in modernist architect Frank Lloyd Wright's design of the central gallery in the Guggenheim Museum, where visitors experience the display of art, design, and architecture—often curated in chronological order—along a ramp that spirals around a sunlit monumental atrium. By eschewing documentary photography in favor of mise-en-scène explorations of history, place, and meaning, Weems constructs counter-histories that expose how photography became a tool in the arsenal of racialization.[6] In her explorations of historic cities, landscapes, archives, studios, and institutions Weems shows me and other viewers why and how photography produces representations of Blackness as evidence of its primitiveness and social pathology on one hand and its eroticism and desirability on the other hand. Across her works Weems asks, is it possible to disengage the racial double bind that melds the ahistoricity of Blackness that located Black people outside of modernity to the primacy of Blackness that kept it fundamental to modernity's historical unfolding and modernism's fertile imagination?

In and Out of Place

In *Roaming* and in her other photographic series *Sea Islands* (1991–1992), *Africa* (1993), *Slave Coast* (1993), *From Here I Saw What Happened and I Cried* (1995–1996), *Not Manet's Type* (1997), *Jefferson Suite* (2001), and *Museums* (2006), Weems travels across three continents—North America, Africa, and Europe. This geography (space) and its history (time) incubated a racial imaginary of the Africa and the African diaspora that formed through the routes of Europe's colonial conquest of land, people, and resources. To better understand how the ability to locate oneself in time and space—self-consciousness—became integral to modern subjectivity, it is helpful to turn to nineteenth-century German philosopher Georg Wilhelm Friedrich Hegel. The German idealist mined narrations of colonial encounters recorded in diaries, reports, and ethnographic writings and drawings of European travelers and colonizers as the basis for his geopolitical thesis that for Africans and New World Negroes consciousness had not yet attained to the realization awareness of any substantial objective existence."[7] Historical consciousness, according to Hegel, was the province of the whitened European mind. For Africans and New World Negroes historical consciousness was unachievable because Blacks in their satisfaction of basic human needs dwelled only in the moment and were therefore outside the "theater of history." Based on this reasoning, Hegel surmised that blackened Africans and New World Negroes could not be modern. Instead, through their metaphorical and viscerally apparent "blackness," they became racialized as Europe's others and thereby cast as the object of domination, exploitation, affectability, and knowledge in science and history.[8]

As millions of people were sold and traded into slavery on the African continent, the dehumanizing journey on the slave ship and the violent confinement of the hold—where captives faced whipping, sickness, or suicide as an ever-present specter of death—gave birth to the modern Black subject—the slave, the nigger, the Negro, and the Black. For poet and philosopher Édouard Glissant, "The belly of this boat dissolves you, precipitates you into a nonworld from which you cry out. This boat is a womb, a womb abyss."[9] In the enclosure of the plantation, its mechanized system of singular crop production to maximize profit of its plant and human commodities gave rise to a new metrics of time and vectors of space. In the process of dehumanizing Africans for trade, labor, and profit, Europeans set the stage for the violence that enabled their freedom. This double bind reared the unreason that imperiled rationality and haunted the discursive ordering of the museal and the archival central to the Enlightenment project. Suspicion of what could or could not be told through historical discourse led poet M. NourbeSe Philip to distrust "the language in which those events took place [which] promulgated the non-being of African peoples, and I distrust its order, which hides disorder; its logic hiding the illogic and its rationality, which is simultaneously irrational."[10] It was the deadly violence mobilized for centuries to subdue the enslaved and contain the colonized in the name of civilization that returned to Europe, for instance, as the theatrical unfolding of modern fascism in the twentieth century.[11] Certainly modern architecture, like the fascist travertine monuments of Rome's E42 that Weems photographed herself within for *Roaming*, bears witness to that relentless will to power unleashing the paradox of reason—madness, death.

From this articulation of Blackness, the European's own body, culture, and episteme, his "whiteness," came to signify what it meant to be virtuous, intelligent, and human—hence, modern. "European bourgeois Man" as theorist Sylvia Wynter argues, "overrepresents itself as if it were the human itself, and that of securing the well-being, and therefore the full cognitive and behavioral autonomy of the human species itself/ourselves."[12] As seen through the eyes of the transcendental typically white male European mind, the dialectic of progress that history produced, as evidenced in the concept of culture and its productions—the arts and the "art of building," that is architecture. These art and cultural forms develop within hierarchical gradations from primitive to civilized. This also spurred cartographic representations of inhabitable temperate regions and forbidding torrid zones that enabled the colonial project of resource extraction and domination while at the same time forming a geopolitical map of moral and intellectual development. In this theater of history's chronological unfolding, the Black body, particularly the Black female body, functioned as the labor—productive and maternal—that sorted racial difference, value, and fungibility. For Spillers, "The captive female body locates precisely a moment of converging political and social vectors that marked the flesh as a prime commodity of exchange."[13]

Captive Black bodies, rendered nonhuman with the enclosure of Blackness signifying what is not modern and ahistorical, become necessary not only for the modern subject's concept of linear time and space, but also for their definition of freedom.[14] It is through this dialectic between slavery and freedom that self-determination becomes enshrined in political discourse, with the ability to move freely becoming a fundamental right guaranteed through modern liberal democracy. Further, the neoclassical architecture of Washington, DC, a capital city dedicated to governance and its monuments symbolic of freedom, though erected by enslaved labor force of men, women, and children, encapsulates this paradox and disavowal at the heart of the American political project.[15] It is this power of belonging to some place that the modern nation state establishes through citizenship and that Weems seeks to challenge. As she has explained, "It's been implied that I have no place in Europe. I find the idea that I'm 'out of place' shocking. There's a dynamic relationship between these places: the power of the state, the emotional manipulation of citizens through architectural means, the trauma of war, genocide, the erasure of Jews, the slave coast, and the slave cabins."[16] Referring to Glissant's abyss, geographer Katherine McKittrick suggests that "the consequences of the Middle Passage rupture, the outcome of annihilation, is a way of knowing and belonging capaciously and generously."[17] Weems's photographic wanderings through coastal regions of the Atlantic Ocean; through cities and towns in Europe, Africa, and the United States; and through her personal archives as well as those of museums and universities, trace the migratory histories and cultures—"the nonworld" and welcoming homeplaces— Black peoples formed in the wake of the transatlantic slave trade.

Wandering the Black Diaspora

As an outcome of colonialism, Western historical narratives are entangled in power relations, ones that are racialized, that have allowed some narratives to speak (and be rendered visible) while silencing others (rendering them invisible).[18] Weems experiments with techniques of appropriation, reframing, and staging to tell counter-histories. She recolors and crops archival photographs and arranges them with her own photographic series, sometimes accompanied by poetic texts and domestic artifacts like wallpaper, dinner plates, or folding screens. These techniques allow Weems to probe the historicized and naturalized lexicon of Blackness through her photographs and the ways she installs her works in museums and galleries. In many of her series Weems performs as witness, as photographer behind the lens and figure inside the frame. Through this approach she problematizes how the historiography of colonialism and slavery has silenced Black narratives and dehumanized Black subjects from the African continent to the African diaspora.[19]

These critical counter-histories are at work in Weems's series *Sea Islands*, *Africa*, and *Slave Coast*, which were shown together in an exhibition at the Museum of Modern Art, New York (MoMA), in 1995. She began these projects with a search for home, a quintessential aspiration of the modern liberal subject to know one's social and cultural origins: "Home for me is both mysterious and mythic—the known and the unknown. My search begins with the *Sea Islands* piece."[20] She turned to folklore and other forms of storytelling that draw upon the intimacy of memory and place, rather than the West's formal language of history writing and erecting monuments: "where I come from, how is that place constructed, what went on there, what was that sort of historical movement about."[21] Weems practices what Audre Lorde called "biomythography," a mixture of myth and truth that entwines heart and mind on a journey to conjure home. In an interview with Weems, scholar bell hooks suggested of the series *Sea Islands*: "You're not looking to 'document' in some scientific, linear, orderly, factual way where we came from, how we got here; you are uncovering these details, but also exploring the gaps, the spaces in the shadows that facts don't allow us to see, the mystery."[22] The three series *Sea Islands*, *Africa*, and *Slave Coast* follow Weems in her search for homeplace, one in which she roams the geography of the transatlantic slave trade, "the womb abyss" and its slave forts and plantations that fueled the industries generating the great wealth of Europeans and Americans, and produced significations of racial difference, a grammar of whiteness, progress, and civilization through dispossession and dehumanization of Black people. To speak back to this monumental historical narrative of nations, race, and modernity Weems created her own counter-histories.

Georgia's coastal Sea Islands; Ghana's Elmina and Cape Coast slave fort castles; Senegal's Goreé Island; and Djenné, Mali's shorelines proved fertile ground for Weems to wander through "the spaces in the shadows that facts don't allow us to see." She photographed places—quotidian and spiritual—that remain as sites of everyday life and the historical points of capture, departure, embarkation, and settlement within the violent geography of transatlantic slave trade. In contrast to mostly voluntary migrations across the Atlantic by Europeans, a white-settler colonial ethos that is celebrated as the bravery and tenacity of American immigrants, these involuntary movements of Black peoples that coalesced into the African diaspora were also routes forged by the greed and brutality of mercantile and industrial capitalism, ones best described by McKittrick as "implicated in the uneven development of space because overarching traditional geographic projects require that they [Black peoples] be placed or displaced."[23] Acutely aware of these geographies, Weems traces how Black bodies were displaced through the middle passage, slavery, and by Jim Crow segregation, and placed within the enclosure of the plantation, Black bottoms, ghetto, and prison.[24]

In places like the Sea Islands, she sees and hears Africanist undertones, fragments of African cultural practices that remain as living memorials to the harrowing middle passage and its aftermath in the "nonworld"—everyday objects arranged in yards to ward off spirits or in the spirituals sung in the local praise house. Her haunting visual narratives enter the interiors of homes and places of worship. She roams cemeteries, roadsides, streams, and fields where West African sensibilities in placemaking persist. In this manner, Weems engages what anthropologist David Scott calls "cultural traditions" that forge relationships to the past—slavery and Africa—within local discourses "constructed around a distinctive group of tropes or figures, which together perform quite specific kinds of rhetorical labor."[25] In Scott's formulation, which is relevant to Weems's visual and verbal counter-histories, cultural traditions do not require anthropological authentication through evidence like those collected and displayed in museums. Rather, cultural traditions make meaning through the ways narratives connect the past, present, and future and valorize particular "dispositions, specific modes of address, specific styles—of dress, of speech, of song, of the body's movements," which all register within the built environments and through texts shown in Weems's photographs.[26]

When Weems installed the three series at MoMA, she also inserted framed panels of text into her counter-historical narratives that directly address the viewer (fig. 3). The texts enunciate what could have happened in spaces like the fortress corridors and door of no return on Goreé Island off the coast of Dakar, Senegal. She stacks words that outline the protocols of capture:

GRABBING
SNATCHING
BLINK
AND YOU
BE GONE

She also drafts a list of Westernized identities and places, as if found on a slave trader's ledger:

CONGO
IBO
MANDINGO
TOGO

Fig. 3 Carrie Mae Weems, *Grabbing, Snatching, Blink and You Be Gone*, from the series *Slave Coast*, 1993, photograph

Courtesy of the artist and Jack Shainman Gallery, New York, NY

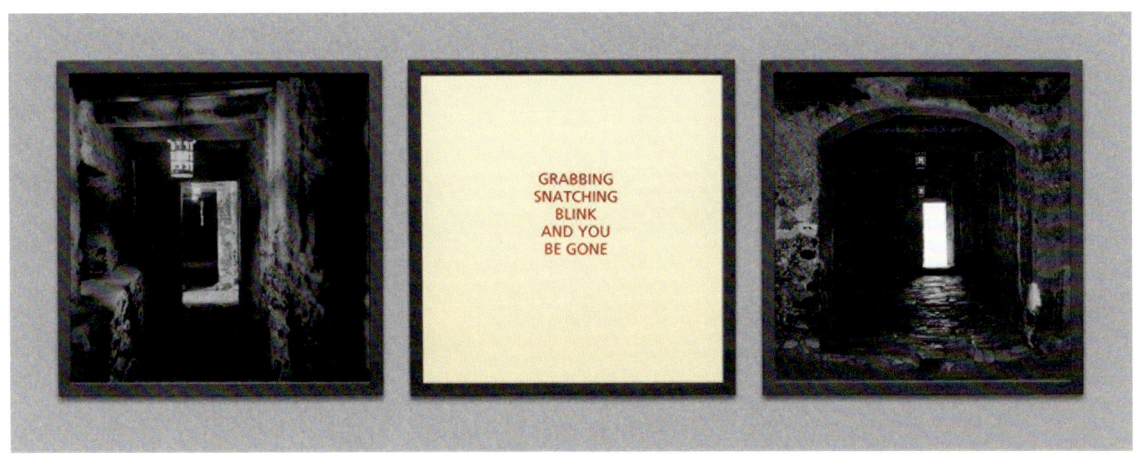

These terms destroyed the culture and lands of distinct people and were necessary to construct a vast slave trading network and enslaved workforce of Negroes for the mono-crop system of plantations whose commodities fed Europe's insatiable appetite for sugar, tobacco, cotton, indigo, rice, and rum.

On the other side of the Atlantic's abyss, on the coasts and marshlands of Georgia and South Carolina, where Creolized Gullah culture flourished, Weems photographed an old brick cottage, perhaps a plantation slave cabin (fig. 4). Adjacent to the three photographs of the house, Weems placed the text, sentences stacked like a sloping roof: "When you move into a new house, remove old spirits by washing around the windows and doors with vinegar water. But, prevent spirits from crossing the doorstep by putting salt and pepper along the door and window sills." These Gullah rituals link back to West African spiritual practices such as forms of collective address and dialogue like the call and response traditions found in Black song and religions. Moreover, her second-person voice allows "you," the viewer, to enter the house, take possession of the rituals that ward off evil influences, and then pass on these cultural traditions. The texts introduce a cadence in her series, like this one found on a ceramic plate from the *Sea Islands* series:

Fig. 4 Carrie Mae Weems, *House*, from the series *Sea Islands*, 1991–1992, photograph

Courtesy of the artist and Jack Shainman Gallery, New York, NY

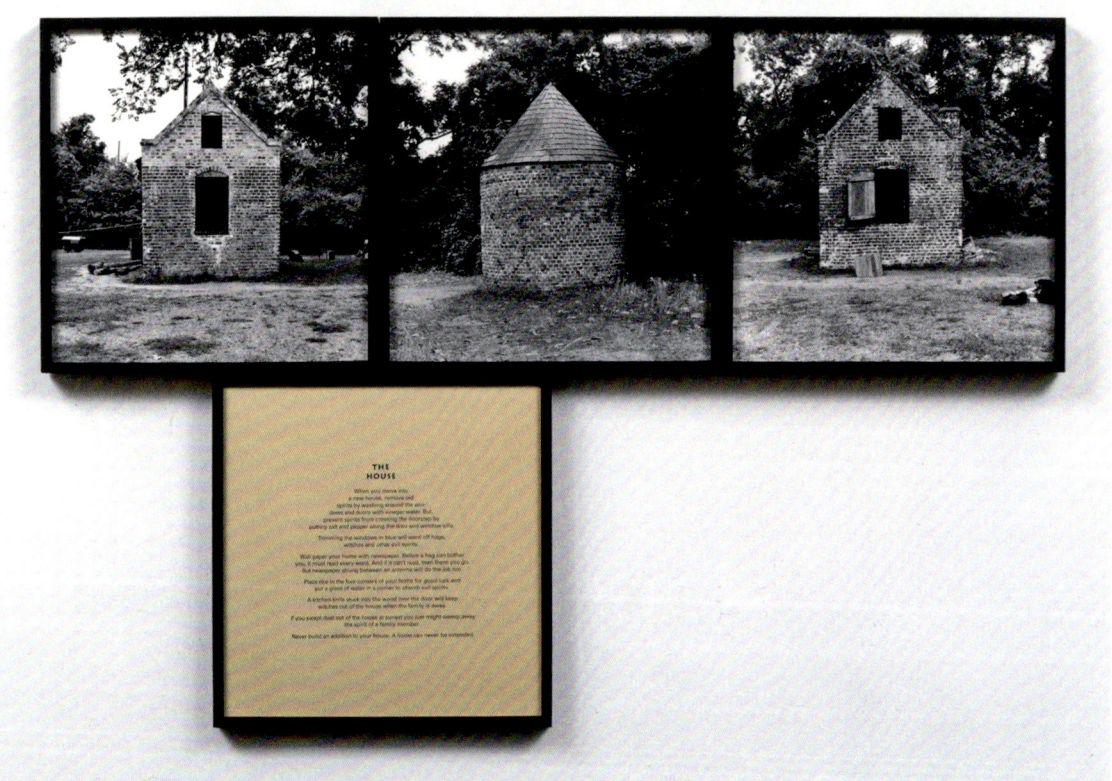

208

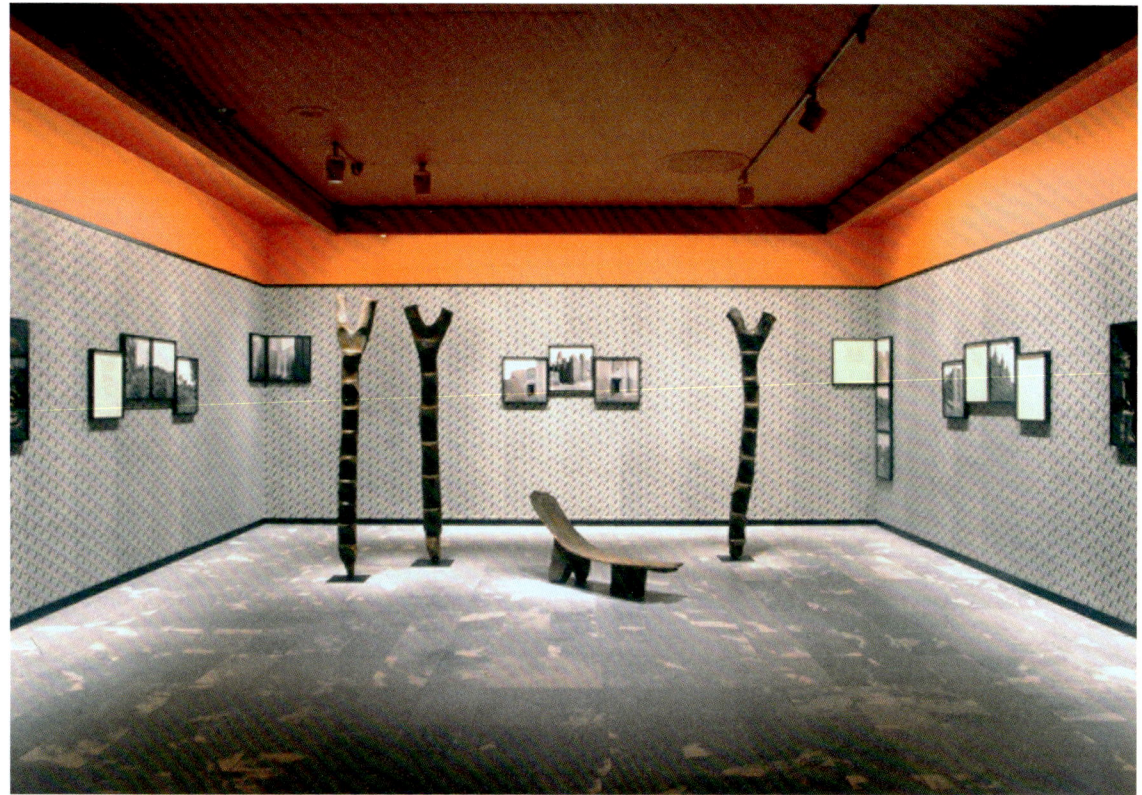

Fig. 5 *Projects 52: Carrie Mae Weems* exhibition, Museum of Modern Art, New York, October 31 (November 1), 1995–March 12, 1996, Museum of Modern Art Archives, Photographic Archive

Courtesy of the artist and Jack Shainman Gallery, New York, NY. Photo by Mali Olatunji. Digital image © The Museum of Modern Art / Licensed by Scala / Art Resource, NY

<u>WENT LOOKING FOR AFRICA</u>
and found Africa
in a wrought iron gate
the design of
the master house
in the shape of a
sweet-grass basket
in a round
smoke house

The verses create a vocal track of sorts, in the form of what curator Franklin Sirmans has identified as "poetic writing that recalls the vernacular and oral narration" in the work of writers like Zora Neale Hurston.[27] Weems calls out to her viewer in the tonalities of cultural traditions, reverberations of sounds and silences across the Black spaces formed in the wake of the transatlantic slave trade.

To organize the photographic groupings *Africa* and *Slave Coast* at MoMA, Weems painted the symbolic white walls of the modernist art gallery a deep yam-like orange (fig. 5). She also lined sections of the gallery walls with an abstract black-and-white patterned wallpaper framed by black molding at the base and at the top not quite covering the entire orange wall. Upon closer inspection the wallpaper features a repeating vignette of a Black woman reaching toward a palm frond amid cascading

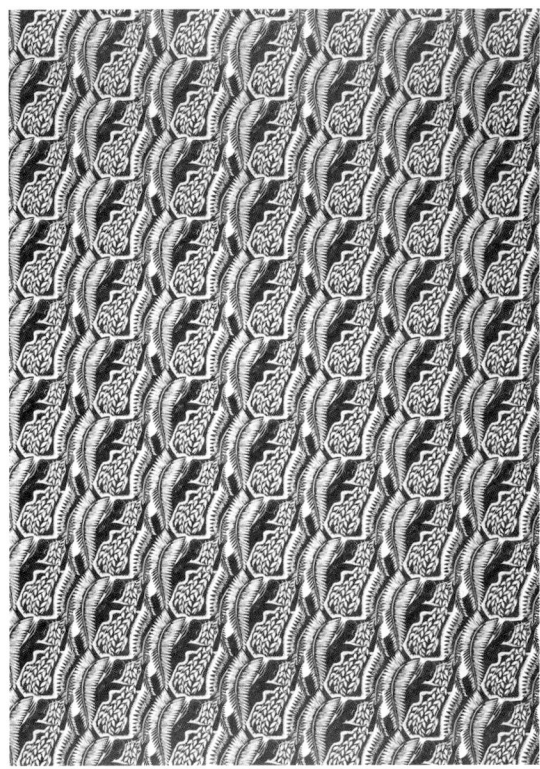

Fig. 6 Carrie Mae Weems, *Looking High and Low*, from the series *Africa*, 1993, screenprint on paper, from an original endpaper design and engraving by John Farleigh in George Bernard Shaw, *The Adventures of the Black Girl in Her Search for God* (New York, 1932), Victoria and Albert Museum, Prints, Drawings, and Paintings Collection, given by the artist

Courtesy of the artist and Jack Shainman Gallery, New York, NY. Image © Victoria and Albert Museum, London

leaves whose design Weems named *Looking High and Low* (fig. 6). She appropriated the pattern, a metaphor for "searching, probing, looking," from the endpapers of a first edition of George Bernard Shaw's satire *The Adventures of the Black Girl in Her Search for God* (1932). Shaw wrote a series of short stories about a young African girl who, after she is converted by white missionaries, goes on a journey to find God.[28] On this patterned backdrop, which from a distance appears as wave patterns of a choppy sea, Weems arranged her works in groupings so that photographs slide upward or around corners to create a dynamic rhythm and movement of her visual and textual series for viewers walking through in the galleries. This kinetic placement unsettles for the viewer the static exhibition space of the museum, one that has historically used white walls and glass vitrines to arrest objects, especially those from the African continent, out of time and location in order to fashion the dialectic between art and artifact central to how modernism distinguished itself from primitivism in institutions like MoMA.

As Seen by Science and History

In her series and installations of *From Here I Saw What Happened and I Cried* Weems appropriated and incorporated rare mid-nineteenth-century daguerreotypes of enslaved men and women who lived and worked on plantations around Columbia, South Carolina, one hundred and fifty miles inland from the Sea Islands. The daguerreotypes commissioned in 1850 by Swiss-born biologist, geographer, and Harvard professor Louis Agassiz resided in the archives of the Harvard University's Peabody Museum, where they had been lost until rediscovered in 1976.[29] Because Weems used the images in her works without permission, Harvard, the images' owner, threatened legal action. Determined, Weems believed that given the racialized nature of Agassiz's research the scientist had violated the humanity of his photographic subjects and Harvard had continued that violation through its possession of the daguerreotypes. Legal scholar Yxta Murray expanded upon this claim to argue that Weems's alleged "theft takes back what Agassiz, Morton, Cuvier, Guyot, Galton, and their ilk stole from African-born people and their descendants in the United States."[30] To be sure, white planters had purchased and owned the persons Jack and his daughter Drana; Renty and his daughter Delia; along with three men, Jem, Alfred, and Fassena; and now Harvard University owned and continued to profit from their likenesses. To expose how photography facilitated the violence of racial subjection Weems guides us through the archives at the Peabody Museum and the J. Paul Getty Art Museum, along with other archives of popular culture and history.

Sketching the history of how the daguerreotypes were created helps explain Weems's strategic appropriation of them. The Peabody Museum, whose curatorial focus was ethnology and archeology, opened in 1866 and marked the mid-nineteenth century's shift to biologically affirmed racial difference, whose origins were in the Enlightenment's examination of human difference that cast Europe's Others as naturally and logically inferior, rationalizing their exploitation and if necessary, their elimination.[31] Of Africans, German philosopher Immanuel Kant observed in his *Observations on the Feeling of the Beautiful and Sublime and Other Writings* (1764): "Negroes of Africa have by nature no feeling that rises above the ridiculous."[32] From this Kant reasons that Europeans (eventually marked phenotypically as white) were superior "in capacities of the mind."[33] Later, Hegel built upon these assertions and christened Africa "the land of childhood, which lying beyond the day of self-conscious history, is enveloped in the dark mantle of the Night."[34] This measure of human and cultural development (racial difference), which for Hegel was the provenance of European mind (historical consciousness), underwrote the modern concept of Progress that became a cultural project as well as a political and economic imperative for nations like the United States. The signifier "whiteness" marked the European body as superior and illuminated him as a man of reason, which led some naturalists and eventually scientists to theorize through polygenesis that the races were in fact distinct species. Though many challenged this assertion, they did not necessarily dispute the natural inferiority of Black persons.

Dedicated to the nascent nineteenth-century disciplines of anthropology, ethnography, and archaeology, institutions such as the Peabody Museum objectified and rationalized the exploitation of Europe's others for the extraction of knowledge, wealth, labor, and delight. While nineteenth-century American and European abolitionist movements sought to end the odious trade in human flesh, there nonetheless emerged aesthetic ideas linking beauty, whiteness, and European superiority within racial science. The "ideal physiognomy, which had been unattainable on earth for those who believed in the brotherhood of man," writes art historian David Bindman, "became increasingly as the nineteenth century progressed a European or 'Caucasian' norm, to be contrasted with the inferior physiognomy, morality, and 'intelligence' of other races."[35] The aesthetics of these comparative classificatory systems, which would become the biological and thus innate basis for racial difference, can be traced to the Enlightenment anthropology of Kant and can be found in the writings of Johann Joachim Winckelmann, a founding scholar of art history, who believed that the perfect lines and proportions of Greek physiognomy accounted for the beauty of Greek art.[36] By the mid-nineteenth century a racialized conception of beauty was more explicitly rendered in painting and sculpture, particularly in the articulation of skin, hair, facial, and other physical attributes, which not only represented the most revered aesthetic characteristics but also conveyed a virtuous moral character of those possessing refined cultural taste.[37]

Regardless of whether it could be proven through scientific evidence, Agassiz's concept of racial difference rooted in antiblack racism boosted nationalist claims that the intellectually superior Europeans (and their hereditary descendants, white Americans, primarily those claiming Anglo-Saxon lineage) would advance modern civilization (liberal democracy, culture, and industrial capitalism) in the project of nation building. Whereas those labeled as the inferior races—the primitive Africans (including America's Negroes), Asians, Southeast Asians, and Native Americans—were either degenerating toward disappearance, as with Indigenous peoples of the New World, or if not, were appropriately consigned to labor on plantations or compartmentalized, as Frantz Fanon described of the colony into "the native town, the Negro village, the medina, the reservation, is a place of ill fame, peopled by men of evil repute. They are born there, it matters little where or how; they die there, it matters not where, nor how. It is a world without spaciousness."[38]

For practitioners of nineteenth-century ethnography like Agassiz, photography became an important tool for the close study of the modern racial type. "Typological photography" like Agassiz's objectified and racialized individuals by analyzing, as curator Brian Wallis writes, "the exterior form of the human body in an attempt to understand the connections between different human groups as well as the inner workings of the mind and spirit."[39] For Agassiz's study and collection, J. T. Zealy, a white photographer, made several sets of daguerreotypes of two women, Drana and Delia, and five men, Renty, Jack, Jem, Alfred, and Fassena—all from plantations near Columbia, South Carolina. Zealy made two daguerreotypes of Jack and his daughter Drana and two of Renty and his daughter Delia. In the classification notes made by Robert W. Gibbes, a fellow naturalist and a local doctor who tended enslaved communities at the behest of enslavers, this group were believed to possess distinctly African physiognomic characteristics, including temperament, that could be assumed to be "Mandingo,"

"Guinea," "Foulah," or "Gullah," labels culled from the decades of slave trading and ownership in the region.[40] By taking a frontal and profile portrait of each father and daughter, Agassiz hoped to document and prove through comparative analysis the character of pure Africans, as opposed to Negroes who were a mixture of Africans, Europeans, and/or Native Americans. These daguerreotypes along with a physical exam would provide evidence that these specimens bore attributes of a separate species.[41] At the behest of Agassiz and with the consent of their enslavers, Zealy photographed the two daughters naked from the waist up, their breasts exposed and clothing bunched around their waists. And he photographed the two men Jack and Renty with naked upper torsos, their veins and taut muscles disclosing a life in bondage.

I can assume that neither the men nor the women were asked by any of their white interrogators if they wished to be photographed in this manner or at all. In pointing out the sexualized and racialized violence of the pictures, scholar Ariella Azoulay observes how the fathers and daughters "stand motionless, like statues—upright and balanced, mouths shut, eyes, staring ahead, heads held high on tall necks, arms symmetrically dropped at their sides, palms placed on their thighs pointing toward each other at an angle to the arms and wrists."[42] Posed in front of the camera for long periods to capture an exacting likeness of their Blackness, a mark of their sub-humanity and animality, in turn elevates and equates whiteness with humanness. The half-dressed pose of Drana and Delia illustrates for art historian Sarah E. Lewis how these daguerreotypes conditioned a way of looking that turned the women into scientific specimens primed to be read.[43] In the intimate space of the studio and archive, epistemic motivation and paternal desire joined to enact the power of white supremacy on the Black female body. Rather than toil in the fields, they labored in the photographer's studio, which doubled as a scientific laboratory, to certify the racial type and the superiority of the white mind and body. "In my look at them," scholar Christina Sharpe writes of their pose, "I register in their eyes an 'I' and a 'we' that is and are holding something in, holding on, and held, still."[44] The opacity of the gazes of Jack, Drana, Renty, and Delia reminds me of the impenetrable abbreviations entered on the 1850 and 1860 schedules of enslaved people for the US census, which historians and amateur genealogists peruse for clues of African American ancestry. These documents list the enslaver's first and last names, below them appear the sex and age of their human property, ciphers that veil enslaved identities—like those of my ancestors whose actual names were later recorded in the 1870 census as Miles Barnhill and his daughter Fannie. Whether a census, a daguerreotype, or a ledger, these documents exist as a "meeting ground of investment and privation in the national treasure of rhetorical wealth," as noted by Spillers.

Weems incorporated the images of Jack, Drana, Renty, and Delia into her work *From Here I Saw What Happened and I Cried*, which takes a critical arc through how the signs and signifiers within portraiture, anthropological, and documentary photography produced the visuality of Blackness.

The J. Paul Getty Museum commissioned Weems to create a response to an exhibition of rare antebellum daguerreotypes, ambrotypes, and tintypes of mostly free African Americans from its collection and from a private collection owned by Jackie Napoleon Wilson, a Black historian and attorney. That exhibition, *Hidden Witness: African Americans in Early Photography*, along with *From Here I Saw What Happened and I Cried*, was exhibited at the Getty Museum in Malibu, California, in the first half of 1995. From the Getty Museum's photography collection, Weems selected a series of early photographs as well as iconic works by Garry Winogrand and Robert Mapplethorpe that she rephotographed. She also included images from the Peabody and others from advertising and popular culture. She resized, cropped, and colored the photographs. She added a red tint—symbolic of anger and of blood—to thirty-one of the thirty-three prints. The red amplified the violence of photographic process in its enforcement of racial subjection, while at the same time the way she cropped or labeled the image liberates some small semblance of their humanity.[45] Weems tinted the photographs of her earlier series *Colored People* (1989–1990) to emphasize how "Blackness" encompasses a range of hues.[46] To implicate the photographic apparatus and process, Weems placed her new portraits for *From Here I Saw What Happened and I Cried* in circular frames to reinscribe the lens that captured them as the object of study, highlighting the gaze of not only Zealy and Agassiz, but also Weems and the viewer. Her reframing reconstitutes the racialized gazes of mid-nineteenth-century science and modern photography—as each person or group, now shaded in red or blue, draw my gaze into the production of racialized knowledge.

Weems began and ended the sequence of portraits with a witness. She incorporated two large photographs of an existing iconic photograph, *Nobosodru, Femme Mangbetu* (1925), by white filmmaker Léon Poirier, who with photographer and cinematographer Georges Specht took the photo during the making of their film *La crosière noire* (*Black Journey*), an automotive expedition, a modern colonial adventure to discover a route connecting French Algeria to Madagascar.[47] Poirier and Specht's well-known image depicts, in profile, the wife of the king of the Mangbetu in Belgian Congo (today the Democratic Republic of the Congo), who became known as the "Venus Noire," a "Black beauty" associated with the exotic and erotic, thus available for the projection of imperial desire and fantasy (fig. 7). This "Venus Noire" is but one in a long history in France that employs the figure of Black women, especially by white men, in the "creation of racist-sexist ideologies, images (sexual savages and prostitutes), and institutions (slavery and motherhood) to produce and sustain the illusion of realism, of absolute truth, thereby effecting mastery of otherness."[48] Nobosodru's distinct profile became a popular icon used to advertise all types of French products.[49] Because these ideas and images circulated globally, Nobosodru can be found in a range of artworks in the United States, from ones that contributed to racial scientific discourse to those by Black artists that honored a mythic Africa to counter popular stereotypes of savagery and barbarism.[50]

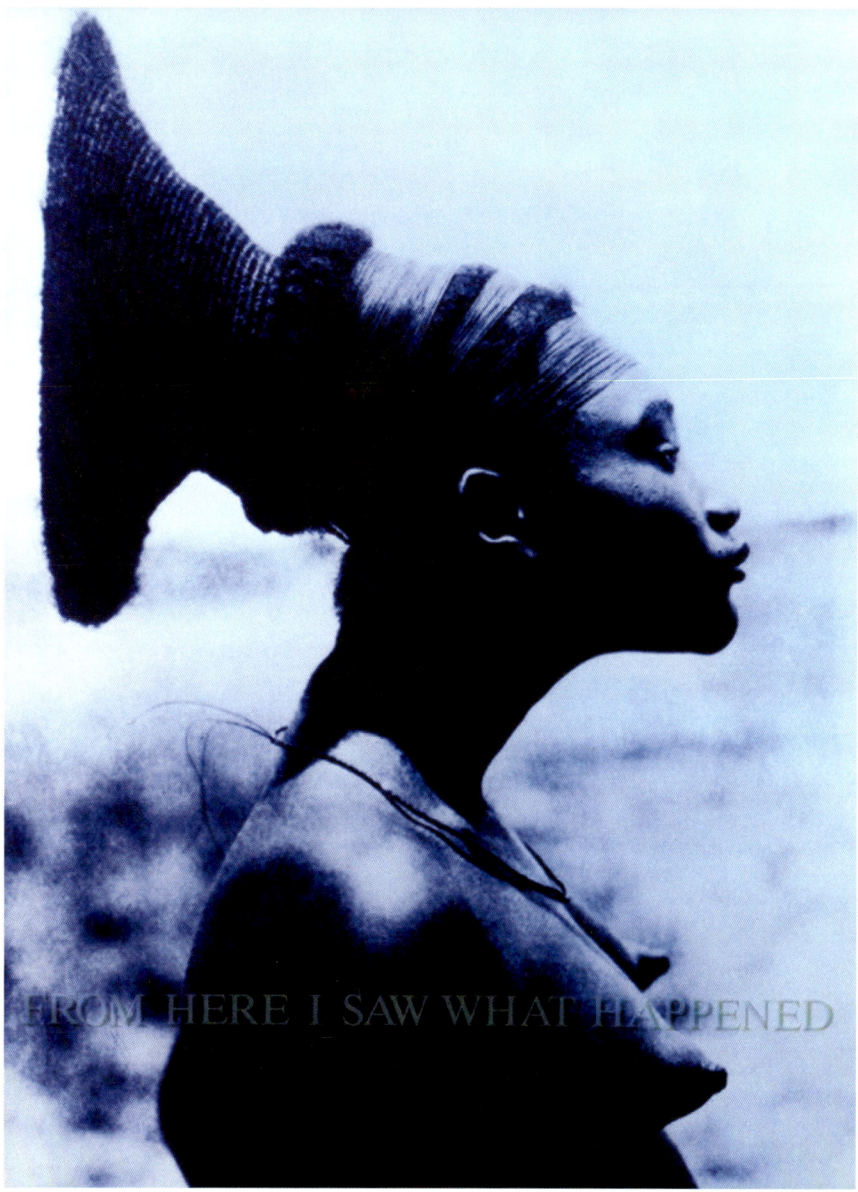

Fig. 7 Carrie Mae Weems, *From Here I Saw What Happened*, from the series *From Here I Saw What Happened and I Cried*, 1995–1996, photograph

Courtesy of the artist and Jack Shainman Gallery, New York, NY

Weems bathed the two photographs of *Nobosodru, Femme Mangbetu* with a blue tint, projecting a melancholic mood of being captured by the ethnographic gaze. On the glass of this first photograph of the series, Weems etched "FROM HERE I SAW WHAT HAPPENED." Looking across the vast history of how Blackness was typecast in the photographic archive, Nobosodru, a stand-in for Weems, bears witness. These twin witnesses bracket Weems's panorama of appropriated photographs. Each is accompanied by a short text, always in uppercase letters, sandblasted on the glass. For the texts, which mimic labels identifying racial types and character, Weems again deploys the second person to implicate the viewer "you" in the production of stereotypes. Inscribed on the photograph of Delia posed in profile, for example, Weems writes: "YOU BECAME A SCIENTIFIC PROFILE" (fig. 8). She sandblasted the text "NEGRO TYPE"

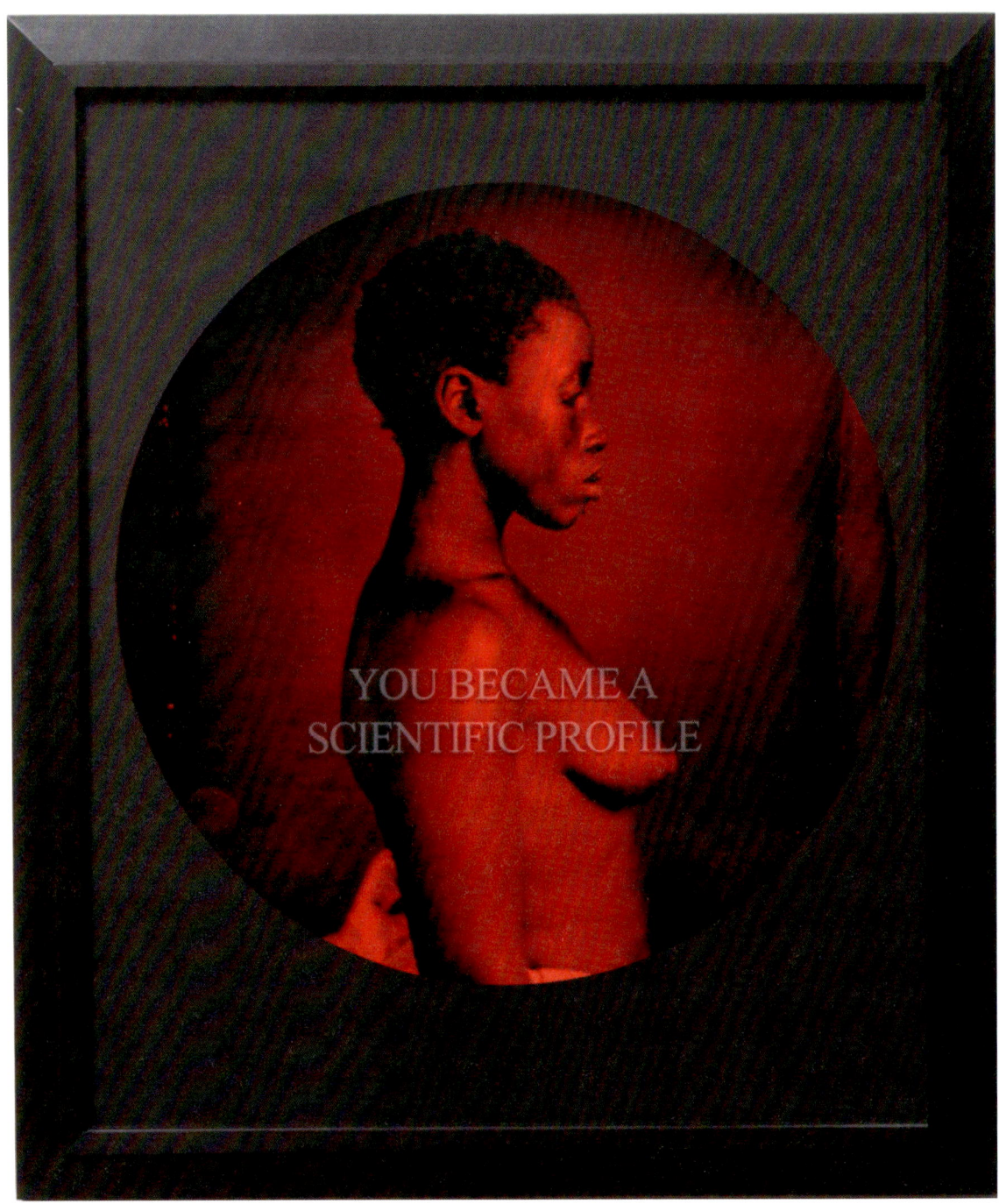

Fig. 8 Carrie Mae Weems, *You Became a Scientific Profile*, from the series *From Here I Saw What Happened and I Cried*, 1995–1996, photograph

Courtesy of the artist and Jack Shainman Gallery, New York, NY

on the portrait of Jack. "AN ANTHROPOLOGICAL DEBATE" appears on the picture of Renty. Weems inscribed "& PHOTOGRAPHIC SUBJECT" on the photograph of Drana. These labels remind viewers of the original intent of the daguerreotypes in the production of racial knowledge and antiblackness.

The series unfolds a chronology of how Black men, women, and children, regardless of intellect, ambition, or social standing, were subject to degradation through visuality of Blackness. Weems labels four antebellum portraits of Black women, including an ambrotype of a well-dressed seated Black woman from the Getty's photography collection, "HOUSE," "YARD," "FIELD," and "KITCHEN." Her words illustrate slavery's geography of the plantation overlaid onto the Black female body, regardless of whether one was free or wealthy—Blackness is what defined one's status over all else. On an 1856 daguerreotype of a dapper young man in a hat, from the Getty's collection, Weems writes: "YOU BECAME UNCLE TOM/JOHN & CLEMON'S JIM." She etches "DRIVERS" on an 1850 daguerreotype, also from the Getty's collection, of a young boy wearing a suit. As I walked and read the texts when the series was on view at Weems's retrospective at the Guggenheim, the second-person address made me the subject of racialization and amplified the objectifying work of the racist stereotypes and signifiers; the words called out for a response, an eruption of outrage, melancholy, and empathy. This effect of interpellation is similar to the way that Claudia Rankine employs the second person throughout her book of lyrical essays *Citizen: An American Lyric* (2014), which includes among its artworks Weems's *Blue Black Boy* (1987–1988) from her *Colored Peoples* series.

From the Getty's collection Weems placed into her panorama of racial types contemporary works such as *Man in Polyester Suit* (1980) by photographer Robert Mapplethorpe, with its singular focus on the exposed genitals of his lover Milton Moore. Because Mapplethorpe's photo reinforced in part stereotypical imagery of Black virility Weems added "ANYTHING BUT WHAT YOU WERE HA" to the image. Onto Garry Winogrand's photograph *New York 1967* that captured an interracial couple—a white woman and Black man—each carrying clothed chimpanzees from a New York City zoo, she overlaid the phrase "SOME LAUGHED LONG & HARD & LOUD" (fig. 9). Weems mined this iconic photograph from the Getty's collection for its perhaps unintended inference that miscegenation would lead to the birth of primate progeny—traces of polygenesis theories that resonate in racist caricatures. At the end of her series, Weems placed the other blue-tinted image of *Nobosodru, Femme Mangbetu*, this time gazing to the left with the label "AND I CRIED."

As I move among Weems's gallery of racial types, I read a narrative about how Black stereotypes have the power to devalue and dehumanize, to possess and desire. Weems said of *From Here I Saw What Happened and I Cried* that she wanted to "give them a different kind of status first and foremost, and heighten their beauty and their pain and sadness, too, from the ordeal of being photographed."[51] Weems used the series to chart

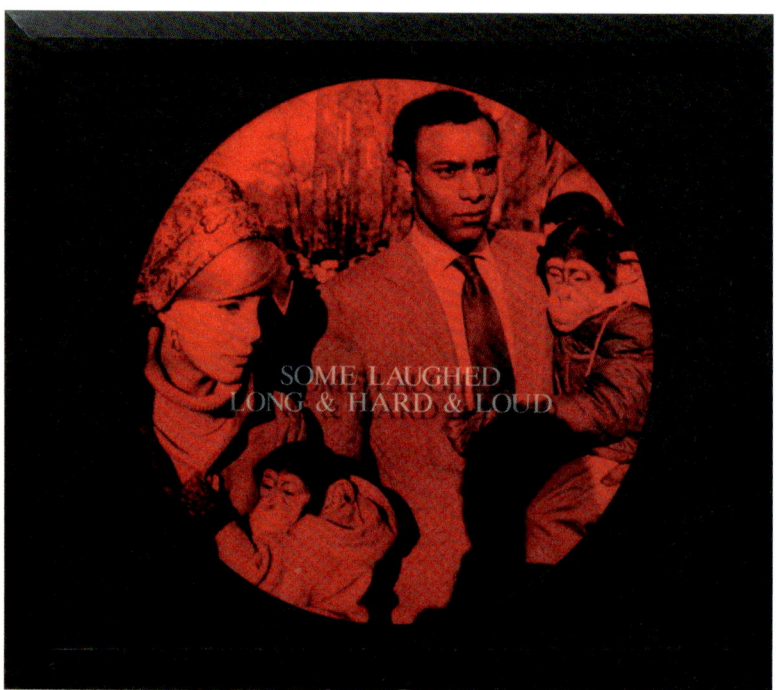

Fig. 9 Carrie Mae Weems, *Some Laughed Long & Hard & Loud*, from the series *From Here I Saw What Happened and I Cried*, 1995–1996, photograph

Courtesy of the artist and Jack Shainman Gallery, New York, NY

a historical arc of the complicity of photography found in the archives of institutions like the Getty and Peabody, and in popular culture. These images have contributed to the modern visual lexicon of antiblack racism, which in turn bolsters and validates the superiority of whiteness definitive of Euro-American culture.

The oeuvre of seminal painters found in major museum collections is central to Weems's series *Not Manet's Type*, which followed *From Here I Saw What Happened and I Cried*. The scopic frame in this series of vignettes appears courtesy of a circular mirror atop a dresser that reflects Weems in various poses sitting on or in front of a brass bed, some with her back to the camera. These are staged in a bedroom—the private domain of male pleasure, domination, and possession. Below each of the five images she narrates being the object of the artist's gaze: "Standing On Shaky Ground / I Posed Myself For Critical Study / But Was No Longer Certain Of The Questions To Ask." She cites white male painters who were known for painting the female nude: "Picasso—who had a way with women—only used me"; "Duchamp never even considered me"; and "It could have been worse . . . had De Kooning gotten hold of me." For Weems, "it was clear I was not Manet's type," a reference to the artist's famous painting of Olympia, in which a Black maid, the model Laure, stands nearby and carries a bouquet as an erotic symbol of the white sex worker's fecundity (see "Introduction: A Troubled Conjuncture," fig. 6). Art historian Darcy Grigsby points out that Manet makes the viewer scrutinize two working-class women, one Black and one white. However, for Laure, a free Black woman in Paris, the professions of model, wet nurse, sex worker, and governess were interchangeable, and as Grigsby astutely writes, "One woman connoted objecthood and dispossession—the Black woman whom art historians have failed to see."[52] Acutely aware, Weems refuses their (desirous and violating) gaze, this time of the artistic one and that of the art historian.

Weems returned to the themes of history, slavery, race, and science in her series and installation *Jefferson Suite*, formed out of a mix of archival images and her own photographs. For her DNA series in *Jefferson Suite*, Weems presented photographs of two men and two women from the waist up overlaid with a letter signifying a DNA code. In contrast to Agassiz's exploited quartet of fathers and daughters, these photographic subjects have turned their backs to the camera. First and foremost, they have refused to be seen, profiled, and, hence, known. They have refused the ethnographic gaze.

In another photograph from *Jefferson Suite*, Weems dressed revealingly in a corset and head wrap with her exposed back turned to the camera. A white man sits at a desk with a quill pen in hand. His back is to the camera, hence his gaze is directed at Weems. Although we cannot see their faces, we can assume that the man is Founding Father, natural philosopher, and enslaver Thomas Jefferson, and that she is performing the role of Sally Hemings, his enslaved concubine and mother of six of his children. With the mind and eye of a naturalist, the precursor to Agassiz's ethnographer, Jefferson cited "the preference of the Oranootan for the black women over those of his own species."[53] While we have thousands of likenesses and handwritten letters by Jefferson in the nation's revered archives, we know nothing about Hemings's appearance nor what she might have thought or said. Legally rendered property not person, Hemings had been purposefully redacted from history and excluded from the archives, until recent archeological excavations at Jefferson's home at Monticello, Virginia, revealed a room she is believed to have inhabited. Equally absent are their children, whose fate remains unknown, presumed to have been manumitted after his death in 1826. More recently, DNA testing confirmed familial ties between the descendants of the Hemings and Jefferson families.[54] Though built on the problematic legacy of racial science, genetic tests have scientifically unmasked the violence of white men who raped Black women for pleasure and profit.[55] It is a history of sexual violence that has been silenced by the social protocols of denial and respectability even though it was nonetheless an effective form of domination and racial subjection.

In a poetic turn of the title, "suite" aptly encapsulates Weems's series of photographic set pieces. "Suite" also describes the entourage of enslaved persons—Jefferson enslaved more than six hundred people in his lifetime—that made the plantation owner's life comfortable and prosperous. Further, "suite" refers to the rooms in Monticello where Jefferson took his pleasure from his property and concubine "Dusky Sally," her racist nickname that circulated in the press at the time. In *Jefferson Suite*, a dance of masks and masquerades, Weems rejected the desire of Agassiz and a host of others like Jefferson who took great pains to characterize Blackness as aesthetically abject and ugly, while remaining desirous of its sexual, epistemic, and economic value. In doing so, she challenged ethnographic, historiographic, and artistic scrutiny by turning her back to the camera—refusing to be known and typologically identified.[56] Weems was not "beholden to taxonomic truth" according to McKittrick, and instead she turns toward "the nonworld [after the Middle Passage that] engenders the urgent praxis of unwriting racial taxonomies and its attendant spatial violences."[57]

Roaming the Canon

That desire to draw the viewer into the frame and the production of counter-histories led Weems to incorporate and perform the figure of the wanderer and witness in her photographic series. She not only roams through the archive of history to address the West's spectrum of valuation that sorts who and what is modern against who and what is either still developing or degenerating into oblivion, but also wanders through public spaces that are produced by and productive of regimes of power, whether they be religious, national, cultural, racial, or economic. In her series *Museums* and *Roaming*, Weems performs as the witness of history standing in front of institutions and monuments. No longer captured and captivated by the objective gaze of science and history, her mysterious figure crosses thresholds of time and space as if emerging into the city from "the spaces in the shadows that facts don't allow us to see, the mystery."[58]

For her series *Museums*, Weems adopted the guise of the witness to address institutional power. Most if not all public museums have functioned as custodians of the bounty gleaned from Europe and America's colonial conquests and scientific expeditions. Their immense collections of artifacts, specimens, and artworks serve as the keepers of imperial time that established the stature of the metropole over the colony, colonized, and dominated.[59] Depending on whether scientific and historical evidence designated a cultural group primitive or civilized, its cultural artifacts were exhibited in natural history museums like the Peabody as fetish and craft, or put on display in art museums like the Getty, MoMA, or Guggenheim as an expressions of genius and beauty. To directly address the architectural expression of this power, Weems donning a somber black dress pauses in front of the distinct neoclassical facades of Dresden's Zwinger Museum, Paris's Louvre Museum, Berlin's Pergamon Museum, London's British Museum, Rome's National Gallery of Modern Art, and Philadelphia's Museum of Art, along with the contemporary designs of Bilbao's Guggenheim Museum and London's Tate Modern (fig.10). These collections hold artworks that portray the desirability of the Black female body, such as the Louvre's *Portrait d'une Negrésse* (1800) by Marie-Guilhelmine Benoist, or provide evidence of her fungibility and degradation, as found in the British Museum's collection of abolition prints. In each photograph, the museum's edifice looms over Weems's diminutive and motionless black-clad figure, as if she refuses its allure. As a Black woman, who has historically been characterized as lacking the

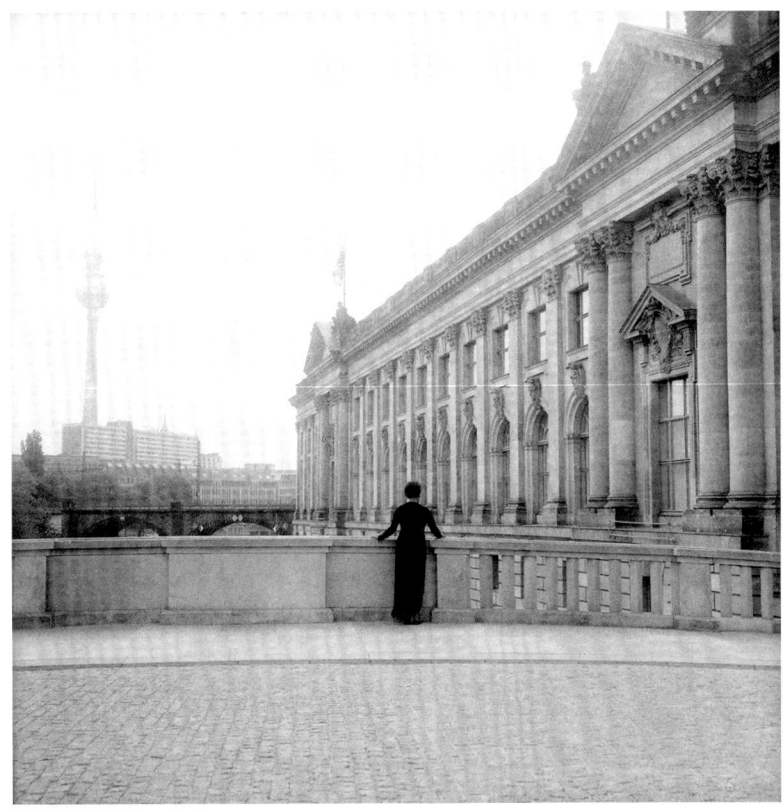

Fig. 10 Carrie Mae Weems, *Pergamon Museum*, from the series *Museums*, 2006, photograph

Courtesy of the artist and Jack Shainman Gallery, New York, NY

mental capacity for aesthetic reflection and historical consciousness, what does Weems witness standing before these symbols of power in the city?

In *Roaming* Weems guides me through monumental Rome, a city that has produced seminal works in the Western canons of art, architecture, and cinema, in both the ancient and modern eras. Rome has served as a living archive in marble, travertine, and concrete through which scholars and artists have imagined the origins of the West's culture and politics. This historical knowledge and aesthetic interpretation of antiquity was foundational to the racial and developmental theories posited by the scholarship of Winckelmann, Owen Jones, Eugène Viollet-le-Duc, and others, which in part informed how racial scientists like Agassiz viewed Black bodies as distasteful and abject.[60] This storied significance of Rome was compelling enough for Americans artists Daniel Chester French, John La Farge, Francis Millet, and Augustus Saint-Gaudens, along with architects Daniel Burnham and Charles Follen McKim, who were all organizers and contributors to Chicago's World's Columbia Exposition (1893), to establish a study center there. Desirous of validating America's imperial prowess by reclaiming European cultural (and racial) lineage and elevate American tastes, the group chose Rome because, as they explained: "With the architectural and sculptural monuments and mural paintings, its galleries filled with the chef d'oeuvres of every epoch, no other city offers such a field of study or an atmosphere so replete with precedents."[61] While on her fellowship at the academy in 2005 and 2006, in part as a respite away from the unrelenting demands of her career, Weems toured Rome, including the vistas of the ancient imperial era and the Fascist monuments erected when the city was reimagined through art and architecture as a modern empire. As a witness she stands at the threshold of several historical buildings and urban spaces in Rome and around southern Italy—including the ancient hill town of Matera and the artworks of Niki de Saint Phalle.

To return to Weems's *Pyramids of Rome—Ancient Rome*, the layering of the Cestius pyramid adjacent to the city's later Aurelian Walls and gateways like the Porta San Paolo conveys a sense of time passing. The idea that antiquity was the root of European culture took shape through the scholarly study of the ruins and fragments of statuary from the many ancient civilizations—Greek, Roman, Phoenician, Egyptian, and others—that ringed the Mediterranean Sea. Engraver Giuseppe Vasi depicted the unusual assemblage at the Piazzale Ostiense in the first book of his mid-eighteenth-century *Delle Magnificenze di Roma antica e moderna*—a primer on popular ancient sites along the Grand Tour route. Vasi's peer Giovanni Battista Piranesi also included the Pyramid of Cestius—laden with vines and other vegetation—in his engravings of Rome in various stages of ruination (fig. 11). At the same time that the ethnographic gaze labeled Africa, Asia, and the Americas as undeveloped and primitive, archeological and art historical scrutiny of Greece and Rome crafted an origin story of white European civilization and genius.

Weems takes me to other sites around Rome. In another photograph from *Roaming*, titled *Sabatini Gate—Ancient Rome* (2006), my guide in black stands framed by the Arch of Drusus, which leads to the Porta San Sebastiano, another southern gate in the Aurelian Walls. In Piranesi's engraving of the Arch of Drusus from his series *Roman Antiquity of the Time of the Republic and the First Emperors* (1748) the chiaroscuro depicts the monstrous decrepit archway as an allegory of Rome's ruin. To the eyes of the grand tourist, these ruins made legible and knowable the chronology

Fig. 11 Giovanni Battista Piranesi, *The Pyramid of Caius Cestius, with the Porta S. Paolo and adjoining road (Veduta del Sepolcro di Cajo Cestio)*, from *Vedute di Roma (Views of Rome)*, 1755, etching, Metropolitan Museum of Art, Harris Brisbane Dick Fund, 1937

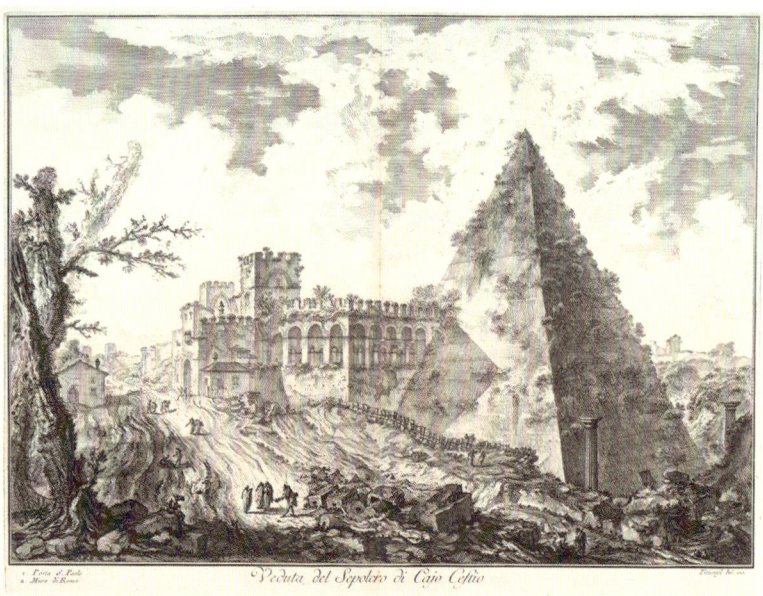

of events through which Europe constructed its past. Echoing Piranesi's aesthetics, the overgrown vegetation on the Arch of Drusus, along with its dark contrast in Weems's photo, casts a funereal mood. As for Weems's dress, it is possible to interpret her clothing as widow's weeds. Has she wandered from places formed in the wake of slavery, to, as Sharpe writes, "tend to the Black person, to Black people, always living in the push toward our death?"[62]

With Weems, I traverse Porta del Popolo, a northern gate in Aurelian Walls that connects to the Via Flaminia, a northern road to the Adriatic coast. Here, she/we witness the condensation of time. In the foreground of the photograph, two tents fill the piazza along with crates, what appear to be stage flats, and a portable toilet. These makeshift elements indicate that a fair or perhaps film shoot was about to take place or has just ended. The tents and other artifacts of daily Roman life contrast with the grandiosity of the piazza's architecture. On the northern corner of the Piazza del Popolo, the partial façade of the ornate fifteenth-century Basilica of Santa Maria del Popolo and the nineteenth-century palazzo that gave the piazza its oval configuration towers, their enormity almost subsuming Weems's figure. This assemblage of monuments to imperial and papal power also fascinated Piranesi and Vasi in their Roman *vedute* (views). Unlike Piranesi and Vasi, Weems's close cropping of the frame of the piazza and perspective is partial rather than panoramic. Unseen and just outside of the frame is the Egyptian Obelisk of Ramses, brought to the city by the emperor Augustus in 10 BCE, which dominates the center of the sprawling piazza. In the historical chain of power and domination, a monument to a pharaoh that was looted as tribute to a Roman emperor eventually became a testament to the pontifical power remaking Rome in the image of the imperial ambitions of the Catholic Church. This shift in meaning reflects how Rome has served as an urban museum where the bounty of war and the ruins of ancient cultures were appropriated and put on display to validate the authority of the most recent political regime, and it affirms Weems's observation that "architecture in its essence is very much about power."[63]

Along with the monuments of imperial Rome, Weems also stands in front of the monuments of fascist prime minister Benito Mussolini's Rome. Parts of the city's architectural landscape were reshaped by the Fascist state's modernist revival of imperial Rome in the 1930s and 1940s.[64] Weems wanders through EUR or E42, the site of the Esposizione Universale Roma, commissioned by Mussolini and scheduled to open in 1942. The spare neoclassical lines of E42's rationalist architecture was conceived, according to architectural historian Brian McLaren, as a "racial idea of ancient renewal," which meant that the "architectural taste during the late-Fascist era was similarly shaped along eugenic lines."[65] Elsewhere in the EUR, Weems walks toward the large equestrian statue in *Department of Lavorare—Mussolini's Rome* (2006, fig. 12). The abstract ensemble of the arched multitiered loggia of the Palazzo della Civiltà del Lavoro frames the statue along with the rectangular fluted columns in the Hall of Italian

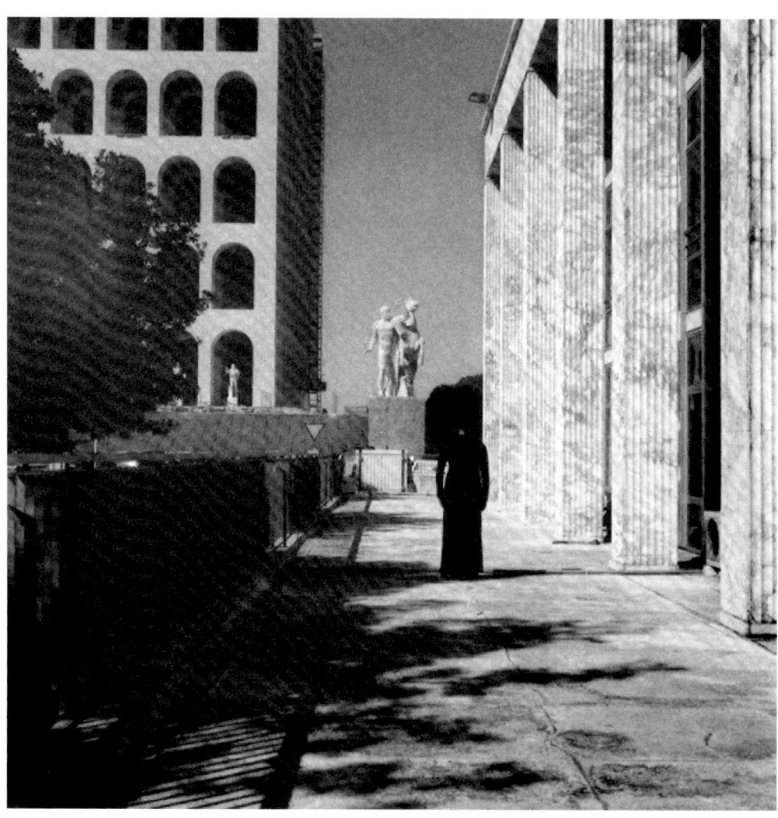

Fig. 12 Carrie Mae Weems, *Department of Lavorare—Mussolini's Rome*, from the series *Roaming*, 2006, photograph

Courtesy of the artist and Jack Shainman Gallery, New York, NY

Civilization's colonnade. All three edifices dominate Weems's black-clad figure. In *Palazzo dei Congressi—Mussolini's Rome* (2006), Weems's regal Black figure halts in front of the spare white geometries of the Hall of Congress. The massive columns that stretch across the building's portico extend beyond the frame to evoke the all-encompassing power of the state. In confronting these monuments, Weems asks, "What is this relationship of power to you, and what is your relationship to power? And how do you contest it?"[66]

For *When and Where I Enter—Mussolini's Rome* (2006), Weems stands within a film set at Cinecittà Studios built by Mussolini (fig. 13). Amid fragments of columns, Weems ascends a small stair that leads to a balcony and fake vista, her body diminished by the large opening and depth of the sound stage. A camera tripod, rolling studio lamps, and tracks of studio lighting set the stage, but we are unsure what is about to happen? It should be noted that Mussolini's slogan for Cinecittà was that "Cinema is the strongest weapon." This put Italy's film industry in service of the aesthetic project of fascism and the production of its authoritarian images and myths. Photographs like these make clear Weems's critique of monumentality and its staging of authority, where one feels "the power of the State in relationship to the lower subject, the general populace."[67] "You are always aware," Weems asserts, "that you are a minion in relationship to enormous edifice. The edifice of power."[68] And yet, the photograph's title, *When and Where I Enter*, which refers to a quote from educator and activist Anna Julia Cooper about her struggle for dignity and rights in the

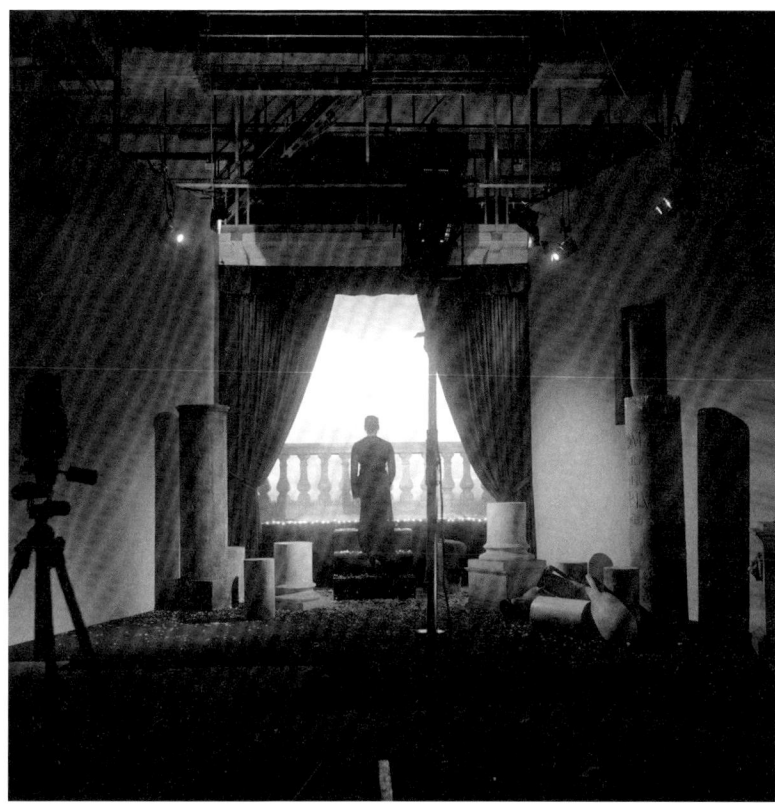

Fig. 13 Carrie Mae Weems, *When and Where I Enter— Mussolini's Rome*, from the series *Roaming*, 2006, photograph

Courtesy of the artist and Jack Shainman Gallery, New York, NY

Jim Crow era, offers a counter narrative. Historian Paula Giddings also used the phrase as the title for her book *When and Where I Enter: The Impact of Black Women on Race and Sex in America* (1984), which excavates how Black women like Cooper, journalist Ida B. Wells, politician Shirley Chisholm, and others led social movements against racism and sexism. It is through these potent references that Weems constructs a genealogy, a counter-history against antiblackness and patriarchy in order to claim kinship with Black women—known and unknown—who shared a transformative vision of the past and the future.

Weems also visits the sea. Rome's nearby Tyrrhenian Sea melds into the Libyan Sea and the Sea of Sicily. In ancient times, Rome's empire stretched across the Mediterranean Sea to Egypt, Libya, and Tunisia. Centuries later, Mussolini's Rome held imperial ambitions and an agenda of racial domination by its brief colonial occupation of Ethiopia. In the twenty-first century, migrants from northern Africa arrive by sea to Italy's shores, many risking death to be ferried by ruthless smugglers exacting once again a profit for the dangerous passage to Lampedusa, a small island between Tunisia and Malta. In 2005, the year before Weems's photograph *A Broad and Expansive Sky—Ancient Rome* (2006, fig. 14), the United Nations High Commissioner for Refugees (UNHCR) estimated that 25,000 African men, women, and children embarked on the dangerous journey to Italy.[69] In *A Broad and Expansive Sky—Ancient Rome* Weems stages a similar photograph to Caspar David Friedrich's *Wanderer Above the Sea of Fog* (c.1817). A cloudy sky dominates more than half the frame

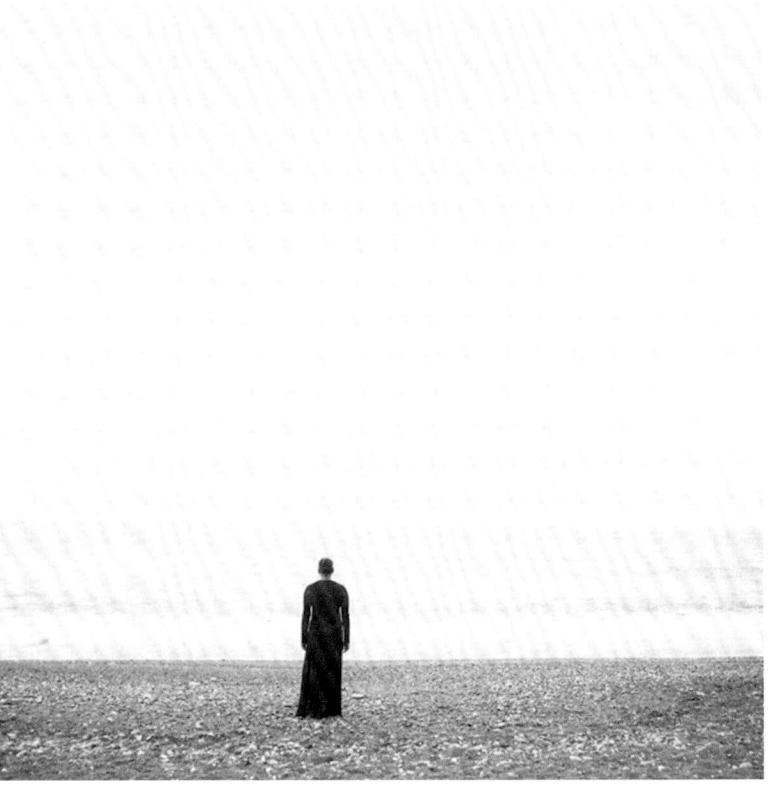

Fig. 14 Carrie Mae Weems, *A Broad and Expansive Sky—Ancient Rome*, from the series *Roaming*, 2006, photograph

Courtesy of the artist and Jack Shainman Gallery, New York, NY

where its horizon touches the dark gray sea suspending her motionless figure; when I viewed it in the Guggenheim's exhibition I felt as if I could drift into its atmospheric scene. This transcendental moment evokes what theorist Denise Ferreira da Silva describes as "a temporality of the knowing subject, acquiring their own historicity."[70] From Europe's shores Weems gazes out across the sea, however, rather than affirm the bourgeois self; her presence, stature, and Blackness portend an estrangement from modernity. With the African continent beyond the vista's edge, across the "womb abyss" there emerges for Weems the possibility of imagining the world differently.

Weems's oeuvre bears witness to the historical traces of the transatlantic slave trade—fragments filed away, forgotten, or hidden in the shadows, displaced peoples whose capture made modernity possible. The archive and the museum function for Weems as reservoirs of representations that conjure the impossibility of Black humanity. But these institutions, along with cities and landscapes, are spaces from which Weems creates other possible narratives through her counter-histories. To disrupt racialized visuality and images that cast Blackness in time—as (1) a primitive form of being, and (2) a form of enclosure to extract value and meaning—she employs "biomythography" and storytelling in her various photographic series.

The geopolitical dimension of history divided those of European origin from its subaltern others encountered in Africa, Asia, and the Americas in the centuries-long colonial expansion that gave rise to modernity.

Attentive to the power dynamics established not only through the cartographic scale, but also by Western architecture and vernacular building's ability to place and displace, Weems compels her viewers to reckon with "living in the wake," as Sharpe writes, "living the history and present of terror, from slavery to the present, as the ground of our everyday Black existence."[71] In her performances, Weems bears witness to those sites of terror taking in the psychological violence deployed in racial subjection and retaking representations and narratives through her own appropriations, stagings, and wanderings. We encounter this strategy in her use of the second-person voice, which implicates the viewer (me) in how images racialize, and in her first-person evocations of anger and refusal, insight and joy. Weems places her own body in the frame as if her sheath were a surface absorbing the myriad ways that the West has projected the contours that define Blackness. It is through her mien and stature that she embodies how "enslaved and post slave subjects," writes McKittrick, "are tasked to imagine and live the world differently."[72] Weems's presence as witness, as a displaced subject in the historical landscape of the West, as a Black woman in public and private spaces, complicates the reading of modernity's linear unfolding of time—its power and its place.

NOTES

INTRODUCTION: A TROUBLED CONJUNCTURE
HUEY COPELAND AND STEVEN NELSON

1. See, for instance, Tanya Barson and Peter Gorschlüter, eds., *Afro Modern: Journeys through the Black Atlantic* (Liverpool, 2010); Kimberly W. Benston, *Performing Blackness: Enactments of African-American Modernism* (London, 2000); Maurice Berger, ed., *Modern Art and Society: An Anthology of Social and Multicultural Readings* (New York, 1994); Huey Copeland, "In the Wake of the Negress," in *Modern Women: Women Artists at the Museum of Modern Art*, ed. Cornelia Butler and Alexandra Schwartz (New York, 2010), 480–497; Jacqueline Francis, *Making Race: Modernism and "Racial Art" in America* (Seattle, 2012); Ann Eden Gibson, *Abstract Expressionism: Other Politics* (New Haven, CT, 1997); Simon Gikandi, "Picasso, Africa, and the Schemata of Difference," *Modernism/modernity* 10, no. 3 (September 2003): 455–480; Paul Gilroy, *The Black Atlantic: Modernity and Double Consciousness* (Cambridge, MA, 1993); Stuart Hall and Sarat Maharaj, *Modernity and Difference* (London, 2001); Kobena Mercer, ed., *Cosmopolitan Modernisms* (Cambridge, MA, 2005); Elaine O'Brien et al., eds., *Modern Art in Africa, Asia, and Latin America: An Introduction to Global Modernisms* (Chichester, West Sussex, 2013); Sylvester Okwunodu Ogbechie, *Ben Enwonwu: The Making of an African Modernist* (Rochester, NY, 2008); Griselda Pollock, *Differencing the Canon: Feminist Desire and the Writing of Art's Histories* (London, 1999), 246–315; and James Smethurst, *The African American Roots of Modernism: From Reconstruction to the Harlem Renaissance* (Chapel Hill, NC, 2011).

2. Here, we think first and foremost of Saidiya V. Hartman, *Scenes of Subjection: Terror, Slavery, and Self-Making in Nineteenth-Century America* (Oxford, 1997), and Fred Moten, *In the Break: The Aesthetics of the Black Radical Tradition* (Minneapolis, 2003).

3. See T. J. Clark, "Clement Greenberg's Theory of Art," *Critical Inquiry* 9, no. 1 (September 1982): 139–156.

4. See, respectively, Darcy Grimaldo Grigsby, "Revolutionary Sons, White Fathers, and Creole Difference: Guillaume Guillon-Lethière's 'Oath of the Ancestors' (1822)," *Yale French Studies*, no. 101 (2001): 201–226; Lisa Gail Collins, "Cycles of Mourning and Memory: Quilts by Mother and Daughter in Gee's Bend Alabama," *The Journal of Childhood and Youth* 8, no. 3 (Fall 2015): 345–352; and Athi Mongezeleli Joja, "Jafta Masemola's Master Key," *Theoria* 68, no. 168 (September 2021): 160–195.

5. See Huey Copeland, *Bound to Appear: Art, Slavery, and the Site of Blackness in Multicultural America* (Chicago, 2013); Sampada Aranke, "Objects Made Black," *Art Journal* 73, no. 3 (Fall 2014): 66–68; and Krista Thompson, "A Sidelong Glance: The Practice of African Diaspora Art History in the United States," Centennial Essay, *Art Journal* 70, no. 3 (Fall 2011): 7–31.

6. Clement Greenberg, "Avant-Garde and Kitsch," in *Art and Culture: Critical Essays* (Boston, 1961), 18, n. 5.

7. Hannah Black, "Fractal Freedoms," *Afterall: A Journal of Art, Context, and Enquiry* 41 (Spring/Summer 2016): 2–6. Also see Cauleen Smith and Sophia Kishkovsky, "There Is More to Malevich's Black Square than a Hidden Racist Joke, Moscow Curators Reveal," *Art Newspaper*, November 18, 2015, https://www.theartnewspaper.com/2015/11/18/there-is-more-to-malevichs-black-square-than-a-hidden-racist-joke-moscow-curators-reveal.

8. In these specific emphases, *Black Modernisms in the Transatlantic World* also departs from previous groundbreaking volumes such as Kymberly N. Pinder, ed., *Race-ing Art History: Critical Readings in Race and Art History* (New York, 2002). For contemporaneous exhibitionary interventions that rhyme with and anticipate the present volume, see Adrienne Childs, *Riffs and Relations: African American Artists and the European Modernist Tradition* (New York, 2020), and Adrienne Edwards, *Blackness in Abstraction* (New York, 2016).

9. Darby English, *1971: A Year in the Life of Color* (Chicago, 2016).

10. Richard J. Powell, *Black Art: A Cultural History*, 3rd ed. (New York, 2021).

11. Karen Barad, *What Is the Measure of Nothingness: Infinity, Virtuality, Justice* (Ostfildern, 2012), 17.

12. Brent Hayes Edwards, *The Practice of Diaspora: Literature, Translation, and the Rise of Black Internationalism* (Cambridge, MA, 2003), 44.

13 T. J. Clark, *Farewell to an Idea: Episodes from a History of Modernism* (New Haven, CT, 1999), and Hortense J. Spillers, "Mama's Baby, Papa's Maybe: An American Grammar Book," *Diacritics* 17, no. 2 (Summer 1987): 64–81.

14 T. J. Clark, "Preface," in *The Painting of Modern Life: Paris in the Art of Manet and His Followers*, rev. ed. (Princeton, NJ, 1999), xxvii, and Hortense J. Spillers, "Art Talk and the Uses of History," *Small Axe* 19, no. 3 (November 2015): 178.

15 For a recent consideration of these dynamics from a Black feminist perspective, see Denise Ferreira da Silva, *Unpayable Debt* (London, 2022).

16 Clark, *Farewell to an Idea*, 7; Édouard Glissant, "The Open Boat," in *Poetics of Relation*, trans. Betsy Wing (Ann Arbor, MI, 1997), 5–9; and Paul Gilroy, "Living Memory: A Meeting with Toni Morrison," in *Small Acts: Thoughts on the Politics of Black Cultures* (London, 1993), 175–182. We borrow the notion of the Black fem from Chelsea Frazier, "Thinking Red, Wounds, and Fungi in Wangechi Mutu's EcoArt," in *Ecologies, Agents, Terrains*, ed. Christopher P. Heuer and Rebecca Zorach (New Haven, CT, 2018), 167–194.

17 Clark, *Farewell to an Idea*, 9.

18 Spillers, "Mama's Baby, Papa's Maybe," 79, 68.

19 For Spillers, "Before the 'body' there is the 'flesh,' that zero degree of social conceptualization that does not escape concealment under the brush of discourse, or the reflexes of iconography. Even though the European hegemonies stole bodies—some of them female—out of West African communities in concert with the African 'middleman,' we regard this human and social irreparability as high crimes against the *flesh*, as the person of African females and African males registered the wounding. If we think of the 'flesh' as a primary narrative, then we mean its seared, divided, ripped-apartness, riveted to the ship's hole, fallen, or 'escaped' overboard." See Spillers, "Mama's Baby, Papa's Maybe," 67.

20 Gilroy, "Living Memory," 178.

21 Fred Moten, "The Case of Blackness," *Criticism* 50, no. 2 (Spring 2008): 177–218.

22 Harriet Jacobs, *Incidents in the Life of a Slave Girl* [1861], ed. Jean Fagan Yellin (Cambridge, MA, 1987). The present accounting of Jacobs's tactics revisits and extends Huey Copeland, "Flow and Arrest," *Small Axe* 19, no. 3 (November 2015): 220.

23 Orlando Patterson, *Slavery and Social Death: A Comparative Study* (Cambridge, MA, 1982).

24 Judith Wilson, "Getting Down to Get Over: Romare Bearden's Use of Pornography and the Problem of the Black Female Body in Afro-U.S. Art," in *Black Popular Culture*, ed. Gina Dent (Seattle, 1992), 114.

25 Lorraine O'Grady, "Olympia's Maid: Reclaiming Black Female Subjectivity*," in *New Feminist Criticism: Art, Identity, Action*, ed. Joanna Frueh, Cassandra L. Langer, and Arlene Raven (New York, 1994), 153. For two lines of inquiry that follow and expand upon O'Grady's insights about the social production of Black womanhood, see T. Denean Sharpley-Whiting, *Black Venus: Sexualized Savages, Primal Fears, and Primitive Narratives in French* (Durham, NC, 1999), and Nicole R. Fleetwood, *Troubling Vision: Performance, Visuality, and Blackness* (Chicago, 2011).

26 Spillers, "Mama's Baby, Papa's Maybe," 65.

27 On this score, see Zakiyyah Iman Jackson, *Becoming Human: Matter and Meaning in an Antiblack World* (New York, 2020).

28 On the structuring importance of Black female reproductive capacity in the making of modern capitalism, see Saidiya Hartman, "The Belly of the World: A Note on Black Women's Labors," *Souls* 18, no. 1 (January–March 2016): 166–173.

29 Kimberlé Williams Crenshaw, "Demarginalizing the Intersection of Race and Sex: A Black Feminist Critique of Antidiscrimination Doctrine, Feminist Theory, and Antiracist Politics," *University of Chicago Legal Forum*, no. 1 (1989): 139–167; Kimberlé Williams Crenshaw, "Mapping the Margins: Intersectionality, Identity, and Violence Against Women of Color," *Stanford Law Review* 43, no. 6 (July 1991): 1241–1300; Leslie McCall, "Toward a Field of Intersectionality Studies: Theory, Applications, and Praxis," *Signs: Journal of Women in Culture and Society* 38, no. 4 (June 2013): 785–810; and Jennifer C. Nash, "Intersectionality and Its Discontents," *American Quarterly* 69, no. 1 (March 2017): 117–129.

30 For an incisive critique of contemporary art world structures along these lines, see C. Riley Snorton and Hentyle Yapp, "'Sensuous Contemplation': Thinking Race at Its Saturation Points," in *Saturation: Race, Art, and the Circulation of Value* (Cambridge, MA, 2020), 1–12.

31 James Baldwin, "In Search of a Majority: An Address," in *James Baldwin: Collected Essays*, ed. Toni Morrison (New York, 1998), 221.

SIMONE LEIGH: ACTS OF TRANSFORMATION
STEVEN NELSON

1 Simone Leigh, email message to Steven Nelson, January 2, 2020.

2 Leigh to Nelson, January 2, 2020.

3 Leigh to Nelson, January 2, 2020.

4 Simone Leigh, email message to Steven Nelson, December 28, 2019.

5 Audre Lorde, "The Master's Tools Will Never

Dismantle the Master's House," in *Sister Outsider: Speeches and Essays* (Freedom, CA, 1984), 111. Emphasis in original.
6 Lorraine O'Grady, "Olympia's Maid: Reclaiming Black Female Subjectivity," *Afterimage* (Summer 1992): 14.
7 Leigh to Nelson, January 2, 2020.
8 O'Grady, "Olympia's Maid," 14.
9 O'Grady, "Olympia's Maid," 14.
10 Hortense J. Spillers, "Mama's Baby, Papa's Maybe: An American Grammar Book," *Diacritics* 17, no. 2 (Summer 1987): 66.

LEAVE NO MARK: BLACKNESS AND INSCRIPTION IN THE INQUISITORIAL ARCHIVE
MATTHEW FRANCIS RAREY

1 A *comissário* was a mid-level bureaucrat responsible for taking action on denunciation letters received from across the empire. The comissário would forward particular cases to prosecutors if they believed the instances warranted further investigation.
2 Throughout this essay I refer to the amulets as *bolsa* and *mandinga*. While "bolsa" literally translates as "pouch" or "bag," it here marks those that function as amulets. In turn, I only use "mandinga" when archival documents refer to bolsas using that term.
3 Arquivo Nacional da Torre do Tombo, Inquisição de Lisboa (hereafter ANTT-IL), Correspondência Recebida de Comissários, Livro 922, fol. 378r.
4 Hortense J. Spillers, "Mama's Baby, Papa's Maybe: An American Grammar Book," *Diacritics* 17, no. 2 (Summer 1987): 67.
5 Sherwin K. Bryant, *Rivers of Gold, Lives of Bondage: Governing Through Slavery in Colonial Quito* (Chapel Hill, NC, 2014), 52.
6 Spillers, "Mama's Baby, Papa's Maybe," 67. Spillers's formulation undergirds much scholarship of recent authors who, as the editors of a 2015 issue of *Social Text* summarize, analyze how "imperial archives . . . often record blackness or black life only as an absence of human subjecthood, as when the enslaved enter the historical record as a number, a mark, or a notice of death." See Laura Helton, Justin Leroy, Max Mishler, Samantha Seeley, and Shauna Sweeney, "The Question of Recovery: An Introduction," *Social Text* 33, no. 4 (2015): 4. For the scholarship they summarize, see Saidiya Hartman, *Lose Your Mother: A Journey Along the Atlantic Slave Route* (New York, 2007); Saidiya Hartman, "Venus in Two Acts," *Small Axe* 12, no. 2 (2008): 1–14; Stephanie Smallwood, *Saltwater Slavery: A Middle Passage from Africa to American Diaspora* (Cambridge, MA, 2008); and Christina Sharpe, *In the Wake: On Blackness and Being* (Durham, NC, 2016).
7 Spillers, "Mama's Baby, Papa's Maybe," 67.
8 On the *Scourged Back* photograph, see Zoe Trodd, "Am I Still Not a Man and a Brother? Protest Memory in Contemporary Antislavery Visual Culture," *Slavery and Abolition* 34, no. 2 (2013): 338–352, and Matthew Fox-Amato, *Exposing Slavery: Photography, Human Bondage, and the Birth of Modern Visual Politics in America* (New York, 2019), 119–121.
9 *Mandinga* is the Portuguese rendering of *mandinka* or *mande*. On the use of this ethnonym in reference to bolsas, see Vaniclèia Silva Santos, "Mandingueiro não é Mandinga: o debate entre nação, etnia, e outras denominações atribuídas aos africanos no contexto do tráfico," in *África e Brasil no Mundo Moderno*, vol. 1, ed. Eduardo França Paiva and Vaniclèia Silva Santos (São Paulo, 2012), 11–27, and Matthew Francis Rarey, "Assemblage, Occlusion, and the Art of Survival in the Black Atlantic," *African Arts* 51, no. 4 (2018): 20–33.
10 ANTT-IL, Correspondência Recebida de Comissários, Livro 922, fol. 378r.
11 On *bolsas de mandinga*, see Daniela Buono Calainho, *Metrópole das Mandingas: Religiosidade Negra e Inquisição Portuguesa no Antigo Regime* (Rio de Janeiro, 2008); Laura de Mello e Souza, *The Devil and the Land of the Holy Cross: Witchcraft, Slavery, and Popular Religion in Colonial Brazil*, trans. Diane G. Whitty (Austin, TX, 2003); Roger Sansi, "Sorcery and Fetishism in the Modern Atlantic," in *Sorcery in the Black Atlantic*, ed. Luis Nicolau Parés and Roger Sansi (Chicago, 2011), 19–39; and James H. Sweet, "Slaves, Convicts, and Exiles: African Travellers in the Portuguese Atlantic World, 1720–1750," in *Bridging the Early Modern Atlantic World: People, Products, and Practices on the Move*, ed. Caroline A. Williams (Burlington, VT, 2009), 193–202.
12 ANTT-IL, Cadernos do Promotor, No. 72, Livro 266, fol. 77–91.
13 *Natural* is a Portuguese term designating the originating port of departure for enslaved Africans. In this case, the term indicates that Jacques entered a ship at or near Ouidah.
14 ANTT-IL, Cadernos do Promotor, No. 72, Livro 266, fol. 291r–291v.
15 ANTT-IL, Correspondência Recebida de Comissários, Livro 922, fol. 626r.
16 ANTT-IL, Correspondência Recebida de Comissários, Livro 922, fol. 619r.
17 ANTT-IL, Processo 2355.
18 ANTT-IL, Processo 502, fol. 8r–8v.
19 While scores of extant trials involving bolsa users survive, fewer than five describe the objects' users as women. Rather than (and sometimes in addition to) explicitly protecting the owner from physical violence, the pouches these women

used often facilitated sexual relationships or denied unwanted advances. Broadly speaking, women less frequently appeared in Inquisition trials accused of *feitiçaria* (recourse to fetishes, the accusation most commonly associated with the bolsas) than *bruxaria* (witchcraft), which indicates the perceived gendered dimensions of Inquisitorial accusations. While this fact possibly suggests that far more men than women used the pouches, it is more likely that Inquisitorial authorities felt the public dimensions of Black men's performances of bodily inviolacy posed a much more significant threat than that posed by searches for personal relationships.

20 In 1693, for example, the Lisbon Inquisition sent twenty-five *editais* concerning the bolsas to Rio de Janeiro. ANTT-IL, Registro de Correspondência Expedida, Livro 20, fol. 3v.
21 ANTT-IL, Maço 27, No. 41, fol. 1v.
22 ANTT-IL, Cadernos do Promotor, No. 113, Livro 305, fol. 251r.
23 ANTT-IL, Maço 27, No. 20.
24 ANTT-IL, Processo 11767. For a summary of this case, see Luiz R. Mott, "A vida mística e erotica do escravo José Francisco Pereira, 1705–1736," *Revista Tempo Brasileiro* 92/93 (1988): 85–104.
25 José Francisco Pedroso's and José Francisco Pereira's respective enslavers were brothers. It is possible that the pair already knew each other in Africa, given this close connection and their shared passage through Ouidah.
26 For an analysis of the shifting interpretations of the Caravaca Cross in seventeenth-century Iberia, see Mercedes García-Arenal and Fernando Rodríguez Mediano, *The Orient in Spain: Converted Muslims, the Forged Lead Books of Granada, and the Rise of Orientalism*, trans. Consuelo López-Morillas (Leiden, 2013), 215–219.
27 ANTT-IL, Processo 11767, fol. 10r; ANTT-IL, Processo 11774, fol. 33v.
28 Robert Edgar Conrad, "Preface," in *Children of God's Fire: A Documentary History of Black Slavery in Brazil*, ed. Robert Edgar Conrad (University Park, PA, 1984), xviii. Reliable data on literacy rates among the enslaved people in Brazil prior to this census are notoriously difficult to uncover. For a speculative analysis of literacy rates for enslaved and free Black people in colonial Brazil, see Christianni Carodoso Morais, "Ler e escrever: Habilidades de escravos e forros? Comarca do Rio das Mortes, Minas Gerais, 1731–1850," *Revista Brasileira de Educação* 12, no. 36 (2007): 493–504.
29 For António Guedes's trial, see ANTT-IL, Processo 2137.
30 José Francisco testified as to the location of his own baptism in ANTT-IL, Processo 11767, fol. 9v.
31 James H. Sweet, *Recreating Africa: Culture, Kinship, and Religion in the African-Portuguese World, 1441–1770* (Chapel Hill, NC, 2003), 186.
32 "A Narrative of the Most Remarkable Particulars in the Life of James Albert Ukawsaw Gronniosaw, an African Prince, as related by Himself," in *Slave Narratives*, ed. William Andrews and Henry Louis Gates Jr. (New York, 2000), 11–12.
33 Cécile Fromont, "Paper, Ink, Vodun, and the Inquisition: Tracing Power, Slavery, and Witchcraft in the Early Modern Portuguese Atlantic," *Journal of the American Academy of Religion* 88, no. 2 (2020): 1–45.
34 Nuno Marques Pereira, *Compendio narrativo do peregrino da America: Em que se tratam varios discursos espirituaes, e moraes, com muitas advertencias, e documentos contra os abusos, que se achaõ introduzidos pela malicia diabolica no Estado do Brasil* (Lisbon, 1760), 123.
35 ANTT-IL, Maço 27, No. 41, fol. 1r.
36 ANTT-IL, Maço 27, No. 41, fol. 1r.
37 Souza, *The Devil and the Land of the Holy Cross*, 126.
38 See, for example, ANTT-IL, Processo 9972.
39 ANTT-IL, Cadernos do Promotor, No. 51, Livro 248, fol. 283–285v.
40 ANTT, Inquisição de Coimbra, Processo 1630.
41 ANTT-IL, Maço 27, No. 20.
42 This point dialogues with some of my previous work where I argued that colonial authorities in Brazil, and the Portuguese Atlantic more broadly, defined Black bodies in general through their capacity to endure pain. See Matthew Francis Rarey, "Counterwitnessing the Visual Culture of Brazilian Slavery," in *African Heritage and Memories of Slavery in Brazil and the South Atlantic World*, ed. Ana Lucia Araujo (Amherst, NY, 2015), 71–108.
43 ANTT-IL, Maço 27, No. 41, fol. 1v.
44 A series of first-person accounts of Lisbon's autos-da-fé survive. See Phyllis S. Lachs, "An English Account of an Auto da Fe: Lisbon, 1669," *The Jewish Quarterly Review* 57, no. 4 (1967): 319–326, and Samuel Oppenheim, "A Newspaper Account of an Auto da Fe in Lisbon in 1726, in which a Jew, a Native of Bahia, South America, was Burnt," *Publications of the American Jewish Historical Society* 22 (1914): 180–182.
45 António José Saraiva, *The Marrano Factory: The Portuguese Inquisition and Its New Christians, 1536–1765*, trans. H. P. Salomon and I. S. D. Sassoon (Leiden, 2001), 114.
46 Saraiva, *The Marrano Factory*, 113.
47 ANTT-IL, Lista dos Autos da Fé, fol. 290r.
48 ANTT-IL, Processo 502.

49 ANTT-IL, Processo 502, fol. 48v.
50 ANTT-IL, Processo 15628, fol. 2r.
51 Hartman, *Lose Your Mother*, 36, and Krista Thompson, *Shine: The Visual Economy of Light in African Diasporic Aesthetic Practice* (Durham, NC, 2015). See also Agnes Lugo-Ortiz and Angela Rosenthal, "Introduction," in *Slave Portraiture in the Atlantic World*, ed. Agnes Lugo-Ortiz and Angela Rosenthal (New York, 2016).
52 I am not the first to make this point; see Sweet, *Recreating Africa*, 185–186.
53 Tania Andrade Lima, Marcos André Torres de Souza, and Glaucia Malerba Sene, "Weaving the Second Skin: Protection against Evil among the Valongo Slaves in Nineteenth-Century Rio de Janeiro," *Journal of African Diaspora Archaeology and Heritage* 3, no. 2 (2014): 108.
54 Aldair Rodrigues, "Deciphering Scarification in West Africa and Brazil During the Eighteenth Century," public lecture, Program of African Studies, Northwestern University, February 20, 2019.
55 Simone Browne, *Dark Matters: On the Surveillance of Blackness* (Durham, NC, 2015), 42.
56 ANTT-IL, Correspondência Recebida de Comissários, Livro 922, fol. 378r.
57 Hartman, "Venus in Two Acts," 2.
58 Hartman, "Venus in Two Acts," 5. Emphasis in original.
59 Hartman, "Venus in Two Acts," 14.

BARE FEET, OR, THE AMBIVALENCE OF EMANCIPATION: CAMILLE PISSARRO AND THE CARIBBEAN
C. C. MCKEE

1 C. C. McKee, "Cultivating Visible Order: Representations of Race and Ecology in the French Atlantic" (PhD diss., Northwestern University and l'École des hautes études en sciences sociales, 2019). This essay draws from a chapter in my forthcoming monograph that takes a comparative and ecocritical approach to representations of Blackness and the tropical landscape from the 1848 abolition of slavery in the French and Danish Empires through the 1878 labor strike dubbed "Fireburn" on the island of St. Croix and another labor strike on Martinique in 1900. Camille Pissarro's oeuvre represents one node in a transatlantic visual cultural network and attempts to restructure the relationship between race and the environment during the rise of a post-emancipation wage economy.
2 Linda Nochlin, "Camille Pissarro: The Unassuming Eye," in *The Politics of Vision: Essays on Nineteenth-Century Art and Society* (New York, 1989), 73.
3 T. J. Clark, *Farewell to an Idea: Episodes from a History of Modernism* (New Haven, CT, 1999), 101, 824.
4 Clark, *Farewell to an Idea*, 101.
5 Clark, *Farewell to an Idea*, 6.
6 Clark, *Farewell to an Idea*, 121.
7 Clark, *Farewell to an Idea*, 122.
8 This provocation is informed by contemporary scholarship that reframes the overwhelmingly singular and Eurocentric vision of modernism to include a multitude of non-Western *modernisms*. Simon Gikandi, "Picasso, Africa, and the Schemata of Difference," *Modernism/modernity* 10, no. 3 (September 2003): 455–480; Michele Greet, *Transatlantic Encounters: Latin American Artists Between the Wars* (New Haven, CT, 2018); Samantha Noel, "Envisioning New Worlds: The 'Tropical Aesthetics' in the Art of Wifredo Lam and Aaron Douglas," *Art Journal* 77, no. 3 (Fall 2018): 76–91; and Elizabeth Harney and Ruth B. Phillips, eds., *Mapping Modernisms: Art, Indigeneity, Colonialism* (Durham, NC, 2019).
9 Ludovic-Rodo Pissarro and Lionello Venturi, *Pissarro: Son art, son oeuvre* (Pissarro: His art, his oeuvre) (Paris, 1939), quoted in Joachim Pissarro and Claire Duran-Ruel Snollaerts, *Pissarro: Critical Catalogue of Paintings*, vol. 2 (New York, 2005), 49.
10 Sigmund Freud, "Screen Memories," in *The Standard Edition of the Complete Psychological Works of Sigmund Freud*, vol. 3 (London, 1953), 299–322.
11 Anne Cheng's theorization of melancholia as a racialized cultural formation provides an essential precedent for this approach. See Anne Anlin Cheng, *The Melancholy of Race* (New York, 2000).
12 Sarah Linger, *Peintures des lointains: La collection du Musée du Quai Branly Jacques Chirac* (Paintings from afar: The collection of the Musée du Quai Branly Jacques Chirac) (Paris, 2018).
13 Sigmund Freud, *Beyond the Pleasure Principle*, trans. James Strachey (London, 1950), 28.
14 Jean Laplanche and Jean-Bertrand Pontalis, *The Language of Psychoanalysis* (London, 1973), 1002–1017.
15 Gunvor Simonsen, *Slave Stories: Law, Representation, and Gender in the Danish West Indies* (Aarhus, 2017), 46.
16 Sigmund Freud, "The Unconscious," in *The Standard Edition*, vol. 14, 191.
17 Hortense J. Spillers, *Black, White and in Color: Essays on American Literature and Culture* (Chicago, 2003), 155.
18 T. Denean Sharpley-Whiting, *Black Venus: Sexualized Savages, Primal Fears, and Primitive Narratives in French* (Durham, NC, 1999), 16–31.
19 Spillers, *Black, White and in Color*, 155.
20 Martha Ward, *Pissarro, Neo-Impressionism,*

21. Janine Bailly-Herzberg, ed., *Correspondance de Camille Pissarro*, vol. 1 (Paris, 1980), 123. All translations are my own.
22. Neville A. T. Hall, *Slave Society in the Danish West Indies: St. Thomas, St. John, and St. Croix* (St. Augustine, Trinidad, 1994), 125, 180. Hall lists 4,077 whites and 10,317 free people of color in the Danish West Indies in 1835.
23. West Indian Census 1841 and West Indian Census 1846, Chamber of Revenue, Danish Department, The Table Commission, Rigsarkivet, Copenhagen.
24. West Indian Census 1841 and West Indian Census 1846.
25. Richard Brettell and Karen Zukowski, *Camille Pissarro in the Caribbean 1850–1855: Drawings from the Collection at Olana* (St. Thomas, 1996), 8.
26. Hall, *Slave Society in the Danish West Indies*, 209.
27. Hall, *Slave Society in the Danish West Indies*, 216.
28. *St. Croix Avis*, July 18, 1848.
29. Laurent Dubois, *Avengers of the New World: The Story of the Haitian Revolution* (Cambridge, MA, 2004).
30. Jennifer Van Horn, "'The Dark Iconoclast': African Americans' Artistic Resistance in the Civil War South," *Art Bulletin* 99, no. 4 (2017): 150. Van Horn has also emphasized the political and symbolic role of iconoclasm for American bondspeople during the Civil War: iconoclasm "emerges as a tactic that effectively sabotaged . . . a visual culture that was based on exclusion, and it did so . . . by alterations to the work of art or its context that brought the experience of the subaltern to bear on the artwork, thereby asserting the new user's humanity."
31. Throughout the 1850s and early 1860s Pissarro frequently used variant spellings of his last name in his signature. For more information see Pissarro and Durand-Ruel Snollaerts, *Pissarro*.
32. Saidiya Hartman, "The Belly of the World: A Note on Black Women's Labors," *Souls* 18, no. 1 (2016): 167.
33. Cora Michael, "'As Much as the Light': The Importance of Shadows in the Art of Camille Pissarro" (PhD diss., New York University, 2006), 17–20.
34. Bernhard von Petersen, *En historisk Beretning om de Dansk-Vestindiske Öer St. Croix, St. Thomas og St. Jan* (Copenhagen, 1855), 117, quoted and translated in Hall, *Slave Society in the Danish West Indies*, 225.
35. Hall, *Slave Society in the Danish West Indies*, 226.
36. Hall, *Slave Society in the Danish West Indies*, 226.
37. Daphne A. Brooks, *Bodies in Dissent: Spectacular Performances of Race and Freedom, 1850–1910* (Durham, NC, 2006), 6. I take my cue from Brooks's emphasis on the quotidian performances and aesthetic means with which freedmen and women "imagined and stylized ways to make their subjugated bodies move more freely."
38. Hartman, "The Belly of the World," 170.
39. Krista Thompson, *An Eye for the Tropics: Tourism, Photography, and Framing the Caribbean Picturesque* (Durham, NC, 2006), 5, 12.
40. *St. Tomæ Tidende*, June 26, 1848.
41. Nicholas Mirzoeff, *The Right to Look: A Counterhistory of Visuality* (Durham, NC, 2011), 158.
42. This watercolor dates to about 1859, well after emancipation in the British, Danish, and French empires, but before abolition in the Dutch territories (1863), the United States (1865), or Cuba (1886).
43. Tim Barringer et al., *Art and Emancipation in Jamaica: Isaac Mendes Belisario and His Worlds* (New Haven, CT, 2007), 41.
44. Richard Brettell and Christopher Lloyd, *Catalogue of Drawings by Camille Pissarro in the Ashmolean Museum, Oxford* (Oxford, 1980), 99. Brettell and Lloyd argue that this drawing was made toward the end of Pissarro's Venezuelan sojourn based on "the subtlety of the tonal effects," but one cannot verify the dates of these works.
45. Alfredo Boulton, *Camille Pissarro en Venezuela* (Caracas, 1966), 88–89.
46. The woman cooking with a cauldron is repeated in *Studies of female figures with children by a fire* (Ashmolean Collection, verso of B&L, 15). This iteration of the Black washerwoman is a leitmotif in Pissarro's Caribbean drawings, watercolors, and paintings (see the Ashmolean Collection, B&L, 13–16, among others).
47. Mirzoeff, *The Right to Look*, 158. Emphasis mine.
48. Mirzoeff, *The Right to Look*, 159.
49. Seymour Drescher, *Abolition: A History of Slavery and Antislavery* (New York, 2009), 190.
50. John V. Lombardi, *The Decline and Abolition of Negro Slavery in Venezuela, 1820–1854* (Westport, CT, 1971).
51. Ralph E. Shikes and Paula Harper, *Pissarro: His Life and Work* (New York, 1980), 56.
52. Helena Scannone, *Pissarro in Venezuela: Works in Venezuelan Collections of Camille Pissarro's Venezuelan Oeuvre (1852–1854)* (London, 1997), 24.
53. Clark, *Farewell to an Idea*, 70.
54. Huey Copeland, "In the Wake of the Negress," in *Modern Women: Women Artists at the Museum of Modern Art*, ed. Cornelia Butler and Alexandra Schwartz (New York, 2010), 482, 484.

55. Christopher Miller, *Blank Darkness: Africanist Discourse in French* (Chicago, 1985), 115–124.
56. Charles Baudelaire, *Le spleen de Paris, ou les cinquante petits poèmes en prose de Charles Baudelaire* (The spleen of Paris, or the fifty little prose poems of Charles Baudelaire) (Paris, 1917), 80.
57. Sharpley-Whiting, *Black Venus*, 68.
58. Baudelaire, *Le spleen de Paris*, 80–81.
59. Baudelaire, *Le spleen de Paris*, 81.
60. Baudelaire, *Le spleen de Paris*, 82.
61. Sharpley-Whiting, *Black Venus*, 69.
62. Baudelaire, *Le spleen de Paris*, 82.
63. Hartman, "The Belly of the World," 171.

ON EUROPEAN MODERNISM AND BLACK BEING
SIMON GIKANDI

I would like to thank Steven Nelson and Huey Copeland for their help with the final draft of this essay.

1. For the centrality of Blackness in the art of early modernism, see Denise Murrell, *Posing Modernity: The Black Model from Manet and Matisse to Today* (New Haven, CT, 2018).
2. Fredric Jameson has discussed how the ideology of modernism "imposes its conceptual limitations on our aesthetic thinking and our tastes and judgments." Fredric Jameson, "Beyond the Cave: Demystifying the Ideology of Modernism," in *The Ideologies of Theory: Essays 1971–1986*, vol. 2, *Syntax of History* (Minneapolis, 1988), 11.
3. Frantz Fanon called it "L'expérience vécue du Noir." See *Peau noire, masques blancs*, 88–114. For the English translation, see *Black Skin, White Masks*, trans. Charles Lam Markmann (New York, 1967), 109–140.
4. Sigmund Freud, *Civilization and Its Discontents*, trans. and ed. James Strachey (New York, 1961). For a discussion on modernity's violence, see Debarati Sanyal, *The Violence of Modernity: Baudelaire, Irony, and the Politics of Form* (Baltimore, 2006), 1–19.
5. Judith Wilson, "Hager's Daughters: Social History, Cultural Heritage, and Afro-US Women's Art," in *Bearing Witness: Contemporary Works by African American Women Artists*, ed. Jontyle Theresa Robinson (New York, 1996), 95–112.
6. W. E. B. Du Bois, *The Souls of Black Folk* (New York, 1990), 34–35.
7. Jean Franco, *Cruel Modernity* (Durham, NC, 2013).
8. The decree declares: "The Herero are no longer German subjects. They have murdered and stolen, they have cut off the ears, noses and other body-parts of wounded soldiers, now out of cowardice they no longer wish to fight. . . . Within the German borders every Herero, with or without a gun, with or without cattle, will be shot. I will no longer accept women and children, I will drive them back to their people or I will let them be shot at." Quoted by Jan-Bart Gewald, "The Great General of the Kaiser," *Botswana Notes and Records* 26, no. 1 (January 1994): 72.
9. I discussed these issues in "Race and the Modernist Aesthetic," in *Writing and Race*, ed. Tim Youngs (London, 1997), 147–165, and in "Picasso, Africa, and the Schemata of Difference," *Modernism/modernity* 10, no. 3 (September 2003): 455–480.
10. Walter Benjamin, "Critique of Violence," in *Reflections: Essays, Aphorisms, Autobiographical Writings*, ed. Peter Demetz, trans. Edmund Jephcott (New York, 1978), 300.
11. Theresa Leininger-Miller, *New Negro Artists in Paris: African American Painters and Sculptors in the City of Light, 1922-1934* (New Brunswick, NJ, 2001), 1–15.
12. Sharon F. Patton, *African-American Art* (Oxford, 1998), 99.
13. James A. Porter, *Modern Negro Art* [1943], Moorland-Spingarn Series (Washington, DC, 1992), 58.
14. The terms here are borrowed from William Wordsworth's manifesto for Romantic poetry: "Poetry is the spontaneous overflow of powerful feelings: it takes its origin from emotion recollected in tranquility." See "Preface," in William Wordsworth and Samuel Taylor Coleridge, *Lyrical Ballads: 1798 and 1802* (Oxford, 2013), 98.
15. Porter, *Modern Negro Art*, 58.
16. See Richard J. Powell, *Black Art and Culture in the 20th Century* (London, 1997), 26.
17. Leininger-Miller, *New Negro Artists*, 15, 16.
18. David Scott, *Conscripts of Modernity* (Durham, NC, 2004), 4.
19. See Henry Louis Gates Jr., "The Face and Voice of Blackness," in Guy C. McElroy, *Facing History: The Black Image in American Art 1710–1940*, ed. Christopher French (Washington, DC, 1990), xxix–xliv.
20. Powell, *Black Art and Culture*, 26.
21. Alain Locke, "The Negro as Artist," in *The Negro in Art: A Pictorial Record of the Negro Artist and of the Negro Theme in Art* (New York, 1979), 9.
22. This dilemma has been laid out clearly by Dipesh Chakrabarty writing on cultural movements in West Bengal in about the same period. See Dipesh Chakrabarty, *Provincializing Europe* (Princeton, NJ, 1999), 150.
23. I have discussed the cultural project of Black elites in "Afro-Victorian Worlds," in *The Victorian World*, ed. Martin Hewitt (London, 2012), 671–690.
24. For Kristeva, the state of the depressive is the feeling of simultaneously being absent from "other people's meaning" and of being

a witness "to the meaninglessness of being." See Julia Kristeva, *Black Sun: Depression and Melancholia*, trans. Leon S. Roudiez (New York, 1989), 4.

25 Du Bois, *The Souls of Black Folk*, 9.
26 Kristeva, *Black Sun*, 5.
27 Edward Wilmot Blyden, "Ethiopia Stretching Out Her Hand unto God (African's Services to the World)," in *Christianity, Islam, and the Negro Race* (Baltimore, 1994), 146–147. For Ethiopianism as a discursive category, see William Jeremiah Moses, *The Wings of Ethiopia* (Iowa City, IA, 1990).
28 Anna Julia Cooper, *A Voice from the South* (New York, 1988), 1.
29 Du Bois, *The Souls of Black Folk*, 9.
30 J. E. Casely Hayford, *Ethiopia Unbound: Studies in Race Emancipation* [1911] (London, 1969), 160.
31 See Renée Ater, "Making History: Meta Warrick Fuller's 'Ethiopia,'" *American Art* 17, no. 3 (Autumn 2003): 12–31.
32 See Brent Hayes Edwards, *The Practice of Diaspora: Literature, Translation, and the Rise of Black Intellectualism* (Cambridge, MA, 2003), and Michelle Ann Stephens, *Black Empire: The Masculine Global Imaginary of Caribbean Intellectuals in the United States, 1914–1962* (Durham, NC, 2005).
33 Paul De Man, "The Rhetorical of Temporality," in *Blindness and Insight: Essays in the Rhetoric of Contemporary Criticism* (Minneapolis, 1983), 207.
34 Ater, "Making History," 19.
35 De Man, "The Rhetorical of Temporality," 219.
36 Northrop Frye, *Anatomy of Criticism* (Princeton, NJ, 1971), 193, and Fredric Jameson, *The Political Unconscious: Narrative as a Socially Symbolic Act* (Princeton, NJ, 1981), 104.
37 Meta Vaux Warrick Fuller, quoted in Ater, "Making History," 17.
38 Clement Greenberg, "Modern and Postmodern," William Dobell Memorial Lecture, Sydney, Australia, October 31, 1979, *Arts* 54, no. 6 (February 1980), http://www.sharecom.ca/greenberg/postmodernism.html.
39 Aaron Douglas, quoted in Patton, *African-American Art*, 144–145.
40 I'm echoing Virginia Woolf, *A Room of One's Own* (New York, 1981).
41 Martin Heidegger, "Building Dwelling Thinking," in *Poetry, Language, Thought*, trans. Albert Hofstadter (New York, 1975), 147.
42 Alain Locke, ed., *The New Negro: Voices of the Harlem Renaissance* (New York, 1997). The manifesto of the movement can be found in Alain Locke, "The New Negro," in *The New Negro*, 3–16. For the Harlem Renaissance and its influence, see Nathaniel Irvin Huggins, *Harlem Renaissance* (Oxford, 1971); David Levering Lewis, *When Harlem Was in Vogue* (New York, 1981); Houston Baker, *Modernism and the Harlem Renaissance* (Chicago, 1989); Cheryl A. Wall, *Women of the Harlem Renaissance* (Bloomington, IN, 1995); Caroline Goeser, *Picturing the New Negro: Harlem Renaissance Print Culture and Modern Black Identity* (Lawrence, KS, 2007); and Wil Haywood, *I Too Sing America: The Harlem Renaissance at 100* (New York, 2018).
43 Locke, "The New Negro," 7.
44 T. J. Clark, *Farewell to An Idea: Episodes from a History of Modernism* (New Haven, CT, 1999).
45 Locke, "The New Negro," 3.
46 Archibald John Motley Jr., quoted in Patton, *African-American Art*, 124.
47 Alain Locke, *Negro Art: Past and Present* (Washington, DC, 1936), 67–68.
48 My discussion here is indebted to Patton, *African-American Art*, 119–120.
49 Georg Lukács, *The Theory of the Novel: A Historico-Philosophical Essay in the Forms of Great Epic Literature*, trans. Anna Bostock (Cambridge, 1971), 41.
50 Lukács, *The Theory of the Novel*, 129.
51 The violent dispossession and displacement of Black communities engendered by the 1913 Natives Lands Act in South Africa is captured vividly by Sol T. Plaatje in *Native Life in South Africa* (London, 1916). Huey Copeland has also focused on Blackness and homelessness within modernity. See Huey Copeland, *Bound to Appear: Art, Slavery, and the Site of Blackness in Multicultural America* (Chicago, 2013), 145.
52 Aimé Césaire, *Journal of a Homecoming/Cahier d'un retour au pays natal*, trans. N. Gregson Davies with an introduction by F. Abiola Irele (Durham, NC, 2017), 148–149. I have modified the translation slightly.
53 Claude McKay, *Banjo: A Story without a Plot* (New York, 1929), 5.
54 Édouard Glissant, *Poetics of Relation*, trans. Betsy Wing (Ann Arbor, MI, 1997), 19.
55 This point has been made by Fredric Jameson in "Beyond the Cave," 117.
56 Marianne Dekoven, "Modernism and Gender," in *The Cambridge Companion to Modernism*, ed. Michael Levenson (Cambridge, 1999), 174.
57 For Josephine Baker, see Petrine Archer-Straw, *Negrophilia: Avant-Garde Paris and Black Culture in the 1920s* (London, 2000), and Anne Anlin Cheng, *Second Skin: Josephine Baker and the Modern Surface* (Oxford, 2013).
58 See Harry Harootunian, "Foreword: The Exotics of Nowhere," in Victor Segalen, *Essay on Exoticism: An Aesthetics of Diversity*, trans. and ed. Yael Rachel Schlick (Durham, NC, 2002), xiii.
59 Claude McKay, "The Harlem Dancer," in *Harlem Shadows: The Poems of Claude McKay* (New York, 1922), 42.

60 Léopold Sédar Senghor, "To New York" ("À New York"), in *The Collected Poetry*, trans. Melvin Dixon (Charlottesville, VA, 1998), 88, 370.
61 Stephens, *Black Empire*, 43.
62 Harootunian, "Foreword," xi.
63 Nicolás Guillén, "Sóngoro cosongo" [1931], Biblioteca Miguel Cervantes, accessed April 14, 2020, http://www.cervantesvirtual.com/obra-visor/songoro-cosongo-1931--0/html/ff47ec48-82b1-11df-acc7-002185ce6064_2.html#I_8. My translation.
64 Wifredo Lam, "'My Painting Is an Act of Decolonization': An Interview with Wifredo Lam by Gerardo Mosquera (1980)," trans. Colleen Kattau and David Craven, *Journal of Surrealism and the Americas* 3, no. 1 (2009): 3.
65 For the idea of the short circuit and interpretation, see Slavoj Žižek, "Series Forward," in *The Parallax View* (Cambridge, MA, 2009), ix.
66 McKay, *Banjo*, 96.
67 McKay, *Banjo*, 97.

NANCY ELIZABETH PROPHET AND AUGUSTA SAVAGE: SCULPTURAL HABITS OF BLACK MODERNISM
KELLIE JONES

For Margaret Rose Vendryes, artist, scholar, classmate. And in memory of David C. Driskell, Cheryl A. Wall, and Joan Sandler. With thanks to Mya Chau, Dana Suzanne Rodriguez, and Madeline Weisburg for research assistance.

1 Brittney C. Cooper, *Beyond Respectability: The Intellectual Thought of Race Women* (Urbana, IL, 2017), 2. Brittney Cooper's work is part of an impressive lineage by and about Black women, their cultural production, and their histories. For instance, see the introduction to Farah Jasmine Griffin, ed., *Beloved Sisters and Loving Friends: Letters from Rebecca Primus of Royal Oak, Maryland, and Addie Brown of Hartford, Connecticut, 1854–1868* (New York, 1999), and Mia Bey, Farah J. Griffin, Martha S. Jones, and Barbara D. Savage, eds., *Toward an Intellectual History of Black Women* (Chapel Hill, NC, 2015).
2 Cooper, "Introduction," in *Beyond Respectability*. See also Hazel V. Carby, "The Sexual Politics of Black Women's Blues" [1987], in Carby, *Cultures in Babylon: Black Britain and African America* (London, 1999), 7–21.
3 Cooper, *Beyond Respectability*, 7. See also Elizabeth Alexander, "'We Must Be about Our Father's Business': Anna Julia Cooper and the In-Corporation of the Nineteenth Century African-American Female Intellectual," *Signs* 20, no. 2 (1995): 336–356.
4 Cooper, *Beyond Respectability*, 8.
5 Meta Vaux Warrick Fuller was another Black woman sculptor working with themes similar to those of Prophet and Savage. However, she was almost a generation older (b. 1877, Philadelphia) and from a middle-class background that offered more support than that afforded her younger colleagues. See Renée Ater, *Remaking Race and History: The Sculpture of Meta Warrick Fuller* (Berkeley, CA, 2011).
6 Ironically, it was France's Exposition Coloniale of 1931 that seems to have provided inspiration. Prophet raved about the African art and material culture she found there. Theresa Leininger-Miller, *New Negro Artists in Paris: African American Painters and Sculptors in the City of Light, 1922–1934* (New Brunswick, NJ, 2001), 54–58. On cosmopolitanism as a fraught concept see Judith R. Walkowitz, "The 'Vision of Salome': Cosmopolitan and Erotic Dancing in Central London, 1980–1918," *The American Historical Review* 108, no. 2 (April 2003): 337–376.
7 The Whitney Museum of American Art acquired *Congolais* in 1932, the year after the Whitney opened to the public. Theresa Leininger-Miller, "'Heads of Thought and Reflection': Busts of African Warriors by Nancy Elizabeth Prophet and Augusta Savage, African America Sculptors in Paris, 1922–1934," in *Out of Context: American Artists Abroad*, ed. Laura Felleman Fattal and Carol Salus (Westport, CT, 2004), 104.
8 While Prophet's *Congolais* was purchased by the Whitney Museum of American Art, *The Harp* was destroyed because Savage lacked funds to cast the large plaster in bronze. For more on the song and its history, see Imani Perry, *May We Forever Stand: A History of the Black National Anthem* (Chapel Hill, NC, 2018).
9 T. J. Clark, *Farewell to an Idea: Episodes from a History of Modernism* (New Haven, CT, 1999), 7–8.
10 Erica Moiah James, "Decolonizing Time, Nineteenth Century Haitian Portraiture and the Critique of Anachronism in Contemporary Art," *NKA, Journal of Contemporary African Art* 44 (May 2019): 21.
11 Meg Onli, in conversation with Huey Copeland, in Huey Copeland, "About Time," *Artforum* 57, no. 9 (2019).
12 Joanne Winning, "The Sapphist in the City: Lesbian Modernist Paris and Sapphic Modernity," in *Sapphic Modernities: Sexuality, Women and National Culture*, ed. Laura Doan and Jane Garrity (New York, 2006), 20.
13 T. Denean Sharpley-Whiting, *Bricktop's Paris: African American Women in Paris between the Two World Wars* (Albany, NY, 2015), 5–6.
14 Sharpley-Whiting, *Bricktop's Paris*, 5–6.
15 Brent Hayes Edwards, *The Practice of*

Diaspora: Literature, Translation, and the Rise of Black Internationalism (Cambridge, MA, 2003), 125.

16 Painter Romaine Brooks, for instance, never needed to sell her work to live. Her lover Natalie Barney also supported the fascist movement. Sharpley-Whiting, *Bricktop's Paris*, 9–11, and Tirza True Latimer, "Romaine Brooks and the Future of Sapphic Modernity," in Doan and Garrity, *Sapphic Modernities*, 40. See also Joanne Winning, "The Sapphist in the City: Lesbian Modernist Paris and Sapphic Modernity," in Doan and Garrity, *Sapphic Modernities*, 17–33.

17 Sharpley-Whiting, *Bricktop's Paris*, 9.

18 Edouard Roditi, quoted in Richard Bruce Nugent and Thomas Wirth, *Gay Rebel of the Harlem Renaissance: Selections from the Work of Richard Bruce Nugent* (Durham, NC, 2002), 18; George Chauncey, *Gay New York: Gender, Urban Culture, and the Making of the Gay Male World, 1890–1940* [1994] (New York, 2019), 264; Theresa Leininger-Miller, "Modern Dancers and African Amazons: Augusta Savage's Daring Sculpture of Women, 1929–1930," in *The Modern Woman Revisited: Paris Between the Wars*, ed. Whitney Chadwick and Tirza True Latimer (New Brunswick, NJ, 2003), 193; and "Beth Prophit [sic] Is Hailed in Paris as Real Artist," *Baltimore Afro-American*, August 3, 1929, 8. Prophet also maintained a correspondence with Cullen. For excerpts, see Leininger-Miller, *New Negro Artists in Paris*, 47–49, and Countee Cullen Papers, Amistad Research Center, Tulane University, New Orleans. On Paulette Nardal's Paris, see Edwards, *The Practice of Diaspora*, chap. 3. Cullen, Alain Locke, and Hale Woodruff were frequent guests at the gatherings that Nardal held in her home. Edwards, *The Practice of Diaspora*, 120.

19 Edwards, *The Practice of Diaspora*, 156–157.

20 Elizabeth Alexander, *The Black Interior* (Minneapolis, 2004), 9.

21 Edwards, *The Practice of Diaspora*, 157.

22 Paulette Nardal, "Une femme sculpteur noire," *La Dépêche africaine* 3, nos. 27–28 (August–September 1930): 5; "Paris Gossip," *Philadelphia Tribune*, May 22, 1930, 6; and Leininger-Miller, *New Negro Artists in Paris*, 185–190. On Black models in Paris during this era see Denise Murrell, *Posing Modernity: The Black Model from Manet and Matisse to Today* (New Haven, CT, 2018).

23 Leininger-Miller, *New Negro Artists in Paris*, 185–190.

24 After all women were not political or voting citizens in ancient Athens.

25 Ironically, as with Prophet, France's Exposition Coloniale of 1931 provided encouragement for making these works, and it is possible that Savage showed at least one of her Amazon series within the fair itself.

Leininger-Miller, *New Negro Artists in Paris*, 185–190.

26 *Augusta Savage: Renaissance Woman* was organized by Jeffreen M. Hayes for the Cummer Museum of Art and Gardens, Jacksonville, Florida, in 2018 and traveled into 2020. The most recent comprehensive exhibition of work by Nancy Elizabeth Prophet was *Hale Woodruff, Nancy Elizabeth Prophet, and the Academy*, organized by the Spelman College Museum of Fine Art, Atlanta, Andrea Barnwell Brownlee, director, in 2007.

27 Hazel V. Carby, "Policing the Black Woman's Body in an Urban Context" [1992], in Carby, *Cultures in Babylon*, 23.

28 Carby, "Policing the Black Woman's Body," 36.

29 Prophet resided in Paris for one of the longest periods (1922–1934) of the major circle of expatriate African American creators of her generation.

30 Kai M. Green, "Troubling the Waters, Mobilizing a Trans* Analytic," in *No Tea, No Shade: New Writing in Black Queer Studies*, ed. E. Patrick Johnson (Durham, NC, 2016), 76, and Leininger-Miller, *New Negro Artists in Paris*, 17.

31 Countee Cullen, "Elizabeth Prophet: Sculptress," *Opportunity* (July 1930): 204–205.

32 Saidiya Hartman, *Wayward Lives, Beautiful Experiments: Intimate Histories of Social Upheaval* (New York, 2019), x–xv. Prophet's lovers included W. E. B. Du Bois, an ardent supporter of this generation of African American artists. Amalia Amaki, "The Unfulfilled Promise of Elizabeth Prophet," *International Review of African American Art* 18, no. 3 (2002): 22–31, and Leininger-Miller, *New Negro Artists in Paris*, chap. 2.

33 Carby, "The Sexual Politics of Black Women's Blues," 18.

34 Dan Burley, "Augusta Savage Realizes Dream," *The New York Amsterdam News*, December 18, 1937, 24. Barthé crafts the female dancer as the more active and aggressive, pushing into the body of her male partner. Barthé, an excellent dancer himself, noted that the dance floor was indeed a place for women to expose sexual power by revealing more of their body as well as lingerie. Margaret Rose Vendryes, *Barthé: A Life in Sculpture* (Jackson, MS, 2008), 73–74.

35 Walkowitz, "'Vision of Salome,'" 340.

36 Norah Waugh, *Corsets and Crinolines* (London, 1954), quoted in Walkowitz, "'Vision of Salome,'" 360.

37 Walkowitz, "'Vision of Salome,'" 360.

38 Maud Allan, quoted in Walkowitz, "'Vision of Salome,'" 356.

39 Clark, *Farewell to an Idea*, 7–8.

40. Vendryes, *Barthé*, 7.
41. Hartman, *Wayward Lives*, 308.
42. Vendryes, *Barthé*, 63, 72. However, Bourdelle was also known for his indeterminant figures. On transgender or what they call Trans* aesthetics, see Green, "Troubling the Waters," 65–82.
43. Laura Doan and Jane Garrity, "Introduction," in Doan and Garrity, *Sapphic Modernities*, 3.
44. In the United Kingdom women donning male attire was considered humorous more than anything else. See Laura Doan, "Passing Fashions: Reading Female Masculinities in the 1920s," *Feminist Studies* 24, no. 3 (Autumn 1998): 663–700, and Lillian Faderman, *Odd Girls and Twilight Lovers: A History of Lesbian Life in Twentieth Century America* (New York, 1991).
45. Leininger-Miller, "Modern Dancers and African Amazons," 185, and Edwards, *The Practice of Diaspora*, 130.
46. James T. Wilson, *Bulldaggers, Pansies, and Chocolate Babies: Performance, Race, and Sexuality in the Harlem Renaissance* (Ann Arbor, MI, 2010), 123, 126, 127. Hartman, *Wayward Lives*, 193–205.
47. Green, "Troubling the Waters," 76. As Hartman informs us, "In the 1930s, state law would require female performers to apply for a license to wear men's clothing in their acts." Hartman, *Wayward Lives*, 200. High-profile cases in Britain that put women, sexuality, queerness, and art on trial include that of Maud Allan (1918) and Radclyffe Hall (1928). On Allan, see Walkowitz, "'Vision of Salome'"; on Hall, see Jodie Medd, "Séances and Slander: Radclyffe Hall in 1920," in Doan and Garrity, *Sapphic Modernities*, 201–216. On violence in this period, see Hartman, *Wayward Lives*, and Chauncey, *Gay New York*.
48. Krista Thompson, "Preoccupied with Haiti, The Dream of Diaspora in African American Art, 1915–1942," *American Art* 21, no. 3 (Fall 2007): 77–78.
49. Jafari S. Allen, "Black/Queer/Diaspora at the Current Conjuncture," *GLQ: A Journal of Lesbian and Gay Studies* 18, nos. 2–3 (2012): 215.
50. José Esteban Muñoz, *Disidentifications: Queers of Color and the Performance of Politics* (Durham, NC, 1999), 31.
51. Chauncey, *Gay New York*, xxi.
52. Chauncey, *Gay New York*, 263.
53. Henry Louis Gates Jr., "The Black Man's Burden," in *Fear of a Queer Planet: Queer Politics and Social Theory*, ed. Michael Warner (Minneapolis, 1993), 233.
54. Gates, "The Black Man's Burden," 238. See also Henry Louis Gates Jr., "Foreword," in Nugent and Wirth, *Gay Rebel of the Harlem Renaissance*, xi–xii.
55. Green, "Troubling the Waters," 80. See also Alden Reimoneng, "Countee Cullen's Uranian 'Soul Windows,'" in *Critical Essays: Gay and Lesbian Writers of Color*, ed. Emmanuel S. Nelson (New York, 1993), 145.
56. Vendryes, *Barthé*, 70. See also Manthia Diawara, "The Absent One: The Avant-Garde and the Black Imaginary in Looking for Langston," in *Representing Black Men*, ed. Marcellus Blount and George O. Cunningham (New York, 1996), 205–224.
57. Walkowitz, "'Vision of Salome,'" 363.
58. Jane Garrity, "Mary Butts's 'Fanatical Pédérérastie': Queer Urban Life in 1920s London and Paris," in Doan and Garrity, *Sapphic Modernities*, 235.
59. Vendryes, *Barthé*, 90–91.
60. "Augusta Savage Gives Her Views on Negro Art," *The Pittsburgh Courier*, September 26, 1936, 6. Thinking back to the elements of a harp, the head of Savage's largest figure is where the crown or head of the instrument might indeed be; it is placed on a shaft also referred to as a pillar or column.
61. One exception is James Smalls, *The Homoerotic Photography of Carl Van Vechten: Public Face, Private Thoughts* (Philadelphia, 2006).
62. Edward G. Perry, "Augusta Savage Has Art Exhibit," *The Pittsburgh Courier*, July 28, 1928, A2.
63. Chauncey, *Gay New York*, 252.
64. Susan Manning, *Modern Dance, Negro Dance: Race in Motion* (Minneapolis, 2004), 37, 57.
65. Thomas Wirth, "Introduction," in Nugent and Wirth, *Gay Rebel of the Harlem Renaissance*, 31.
66. Walkowitz, "'Vision of Salome,'" 351.
67. Sarah Ahmed, *Willful Subjects* (Durham, NC, 2014).
68. Walkowitz, "'Vision of Salome,'" 367–368.
69. Walkowitz, "'Vision of Salome,'" 367–370.
70. Green, "Troubling the Waters," 75.
71. Walkowitz, "'Vision of Salome,'" 367–376.
72. Leah Lehmbeck, "All the World's a Stage: Manet's Images of Model-Actresses," in *Manet and Modern Beauty: The Artist's Last Years*, ed. Scott Allen, Emily A. Beeny, and Gloria Groom (Los Angeles, 2019), 57, and Murrell, *Posing Modernity*.
73. Doan and Garrity, "Introduction," 6.
74. Charles Baudelaire cited in Doan and Garrity, "Introduction," 6.
75. Helen Burnham, "'The Type of an Era': Manet and the Parisienne," in Allen, Beeny, and Groom, *Manet and Modern Beauty*, 50.
76. Burnham, "'The Type of an Era,'" 50–51.
77. Latimer, "Romaine Brooks," 37.
78. Jeffrey C. Stewart, *The New Negro: The Life of Alain Locke* (New York, 2018), 729. See also Stewart's chap. 37. Gary J. Reynolds, Beryl J. Wright, and David C. Driskell, eds., *Against the Odds: African American Artists and the Harmon Foundation* (Newark, NJ, 1990).

On Prophet and her patrons, see Leininger-Miller, *New Negro Artists in Paris*, 39–49.

79 The statements Hughes and Bearden penned announcing this modern turn are legendary. Langston Hughes, "The Negro Artist and the Racial Mountain," *The Nation*, June 23, 1926; Romare Bearden, "The Negro Artist and Modern Art," *Opportunity* (December 1934); and N. Elizabeth Prophet, "Art and Life," *Phylon* 1, no. 4 (1940): 325.

80 Stewart, *The New Negro* (New York, 2018), 721.

81 Chauncey, *Gay New York*, 230.

82 Barthé would eventually move to Greenwich Village, another site of creativity, and social and sexual openness, linking him to another, whiter patronage base. Vendryes, *Barthé*, 90–91, and Stewart, *The New Negro*, chap. 37. See also Cheryl A. Wall, *Women of the Harlem Renaissance* (Bloomington, IN, 1995).

83 Prophet was a rigorous teacher by many accounts, training students such as Eugene Grigsby, Wilmer Jennings, and Hayward L. Oubre. The first art department in a historically Black college or university was inaugurated at Howard University in 1921. Spelman began offering design courses that year also. Amalia K. Amaki, "Nancy Elizabeth Prophet: Carving a Niche at Spelman College and Beyond," in *Hale Woodruff, Nancy Elizabeth Prophet, and the Academy* (Atlanta, 2007), 43–59.

84 Sharif Bey, "Augusta Savage: Sacrifice, Social Responsibility, and Early African American Art Education," *Studies in Art Education* 58, no. 2 (2017): 125–140.

85 These funded projects included the Harlem Art Workshop (held at the 135th Street Library, later the Schomburg Center for Research in Black Culture); the 306 Group, which supported Works Progress Administration (WPA) murals, particularly those at Harlem Hospital (and named after its location at 306 West 141st Street, painter Charles Alston's studio); The Harlem Artists Guild begun in 1935 to advocate for more African American hiring on the Federal Art Project; and the Uptown Art Laboratory, which would later become the WPA Harlem Community Art Center in 1937. Savage's many students included William Artis, Robert Blackburn, Ernest Crichlow, Gwendolyn Knight, Jacob Lawrence, Norman Lewis, and brothers Morgan and Marvin Smith.

With the creation of the Federal Art Project, African American artists finally found alternate means to finance their art making and at the same time were included in exhibitions redefining *American* art. In the wake of the Harlem riot of 1935, the WPA committed to funding the Harlem Community Art Center with Augusta Savage at its helm. Locke, who had apparently battled Savage and Ernestine Rose (of the 135th Street Library) for years over art and education in the community, was none too pleased. However, Savage's control and the WPA itself would soon come to an end. Stewart, *The New Negro*, chap. 37; Jeffreen M. Hayes, ed., *Augusta Savage: Renaissance Woman* (Jacksonville, FL, 2019); and Deirdre Bibby, *Augusta Savage and the Art Schools of Harlem* (New York, 1988), 7–11. For more on African American woman sculptors of the nineteenth and twentieth centuries, see Leslie King-Hammond and Tritobia Hayes Benjamin, *Three Generations of African American Women Sculptors: A Study in Paradox* (Washington, DC, 1996).

86 It is not known whether it was the Salon or Prophet that decided to present Prophet as male. Leininger-Miller, *New Negro Artists in Paris*, 43–44.

87 The Harmon Foundation awarded a prize to Prophet though not to Savage, which was not surprising given Locke's connection to the foundation and his animosity toward Savage.

88 For discussions of these artists' exhibitions, see Leininger-Miller, *New Negro Artists in Paris*, 50; Juanita Marie Holland, "Augusta Christine Savage: A Chronology of Her Art and Life, 1892–1962," in Schomburg Center for Research in Black Culture, *Augusta Savage and the Art Schools of Harlem* (New York, 1988), 12–19; Cullen, "Elizabeth Prophet: Sculptress"; "Beth Prophit [sic] Is Hailed in Paris as Real Artist," *Baltimore Afro-American*, August 3, 1929, 8; "Can I Become a Sculptor? The Story of Elizabeth Prophet," *The Crisis*, October 1932, 315; and "Miss Savage's Art Exhibit Wins Praise," *The Chicago Defender*, May 7, 1932, 11.

89 On Chicago's American Negro Exposition of 1940, see Adam Green, *Selling the Race: Culture, Community, and Black Chicago, 1940–1955* (Chicago, 2007), chap. 1. See also Mabel O. Wilson, *Negro Building: Black Americans in the World of Fairs and Museums* (Berkeley, CA, 2012).

90 The other Cinque Gallery founders included Romare Bearden and Ernest Crichlow. For a discussion of such artists initiatives in Los Angeles, see Kellie Jones, *South of Pico: African American Artists in Los Angeles in the 1960s and 1970s* (Durham, NC, 2017), chap. 3.

91 Hartman, *Wayward Lives*, 336; Amaki, "The Unfulfilled Promise of Elizabeth Prophet," 22–31; and Amaki, "Nancy Elizabeth Prophet," 43–59.

92 Green, "Troubling the Waters," 79.

93 Cooper, *Beyond Respectability*, 7.

94 Hortense J. Spillers, "Mama's Baby, Papa's Maybe: An American Grammar Book," *Diacritics* 17, no. 2 (Summer 1987): 64–81.

95 Omise'eke Natasha Tinsley, "Black Atlantic, Queer Atlantic: Queer Imaginings of the Middle Passage," *GLQ* 14, nos. 2–3 (June 1, 2008): 199.
96 It was also a locale where men suffered surveillance and arrest, as did Savage's friend writer Wallace Thurman. Chauncey, *Gay New York*, 265.
97 Hartman, *Wayward Lives*, 59.
98 Muñoz, *Disidentifications*, 170.
99 Prophet, "Art and Life," 325.

NUMINOUS AFFECT IN BLACK ATLANTIC MODERNISMS
SYLVESTER OKWUNODU OGBECHIE

Thanks to Elizabeth Smith, Victoria Jennings, and Nathan Segura for assisting with research for this essay. The epigraph is from the King James Version of the Bible. It was also posted on the wall of James Hampton's garage studio.

1 Henry Louis Gates Jr., *The Signifying Monkey: A Theory of African American Literary Criticism* (Oxford, 1988), 5.
2 German theologian Rudolf Otto was the first to coin and theorize "numinous." See Rudolf Otto, *The Idea of the Holy: An Inquiry into the Non-rational Factor in the Idea of the Divine and Its Relation to the Rational*, 2nd ed. (New York, 1958), 42.
3 Although official documents date Enwonwu's birth to 1921, documentary evidence and the testimony of the artist, his brothers, and other family members support the fact that Enwonwu was born on July 14, 1917. On the debate about Enwonwu's birthday, see Sylvester Okwunodu Ogbechie, *Ben Enwonwu: The Making of an African Modernist* (Rochester, NY, 2008), 24, 230.
4 Gerardo Mosquera, "Modernidad y Africanidad: Wifredo Lam in His Island," *Third Text* 6, no. 20 (1992): 44.
5 See "A Myth of Origins: Esu-Elegbara and the Signifying Monkey," in Gates, *The Signifying Monkey*, 3–43.
6 Gates, *The Signifying Monkey*, 29.
7 Gates, *The Signifying Monkey*, 6. I use "Pan-African" to describe a commonality of cultural practices in Africa and the African diaspora rather than the political ideology of Pan-Africanism.
8 The Eurocentric narrrative of modern art is exemplified by Alfred Barr's genealogy of modern artists in the Museum of Modern Art's 1936 exhibition *Cubism and Abstract Art*.
9 Gates, *The Signifying Monkey*, 51.
10 Ogbechie, *Ben Enwonwu*, 8.
11 Ogbechie, *Ben Enwonwu*, 198.
12 Ogbechie, *Ben Enwonwu*, 201.
13 Gates, *The Signifying Monkey*, xxiv.
14 Eric Newton, "Enwonwu," *Sunday Times* (London), August 6, 1950.
15 For a description of the Igbo *Ozo* title system, see M. Angulu Onwuejeogwu, "The Genesis, Diffusion, Structure and Significance of Ozo Title in Igboland," *Paideuma* 25 (1979): 117–143.
16 Gerald Aching, *Masking and Power: Carnival and Popular Culture in the Caribbean* (Minneapolis, 2002), 3.
17 For a definition of "African diaspora" see Genevieve Fabre and Klaus Benesch, eds., *African Diasporas in the New and Old Worlds* (Amsterdam, 2004), xiii–xxi.
18 John Peffer, "Notes on African Art, History, and Diasporas Within," *African Arts* 38, no. 4 (2005): 70–77, 95–96.
19 Sylvester Okwunodu Ogbechie, "Ben Enwonwu: Aesthetics and Artistic Identity in Modern Nigerian Art," *Nka: Journal of Contemporary African Art* (2002): 24–31.
20 Ogbechie, "Ben Enwonwu: Aesthetics and Artistic Identity," 30.
21 Paul Gilroy, *The Black Atlantic: Modernity and Double Consciousness* (Cambridge, MA, 1993), 6.
22 For analysis of Santería, see Migene González-Wippler, *Santería: The Religion: Faith, Rites, Magic* (Woodbury, MN, 2004), 28–33.
23 Paula Sato, "Wifredo Lam, the Shango Priestess, and the Femme Cheval," *Journal of International Women's Studies* 17, no. 3 (2016): 92. Eshu, Orisa, and Shango are anglicized spellings of Eṣu, Oriṣa, and Ṣango: in Yoruba orthography, the "sh" sound is represented by an "s" with a diacritical mark (in this case, a dot) under the letter.
24 Mark Hudson, "Wifredo Lam: The Unlikely Comeback of the Cuban Picasso," *The Telegraph*, August 31, 2016, https://www.telegraph.co.uk/art/what-to-see/wifredo-lam-the-unlikely-comeback-of-the-cuban-picasso/.
25 Hudson, "Wifredo Lam."
26 Sato, "Wifredo Lam," 93.
27 The quote is from Aimé Césaire, "Moi Laminaire," in *Lyric and Dramatic Poetry, 1946–1982*, trans. Clayton Eshleman and Annette Smith, with an introduction by James Arnold (Charlottesville, VA, 1990), 207.
28 Doris Maria-Reina Bravo, "Lam, The Jungle," Khan Academy, accessed January 18, 2021, https://www.khanacademy.org/humanities/ap-art-history/later-europe-and-americas/modernity-ap/a/lam-the-jungle.
29 Sato, "Wifredo Lam," 97. See also Sabine Rewald and Magdalena Dabrowski, *The American Matisse: The Dealer, His Artists, His Collection* (New York, 2010), 67.
30 Max-Pol Fouchet, *Wifredo Lam* (New York, 1976), 188–189.
31 "Who Is Wifredo Lam?," Tate Modern,

London, accessed February 22, 2022, https://www.tate.org.uk/whats-on/tate-modern/exhibition/ey-exhibition-wifredo-lam/who-is.

32 Sato, "Wifredo Lam," 97.
33 Valerie J. Fletcher, "Wifredo Lam," in *Crosscurrents of Modernism: Four Latin American Pioneers; Diego Rivera, Joaquin Torres-Garcia, Wifredo Lam, Matta*, ed. Olivier Debroise et al. (Washington, DC, 1992), 183.
34 David H. Brown, *Santería Enthroned: Art, Ritual, and Innovation in an Afro-Cuban Religion* (Chicago, 2003), 136, 341.
35 Fouchet, *Wifredo Lam*, 31.
36 Sato, "Wifredo Lam," 98.
37 "Wifredo Lam, The Jungle (La Jungla), 1943," Museum of Modern Art, New York, accessed October 3, 2021, https://www.moma.org/collection/works/34666.
38 "The Jungle (La Jungla)," Museum of Modern Art, New York, accessed June 2, 2021, https://www.moma.org/learn/moma_learning/wifredo-lam-the-jungle-1943/.
39 Gerardo Mosquera, "Mi pintura es un acto de descolonización: Entrevista con Wifredo Lam," *Bohemia* 92, no. 25 (1980): 10–13.
40 Fernando Ortiz, *Visiones sobre Lam* (Havana, 2002), 24–25.
41 Roberto S. Goizueta, "Mysterium Tremendum et fascinans: The Pre-Theistic Art of Wifredo Lam," in *Wifredo Lam: Imagining New World*, ed. Elizabeth T. Goizueta (Chicago, 2014), 79.
42 Michel Leiris, *Wifredo Lam* (New York, 1970).
43 Lowery Stokes Sims, *Wifredo Lam and the International Avant-Garde, 1923–1982* (Austin, TX, 2002), 57.
44 Goizueta, "Mysterium Tremendum et fascinans," 85.
45 For a review of how Lam's Chinese background influenced his art, see Mey-Yen Moriuchi, "Locating Chinese Culture and Aesthetics in the Art of Wifredo Lam," in *Afro-Asian Connections in Latin America and the Caribbean*, ed. Luisa Marcella Ossa and Debbie Lee-DiStefano (Lanham, MD, 2019), 27–60.
46 See Lowery Stokes Sims, "Myths and Primitivism: The Work of Wifredo Lam in the Context of the New York School and the School of Paris, 1942–1952," in *Wifredo Lam and His Contemporaries 1938–1952*, ed. Giulio V. Blanc and Maria R. Balderrama (New York, 1992), 71–90.
47 The concept of "double vision" is a widespread African and African diaspora belief in an ability to simultaneously perceive both physical and spiritual dimensions.
48 Mosquera, "Modernidad y Africanidad," 53.
49 Robert Farris Thompson, *Flash of the Spirit: African and Afro-American Art and Philosophy* (New York, 1984), 146.
50 Casey N. Cep, "Cracking the Code of James Hampton's Private Language," *Pacific Standard*, June 14, 2017, https://psmag.com/social-justice/cracking-code-james-hamptons-private-language-96278.
51 Grey Gundaker and Judith McWillie, *No Space Hidden: The Spirit of African American Yard Work* (Knoxville, TN, 2005), 35.
52 See Mark Stamp and Ethan Le, "Hamptonese and Hidden Markov Models," in *New Directions and Applications in Control Theory*, ed. Wijeshuriya P. Dayawansa, Anders Lindquist, and Yishao Zhou (Berlin, 2005), 367–378. For analysis of precolonial African writing systems, see Christine Mullen Kreamer, Mary Nooter Roberts, Elizabeth Harney, and Allyson Purpura, *Inscribing Meaning: Writing and Graphic Systems in African Art* (Washington, DC, 2007).
53 Betty M. Kuyk traces specific African American religious and cultural practices to West and Central African antecedents, in Betty M. Kuyk, *African Voices in the African American Heritage* (Bloomington, IN, 2003).
54 Grey Gundaker, *Signs of Diaspora, Diaspora of Signs: Literacies, Creolization, and Vernacular Practice in African America* (New York, 1998), 172.
55 Gundaker, *Signs of Diaspora, Diaspora of Signs*, 183.
56 Gundaker, *Signs of Diaspora, Diaspora of Signs*, 183.
57 "The Throne of the Third Heaven of the Nations' Millennium General Assembly," Smithsonian American Art Museum, accessed January 30, 2022, https://americanart.si.edu/artwork/throne-third-heaven-nations-millennium-general-assembly-9897.
58 Lynda Roscoe Hartigan, "*The Throne of the Third Heaven of the Nations' Millennium General Assembly,*" accessed October 24, 2022, http://www.fredweaver.com/throne/throneessay.html.
59 Robert Farris Thompson, "The Song That Named the Land: The Visionary Presence of African American Art," in *Black Art Ancestral Legacy: The African Impulse in African American Art* (Dallas, TX, 1989), 124.
60 Donald J. Cosentino, "On Looking at Vodou Altars," *African Arts* 29, no. 2 (1996): 67.
61 Charles Merewether, "A Matter of Recognition," *African Arts* 29, no. 2 (1996): 72.
62 The relevance of sonics/aurality is an understudied aspect of African and African diaspora art. For a recent attempt to incorporate sonics into analysis, see Henry John Drewal, "Sensiotics, or the Study of the Senses in Material Culture and History in Africa and Beyond," in *The Oxford Handbook of History and Material Culture*, ed. Ivan Gaskell and Sarah-Anne Carter, May 2020, https://www

.oxfordhandbooks.com/view/10.1093/oxfordhb/9780199341764.001.0001/oxfordhb-9780199341764-e-24, and Krista A. Thompson, "The Sound of Light: Reflections on Art History in the Visual Culture of Hip-Hop," *Art Bulletin* 91, no. 4 (2009): 481-505.

63 Stamp and Le, "Hamptonese and Hidden Markov Models," 8.

64 For a definition of *Nkisi*, see Wyatt MacGaffey, "Complexity, Astonishment and Power: The Visual Vocabulary of Kongo Minkisi," *Journal of Southern African Studies* 14, no. 2 (1988): 188-203.

65 Vasily [Wassily] Kandinsky, *Über das Geistige in der Kunst* (Munich, 1911), and Wassily Kandinsky, *Concerning the Spiritual in Art*, trans. and with an introduction by M. T. H. Sadler (New York, 1977). For analysis of Klint's abstract art, which predates Kandinsky's, see Tracey Bashkoff, *Hilma af Klint: Paintings for the Future* (New York, 2018).

66 Thomas Crow, *No Idols: The Missing Theology of Art* (Sydney, 2017).

67 John Picton, "Fetishizing Modernity: Bricollage Revisited," in *Art History and Fetishism Abroad: Global Shifts in Media and Methods*, ed. Gabriele Genge and Angela Stercken (Bielefeld, 2014), 205-234.

68 Moyo Okediji, *Western Frontiers of African Art* (Rochester, NY, 2011).

69 For recent efforts to read Blackness beyond the framework of race, see Huey Copeland, *Bound to Appear: Art, Slavery, and the Site of Blackness in Multicultural America* (Chicago, 2013); Krista Thompson, *Shine: The Visual Economy of Light in African Diaspora Aesthetic Practices* (Durham, NC, 2015); and Darby English, *How to See a Work of Art in Total Darkness* (Boston, 2010).

70 See for example Gilroy, *The Black Atlantic*, and Celeste-Marie Bernier, *Stick to the Skin: African American and Black British Art, 1965-2015* (Oakland, 2019). However, these texts interpret Blackness in relation to African American interrogations of slavery and its aftermath. Black Africans mostly subscribe to a different ontology of being, in which subjecthood and agency are taken for granted, albeit also contested.

71 Sonal Khullar, *Worldly Affiliations: Artistic Practice, National Identity, and Modernism in India, 1930-1990* (Berkeley, CA, 2015), 16.

72 Kobena Mercer, *Cosmopolitan Modernisms* (Cambridge, MA, 2005), 11.

73 Mercer, *Cosmopolitan Modernisms*, 19.

74 Philip Kaisary, "The Black Atlantic: Notes on the Thought of Paul Gilroy," *Critical Legal Thinking*, September 15, 2014, http://criticallegalthinking.com/2014/09/15/black-atlantic-notes-thought-paul-gilroy/.

DARKNESS AND THE *UNVISIBLE*: NORMAN LEWIS, ROY DECARAVA, AND POSTWAR ABSTRACTION

KOBENA MERCER

1 Ivor Miller, "'If It Hasn't Been One of Color': An Interview with Roy DeCarava," *Callaloo* 13, no. 4 (Autumn 1990): 849-850.

2 Karli Wurzelbacher, "*Black Monolith II* (Homage to Ralph Ellison *The Invisible Man*)," in *Odyssey: Jack Whitten Sculpture, 1973-2017*, ed. Katy Siegel (New York, 2018), 116.

3 Adrienne Edwards, *Blackness in Abstraction* (New York, 2016), 9; and Mark Godfrey, "Notes on Black Abstraction," in *Soul of a Nation: Art in the Age of Black Power, 1963-1983*, ed. Mark Godfrey and Zoe Whitley (London, 2017), 147-188.

4 Ann Eden Gibson, "Two Worlds: African American Abstraction in New York at Mid-Century," in *The Search for Freedom: African American Abstract Painting, 1945-1973* (New York, 1991), 11-53; Ann Eden Gibson, "Black Is a Color: Norman Lewis and Modernism in New York," in *Norman Lewis: Black Paintings, 1946-1977* (New York, 1998), 24-25; and Ann Eden Gibson, "Norman Lewis: How to Get Black," in *Cosmopolitan Modernisms*, ed. Kobena Mercer (Cambridge, MA, 2005), 102-123.

5 Michael Leja, *Reframing Abstract Expressionism: Subjectivity and Painting in the 1940s* (New Haven, CT, 1993), esp. "Modern Man Discourse and the New York School," 249-268.

6 Hortense J. Spillers, "Mama's Baby, Papa's Maybe: An American Grammar Book," *Diacritics* 17, no. 2 (Summer 1987): 67.

7 Norman Lewis, Alfred Barr Jr., and Ad Reinhardt in *The Artists' Sessions at Studio 35* [1950] (Chicago, 2009), 32-33.

8 The Jefferson School is discussed in Marvin Gettleman, "The Lost World of United States Labor Education: Curricula at East and West Coast Communist Schools, 1944-1957," in *American Labor and the Cold War: Grassroots Politics and Postwar Political Culture*, ed. Robert Cherney, William Essel, and Kieran Walsh Taylor (New Brunswick, NJ, 2004), 205-215. Gwendolyn Bennett's FBI file is available at https://archive.org/stream/GwendolynBennettFBIFile/Gwendolyn%20Bennett%20001_djvu.txt, accessed January 29, 2020.

9 See Andrew Carnduff Ritchie, *Abstract Painting and Sculpture in America* (New York, 1951), and Katharine Kuh, *American Artists Paint the City*, 28th Venice Biennale (Chicago, 1956); see also Mary Caroline Simpson, "American Artists Paint the City: Katherine Kuh, the 1956 Venice Biennale, and New York's Place in the Cold War Art World,"

American Studies 48, no. 4 (Winter 2007): 31–57.

10 Ad Reinhardt, "Twelve Rules for a New Academy," *ARTnews* 56, no. 3 (May 1953): 37–38.

11 Reinhardt, "Twelve Rules," 37.

12 Reinhardt quoted in "1957," in Hal Foster, Rosalind Krauss, Yve-Alain Bois, Benjamin H. D. Buchloh, and David Joselit, eds., *Art Since 1900*, 2nd ed. (New York, 2011), 436.

13 Henri Ghent, "Oral History Interview with Norman Lewis, 1968, July 14," Smithsonian Archives of American Art, accessed January 29, 2020, https://www.aaa.si.edu/collections/interviews/oral-history-interview-norman-lewis-11465#transcript.

14 Harold Rosenberg, "American Action Painters," *ARTnews* (December 1952): 22–23, 48–50.

15 Gibson, "How to Get Black," 107–119.

16 Norman Lewis, "Thesis, 1946," in *Norman Lewis: From the Harlem Renaissance to Abstraction*, ed. Corrine Jennings (New York, 1989), 63.

17 Clement Greenberg, "Modernist Painting" [1961], in *Clement Greenberg: The Collected Essays and Criticism*, vol. 4, *Modernism with a Vengeance*, ed. John O'Brian (Chicago, 1995).

18 Mark Cheetham, *The Rhetoric of Purity: Essentialist Theory and the Advent of Abstract Painting* (Cambridge, 1994).

19 Jean-François Lyotard, *Discourse, Figure* [1971], trans. Anthony Hudeck and Mary Lydon (Minneapolis, 2011).

20 Gibson, "Black Is a Color," 19.

21 Katy Siegel, *Since '45: America and the Making of Contemporary Art* (London, 2011), 58.

22 Joan [Murray] Weissman, interview by Ann Eden Gibson, June 1987, quoted in Gibson, "Black Is a Color," 20.

23 Ralph Waldo Emerson, *Complete Works: Essays, Second Series* [1844] (New York, 1903), 167.

24 Andriana Campbell, "One World or None: Hints of the Future in Norman Lewis's Abstract Expressionism," in *Procession: The Art of Norman Lewis*, ed. Ruth Fine (Philadelphia, 2015), 226.

25 W. E. B. Du Bois and Langston Hughes, quoted in Paul Boyer, *By the Bomb's Early Light: American Thought and Culture at the Dawn of the Atomic Age* (Chapel Hill, NC, 1985), 268, 199.

26 Willem de Kooning, "What Abstract Art Means to Me," *Bulletin of the Museum of Modern Art* 18, no. 3 (Spring 1951): 7.

27 Leonardo da Vinci, quoted in Irene Earls, *Renaissance Art: A Topical Dictionary* (Westport, CT, 1987), 7, and in Alexander Nagel, "Leonardo and *Sfumato*," *Res* 24 (Autumn 1993): 8.

28 Norman Lewis, quoted in Gibson, "Black Is a Color," 11. Gibson draws from Lewis's October 10, 1973, interview with Romare Bearden, which appears in redacted form in Romare Bearden and Harry Henderson, *A History of African-American Artists, 1796 to the Present* (New York, 1993), 322.

29 Bearden and Henderson, *A History of African-American Artists*, 322.

30 Akira Lippit, *Atomic Light (Shadow Optics)* (Minneapolis, 2005), esp. 81–103.

31 Leonardo da Vinci, quoted in Nagel, "Leonardo and *Sfumato*," 8.

32 Norman Lewis, quoted in Bearden and Henderson, *A History of African-American Artists*, 322.

33 Sharon F. Patton, *African-American Art* (New York, 1999), 175.

34 Kiff Bamford, *Lyotard and the Figural in Performance, Art and Writing* (London, 2012), 20.

35 Stuart Hall with Bill Schwarz, "Living with Difference: Stuart Hall in Conversation with Bill Schwarz," *Soundings* 37 (2007): 153.

36 See Michael Raz-Russo, ed., *Invisible Man: Gordon Parks and Ralph Ellison in Harlem*, (Göttingen, 2017), 155–159.

37 T. J. Clark, *Farewell to an Idea: Episodes from a History of Modernism* (New Haven, CT, 1999), 7.

38 Godfrey, "Notes on Black Abstraction," 159.

39 Peter Galassi, ed., *Roy DeCarava: A Retrospective* (New York, 1996).

40 Roy DeCarava, quoted in Sherry Turner DeCarava, "Celebration," in *Roy DeCarava: Photographs*, ed. James Alinder (Carmel, CA, 1981), 14–15.

41 Maren Stange, "'Illusion Complete within Itself:' Roy DeCarava's Photography," *Yale Journal of Criticism* 9, no. 1 (Spring 1996): 73.

42 Roy DeCarava, in Turner DeCarava, "Celebration," 13.

43 Roy DeCarava, in Turner DeCarava, "Celebration," 15.

44 Ralph Ellison, *Invisible Man* [1952] (London, 1982), 469. The starting point for further inquiry into underground spaces as vestibular form in Black modernism would be Richard Wright, "The Man Who Lived Underground" [1942], in Wright, *Eight Men: Short Stories* (New York, 1961).

45 Paul Gilroy, *The Black Atlantic: Modernity and Double Consciousness* (Cambridge, MA, 1993), 37.

46 Darby English, *How to See a Work of Art in Total Darkness* (Cambridge, MA, 2007); Kellie Jones, *Energy/Experimentation: Black Artists and Abstraction, 1964–1980* (New York, 2006); and Courtney J. Martin, ed., *Four Generations: The Joyner/Giuffrida Collection of Abstract Art* (New York, 2017).

47 Penny M. von Eschen, *Race Against Empire:*

Black Americans and Anticolonialism, 1937–1957 (Ithaca, NY, 1997).

48 Spillers, "Mama's Baby, Papa's Maybe," 74.
49 Graham Lock and David Murray, eds., *The Hearing Eye: Jazz and Blues Influences in African American Visual Art* (New York, 2009).
50 Fred Moten, "The Case of Blackness," *Criticism* 50, no. 2 (Spring 2008): 177–218. The debate was published in *ArtsCanada*, no. 113 (October 1967). See Krys Verral, "*artscanada*'s 'Black' Issue: 1960s Contemporary Art and African Liberation Movements," *Canadian Journal of Communication* 36, no. 4 (2011): 539–558. For a cultural history approach to the multiple meanings of "black," see John Harvey, *The Story of Black* (London, 2013).
51 Cedric Robinson, *Black Marxism: The Making of the Black Radical Tradition* [1983], 2nd ed. (Chapel Hill, NC, 2000).
52 Clark, *Farewell to an Idea*, 3.
53 Terry Smith, "Contemporary Art and Contemporaneity," *Critical Inquiry* 32, no. 4 (Summer 2006): 681–707; see also responses by Okwui Enwezor and Terry Smith to "Questionnaire on 'The Contemporary,'" *October* 130 (Fall 2009): 33–40, 46–54.
54 Okwui Enwezor, Katy Siegel, and Ulrich Wilmes, eds., *Postwar: Art between the Pacific and the Atlantic, 1945–1964* (Munich, 2017).
55 See my previous article "Black Atlantic Abstraction," in Kobena Mercer, ed., *Discrepant Abstraction* (Cambridge, MA, 2005), 182–205.
56 The influence of Lewis's *Seachange* series is discussed in Kellie Jones, "Mediterranean Conversations," *Odyssey: Jack Whitten Sculpture*, 40–51.

AT THE THRESHOLD OF WITHHOLDING: STANLEY BROUWN'S MODERNIST REPETITIONS
ADRIENNE EDWARDS

Special thanks to Ellen Gallagher. As in the epigraph, most catalogs of Brouwn's work feature such a statement or a variation thereof. See Christophe Cherix, *In and Out of Amsterdam: Travels in Conceptual Art 1960–1976* (New York, 2009).

1 Cherix, *In and Out of Amsterdam*, 21.
2 Benjamin H. D. Buchloh, "Conceptual Art 1962–1969: From the Aesthetic of Administration to the Critique of Institutions," *October* 55 (Winter 1990): 124.
3 Denise Ferreira da Silva, "Toward a Black Feminist Poethics: The Quest(ion) of Blackness Toward the End of the World," *The Black Scholar* 44, no. 2 (Summer 2014): 81.
4 Gilles Deleuze and Félix Guattari, *A Thousand Plateaus: Capitalism and Schizophrenia*, trans. Brian Massumi (Minneapolis, 1987), 105.
5 See Cherix, *In and Out of Amsterdam*; Ludo van Halem, "Elementaire belevenissen: Het vroege werk van Stanley Brouwn," *Jong Holland*, no. 3 (1991); and Oscar van den Boogaard, "In Search of Stanley Brouwn," *Frieze* 161 (March 2014).
6 Van Halem, "Elementaire belevenissen."
7 Eric de Bruyn, "Topological Pathways of Post-Minimalism," *Grey Room*, no. 25 (Fall 2006): 39.
8 Cherix, *In and Out of Amsterdam*, 21.
9 Édouard Glissant, *Poetics of Relation*, trans. Betsy Wing (Ann Arbor, MI, 1997), 20.
10 Glissant, *Poetics of Relation*, 11.
11 Glissant, *Poetics of Relation*, 14.
12 Glissant, *Poetics of Relation*, 18.
13 Glissant, *Poetics of Relation*, 3.
14 Glissant, *Poetics of Relation*, 20.
15 Gert Oostindie and Inge Klinkers, "A Caribbean Exodus," in *Decolonising the Caribbean: Dutch Policies in a Comparative Perspective* (Amsterdam, 2003), 178.
16 Oostindie and Klinkers, "A Caribbean Exodus," 180.
17 Oostindie and Klinkers, "A Caribbean Exodus," 181.
18 Oostindie and Klinkers, "A Caribbean Exodus," 181.
19 Oostindie and Klinkers, "A Caribbean Exodus," 181.
20 Oostindie and Klinkers, "A Caribbean Exodus," 182.
21 Oostindie and Klinkers, "A Caribbean Exodus," 182.
22 Oostindie and Klinkers, "A Caribbean Exodus," 183.
23 Oostindie and Klinkers, "A Caribbean Exodus," 184.
24 Kwando M. Kinshasha, "From Surinam to the Holocaust: Anton de Kom, A Political Migrant," *The Journal of Caribbean History* 36, no. 1 (2002): 61.
25 Oostindie and Klinkers, "A Caribbean Exodus," 185.
26 Oostindie and Klinkers, "A Caribbean Exodus," 185.
27 Oostindie and Klinkers, "A Caribbean Exodus," 186.
28 Oostindie and Klinkers, "A Caribbean Exodus," 186.
29 Mies van Niekerk, "Afro-Caribbeans and Indo-Caribbeans in the Netherlands: Premigration Legacies and Social Mobility," *The International Migration Review* 38, no. 1 (Spring 2004): 162.
30 Van Niekerk, "Afro-Caribbeans and Indo-Caribbeans in the Netherlands," 162.
31 Van Niekerk, "Afro-Caribbeans and Indo-Caribbeans in the Netherlands," 162.
32 Van Niekerk, "Afro-Caribbeans and Indo-Caribbeans in the Netherlands," 164.

33 Kinshasha, "From Surinam to the Holocaust," 34.
34 Kinshasha, "From Surinam to the Holocaust," 37, 39.
35 Kinshasha, "From Surinam to the Holocaust," 40.
36 De Bruyn, "Topological Pathways of Post-Minimalism," 39.
37 Buchloh, "Conceptual Art 1962–1969," 129, 142.
38 Ian Baucom, *Specters of the Atlantic: Finance Capital, Slavery, and the Philosophy of History* (Durham, NC, 2005), 29.
39 Baucom, *Specters of the Atlantic*, 29.
40 Baucom, *Specters of the Atlantic*, 24.
41 Richard Price and Sally Price, eds., "Introduction," in John Gabriel Stedman, *Narrative of a Five Years Expedition against the Revolted Negroes of Surinam* [1790] (Baltimore, 2010), xiii.
42 Price and Price, "Introduction," xxi.
43 Price and Price, "Introduction," xxi.
44 Price and Price, "Introduction," xiv, xxii.
45 Price and Price, "Introduction," xiv.
46 Price and Price, "Introduction," xxxviii.
47 Price and Price, "Introduction," xl. Unsigned engravings by Blake were possibly made as early as 1791.
48 See Christine Gallant, "Blake's Antislavery Designs for 'Songs of Innocence and of Experience,'" *The Wordsworth Circle* 39, no. 3 (Summer 2008): 123.
49 Emily Senior, "'Perfectly Whole': Skin and Text in John Gabriel Stedman's Narrative of a Five Years Expedition Against the Revolted Negroes of Surinam," *Eighteenth-Century Studies* 44, no. 1 (Fall 2010): 39–40.
50 Senior, "'Perfectly Whole,'" 40.
51 Senior, "'Perfectly Whole,'" 40.
52 Senior, "'Perfectly Whole,'" 40.
53 Senior, "'Perfectly Whole,'" 41.
54 Senior, "'Perfectly Whole,'" 42.
55 "A Paradox in Caribbean Cinema? An Interview with Minimal Movie Filmmaker Pim de la Parra, Pragmatic Dreamer from Suriname," *Imaginations* (December 7, 2015), https://journals.library.ualberta.ca/imaginations/index.php/imaginations/article/view/27428.
56 See Price and Price, "Introduction," xxxii–xxxvi. "Surinamese marriage" is a colloquialism particular to colonial time and place to describe long-time, often commercial transactions for sexual relations between European men and enslaved women.
57 Frantz Fanon, *The Wretched of the Earth* [1961], trans. Richard Philcox (New York, 2004), 145.
58 Fanon, *The Wretched of the Earth*, 149.
59 Fanon, *The Wretched of the Earth*, 157–158.
60 Van Halem, "Elementaire belevenissen," 10.
61 Van Halem, "Elementaire belevenissen," 10.
62 Fanon, *The Wretched of the Earth*, 175.
63 Van Halem, "Elementaire belevenissen," 10.
64 Van Halem, "Elementaire belevenissen," 11.
65 Fanon, *The Wretched of the Earth*, 161.
66 Van Halem, "Elementaire belevenissen," 15–16.
67 Homi K. Bhabha, "Of Mimicry and Man: The Ambivalence of Colonial Discourse," in *The Location of Culture* (London, 1994), 131.
68 Bhabha, "Of Mimicry and Man," 122.
69 Bhabha, "Of Mimicry and Man," 122.
70 Bhabha, "Of Mimicry and Man," 122–123.
71 Bhabha, "Of Mimicry and Man," 123.
72 Bhabha, "Of Mimicry and Man," 123.
73 Bhabha, "Of Mimicry and Man," 125.
74 See Lauren Berlant, "Showing Up to Withhold: Pope.L's Deadpan Aesthetic," in *Showing Up to Withhold*, ed. William Pope.L and Karen Reimer (Chicago, 2014).
75 De Bruyn, "Topological Pathways of Post-Minimalism," 45.

SPACES IN THE SHADOWS: ARCHIVES AND ARCHITECTURES IN THE WORK OF CARRIE MAE WEEMS

MABEL O. WILSON

Anna Julia Cooper, quoted in Paula Giddings, *When and Where I Enter: The Impact of Black Women on Race and Sex in America* (New York, 1984), and Hortense J. Spillers, "Mama's Baby, Papa's Maybe: An American Grammar Book," *Diacritics* 17, no. 2 (Summer 1987).

1 See Richard Krautheimer, *Rome: Profile of a City, 312–1308* (Princeton, NJ, 1980), and Andrea Palladio, *Palladio's Rome: A Translation of Andrea Palladio's Two Guidebooks to Rome*, trans. Vaughn Hart and Peter Hicks (New Haven, CT, 2006).
2 Spillers, "Mama's Baby, Papa's Maybe," 65.
3 Manfredo Tafuri, *Architecture and Utopia: Design and Capitalist Development* [1976] (Cambridge, MA, 1985), 15.
4 Kathryn E. Delmez, ed., *Carrie Mae Weems: Three Decades of Photography and Video* (Nashville, TN, 2012), 220.
5 Cervenak characterizes "spectacular opacity" as "the undetectable place of an errant movement, an interior kinesis that resists forces attempting to trace, follow, and read." Sarah Jane Cervenak, *Wandering: Philosophical Performances of Racial and Sexual Freedom* (Durham, NC, 2014), 14, 165.
6 bell hooks, "Talking Art with Carrie Mae Weems," in *Art on My Mind: Visual Politics* (New York, 1995), 67.
7 Georg Wilhelm Friedrich Hegel, *The Philosophy of History* (Kitchner, Ontario, 2001), 111. See also Susan Beck-Morss, *Hegel, Haiti, and Universal History* (Pittsburgh, 2009).

8 Denise Ferreira da Silva, *Toward a Global Idea of Race*, Borderlines Series 27 (Minneapolis, 2007), 31–33. See also Lisa Lowe, *The Intimacies of Four Continents* (Durham, NC, 2015), 139–148.

9 Édouard Glissant, *Poetics of Relation*, trans. Betsy Wing (Ann Arbor, MI, 1997), 6.

10 M. NourbeSe Philip, *Zong!* (Middletown, CT, 2008), 197.

11 Aimé Césaire, *Discourse on Colonialism*, trans. Joan Pinkham, introduction by Robin D. G. Kelley (New York, 2000), 36.

12 Sylvia Wynter, "Unsettling the Coloniality of Being/Power/Truth/Freedom: Towards the Human, After Man, Its Overrepresentation—An Argument," *The New Centennial Review* 3, no. 3 (Fall 2003): 260.

13 Spillers, "Mama's Baby, Papa's Maybe," 75.

14 See Saidiya V. Hartman, *Scenes of Subjection: Terror, Slavery, and Self-Making in Nineteenth-Century America* (Oxford, 1997), 119–123.

15 See Peter Minosh, "American Architecture and the Black Atlantic: William Thornton's Design for the United States Capitol," in *Race and Modern Architecture: A Critical History from the Enlightenment to Today*, ed. Irene Cheng, Charles L. Davis II, and Mabel O. Wilson (Pittsburgh, 2020), 43–58, and Mabel O. Wilson, "'Home of the Oppressed': Democracy, Slavery, and American Civic Architecture," Eduard F. Sekler Talk, Society of Architectural Historians' 2020 Virtual Conference, April 30, 2020, https://vimeo.com/413127567.

16 Dawoud Bey, "Carrie Mae Weems," *Bomb Magazine*, July 1, 2009, https://bombmagazine.org/articles/carrie-mae-weems/.

17 Katherine McKittrick, "Footnotes (Books and Papers Scattered about the Floor)," in *Dear Science and Other Stories* (Durham, NC, 2021), 33.

18 In the exhibition and publications of these photographic series, Weems invites viewers to join her in the process of articulating what historian Michel-Rolph Trouillot calls "retrospective significance" through her visual narratives. For Trouillot the process of historical production occurs in the four moments of fact creation (sources), fact assembly (archives), fact retrieval (narratives), and retrospective significance (history). Michel-Rolph Trouillot, *Silencing the Past: Power and the Production of History* (Boston, 1995), 25-26.

19 Weems's early series *Kitchen Table* (1990) plumbs the performance of gendered, racialized, classed, and sexualized everyday activities around a kitchen table.

20 hooks, "Talking Art with Carrie Mae Weems," 77.

21 hooks, "Talking Art with Carrie Mae Weems," 77.

22 hooks, "Talking Art with Carrie Mae Weems," 75.

23 Katherine McKittrick, *Demonic Grounds: Black Women and the Cartographies of Struggle* (Minneapolis, 2006), 12.

24 See St. Claire Drake and Horace Cayton, *Black Metropolis: A Study of Negro Life in a Northern City* (Chicago, 2015), and Wynter, "Unsettling the Coloniality."

25 David Scott, "That Event, This Memory: Notes on the Anthropology of African Diasporas in the New World," *Diaspora: A Journal of Transnational Studies* 1, no. 3 (Winter 1991): 278.

26 Scott, "That Event, This Memory," 278–279.

27 Franklin Sirmans, "A World of Her Own: Carrie Mae Weems and Performance," in Delmez, *Carrie Mae Weems*, 50.

28 The pattern was originally designed by British artist John Farleigh; see *Looking High and Low*, accessed April 3, 2021, https://collections.vam.ac.uk/item/O55082/looking-high-and-low-wallpaper-weems-carrie-mae/.

29 For an extensive examination of the history of the daguerreotypes see Ilisa Barbash, Molly Rogers, and Deborah Willis, eds., *To Make Their Own Way in the World: The Enduring Legacy of the Zealy Daguerreotypes* (Cambridge, MA, 2020), and Molly Rogers, *Delia's Tears: Race, Science, and Photography in Nineteenth-Century America* (New Haven, CT, 2010), 5-7.

30 Yxta Maya Murray, "*From Here I Saw What Happened and I Cried*: Carrie Mae Weems' Challenge to the Harvard Archive," *Unbound: Harvard Journal of the Legal Left* 8, no. 1 (2013): 24.

31 David Bindman, *Ape to Apollo: Aesthetics and the Idea of Race in the 18th Century* (Ithaca, NY, 2002), 12.

32 Immanuel Kant, *Observations on the Feeling of the Beautiful and Sublime and Other Writings*, ed. Patrick R. Frierson and Paul Guyer (Cambridge, 2011), 58–59.

33 Kant, *Observations*, 58–59.

34 Hegel, *The Philosophy of History*, 109.

35 Bindman, *Ape to Apollo*, 221.

36 Brian Wallis, "Black Bodies, White Science: Louis Agassiz's Slave Daguerreotypes," *American Art* 9, no. 2 (Summer 1995): 52, and Bindman, *Ape to Apollo*, 79–91.

37 Simon Gikandi, *Slavery and the Culture of Taste* (Princeton, NJ, 2011).

38 Frantz Fanon, *The Wretched of the Earth* (New York, 1961), 4.

39 Wallis, "Black Bodies, White Science," 49.

40 Gregg Hecimovich, "The Life and Times of Alfred, Delia, Drana, Fassena, Jack, Jem, and

41. Renty," in Barbash, Rogers, and Willis, *To Make Their Own Way in the World*, 76.
42. Christina Elizabeth Sharpe, *In the Wake: On Blackness and Being* (Durham, NC, 2016), 43.
43. Ariella Azoulay, *The Civil Contract of Photography* (New York, 2012), 168, 71–72.
44. See Sarah Elizabeth Lewis, "The Insistent Reveal: Louis Agassiz, Joseph T. Zealy, Carrie Mae Weems, and the Politics of Undress in Photography of Racial Science," in Barbash, Rogers, and Willis, *To Make Their Own Way in the World*, 302–303.
44. Sharpe, *In the Wake*, 118.
45. In an interview with photographer and historian Deborah Willis, Weems explained, "In terms of color, I find myself time and again using blue and red: red implying a history of violence, and blue for the history of the blues." See Deborah Willis, "In Conversation with Carrie Mae Weems," in Barbash, Rogers, and Willis, *To Make Their Own Way in the World*, 397.
46. Delmez, *Carrie Mae Weems*, 70.
47. Sponsored by the automobile company Citroën, the French minister of the colonies, the Museum of Natural History, and the National Geographic Society, the expedition provided visual material of so-called primitive cultures by way of photographs and film imagery that fed the metropole's fantasy of mysterious colonial peoples. Brett A. Berliner, *Ambivalent Desire: The Exotic Black Other in Jazz-Age France* (Amherst, MA, 2002), 189–190.
48. T. Denean Sharpley-Whiting, *Black Venus: Sexualized Savages, Primal Fears, and Primitive Narratives in French* (Durham, NC, 1999), 6.
49. Berliner, *Ambivalent Desire*, 195–199.
50. White American sculptor Malvina Cornell Hoffman created, for example, a bronze likeness of Nobosodru to include in her panorama of fifty racial types placed on view in 1933 at Chicago's Field Museum of Natural History. A 1927 issue of the Urban League's magazine *Opportunity* was dedicated to African artworks that had captured the interest and imagination of modern artists like Aaron Douglas, whose abstract illustration of Nobosodru's profile graced the issue's cover. See Huey Copeland, "In the Wake of the Negress," in *Modern Women: Women Artists at the Museum of Modern Art*, ed. Cornelia Butler and Alexandra Schwartz (New York, 2010), 481.
51. Murray, "*From Here I Saw What Happened and I Cried*," 24.
52. Darcy Grimaldo Grigsby, "Still Thinking about Olympia's Maid," *Art Bulletin* 97, no. 4 (December 2015): 443–447.
53. Thomas Jefferson, *Notes on the State of Virginia* (Richmond, VA, 1853), 149.
54. See Annette Gordon-Reed, *The Hemingses of Monticello: An American Family* (New York, 2008).
55. Keith Wailoo, Alondra Nelson, and Catherine Lee, eds., *Genetics and the Unsettled Past: The Collision of DNA, Race and History* (New Brunswick, NJ, 2012).
56. Weems's act of turning her back to the camera and to the viewer "engages a long history of visual obfuscation" observes art historian Gwendolyn DuBois Shaw, associated with Caspar David Friedrich's *Wanderer Above a Sea Fog* (1818). See Gwendolyn DuBois Shaw, "The Wandering Gaze of Carrie Mae Weems's The Louisiana Project," *Panorama: Journal of the Association of Historians of American Art* 4, no. 1 (Spring 2018): 2.
57. McKittrick, "Footnotes (Books and Papers Scattered about the Floor)," 33.
58. hooks, *Art on My Mind*, 75.
59. Tony Bennett, *The Birth of the Museum: History, Theory, Politics* (London, 1995).
60. Irene Cheng, "Structural Racism in Modern Architectural Theory," in Cheng, Davis, and Wilson, *Race and Modern Architecture*, 134–152.
61. American Academy of Rome, "Overview of American Academy of Rome," accessed April 1, 2021, https://www.aarome.org/about/history/academy.
62. Sharpe, *In the Wake*, 10.
63. "'Roaming' Carrie Mae Weems," art21, September 10, 2010, https://art21.org/watch/extended-play-carrie-mae-weems-roaming-short/.
64. Robert H. Kargon, *World's Fairs on the Eve of War* (Pittsburgh, 2015), 108.
65. See Brian L. McLaren, "Modern Architecture and Racial Eugenics at the Esposizione Universal di Roma," in Cheng, Davis, and Wilson, *Race and Modern Architecture*, 178.
66. "'Roaming' Carrie Mae Weems," art21.
67. "'Roaming' Carrie Mae Weems," art21.
68. "'Roaming' Carrie Mae Weems," art21.
69. "Mapping Mediterranean Migration," BBC News, September 15, 2014, https://www.bbc.com/news/world-europe-24521614.
70. Silva, *Toward a Global Idea of Race*, 68.
71. Sharpe, *In the Wake*, 15.
72. McKittrick, "Footnotes (Books and Papers Scattered about the Floor)," 32.

CONTRIBUTORS

Huey Copeland is BFC Presidential Associate Professor of Modern Art and Black Study at the University of Pennsylvania. His interdisciplinary research and teaching interrogate African/diasporic, American, and European artistic praxis from the late eighteenth century to the present, with an emphasis on visual articulations of Blackness in Western culture.

Adrienne Edwards is Engell Speyer Family Curator and Director of Curatorial Affairs at the Whitney Museum of American Art. She was cocurator of *Whitney Biennial 2022: Quiet as It's Kept*.

Simon Gikandi is Robert Schirmer Professor and Chair of English at Princeton University. He specializes in the literatures, arts, and cultures of Africa and its diasporas in Europe and the Americas, with an emphasis on global modernism. His book *Slavery and the Culture of Taste* was winner of both the Modern Language Association's James Russell Lowell Award and of the African Studies Association's Melville J. Herskovits Award.

Kellie Jones is Hans Hofmann Professor of Modern Art in the departments of art history and archaeology and African American and African diaspora studies at Columbia University. Her research interests include African American and African diaspora artists, Latinx and Latin American artists, and issues in contemporary art and museum theory.

C. C. McKee is assistant professor of history of art at Bryn Mawr College. They specialize in the art, visual, and material culture of the modern Atlantic world (c. 1750–1950), with an emphasis on the French empire and the colonial Caribbean.

Kobena Mercer holds the Charles P. Stevenson Chair in Art History and Humanities at Bard College, where his scholarship on African American, Caribbean, and Black British art cuts across the fields of art history, Black studies, and cultural studies.

Steven Nelson is dean of the Center for Advanced Study in the Visual Arts at the National Gallery of Art and professor emeritus of art history at the University of California, Los Angeles. His writings on the contemporary and historical arts, architecture, and urbanism of Africa and its diasporas; African American art history; and queer studies have appeared in numerous publications.

Sylvester Okwunodu Ogbechie is professor of history of art and architecture at the University of California Santa Barbara. He specializes in the arts and visual cultures of Africa and the African diaspora, modern and contemporary African art, and African cultural patrimony research.

Matthew Francis Rarey is associate professor of art history at Oberlin College. His research explores visual histories of Blackness and enslavement in the long eighteenth century, with an emphasis on material and intellectual dialogues between West Africa, Brazil, and Portugal.

Mabel O. Wilson is the Nancy and George E. Rupp Professor of Architecture, Planning, and Preservation and a professor in African American and African diaspora studies at Columbia University, where she also serves as the director of the Institute for Research in African American Studies.

INDEX

Page numbers in **boldface** indicate illustrations. Titles of specific artworks, publications, and performances will be found under the name of the artist, author, or performer.

A

Abstract Painting and Sculpture in America (MoMA exhibition, 1951), 159
abstraction, Black modernist practices of, 155–157, 172–175. *See also* darkness and luminosity, interplay of; *specific abstract artists*
Agassiz, Louis, 210–213, 219, 221
Allan, Maud, 116, 122, 238n47
American Artists Paint the City (Art Institute of Chicago exhibition, 1956), 159
American Negro Exhibition, Chicago, 125
amulets. See *mandingas/bolsas*
art education, 124–125, 158, 239n83
Artists' Sessions, Studio 35, New York, 157–158, **158**, 159
atomic energy, artists' responses to, 162–168, **163**, **164**, **166**, **167**, 175
aurality/sonics, 149, 174–175, 241–242n62
Azoulay, Ariella, 213

B

Baartman, Saartjie (the Hottentot Venus), 63
backlighting, 166
Baker, Josephine, 82, 97, 117
Baldwin, James, 17
Barney, Natalie, 109, 237n16
Barros, Manuel de, 48, 53
Barthé, Richmond, 114, 117, **119**, 121, 237n34, 239n82
Baudelaire, Charles, 76–77, 81, 123
Bearden, Romare, 121, 123, 124, 159, 165, 166, 239n79, 239n90
Belafonte, Harry, 168
Benjamin, Walter, 82
Benoist, Marie-Guilhelmine, *Portrait d'une Negrésse* (1800), 220
Bentley, Gladys, 117–119
Bey, Sharif, 124–125
Bhabha, Homi K., 194, 195
The Birth of a Nation (film, 1915), 83
Black Arts Movement, 172
Black Atlantic, 9, 16, 51, 87, 94, 131–132, 144–146, 150–151
Black diaspora: Europe, Black expatriation to, 83–85, 108; Great Migration, 92, 113; homelessness, internationalism, and Black relationship to world, 90–97, **94–96**, 235n51; Savage and Prophet in interwar Paris, 107, 108–112; Weems and, 203–205, 206, 225–226, **226**

Black modernisms, 1–17; Clark and Spillers, imagined confrontation between, 10–12, 13; defining, 3–5; engagement of Black artists with modernism, 12–13; inauguration of Blackness, modernity, and Blackness as modernity, 3–9, 37, 40; intersections of gender, sexuality, and race, 9, 104; Laure (African maid in Manet's *Olympia*) and, 10, **11**, 13; multiple dimensions of, 5–9, 80; questions posed by, 9–10; women and, 13–15 (*See also* women and Black modernisms). See also darkness and luminosity, interplay of; *mandingas/bolsas*; racial violence, modernism, and Black being; religion and spirituality; *specific artists*
Black radical studies, 3, 175
Blackness in Abstraction (Pace Gallery exhibition, 2016), 156
Blake, William, 188–189, **189**
Blyden, Edward Wilmot, 86–87
bolsas. See *mandingas/bolsas*
Bourdelle, Émile Antoine, 116, 238n42
Brookes, Romaine, 109, 237n16
Brouwn, Stanley: Blackness, as way of thinking about, 180–181, 195–197; *Cowboybrouwn* (1964) compared, 194; difference, as demonstration of, 194–195; errantry and migration in, **178**, 181–182, 183–187, **186**; evolution of Brouwn's art and, 191–194; *Knipbrouwn* (1964) compared, 194; life and times, 181–182, **182**, 191; nature of work, 180, 182; representational withholding in, 180, 181, 196; Stedman's *Narrative* and, 187–190, **189**, 196; *Steps* (1974) compared, 182, 196; *This Way Brouwn* (1964), 17, 179–197; *Wan Pipel* (1976, film) and, 187, 189–191, **192**, 196

C

Carby, Hazel, 112, 113–114
Caribbean. *See* Brouwn, Stanley; Pissarro, Camille; Suriname
Catholic Church: *bolsa* papers using Catholic symbolism, 41, 42, 43, 50–51, 55; Weems's *Roaming* series (2006) and, 223
Catlett, Elizabeth, 125, 159
Cervenak, Sarah Jane, 202, 245n5
Césaire, Aimé, 96–97
Chicago World's Columbia Exposition (1893), 221
Chisholm, Shirley, 225
Christianity: Black churches in America, 146–148; darkness and light, symbolism of, 167; Hampton's *Throne*, Christian interpretation of, 131–132, 145, 146, 148, 149. *See also* Catholic Church
Civil War, US, 81, 233n30
Clark, T. J., 10–12, 13, 59–61, 74, 93, 117, 168, 175

250

color symbolism, 155-156
Conrad, Joseph, *Heart of Darkness* (1899), 80, 82
contemporaneity versus modernity, 175
Cooper, Anna Julia, 104, 126, 201, 225
Cooper, Brittney, 104, 126, 236n1
Copeland, Huey, 74, 235n51, 242n69
Courbet, Gustave, 60
Crenshaw, Kimberlé, 14
Crichlow, Ernest, 239n85, 239n90
La croisière noire (film, 1925), 214, 247n47
cubism, 80, 82, 131
Cullen, Countee, 109-110, 112, 126, 237n18

D

dance, Black portrayals of, 113-116, 121-122, 237n34
darkness and luminosity, interplay of, 17, 153-175; atomic energy, artists' responses to, 162-168, **163**, **164**, **166**, **167**; different directions of Black artists in midcentury abstraction, 157-162, **158**, **160**, **161**; phenomenological versus color symbolism, approach to, 155-157; race, darkness, and vision, nexus of, 157, 174-175; recontextualizing approaches to midcentury Black artists and, 172-175, **173**, **174**, **176**, **177**; sfumato, 165-167, 170-172; vestibular spaces in DeCarava's photography, 168-172, **169-171**. See also DeCarava, Roy; Lewis, Norman
de Kooning, Willem, 167; *Light in August* (1946), **164**, 164-165
de la Parra, Pim, 187, 189-191, 196
Debret, Jean-Baptiste, 44, **45**
DeCarava, Roy: *Dancers* (1953), **171**, 171-172; darkness and luminosity, interplay of, 17, 155-157; Ellison and, 156; *Face Out of Focus* (1960), 170; *Hallway* (1953), **170**; *Man lying down, subway steps* (1965), **152**, **154**, 155; *Mott Avenue* (1951), 169; *Platform and Light* (1960), 169, **170**; *Subway ceiling, New York* (1965), 169; tonalities of photographs of, 155, 157; *Traffic Light and Fog* (1950), 170; vestibular spaces in photography of, 168-172; *Woman on train* (1961), 169
diaspora. *See* Black diaspora
display and description of Black bodies: Agassiz's daguerreotypes of enslaved people (1850), 210-216, **216**, 219; Baartman, Saartjie (the Hottentot Venus), 63; in census records and other documents, 213; enslavement and inspection/marking/description, 37, 40; female Black bodies, display of/gaze at, 76-77, 213-215, **215**, **216**; at world's fairs and expositions, **85**
Dixon, Thomas, Jr., *The Clansman* (1905), 83
double consciousness, 86, 145
double-voicedness/double vision, 132, 144, 145-146, 150, 194, 241n47
Douglas, Aaron, 91, 93-94, 123, 247n50; *Aspects of Negro Life: The Negro in an African Setting* (1934), **78**, **95**; *The Crucifixion* (1927), 93, **96**; *Invincible Music: The Spirit of Africa* (1926), 93, **94**

Du Bois, W. E. B., 81, 85, 86, 87, 157, 163-164, 237n32
Duchamp, Marcel, *Fountain* (1917), 13, **14**
Dutch Caribbean. *See* Brouwn, Stanley; Suriname

E

Eakins, Thomas, 83-84
Edwards, Brent Hayes, 8-10, 109
Eleggua (deity), 131, 132, 140, 142, 144
Ellison, Ralph, *Invisible Man* (1952), 156, 168-169, **169**, 172
embodied discourse, 104, 126
Emerson, Ralph Waldo, 162-163
English, Darby, 8, 172
Enwezer, Okwui, 175
Enwonwu, Ben, 16, 131-132, 133-137, 150, 151, 240n3; *Agbogho Mmo* (1949), **136**; *Ogolo* (1989), 134, **135**, 142
Eṣu (deity), **130**, 131, 132, 140, 141, 142, 144
Ethiopia, allegory of, 86-90, **88**, **91**
exoticism, 61, 76, 82, 97-99, 109, 122, 141, 191, 193, 214

F

Fanon, Frantz, 157, 190-193, 212, 234n3
Faulkner, William, *Light in August* (1932), 164
Federal Art Project (FAP), 158, 239n85
feminism: Black feminism, 8, 14, 16, 20, 104, 109-110, 117; in interwar years, 109-110, 123; Wilde's *Salome* and, 122
Ferreira da Silva, Denise, 180, 226
fetishes and fetishism, 46, 48, 76, 82, 97, 202, 220, 231n19
Fuller, Meta Vaux Warrick, 16, 89-90, 236n5; *Ethiopia Awakening* (1921), 87, **88**, 89-90

G

Gallagher, Ellen, *Negroes Battling in a Cave* (2016), 5-8, **6-7**
Garrity, Jane, 117, 121
Gates, Henry Louis, Jr., 120, 131, 132, 134
Gauguin, Paul, 80, 140
gender/sexuality: Black expatriation from United States to France and, 83; display of/gaze at Black female bodies, 76-77, 213-215, **215**, **216**; of Eṣu (deity), 132; Hemings and Jefferson, 219; intersections of gender, sexuality, and race, 9, 104; *mandingas/bolsas* and performance of masculinity, 16, 39, 45-46, 230-231n19; masculinism of modernism, Black deployments of, 97, 98-99; modernism's masculinism, misogyny, and ambivalence toward powerful femininity, 97, 124; in Pissarro's *Plaza Mayor de Caracas* (1862), **73**, 73-74; Prophet/Savage and, 112-113, 117-123, 126; queer/queerness, concept of, 126; Surinamese marriages, 190, 245n56; transgender aesthetics, **120**, 122, 238n44, 238n47. *See also* LGBTQ+ community; women and Black modernisms
Getty Museum, 211, 214, 217, 220
Gibbes, Robert W., 212-213
Gibson, Ann Eden, 157, 161, 162

Giddings, Paula, 225
Gilroy, Paul, 12, 151, 172
Glissant, Édouard, 11, 183-184, 204, 205
Great Migration, 92, 113
Greek and Roman classical style, 89-90, 111-112, 116, 121
Green, Kai M., 112, 121
Greenberg, Clement, 3-5, 89, 162
Gronniosaw, James Albert Ukawsaw, 43
Guedes, António, 43, 55
Guggenheim Museums, 203, 220
Guillén, Nicolás, "Canto Negro," 99
Gundaker, Grey, 145
Guy, Edna, 121

H

Haitian Revolution, 64, 70, 119
Hammons, David, *Concerto in Black and Blue* (2002), 172, **173**
Hampton, James, 16, 131-132, 144-150, 151; *The Book of the 7 Dispensation* (c. 1945-1964) and symbol-based writing system, 145, 146, **148**, 149; *Throne of the Third Heaven* (1950-1964), 131-132, 144-150, **146-147**
Harlem Renaissance, 92-93, 99, 104, 120-121, 123
Harmon Foundation, 123, 125, 239n87
Hartman, Saidiya, 50, 53, 66, 77, 112-113, 117, 126-127, 228n2, 229n28
Hayford, Joseph Ephraim, *Ethiopia Unbound* (1911), 85, 87
Hegel, Georg Wilhelm Friedrich, 203, 211
Hemings, Sally, 219
hooks, bell, 206
Hughes, Langston, 123, 124, 164, 239n79
Hurston, Zora Neale, 20, 93, 209

I

Inquisition. See *mandingas/bolsas*
intersections of gender, sexuality, and race, 9, 104

J

Jacobs, Harriet, *Incidents in the Life of a Slave Girl* (1861), 12-13
jazz, African American abstraction analogized to, 174
Jefferson, Thomas, 219
Jones, Lois Mailou, *The Ascent of Ethiopia* (1932), 90, **91**

K

Kandinsky, Wassily, 150
Kant, Immanuel, 211, 212
Kline, Franz, 161
Kongo spirituality, 131, 142, 145, 149
Krasner, Lee, 161
Kristeva, Julia, 86, 234-235n24
Ku Klux Klan, 82, **83**

L

Lam, Wifredo, 16, 131-132, 138-144, 150, 151; *Altar for Eleggua* (1944), 140; *The Awakening* (1938), 99-101, **100**; *Composition* (1940), 138; *Figures with Shears* (1942), 140-141; *La Jungla* (1949), **128**, **141**, 141-142; *Light of the Forest* (1942), 140-141; *Nude on Colored Background* (1942), 140-141; *Ogue Orisa (Euggue Orissa, l'herbe des dieux)* (1943), 140; *Le Présent Éternel* (1944), **143**, 143-144; *The Sombre Malembo: God of the Crossroads* (1943), 140; *Woman with Long Hair* (1938), 138, **139**
Laure (African maid in Manet's *Olympia*), 10, **11**, 13, 218
Lawrence, D. H., 80
Lawrence, Jacob, 159, 239n85
Leigh, Simone, 14-15, 18-33; *Brick House* (2019), 20, **22-25**, 33; *Façade* (2022), **32**, 33; *Figure with Skirt (Face Jug Series)* (2019), **29**, **30**, 33; *Jug* (2022), **18**, **31**, 33; *Loophole of Retreat* (2018/2019), **26**, **28**, 33; *Martinique* (2022), **31**, 33; *Satellite* (2022), **32**, 33; *Sentinel* (2019), bronze and raffia, **27**, 33; *Sentinel* (2022), bronze, **30**, 33; *Sovereignty* (2022), 21
Leininger-Miller, Theresa, 84, 107, 117
Lethière, Guillaume Guillon, *The Oath of the Ancestors* (1822), 3, **4**
Lewis, Edmonia, 87-89, **90**, 107, 116
Lewis, Norman: atomic energy, artists' responses to, 162-168; *Blending* (1952), 165-166, **166**; darkness and luminosity, interplay of, 17, 155-157; Ellison and, 156; *Every Atom Glows: Electrons in Luminous Vibration* (1951), 162-163, **163**, 165, 166; fog, interest in, 167; *Harlem Turns White* (1955), 167-168, **168**; life and times, 158-159, 160-162; *Orpheus* (1953), 155, **156**; Reinhardt and, 157-160; on relationship of darkness and vision, 157; Savage, as student of, 125, 239n85; *Seachange* (1975) and *Seachange* series, 172, **173**, 175, 244n56; *sfumato*, use of, 165-168
LGBTQ+ community, 109, 110, 117-121, **120**, 122, 123, 124, 126, 238n44, 238n47, 240n96. See also gender/sexuality
Ligon, Tom, *The Death of Tom* (2008), 175, **177**
literacy, 43-44, 52, 145, 146, **148**, 149, 231n28
Locke, Alain, 86, 92-93, 123, 124, 235n42, 239n85, 239n87
Lorde, Audre, 20, 206
luminosity. See darkness and luminosity, interplay of

M

Malevich, Kazimir, *Black Square* (1915), 8, **9**
mandingas/bolsas, 15-16, 35-55; African practice and, 44, **45**; archives of slavery and, 52-55, 230n6; *autos-da-fé*, 46-48, **47**, **48**, 52; Catholic symbolism, use of, 41, 42, 43, 50-51, 55; contents of, 40, 41, 46, 48; defined, 37-38, 230n2; *editais* (decrees) against, 39, 231n20; etymology of *mandinga*, 230n9; fetishes and fetishism, association with, 46, 48, 231n19; letters denouncing, **36**, 37-38, 40, 52-53; magical properties attributed to, 37, 38; masculinity, performance of, 16, 39, 45-46, 230-231n19; papers with markings

contained inside, 34, 39-41, **42**, 48-51, **49**, **51**; José Francisco Pereira's case (1730-1731), 41-44, **42**, 48, 53-55, **54**, **55**, 231n25, 231n30; physical violence, as protection against, 38, 44-46, 50; records describing contents, 40; secrecy terms of Inquisition trials, **55**; João da Silva's case (1742), **49**, 50-51, **51**, 53; slavery, providing power to escape, 48-51; António de Sousa's case (1732-1733), 44-48; surviving example, **39**; widespread use of, 38

Manet, Édouard: *La Négresse* (1863), 80; *Olympia* (1863), 10, **11**, 13, 80, 81, 218-219

Mapplethorpe, Robert, 214, 217

McKay, Claude: *Banjo* (1929), 97, 101; "The Harlem Dancer" (1922), 98

McKittrick, Katherine, 205, 206, 220, 227

Melbye, Frederik Georg (Fritz), 69, 73

Mello e Souza, Laura de, 45

migration, **178**, 181-182, 183-187, **186**, 225-226, **226**

Mirzoeff, Nicholas, 68-70

modernism and Blackness, 3-9, 37, 40. *See also* Black modernisms; racial violence, modernism, and Black being

Mondrian, Piet, 12

Morris, Robert, *Untitled (Box for Standing)* (1961), 13, **15**

Morrison, Toni, 11, 12, 157

Moten, Fred, 12, 174, 228n2

Motherwell, Robert, 159

Motley, Archibald John, Jr., 93, 108; *Blues* (1929), **99**, 108, 114

Murray, Joan (later Weissman), 162

Museum of Modern Art (MoMA), 142, 159, 205, **209**, 209-210, 220, 240n8

N

Nardal, Paulette and Jane, 110-112

Negritude, 80, 98, 99, 142

New Negro movement, 86, 89, 92-94, 104, 119, 121

new woman, 117, 119

Newman, Barney, 161

Nkisi, 145, 149, 151

Nobosodru, photograph of (1925), 214-215, **215**, 217, 247n50

Nochlin, Linda, 59, 60-61

nudes in African American Art, 112, 121

Nugent, Richard Bruce, 121-124, **122**

numinous affect. *See* religion and spirituality

O

Orișa (deities), 132, 138, 142

P

Pan-Africanism, 8, 10, 80, 87, 89, 105, 240n7

Parks, Gordon, *Invisible Man Retreat* (1952), 168-169, **169**

Patton, Sharon F., 83, 168

Peabody Museum, Harvard University, 210-211, 214, 220

Pedroso, José Francisco, 41, 43, 48, 231n25

Pereira, José Francisco, 41-44, **42**, 48, 53-55, **54**, **55**, 231n25, 231n30

Perry, Sondra, *Black/Cloud* (2010), 175, **177**

Pettway, Missouri, *Blocks and Strips Work-Clothes Quilt* (1942), **viii**, 3, **5**

Philip, M. NourbeSe, 204

Picasso, Pablo, 80, 82, 131, 138, **140**, 141, 142, 144

Pippin, Horace, 159

Piranesi, Giovanni Battista, 202, **222**, 222-223

Pissarro, Camille: ambivalence of, 61-63, 66, 70, 73-77; artistic precedents and early sketches, 67-72, **68**, **71**, **72**; bare feet in, 62, 68, 75-76; Black women in Caribbean images of, 16, 57-77; Black women's role in end of Danish slavery, 66-67, 72; class delineations in, 62, 66; Danish colonies, end of slavery in, 63-67, 232n1; as fantasized colonial memory, 61-63, 70, 72-77; freedom, relationship to, 58-63, 69-72, 76; *Landscape with Female Figures Washing* (c. 1853-1854), 69-72, **71**; photos of Pissarro in llanero costume, **72**, 72-73; *Plaza Mayor de Caracas* (1862), **73**, 73-74; political radicalism of Pissarro and, 59-60, 63; *Route de Bussy* (1852), **65**, 65-66, 70; *Studies of female figures with children by a fire*, 233n46; *Two Women Chatting by the Sea, St. Thomas* (1856), 57, **57**, **59**, 60, 62, 72, 75, 76-77; *Two Young Peasant Women* (1891-1892), **60**, 74; *Young Seated Negress* (c. 1855-1857), 74-75, **75**

Poirier, Léon, 214

Pollock, Jackson, 161

Porter, James A., 83

pouches (*bolsas*), amuletic. *See mandingas/bolsas*

Powell, Richard J., 8, 85

primitivism and modernism, 80, 97, 99, 138, 203, 204, 210, 212, 220, 222

Prophet, Nancy Elizabeth, 16, 103-127; "Art and Life" (1940), 124; Black art education, production, and exhibition, 123-127, 239n83; Black diaspora in interwar Paris and, 107, 108-110, 112; *Congolais* (1931), **105**, 105-107, 117, 236nn7-8; *Discontent* (1925-1929), 117, **118**; gender/sexuality in work of, 117-123; *Head of a Negro* (before 1927), **106**, 107; life and times, 104-105, 112; *Le Pelerin* (c. 1922-1929), 116, 117; photos of, **113**, **124**; sexual freedom practiced by, 112-113, 237n32; *Silence* (before 1930), **116**; style choices of, 108, 113-117

Q

queer/queerness, concept of, 126

R

race, darkness, and vision, nexus of, 157, 174-175

racial violence, modernism, and Black being, 16, 79-101; atomic energy, artists' responses to, 162-168, **163**, **164**, **166**, **167**, 175; Black homelessness, internationalism, and relationship to world, 90-97, **94-96**, 235n51; European colonial violence against Black people, **82**, 234n8; formation of/entry into modern world based on bodily control, violation, and inscription, 37, 40; freedom and slavery, dialectic between, 204-205; historical theorizations of racial difference, 203, 211–212, 221; Jim Crow regime, 81, 82, **83**, 85, 206; *mandingas/bolsas* as protection against physical violence, 38, 44–46, 50; midcentury racial liberalism and silencing of diversity, 159; nexus among, 80–82, **82**, **83**; pain, Black bodies defined through capacity to endure, 231n42; romanticism and, 82–90, **84**, **90**, 234n14; "Scourged Back" photo, 37, **38**; sins of modernism, reckoning with, 97–101, **99**, **100**; Sphinx/Ethiopia, significance of, 86–90, **88**, **91**

racialization of aesthetics, 211–212, 219, 221

Reinhardt, Ad, 157–160, 174; *Abstract Painting, No. 5* (1962), 159, **161**; *Abstract Painting, No. 34* (1964), **2**, 3; *How to Look at Modern Art in America* (1946), 159, **160**; "Twelve Rules for a New Academy" (1953), 159

religion and spirituality, 16, 129–151; African spirituality in Black Atlantic art, 132–133 (*See also* Kongo spirituality; Yoruba deities; *specific deities*); double-voicedness/double vision and, 132, 144, 145–146, 150, 241n47; Enwonwu and, 16, 131–132, 133–137, **135**, **136**, 150, 151; Eşu (deity) as discursive framework for, **130**, 131, 132; Hampton and, 16, 131–132, 144–150, **146–148**, 151; Lam and, 16, **128**, 131–132, 138–144, **139–141**, **143**, 150, 151; modernist project and, 150–151; numinous affect, deployment of, 16, 131–134, 137, 140–142, 144–146, 148–151; Santería, 131, 132, 138–144, 146, 149, 151; vodou, 132, 149. See also Christianity; *mandingas/bolsas*

Rodin, Auguste, 116

romanticism and Black modernisms, 82–90, **84**, **90**, 108, 234n14

Rothko, Mark, 159

S

Saint Phalle, Niki de, 222
Saint-Gaudens, Augustus, 221
Salome, portrayals of, 121–123, **122**
Şango (deity), 138, 140, 144, 146
Santería, 131, 132, 138–144, 146, 149, 151
São Boaventura, João de, **36**, 37–38, 40, 52–53
Savage, Augusta, 16, 103–127; *The Amazon* (c. 1930), **110**, 111, 123; Amazon series, 112, 116, 122, 123, 237n25; Black art education, production, and exhibition, 123–127, 239n85; Black diaspora in interwar Paris and, 107, 108–112; *La Citadelle (Freedom)* (1930), **114**, 119, 123; dance, portrayals of, 113–116, 121–122; gender/sexuality in work of, 117–123, 126; *The Harp* (or *Lift Every Voice and Sing*) (1939), **107**, 107–108, 121, 125, 236n8, 238n60; life and times, 104–105; *Mourning Victory* (c. 1930), **111**, 111–112, 123; style choices of, 108, 113–117, 121; *Susie Q* and *Truckin'* statuettes, 114; *Terpsichore (or Reclining Nude)* (c. 1932), **102**, 114–116, **115**, 117, 123; *Tête de Jeune Fille* (c. 1930), **110**, 111, 123; *Untitled (bookends)* (1930–1931), **126**
Sawkins, James Gay, *St. Jago de Cuba* (c. 1859), 67–69, **68**, 70
Scott, David, 84, 206–207

Senghor, Léopold Sédar, 98
sex/sexuality. *See* gender/sexuality
sfumato, 165–167, 170–172
Sharpe, Christina, 213, 223, 227
Sharpley-Whiting, T. Denean, 76, 109
Shaw, George Bernard, *The Adventures of the Black Girl in Her Search for God* (1932), 210
Siegel, Katy, 162, 164
Silva, João de, **49**, 50–51, **51**, 53
slavery: archives of, 52–55, 230n6; constitutive import of, 3; Danish colonialism, slavery, and end of slavery, 63–67, 232n1; descriptive marks used to identify enslaved, 37, 51; dialectic between freedom and, 204–205; enslaved persons mentioned only by first name, 37–38, **38**, 46, 48–50, 64, 211–213, 215, **215**; Haitian Revolution, 64; iconoclasm and, 233n30; literacy and, 43; *mandingas/bolsas* providing power to escape, 48–51; Middle Passage, 126, 165, 205, 206, 220; as social death/invisibility, 13, 50, 149; Stedman's *Narrative* on, 187–189, **189**; Surinamese marriages, 190, 245n56; Venezuela, abolition in, 70; Voltaire's satire on, 187, 188
Specht, Georges, 214
Sphinx, as guardian spirit of Blackness, 86–90, **88**, **91**
Spillers, Hortense J.: on Black enslaved female bodies, 204; on documents recording enslaved persons, 213; Leigh's oeuvre and, 21; "Mama's Baby, Papa's Maybe" (1987), 10–14, 37, 229n19; *mandingas/bolsas* and, 37, 39–41, 51; Pissarro's Caribbean images of Black women and, 63, 77; race, darkness, and vision, on nexus of, 157; stereotypes of Black women delineated by, 13, 201, 202; on vestibular spaces, 63, 157, 168, 174
Stedman, John Gabriel, *Narrative . . .* (1796), 187–190, **189**, 196
Suriname: independence and migration to Netherlands from, 181–182, **182**, 183–187; Stedman's *Narrative* (1796) on Maroon Rebellion in, 187–189, **189**; *Wan Pipel* (1976, film), 187, 189–191, **192**
Surinamese marriages, 190, 245n56
surrealism, 131, 138

T

Tanner, Henry Ossawa, 112, 116–117; *The Banjo Lesson* (1893), 83–84, **84**, 86
Thompson, Krista, 50, 119
time, decolonizing, 108
Tinsley, Omise'eke Natasha, 126
Toomer, Jean, 93
transatlantic world, Black modernisms in. *See* Black Atlantic; Black modernisms
transgender aesthetics, **120**, 122, 238n44, 238n47

V

Van Der Zee, James, **120**
Vasi, Giuseppe, 222, 223

Vendryes, Margaret Rose, 117, 120, 121
vestibular spaces, 62, 63, 157, 168-172, 174, 243n44
Viegas, Jacques, 38-39, **39**, 53
violence, racial. *See* racial violence, modernism, and Black being
Viollet-le-Duc, Eugène, 221
vodou, 132, 149
Voltaire, 187, 188

W

Walkowitz, Judith R., 116, 123
Wan Pipel (1976, film), 187, 189-191, **192**, 196
Weems, Carrie Mae: *Africa* series (1993), 203, 205-210, **210**; architecture/architectural history challenged by, 201, 202, 204, 205, 220-227; *Black and Tanned* (1995), 37, **38**; Black diaspora and work of, 203-205, 206, 225-226, **226**; Blackness/Black womanhood, investigation of, 201-203, 205, 226-227; color, use of, 214, 247n45; *Colored People* series (1989-1990), 214, 217; concepts of modernity/Blackness/freedom and, 204-205; *From Here I Saw What Happened and I Cried* series (1995-1996), 203, 210-218, **215**, **216**, **218**; Guggenheim exhibition, New York (2014), **200**, 201; *Jefferson Suite* (2001), 203, 219-220; *Kitchen Table* series (1990), 246n19; MoMA exhibition (1995-1996), 205, **209**, 209-210; *Museums* series (2006), 202-203, 220-221, **221**, 226; *Not Manet's Type* series (1997), 203, 218-219; retrospective significance, interrogating, 246n18; *Roaming* series (2006), 17, **198**, **200**, 201-202, 203, 204, 220, 221-226, **224-226**, 247n56; *Sea Islands* series (1991-1992), 203, 205-210, **208**; *Slave Coast* series (1993), 203, 205, **207**; *When and Where I Enter—Mussolini's Rome*, from *Roaming* series (2006), **198**, **225**
Wells, Ida B., 225
White, Charles, 125, 159
white backlighting, 166
Whitten, Jack, 156, 175; *April's Shark* (1974), 175, **176**
Wilde, Oscar, 123; *Salome* (1891), 121-122
Willard, Marian, 159, 160
Williams, Aubrey, *Death and the Conquistador* (1959), **174**, 175
Wilson, Jackie Napoleon, 214
Wilson, Judith, 13, 81
Winckelmann, Johann Joachim, 212, 221
Winfield, Hemsley, 121-122
Winogrand, Garry, 214, 217, **218**
women and Black modernisms, 13-15; Alphonse Allais racist joke/Malevich response, Black women artists' awareness of implications of, 8; Clark and Spillers, imagined confrontation between, 10-12; display of/gaze at Black female bodies, 76-77, 213-215, **215**, **216**; embodied discourse on, 104; exhibitions, women listing themselves as men for purposes of, 125; intersections of gender, sexuality, and race, 9, 104; *mandingas/bolsas*, limited use of, 230-231n19; Manet's *Olympia*, 10, **11**; modernism's masculinism, misogyny, and ambivalence toward powerful femininity, 97, 124; social role of Black female bodies, 204; stereotypes of Black women delineated by Spillers, 13, 201, 202; Surinamese marriages, 190, 245n56. *See also* feminism; gender/sexuality; Pissarro, Camille: Black women in Caribbean images of
Woodruff, Hale, 109, 124, 125, 159; *The Card Players* (193), **109**
The World, the Flesh and the Devil (film, 1959), 168
world's fairs and expositions, 85, **85**, **107**, 112, 125, 221, 223, 236n6, 237n25
Wynter, Sylvia, 204

Y

yard sales, African American, 148-149
Yeman[j]a (deity), 142
Yoruba deities, **130**, 131, 132, 133, 138, 140, 142, 146, 240n23

Z

Zealy, J. T., 212, 213, 214

Copyright © 2023 Board of Trustees, National Gallery of Art, Washington. All rights reserved. This book may not be reproduced, in whole or in part (beyond that copying permitted by Sections 107 and 108 of the U.S. Copyright Law, and except by reviewers from the public press), without written permission from the publishers.

This volume was produced by the Center for Advanced Study in the Visual Arts and the Office of Content Strategy, Publishing, and Branding, National Gallery of Art, Washington
nga.gov

Series Editor
Steven Nelson

Program Assistants
Annie Miller
Jen Rokoski

Design and Production
Peggy Martin
Mariah Shay
Christina Wiginton

Editors
Lisa Shea
Magda Nakassis
Cynthia Ware
Emily Zoss

Copyediting by Amy Teschner
Design and layout by Jeff Wincapaw
Proofreading by Tanya Heinrich
Indexing by Kate Mertes

Typeset in Whitney
Printed on GardaPat Kiara by Friesens, Canada

Distributed by Yale University Press, New Haven and London
yalebooks.com/art

The Center for Advanced Study in the Visual Arts, founded in 1979, is a research institute that fosters study of the production, use, and cultural meaning of art, artifacts, architecture, urbanism, photography, and film worldwide from prehistoric times to the present. The Center's programs include fellowships, internships, meetings, research, and publications.

Library of Congress Control Number: 2022951435
ISBN 978-0-300-26977-2

Frontispiece: Norman Lewis, *Every Atom Glows: Electrons in Luminous Vibration* (detail), 1951 (page 163)